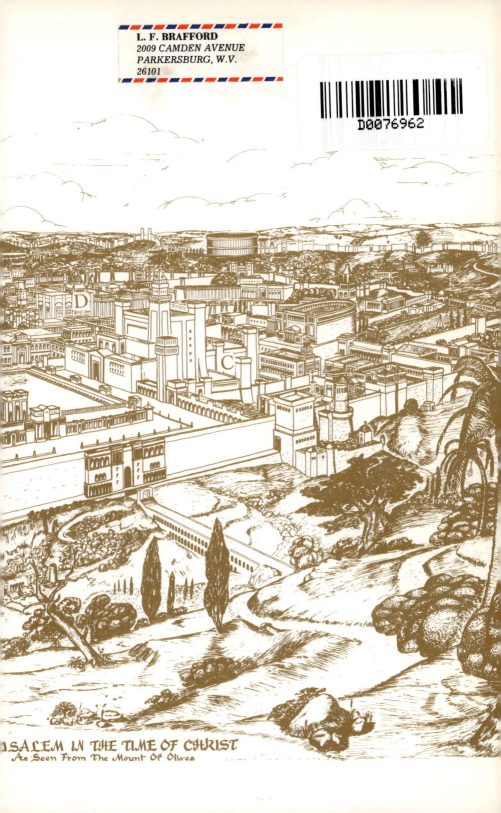

1SALEM IN THE TIME OF CHRIST
As Seen From The Mount Of Olives

ACTS MADE ACTUAL

BIBLE STUDY TEXTBOOK

Acts Made Actual

A New
☆ Commentary,
☆ Workbook,
☆ Teaching Manual.

Don De Welt

Ozark Bible College
Joplin, Missouri

Teacher of New Testament,
Sacred History, Homiletics.

Author of:
The Power Of The Holy Spirit
Romans Realized
The Gospel Of Mark
If You Want To Preach
The Church In The Bible
Paul's Letters To Timothy And Titus

COLLEGE PRESS
Joplin, Missouri

Drawings of Jerusalem by
Frank Stamper

Maps by Robert Huffman

ISBN 0-89900-036-3

DEDICATION

*This book is dedicated to my
dear wife, who has been to me
a constant challenge to a higher
and holier life in Christ.*

PREFACE

HOW THIS BOOK CAME TO BE . . .

This material was prepared to meet a definite need. The need found in the Bible College class room. The same need you find as you teach a Bible class. A simple comprehensive commentary was needed. There was a call for a teaching manual. A certain type of workbook could be used with profit. Several works in print could be combined to meet this three-fold need, but nothing under one cover. And even when combined they left something to be desired.

In 1946, after teaching the book of Acts for several years, a work was begun that it was felt would combine the features of a commentary, manual, and workbook, to be a help both to the student and the teacher. As it was written, it was printed in mimeographed form. The mimeographed material has gone through four or five editions. It has been used by several hundred students of the book of Acts.

NOTE SEVERAL OF THE FEATURES OF THIS BOOK:

☆It is planned that each page be complete within itself. Each page can be read and your knowledge of its contents can be tested by answering the questions at the bottom of the page. (Some questions can be more completely answered by supplemental reading).

☆The entire book of Acts is given in outline form. This can be observed by referring to the opening pages of the book. This outline is memorized by the class members.

☆Eight exams that have been used in class are included with this work.

☆A special study of the Holy Spirit is a feature in the back of the book.

☆Every person, place, and event of the book of Acts can be visualized from the ten chart-maps that appear consecutively.

☆Almost all of the important places in the Acts record are shown in accurate drawings.

☆Large charts for use in the class room are being prepared. These are an enlargement of the chart-maps that appear in the book.

This book is prepared to be practical. The student of the Bible who for the first time begins his study of the wonderful book of Acts will find here a real help in enabling him to comprehend the general outline of the book, as well as a simple verse by verse comment on its contents.

The Bible student who has already studied Luke's second treatise will find here an outline from which he can teach. A wealth of information is given on points that are not usually discussed. With only one or two exceptions the books quoted from are out of print.

With a prayer to our heavenly Father, who has enabled the production of every part of this work, I send this book forth to be used wherever the book of Acts is studied or taught.

Don De Welt

INTRODUCTION TO THE FIRST EDITION

It is my pleasure and great honor to introduce to you the author of this book. I have personally known Brother Don De Welt since 1939. I have found him in every way to be a real consecrated servant of Christ. He has endeavored to put into practice in his own life that which he teaches to others.

Because of his consecration and devotion in his study of the Word of God, and his deep compassion for the souls of men, he was called as a teacher to labor with us at the San Jose Bible College. Since 1943 he has been teaching young people the Word of Life and challenging them to be evangels of the cross of Christ. In this way his ministry has been multiplied a thousand-fold.

His class in the book of Acts has been a high point in the life of each student. Out of his personal experience and storehouse of knowledge he was written this material and presents it to you that you might come to know God's word in a greater way.

I know as you study this book you, too, will come to know the author, for his radiant Christian personality is seen on every page; his evangelistic zeal will be felt as you read through the book. No greater honor can be paid the author and the Christ he serves than to stir you to greater depths of consecration and service as you study this exegesis of the book of Acts.

May God bless this work, and may every reader be richly blessed and led to a closer walk with Christ.

W. L. Jessup
President, San Jose Bible College

INTRODUCTION TO THE REVISED EDITION

Text books for the Bible College classroom that are really usable are not many in number. It was a great joy to me to learn of Brother DeWelt's desire to write. Many have the desire, but Brother De Welt's ambition is being fulfilled not only with this book but several others.

This text book comes from the pen of a scholarly teacher and from one who is unusually practical. Few men are as popular in the classroom, and yet he possesses a rare quality to be equally effective as a preacher. Those of us who know Brother Don were delighted that **Acts Made Actual** was so gladly received, and we were not surprised. We are now rejoicing that it is being published again. May it have a wide reading and study beyond the college classrooms. Churches have used it for study periods and have written to us telling of the blessings which they have received.

The Book of Acts is perhaps the most misunderstood book in the New Testament. If all Christendom would study and practice New Testament Christianity as revealed in the Book of Acts, then the divisions that plague the churches could be eliminated. The Holy Spirit, the plan of Salvation, the purpose and work of the Church are taught in Luke's history of first century Christianity. To see these truths clearly is the purpose of **Acts Made Actual.**

Don Earl Boatman, President,
Ozark Bible College, Joplin, Missouri

GENERAL INTRODUCTION TO THE BOOK OF ACTS

1. The **name** of the book.

   A better term would be simply, "Acts," or "Some of the Acts of Some of the Apostles," for it neither contains all the acts of some of the apostles nor some of the acts of all the apostles. The term "Acts" is applied to the book in some of the ancient manuscripts.

2. The **author** of the book—the Holy Spirit (II Peter 1:21).

3. The **writer** of the book—Luke. Evidence to prove this:
   a. Both Acts and Luke addressed to the same person. Cf. Acts 1:1 and Luke 1:3.
   b. The style the same: Fifty words used, common to the two books and that are not found elsewhere in the New Testament.
   c. Luke was a companion of Paul and was therefore qualified to write this book. Cf. 16:10; 20:4-6; 28:16; Col. 4:14; II Tim. 4:11; Philemon 24.

4. The **date** of writing A.D. 63-64. History supports the thought that Luke lived and wrote at this time. The book closes before the trial of Paul before Nero was completed. The strong inference is that Luke completed the book during Paul's two-year imprisonment and began its circulation before the trial was completed. Since we know the reign of Nero included the years 63-64 A.D. we feel safe in assigning the book this date.

5. A **general** view of its content.
   a. This is the first history of the church.
   b. It covers a period of thirty-two years in twenty-eight chapters.
   c. The book, like Genesis, is one of beginnings and is just as important. It contains the following beginnings:
      1) The beginning of the Holy Spirit's work of evangelization.
      2) The beginning of gospel preaching. (Cf. I Cor. 15:1-4).
      3) The beginning of the church of the Lord.
      4) The beginning of the Christian dispensation.
      5) The beginning of salvation through the blood of Christ.
      6) The beginning of world-wide evangelism.
   d. The book centers around the work of two great apostles:
      1) Peter to the Jews.
      2) Paul to the Gentiles.
   e. The book evolves around four geographical centers:
      1) Jerusalem, 2) Antioch, 3) Ephesus, 4) Rome.
   f. The book gives to us the divine execution of the Great Commission. Cf. Matt. 28:18-20; Mark 16:15, 16; Luke 24:46, 47.

TABLE OF CONTENTS

THE CHURCH IN JERUSALEM
1:1—7:60

THE CHURCH IN JUDEA AND SAMARIA
8:1 — 12:25

THE DISPERSION   THE WORK OF PHILIP
THE WORK OF PETER AND JOHN
8:1-40

11

THE WORK OF PETER   THE ESTABLISHMENT OF THE CHURCH IN ANTIOCH   THE EARLY LABORS OF BARNABAS AND SAUL

9:31 — 12:25

THE CHURCH IN THE UTTERMOST PART OF THE EARTH
13:1—28:31

THE FIRST MISSIONARY JOURNEY
13:1 — 14:28

THE TROUBLE OVER CIRCUMCISION
THE JERUSALEM COUNCIL
15:1—35

THE THIRD MISSIONARY JOURNEY
18:23 — 21:16

THE VOYAGE TO ROME

20

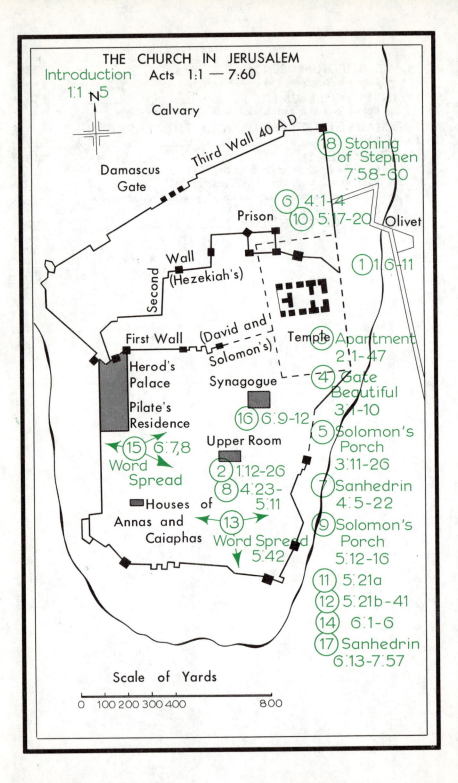

THE CHURCH IN JERUSALEM
Acts 1:1 — 7:60

Introduction
1:1

N5

Calvary

Third Wall 40 AD

Damascus Gate

(18) Stoning of Stephen 7:58-60

Prison

(6) 4:1-4
(10) 5:17-20

Olivet

Wall (Hezekiah's)

(1) 1:6-11

First Wall (David and Solomon's)

Temple

Apartment 2:1-47

Herod's Palace

Synagogue

(4) Gate Beautiful 3:1-10

Pilate's Residence

(16) 6:9-12

(5) Solomon's Porch 3:11-26

(15) 6:7,8
Word Spread

Upper Room

(2) 1:12-26

(8) 4:23-5:11

(7) Sanhedrin 4:5-22

Houses of Annas and Caiaphas

(13)
Word Spread 5:42

(9) Solomon's Porch 5:12-16

(11) 5:21a

(12) 5:21b-41

(14) 6:1-6

(17) Sanhedrin 6:13-7:57

Scale of Yards

0   100 200 300 400   800

THE CHURCH IN JERUSALEM
1:1 — 7:60

All the events of the first seven chapters can be summed up under the heading: **"The Church in Jerusalem."** In the picture of the preceding page you can observe an artist's conception of Jerusalem as it appeared in the time of the events recorded in the book. Within the walls are designated four buildings. These are lettered and named as follows:

A. The Upper Room,
B. The Temple,
C. The Public Ward or Jail,
D. The Synagogue of the Libertines.

In and around these buildings, (which, with the exception of the Temple, are conjecturally located) **all** the events recorded in the first seven chapters took place. These events can be counted as eighteen in number and are so designated on the preceding page. You can follow these events, one by one, as to where they took place and as to what happened by following the numbers on the chart from one through eighteen and reading the scripture references given.

The pages following are simply an enlargement upon the points or numbers you found upon the foregoing picture. The scripture is printed under the heading of the points and the comment following is intended to make the events recorded in the text a living reality to your mind and heart.

INTRODUCTION 1:1-5.

    1 The former treatise I made, O Theophilus, concerning all that Jesus began both to do and to teach,

    2 until the day in which he was received up, after that he had given commandment through the Holy Spirit unto the apostles whom he had chosen:

    3 to whom he also showed himself alive after his passion by many proofs, appearing unto them by the space of forty days, and speaking the things concerning the kingdom of God:

    4 and, being assembled together with them, he charged them not to depart from Jerusalem, but to wait for the promise of the Father, which, said he, ye heard from me:

    5 for John indeed baptized with water; but ye shall be baptized in the Holy Spirit not many days hence.

Here are a few of the points of interest found within these verses Luke penned as an introduction to the history of the church in Jerusalem:

MOUNT OF OLIVES.

In the drawing you are looking at the mount of ascension and the chapel of ascension. The Mount of Olives is a limestone ridge, a little more than a mile in length. There are seven peaks in this ridge that runs the whole length of the city of Jerusalem. On the north the ridge bends around to the west and thus encloses the city on the north and east. David walked down from the city of Jerusalem into the Kidron valley and up the slopes of the Mount of Olives in his flight from Absalom (II Sam. 15:30). Solomon built high places on the Mount of Olives. (II Kings 23:13). Ezekiel saw the Mount of Olives in a vision. Read about that strange sight in Ezekiel 10:4, 19; 11:23. The prophet Nehemiah indicated that at one time there were many trees growing in this valley. (Neh. 8:15). It was on the road up from this valley that our Lord rode in His triumphal entry into Jerusalem. (Mark 11:8) It was on this Mount that Jesus sat when He viewed the city of Jerusalem and wept because of their unbelief. (Mark 13:1; Matt. 23:37). The garden of Gethsemane is in the valley at the foot of the Mount of Olives. (John 18:1; Matt. 26:30, 36). Our Lord last appeared on earth on the fortieth day after His resurrection on the Mount of Olives.

1 He wrote a "former treatise," or book, to the same person to whom this present work is addressed—one "Theophilus." This name is Grecian and is said to mean "lover of God." In this former treatise he discussed all that Jesus did and taught. Notice that he says he wrote "concerning" all that Jesus did and taught. He does not say he recorded every spoken word of Christ nor described every act of the Master. He says that he only wrote "concerning" these things. This is in agreement with John 20:30, 31; 21:25.

2 The former treatise ended with the day in which He (Jesus) was received up. By referring to Luke 24:50-53 we find the events described in exact agreement with the time spoken of in Acts 1:2a. Luke also says that Jesus was received up only after he had "given commandment through the Holy Spirit unto the apostles whom he had chosen." J. W. McGarvey arranges this verse in the following order—"until the day in which, having given commandment through the Holy Spirit unto the apostles whom he had chosen, he was taken up." (Read the verse over and then read McGarvey's comment upon it which follows.) "In this rendering of verse two, the exact order of the clauses in the Greek is followed and the connection between the day of the ascension and the commandment given on that day is expressed as in the original." (**New Commentary on Acts** Vol. I, pages 1 and 2.) Jesus gave the "commandment," or as we so often call it, "the Great Commission," more than once. The time of its giving here was on the ascension day which will be described in the ensuing verses. The fact that the Commission was given "through the Holy Spirit" to "chosen apostles" lends force to its great importance.

3 The words "to whom he also showed himself alive." refer, of course, to the apostles. Notice that the chronological order of events as found in the life of Christ is not here followed. Rather, the thought expressed in verse two, i.e. "the apostles whom he had chosen," suggests the thought of verse three and this thought further suggests those appearances of Jesus "after his passion" to his chosen leaders in which He spoke to them things concerning the kingdom of God.

4 Then the thought of His appearance to His apostles during the

1. To what does the "former treatise" refer?
2. What do you know of Theophilus?
3. How is the word "began" used in verse 1?
4. How is the word "concerning" used?
5. On what day was the former treatise concluded?
6. What advantage is there in the arrangement of verse 2 as given by J. W. McGarvey?
7. Was the Great Commission given more than once? If so where is the other place or places?

forty-day period suggests one of those appearances in which Jesus said something upon the subject which is to follow in the book of Acts, so Luke speaks of that time when, in the upper room, Jesus showed Himself alive. The whole wonderful story is recorded in Luke 24:13-49.

5 Finally in verse five, the writer gives us a little more specific information on the precious comment he made in his former treatise (Luke 24:49) when Jesus said "ye shall be clothed with power from on high." Luke now tells us that this is "the promise of the Father" which they had heard from Jesus (John 14:16) and lest they become confused as to what this promise included, he informs them through the words of John the Baptist (Matthew 3:11, 12) "Ye shall be baptized in the Holy Spirit not many days hence."

Now let us take a backward look at the marvelous progression of connected thoughts in these verses. Luke begins his treatise to Theophilus by saying:

   a. He wrote a former treatise concerning the teaching and acts of of Jesus. 1.

   b. That it ended on the day of His ascension. 2a.

   c. That on this day He gave the Commission to his chosen apostles. 2b.

   d. That He had previously shown Himself alive to these apostles by many (infallible) proofs by the space of forty days and had spoken to them things concerning the kingdom of God. 3

   e. That at one of these appearances He charged them, as He was teaching them concerning the kingdom of God, not to depart from Jerusalem—but to wait for the baptism of the Holy Spirit. 4, 5.

1. **ON THE MOUNT OF OLIVET** 1:6-11.

   6 They therefore, when they were come together, asked him, saying, Lord, dost thou at this time restore the kingdom to Israel?

   7 And he said said unto them, It is not for you to know times or seasons, which the Father hath set within his own authority.

   8 But ye shall receive power, when the Holy Spirit is come upon you: and ye shall be my witnesses both in Jerusalem, and in all Judea and Samaria, and unto the uttermost part of the earth.

   9 And when he had said these things, as they were looking, he was taken up; and a cloud received him out of their sight.

8. State in your own words the connection of verse 2b, 3, and 4.

9. Show the connection of Luke 24:29; Acts 1:5 and John 14:16.

10. From memory give in your own words the five thoughts of verses 1-5.

10 And while they were looking stedfastly into heaven as
    he went, behold, two men stood by them in white ap-
    parel;

11 who also said, Ye men of Galilee, why stand ye look-
    ing into heaven? this Jesus, who was received up from
    you into heaven, shall so come in like manner as ye
    beheld him going into heaven.

6 Luke had already told Theophilus that Jesus appeared "by the space of forty days." Now he describes that last memorable day. Luke had further told him that Jesus spoke things to the eleven concerning the kingdom of God, so the question of the apostles would not be at all strange, when they asked, "Lord, dost thou at this time restore the kingdom to Israel?" Not at all strange, did we say? No? Not as to content, but as to the utter lack of understanding of the kingdom of God, it is indeed strange. We remember that the apostles had walked with and listened to Jesus until they had now come to His last day on earth and **still** they had not freed their minds of the thought of the restoration of the physical kingdom of David to Israel.

7-8 Jesus does not chide them for their misconception, possibly being satisfied that the apostles understood that a kingdom was about to be set up, however distorted might be their view of it. He simply reminds them that their question about the "time" of the coming kingdom was not for them to know and was of secondary importance. The all important truth for them at this time was what He had promised them while they were in the upper room—that they were to wait for power through the Holy Spirit; and that through this power, which was to "come upon them," they were going to be made witnesses for Him "both in Jerusalem, and in all Judea and Samaria, and unto the uttermost part of the earth."

9-11 The inspired writer pictures graphically the ascension of Jesus. A further word can be added to this description by reading his former treatise on this very point. ". . . and he lifted up his hands, and blessed them. And it came to pass, while he blessed them, he parted from them, and was carried up into heaven." (Luke 24:50, 51)

We know of no artist who has successfully painted the scene described in verses 9-11. Possibly this is true because the event therein described is beyond the brush of an artist.

11. On what day do the events of verses 6-11 occur?
12. What is not strange and what is strange about the question of the apostles?
13. Why was the time of the setting up of the kingdom of Israel of secondary importance to the baptism in the Holy Spirit?
14. What is the further word added by Luke in his gospel that is not found in Acts regarding the ascension of Jesus?

We want to notice that the two men or angels did not appear in the heavens into which the apostles were gazing—but while their eyes were cast heavenward the two men "stood beside them in white apparel." With the words, "Ye men of Galilee," the two men probably turned the heads of the apostles from their worshipful gaze into the sky to staring awestruck upon these two heavenly strangers. The two men left with the eleven the same truth that Jesus had spoken to them at the time He had promised them the Holy Spirit(John 14:1-3). But now they could see; now they could understand; now they could know the true meaning of these strange words. In addition to a reiteration of the promise of the second coming made by Jesus, they said He would "come in **like manner** as ye beheld him going."

Now for a backward glance over these verses to formulate an outline as the basis for memorizing the events of Acts 1:6-11.

a. The apostles gather with Jesus on the mount of Olivet on the day of His ascension. 6a.

b. Their conversation together consisted of their misguided question about the kingdom and Jesus' reply that the time was in the authority of the Father—but that their need was to realize the coming power and its results in making them witnesses. 6b-8.

c. The actual ascension of Jesus attended as it was with the amazement of the apostles; the cloud; the two men and their message of His return. 9-11.

Would not you, too, be held by the spell of the moment to the spot on that little hill? To watch before you the bodily form of one you had known so well suddenly begin to rise from the earth; then to see His progress into the sky until He passed out of sight into a cloud? It is true Jesus had told them, before He began this miraculous ascent, that He intended for them to promptly leave for the city—but who wouldn't have forgotten these words for a moment as he stood in the presence of such an event?

2. IN THE UPPER ROOM 1:12-26

    12 Then returned they unto Jerusalem from the mount called Olivet, which is nigh unto Jerusalem, a sabbath day's journey off.

    13 And when they were come in, they went up into the upper chamber, where they were abiding; both Peter and John and James and Andrew, Philip and Thomas, Bartholomew and Matthew, James the son of Alphaeus, and Simon the Zealot, and Judas the son of James.

    14 These all with one accord continued stedfastly in pray-

15. Where did the two men in white apparel appear and why did they chide the apostles?

16. What did the two angels add to the words of Jesus in John 14:1-3?

17. From memory give in your own words the three thoughts of verses 6-11.

er, with the women, and Mary the mother of Jesus, and with his brethren.

15 And in these days Peter stood up in the midst of the brethren, and said (and there was a multitude of persons gathered together, about a hundred and twenty),

16 Brethren, it was needful that the scripture should be fulfilled, which the Holy Spirit spake before by the mouth of David concerning Judas, who was guide to them that took Jesus.

17 For he was numbered among us, and received his portion in this ministry.

18 (Now this man obtained a field with the reward of his iniquity; and falling headlong, he burst asunder in the midst, and all his bowels gushed out.

19 And it became known to all the dwellers at Jerusalem; insomuch that in their language that field was called Akeldama, that is, The field of blood.)

20 For it is written in the book of Psalms,
Let his habitation be made desolate,
And let no man dwell therein: and, His office let another take.

21 Of the men therefore that have companied with us all the time that the Lord Jesus went in and went out among us,

22 beginning from the baptism of John, unto the day that he was received up from us, of these must one become a witness with us of his resurrection.

23 And they put forward two, Joseph called Barsabbas, who was surnamed Justus, and Matthias.

24 And they prayed, and said, Thou, Lord, who knowest the hearts of all men, show of these two the one whom thou hast chosen,

25 to take the place in this ministry and apostleship from which Judas fell away, that he might go to his own place.

26 And they gave lots for them; and the lot fell upon Matthias; and he was numbered with the eleven apostles.

a. Their return. 12

12 Verse twelve is a transition verse linking up the two places designated on the picture on page 22. If you will read Luke 24:52, 53, you will discover that they returned "with great joy" and that they were "continually in the temple blessing God." So, we can say that they spent their time of waiting either in the temple

18. What two points do we find in Luke 24:52, 53 that are not mentioned in Acts 1:12?

or in the upper room. At least, the events described in the text would have taken place in one of these two places. The position of the mount called Olivet, from which Jesus was taken up, is about seven-eights of a mile east of Jerusalem. This distance is called "a sabbath day's journey."

b. The prayer meeting. 13-14.

13 Can you imagine the feeling of joy that must have surged through their hearts as they walked with eager steps down the slope of the mount of Olives, down into the Kidron Valley and looked up to the heights of the wall of Jerusalem? Never had those walls, which were so familiar to them, appeared as they did on that day, for they now were to enclose that place where the risen Lord had told them to wait.

Oh, that today, as we press on towards that new Jerusalem, we might believe in our hearts that Jesus is as much alive as He was in that day! The same holy confidence and joy can be ours for we have the same evidence; yea, more, upon which to found our convictions that "He ever liveth" and will keep His promises now even as He did then.

Verse thirteen speaks of the house in which the apostles had been living. There is good reason to believe that this house is the same one described in Luke 22:7-13. Be that as it may, Luke here tells us who those were that went into that upper chamber. It would be well to learn the names of the twelve apostles if you have not already done so. They are:

Peter and John,
James and Andrew,
Philip and Thomas,
Bartholomew and Matthew,
James the son of Alphaeus,
Simon the Zealot,
Judas the son of James.

Add to this list the name of Matthias and you have the twelve.

14 Immediately upon entering the city and the upper room the eleven along with certain women; Mary, the mother of Jesus; and the brethren of Jesus held a prayer meeting. They were in total accord one with another and so continued steadfastly in prayer for some time.

19. In what two places did the events described in 1:12-26 occur?
20. How far is a sabbath day's journey? How did it come to be called a "sabbath day's journey?"
21. What comparison can we make today with the event in verse 12?
22. What do you know of the upper room spoken of in verse 13?
23. Give from memory the eleven apostles as found in verse 13.
24. What was the first act upon coming into the city and entering the upper room?

c. The place of Judas filled. 15-26.

15 We must remember that all of the events described in the first chapter took place in the ten days that elapsed from the day of ascension to the day of Pentecost. Notice what is said to have happened in this period: (It is heard quite often that the eleven held a ten-day prayer meeting. They did something besides pray.)

a. They held a prayer meeting in the upper room. 14.

b. They were continually in the temple blessing God. Luke 24:52, 53.

c. They transacted the business of filling the office of Judas. 15-26.

The place where the filling of the office of Judas occurred is not mentioned in the text—but the text **does** indicate a lapse of time between the prayer meeting in the upper room and the business of filling the vacancy in the "office" of the twelve. This indication is found by realizing that in verse fifteen we have a multitude of one hundred and twenty persons gathered, whereas in verse fourteen, we find only the eleven, the women, Mary, and the brethren of Jesus.

It seems to the writer altogether possible, if not probable, that the gathering of the one hundred and twenty persons would have been in the "large upper room." Here are the reasons for concluding that the selection of Matthias took place in the upper room and not in the temple or some other place of public assemblage:

a. The fact that this was the place of residence for the eleven, and since this was a personal or private matter, it would not be reasonable to imagine them carrying out this selection in any public place such as the temple.

b. The opposition to the work of Christ would prevent or hinder the apostles from transacting this matter in a public gathering. Their knowledge of the situation would make it unwise to do such a thing.

c. The upper chambers of the city of Jerusalem were such as could accomodate a crowd of one hundred and twenty persons.

16 Notice the content of the sixteenth verse—read it. Let us mark the circumstances: The eleven were promised by Jesus that they would be baptized in the Holy Spirit (1:5), and that they would receive power when the Holy Spirit was come upon them (1:8). With

25. What three things happened in the 10 days from the ascension to Pentecost?

26. How do we know there is a lapse of time between the prayer meeting and the filling of the office of Judas?

27. What reasons do we have for concluding that the filling of the office of the twelve occurred in the upper room?

these promises impressed upon their hearts, they walked into the city to wait for the fulfillment. But here we have them gathered in a formal meeting to carry out a specific work. Isn't it a bit strange? It is, unless we understand that the apostles knew they were going to be baptized in the Holy Spirit according to promise and prophesy and that there should be **twelve** in the group. Because of this, Peter directed the selection of one to fill this vacancy left by the betrayal of Judas. This truth lends still more force to the thought that only the twelve were baptized in the Holy Spirit.

17-20 Seven hundred years before the angels sang of the advent of the Messiah, that man "after God's own heart" wrote these words: "Let his habitation be made desolate, and let no man dwell therein and, His office let another take." Little did David know that it would be seven hundred years before these words would find their fulfillment in Judas, the betrayer of the Christ. But the same Spirit that spoke these words to the mind of the Psalmist directed their fulfillment. Peter arises in the midst of the one hundred and twenty brethren to tell of this "son of perdition" in whom this prophecy finds its consummation. Peter gives five things about Judas in verses sixteen through twenty—note them:

a. "Who was guide to them that took Jesus." 16b.
b. "He was numbered among us" i.e. he was counted as one of the twelve. 17a.
c. "And received his portion in this ministry" i.e., he had as much a part in the ministry to which Jesus called the twelve as any other. 17b.
d. "Obtained a field with the thirty pieces of silver." This was done indirectly through the priests. Although the field was purchased by the priests, it was counted as being purchased by Judas since it was his money that made the transaction. 18a. Cf. Matt. 27:3-8.
e. He fell headlong into the field from his hanging position and burst asunder in the field. Hence, the name given to the field by those living near there: "The Field of Blood."

21-26 In the six remaining verses, we have an account of the actual business at hand. First, Peter very carefully gave the qualifications of the man who could properly occupy the vacancy left by Judas. It would have to be one of those who "have companied with us (them) all the time that the Lord Jesus went in and out among us (them), beginning from the baptism of John, unto the day that he was received up from us (them)." 21, 22a. Peter also specifically stated the purpose of this selection. It was so "this' one" could

28. Show the connection of the selection of one to take the place of Judas and the baptism of the Holy Spirit.
29. Give from memory in your own words the five things concerning Judas mentioned by Peter.

be, along with the eleven, a witness of His resurrection. It is significant to note that even before the day of Pentecost, the apostles took the words of Jesus: "Ye shall be my witnesses" to mean that they were to be witnesses or proclaimers of His resurrection. 21, 22. The apostles were to be witnesses in the sense of ambassadors. Cf. II Cor. 5:20.

Later we are to read in Acts 6:5 "And the saying pleased the whole multitude: and they chose Stephen, ..." A similar incident took place here—the statement of Peter "pleased the whole multitude" of the one hundred and twenty and "they put forward two: Joseph called Barsabbas who was surnamed Justus, and Matthias."

When we know what God said in regard to a certain matter and yet a selection must be made as to how this matter will be executed only prayer can determine God's will. By asking for His providential leadership His will can be made known. This was the procedure in the case of the eleven. Notice the steps and mark them well as an example for our discovery of God's will in some matters.

a. To know that God wants something to be done. In this case it was the filling of the office of the twelve.

b. To know that now is the time for action. This they knew from the coming day of power, "not many days hence."

c. To have a man (or men) who is (are) qualified to occupy the place of God's servant. This they had in Barsabbas and Matthias."

d. To pray an unselfish and dependent prayer for God's leadership. This was surely the prayer of the eleven as recorded in verses twenty-four and twenty-five. It would be well to look closely into the content of the prayer, demonstrating as it does their utter dependence upon God for His knowledge of who was fitted for this place.

"Thou, Lord, **who knowest the hearts of all men,** show of these two the one whom thou hast chosen."

It is also of interest to find within this prayer a reiteration of a very bluntly stated fact: that Judas fell away from this ministry

30. What were the qualifications given by Peter for the one to take the place of the apostle Judas?

31. What was the purpose of this selection?

32. Did the apostles know God's will in the case at hand? If so, why the prayer?

33. State in your own words the five steps in finding the Lord's will in this situation.

34. How can we know God's will today?

35. How can we know the time for action in the will of God?

of apostleship to go to his own place. Being as he was "a son of perdition" we can have no hesitancy as to what place is here meant.

    e. Make, then some move on your part in which the providence of God can be manifested. This was the reason for the casting of lots. Otherwise, there would have been, of necessity, some direct operation of the mind of God upon the mind of man, in which, such information would have been given. But since it is not the nature of Jehovah to thus convey knowledge when there is some other more natural method, we find the eleven casting lots. "And the lot fell upon Matthias and he was numbered with the eleven apostles."

The question as to whether Matthias was in truth an apostle should be settled with these words the Holy Spirit spoke through Luke: ". . . . **and he was numbered with the eleven apostles.**"

3. IN AN APARTMENT IN THE TEMPLE.
    a. The baptism in the Holy Spirit. 2:1-4.

  1 And when the day of Pentecost was now come, they were all together in one place.

  2 And suddenly there came from heaven a sound as of the rushing of a mighty wind, and it filled all the house where they were sitting.

  3 And there appeared unto them tongues parting asunder, like as of fire; and it sat upon each one of them.

  4 And they were all filled with the Holy Spirit, and began to speak with other tongues, as the Spirit gave them utterance.

  1 The great day had arrived. The day toward which the whole plan and program of Jesus had pointed. His death and resurrection would mean nothing unless spread abroad; and here was the day upon which these great facts were to be declared for the first time. When Jesus stood in Caesarea Philippi and made that glorious promise: "I will build my church" (Matt. 16:18), He was looking forward to this day. The word "church" means "called out." On this day of Pentecost certain persons were "called out" of the world by the preaching of the gospel to become the possession of Christ; thus to form His "called out" body, His church. Jesus had not been explicit as to the number of days the apostles were to tarry in the city, He simply said it would be not "many days" (1:5), but it is interesting to note the divine hand in the selection of this particular day: The **proper people** were on this day present: "devout men" (2:5), thus they were more receptive to the divine truth. The **proper**

36. Why can we consider the day of Pentecost the day toward which the whole plan and program of Jesus pointed?

37. Explain how the church was established on the day of Pentecost.

preachers were there: those whom Jesus Himself had designated, His twelve apostles. These were the men Jesus had selected and taught; all the while preparing them for this momentous occasion. The **proper power** was present, that promised power of the baptism in the Holy Spirit. The subject of the baptism in the Holy Spirit is to be taken up in our special study (Cf. pp. 351). Suffice it to say here that:

1. Jesus had promised the apostles that they were to receive this power. (1:5)
2. That the grammatical construction of 1:26 and 2:1 points only to the apostles as the recipients of this experience.
3. When we remember that the original manuscripts did not contain the chapter and paragraph divisions that our English translations do, and then we read from the close of the first chapter ignoring the break of the chapter and paragraph, it becomes very clear who Luke wanted us to understand were immersed in the Holy Spirit. Note how it reads this way:

"And they gave lots for **them;** and the lot fell upon Matthias; and he was numbered with the **eleven apostles.** And when the day of Pentecost was now come, **they** were all together in one place."

The fact that the antecedent of any pronoun is found by referring back to the nearest noun with which it agrees in person, number and case clinches the argument of the baptism of only the apostles in the Holy Spirit.

It might be well to say just a word as to where the apostles were gathered. The scriptures say "they were all together in one place" but where was that place? It is important to notice that it must have been in some other place than the upper room referred to in 1:13, for had it been a continuation of action in the same room there would have been no need to mention that they were gathered together, since that would have already been known.

We are disposed to the opinion that the place spoken of was an **apartment in the temple.** We hold this opinion for the following reasons:

1. The circumstances of preaching to thousands would not lend itself to this taking place in a private residence. Whereas, all the twelve needed to do in the temple apartment, which faced the temple area, was to turn to the patio side of the apartment, and there were the many acres of the temple area to accommodate the crowd.

38. Give three evidences of the divine hand in the selection of the day of Pentecost as the day for the establishment of the church.
39. How can we say that the grammatical construction of 1:26 and 2:1 points only to the twelve as the ones baptized in the Holy Spirit?
40. How can we know that the gathering of the apostles was in some other place than the upper room?

2. Since this was a great feast day for the Jews, the temple was the headquarters for the celebration (Luke 24:53), it would not seem logical that the apostles would be in their homes upon such an occasion.

3. Luke states "they were continually in the temple blessing God." What more appropriate time to be in the temple worshiping God than upon this great day of the feast of the first fruits?

2-4 Notice that there was a "sound as of the rushing of a mighty wind." It does **not** say there was mighty wind, but only the "sound as of the rushing of a mighty wind." This sound was confined to the place wherein they were sitting. Immediately preceding the sound, or appearing simultaneously with the sound, were the tongues like as of fire, or what appeared to be tongues of fire, which upon appearing, immediately distributed themselves over the various parts of the room and came to rest upon the apostles. These tongues of fire were like the sound of the wind, they were not literal flames of fire but only "like as of fire." The reason for these manifestations was, no doubt, to lend splendor to the occasion which would attract attention and interest, and would at the same time manifest to all that saw and heard that the hand of God was in the whole experience. We can know as a dogmatic certainty that verse 4 of the second chapter is the literal fulfillment of verse 5 of the first chapter. Jesus had promised the baptism of the Holy Spirit and here is the fulfillment of His promise.

Consider a point of import: What is meant by the word "baptism" as it is here used? The **objects** of the baptism were the apostles . . . the **element** of the baptism was the Holy Spirit. What **part** of the apostles was immersed in the Holy Spirit? A moment's thought will cause us to say that their minds were the portions of their beings to be immersed in the Holy Spirit. Thus the personality of the Holy Spirit literally immersed the personalities of the twelve and they spake not from their own spirits, but only as their immersed spirits were controlled by the Spirit of God. Indeed Jesus' words in Matt. 10:20 found an actual fulfillment here: "For it is not ye that speak but the Spirit of your Father that speaketh in you."

41. What reasons are given for saying that the baptism in the Holy Spirit occurred in a temple apartment?

42. Was the sound of the rushing of a mighty wind general or local?

43. Why were these miraculous manifestations given at this time?

44. What statement of Jesus finds its fulfillment on this day?

45. Explain the meaning and use of the word "baptism" as used in the baptism of the Holy Spirit.

46. What kind of Jews were present at Pentecost, and what called them together to listen to the words of Peter?

b. The result of the baptism. 5-13.
5 Now there were dwelling at Jerusalem Jews, devout men, from every nation under heaven.
6 And when this sound was heard, the multitude came together, and were confounded, because that every man heard them speaking in his own language.
7 And they were all amazed and marvelled, saying, Behold, are not all these that speak Galilaeans?
8 And how hear we, every man in our own language wherein we were born?
9 Parthians and Medes and Elamites, and the dwellers in Mesopotamia, in Judaea and Cappadocia, in Pontus and Asia,
10 in Phrygia and Pamphylia, in Egypt and the parts of Libya about Cyrene, and sojourners from Rome, both Jews and proselytes,
11 Cretans and Arabians, we hear them speaking in our tongues the mighty works of God.
12 And they were all amazed, and were perplexed, saying one to another, What meaneth this?
13 But others mocking said, They are filled with new wine.

5-13 We have already observed the result of the Holy Spirit baptism upon the apostles. We come now to note its result upon those who beheld this miraculous appearance.

We take note first of those present to witness this scene: "Jews, devout men, from every nation under heaven."

As we have already commented, the day of Pentecost called many Jews from their native homes to Jerusalem to participate in this annual feast. That they were **devout men** indicates their deep interest in the things of Jehovah. A better soil could not be imagined for planting the seed of the kingdom. Luke next tells us what called the congregation together. "The sound of the rushing of a mighty wind." It seemed to be located in a particular portion of the temple. This called a great multitude to this place to investigate. When they arrived imagine their surprise when they found no effects of a great wind, but what they did behold was a sight never before beheld by mortal eye, and they heard things which no man had ever heard.

47. Using a Bible dictionary or encyclopedia, look up a diagram of the temple and formulate in your mind the location of the temple area, apartments, and sanctuary.
48. What three words describe the results of the hearing of every man speaking in his own language?
49. Using a Bible dictionary or encyclopedia, locate upon a map the nations spoken of in Acts 2:9-11.

Will you imagine with me a Jew from the nation of Cappadocia running toward the temple? As he runs he must pause every so often ere he jostle a stranger. There is an ever increasing crowd gathering, hurrying to the same place. He hears as he dodges in and out among the crowd, a babel of voices, and it seems that no two languages or dialects are the same. He thinks: "Ah, to be home among my own people and to hear once again my native tongue." Being near the temple when startled by this sound, he soon comes to the place of interest. There is a little knot of men gathered under the balcony of one of the temple apartments; he looks up through the balcony rail, and there, standing together, are several very ordinary looking men. "But what is that above their heads? It looks like flames of fire, yea, tongues of fire. They are speaking, but what are they saying?" Suddenly, a startled look comes across the face of the Cappadocian Jew, for he can **understand every word these men are saying.** They are speaking to him **in his native dialect!** How good it is to hear it again, and they are declaring the mighty works of God. He listens for a moment and then becomes curious and looks around him. There, written upon the faces of all, is utter astonishment. All seem to be held in a spell of perplexity. Soon the shock of the first impression is worn off, and he sees on every hand signs that all who are there assembled are hearing and seeing exactly what he is. "How can this be? Are not these men upon the balcony Galileans? How can it be then that every man can hear them speaking in his own tongue wherein he was born? Why, there are here assembled: Parthians and Medes and Elamites and dwellers in Mesopotamia, in Judea and I had others from Cappadocia, there are those here from Pontus and Asia, Phrygia, Egypt and parts of Libya about Cyrene, sojourners from Rome, both Jews and proselytes, even Cretans and Arabians. All these are hearing what I am hearing in their own tongue . . . What can this mean?"

Here we leave our imaginary Jew and add that all who were there gathered were amazed and perplexed, and the question of our Cappadocian Jew was the question of every heart. But we, upon reading this account, although we understand its action and import, are amazed and perplexed ourselves, for there were mockers present who dared to mock at this divine demonstration. They said with utter lack of reason:

"They are filled with new wine."

c.　The sermon of Peter. 14-36.

14　But Peter, standing up with the eleven, lifted up his
　　　voice, and spake forth unto them, saying, Ye men

50. Did the apostles speak in fifteen languages or did the Holy Spirit perform a miracle of hearing?
51. What reason would you assign for the words of those who said, "They are filled with new wine?"

THE TOMB OF DAVID

The whole group of buildings is called Neby Daud, which signifies the Sanctuary of the Sepulchre of the Prophet David.

Peter could say in his day: "his tomb is with us unto this day". Persons could go to view the place where David was buried. And so today we are shown in the city of Jerusalem these buildings as the tomb of David. Whether or not this tomb does indeed contain the dust of the king of Israel we know that he both died and was buried, but of the one he spoke He is alive forevermore. Only kings and prophets were buried in cities. (I Kings 2:10; 16:6; I Sam. 25:1; 28.)

of Judaea, and all ye that dwell at Jerusalem, be this
known unto you, and give ear unto my words:

15 For these are not drunken, as ye suppose; seeing it is
but the third hour of the day;

16 but this is that which hath been spoken through the
prophet Joel:

17 And it shall be in the last days, saith God,
I will pour forth of my Spirit upon all flesh:
And your sons and your daughters shall prophesy,
And your young men shall see visions,
And your old men shall dream dreams:

18 Yea and on my servants and on my handmaidens in
those days
Will I pour forth of my Spirit; and they shall prophesy.

19 And I will show wonders in the heaven above,
And signs on the earth beneath;
Blood, and fire, and vapor of smoke:

20 The sun shall be turned into darkness,
And the moon into blood,
Before the day of the Lord come,
That great and notable day:

21 And it shall be, that whosoever shall call on the name
of the Lord shall be saved.

22 Ye men of Israel, hear these words: Jesus of Nazareth, a man approved of God unto you by mighty works
and wonders and signs which God did by him in
the midst of you, even as ye yourselves know;

23 him, being delivered up by the determinate counsel and
foreknowledge of God, ye by the hand of lawless men
did crucify and slay:

24 whom God raised up, having loosed the pangs of
death: because it was not possible that he should be
holden of it.

25 For David saith concerning him,
I beheld the Lord always before my face;
For he is on my right hand, that I should not be
moved:

26 Therefore my heart was glad, and my tongue rejoiced;
Moreover my flesh also shall dwell in hope:

27 Because thou wilt not leave my soul unto Hades,
Neither wilt thou give thy Holy One to see corruption.

28 Thou madest known unto me the ways of life;
Thou shalt make me full of gladness with thy countenance.

29 Brethren, I may say unto you freely of the patriarch

David, that he both died and was buried, and his
tomb is with us unto this day.

30 Being therefore a prophet, and knowing that God had
sworn with an oath to him, that of the fruit of his
loins he would set one upon his throne;

31 he foreseeing this spake of the resurrection of the
Christ, that neither was he left unto Hades, nor did
his flesh see corruption.

32 This Jesus did God raise up, whereof we all are witnesses.

33 Being therefore by the right hand of God exalted, and
having received of the Father the promise of the Holy
Spirit, he hath poured forth this, which ye see and hear.

34 For David ascended not into the heavens: but he saith
himself,
The Lord said unto my Lord, Sit thou on my right
hand,

35 Till I make thine enemies the footstool of thy feet.

36 Let all the house of Israel therefore know assuredly,
that God hath made him both Lord and Christ, this
Jesus whom ye crucified.

14-16 Evidently the jeering of the mockers was loud and distinct enough to be heard by the apostles, for we now find Peter
standing forth among the twelve and giving answer to their charge.
His first words are a bold denial of the accusation and then follows his two-fold reply: "These are not drunken, as ye suppose" because:

1. It is only nine o'clock in the morning; whoever heard of men
   drunk at this hour on a sacred feast day? The drunken charge
   could not have been true for it was a strict violation of Jewish
   law to drink intoxicants on a feast day.

2. This which ye behold is a fulfillment of prophecy. "This is
   that which hath been spoken through the prophet Joel." Then
   he quotes the words of the prophet. We shall notice their import and meaning according to the verses:

17-18 The "last days" spoken of in these verses must be associated
with the context for their meaning. The words of Joel, like those
of a number of other prophets have to do with **Judah** and **Jerusalem,**
hence we can say that the "last days" have reference to the last days
of Judah as a tribe (the term "Judah" has reference also, at times,
to the whole nation of Israel) and to the last days of Jerusalem
as a city. The exact fulfillment of these words becomes apparent

52. How do the words of Peter concerning the time of day answer the charge
of the mockers?

53. To what period of time do the words, "the last days," refer, as used in
verse 17?

when we realize that it was only thirty-five or forty years from the day Peter spoke to the utter destruction of Jerusalem and the dispersion of the nation of Israel.

The pouring forth of the Holy Spirit upon all flesh was **potentially** accomplished upon the day of Pentecost. It is impossible to claim more than this. The reference to "all flesh" doubtless contemplated the reception of the Holy Spirit by both Jew and Gentile. To say that "all flesh" upon this day received the outpouring of the Holy Spirit is an absurdity in view of the fact that all present were Jews. How then can it be said that these words of the prophet can here find fulfillment? It seems best to say that because the apostles were baptized in the Holy Spirit, they were enabled to carry the gospel to the Gentiles as well as the Jews, and through obedience to the gospel both Jew and Gentile received, as a gift from God, the Holy Spirit (2:38, 39). Thus could it be said that "all flesh" received the Holy Spirit through what occurred on Pentecost.

We next find the promise of prophesying and visions. How can these be connected with the day of Pentecost and the events of that day? The answer is found in realizing that through the baptism in the Holy Spirit, the apostles were given the power that upon whomsoever they laid their hands they could impart to those persons certain spiritual powers called "spiritual gifts" (I Cor. 12:1-11). These gifts included prophecy, wisdom, knowledge, etc. The statement in verses 17 and 18 relative to the prophesying and visions can then be understood as the spiritual gifts imparted by the apostles to the persons named.

This all came about as a result of the Holy Spirit baptism.

19-21 Many and various are the remarks upon these verses. We will not enter the arena of controversy, but will content ourselves by stating that it seems altogether probable that the words of these verses could very well be applied to the day of the Pentecostal feast. Note the expressions and how their fulfillment can be found in the celebration:

  1. "I will show wonders in the heavens above, and signs on the earth beneath" . . . then follows the description of the wonders and signs . . . "Blood, and fire, and vapor of smoke: The sun shall be turned into darkness, and the moon into blood, before the day of the Lord come, that great and notable day: And it shall be that whosoever shall call upon the name of the Lord shall be saved."

54. How can it be said that upon the day of Pentecost the words of Joel were fulfilled, i.e. the fulfillment of his words: "I will pour forth of my Spirit upon all flesh?"
55. When were these "last days" consummated?
56. How were the prophesyings and visions connected with the day of Pentecost.

One explanation of Acts 2:19-21 is: The blood and fire, and vapor of smoke, were surely found upon the day of this feast. The blood must have flowed from the altars like rivers, as the thousands of animals were sacrificed. The fire and vapor of smoke ascended from the altars as the same sacrifices were burned. As the great billows of smoke filled the air in Jerusalem the sun was quite literally "turned into darkness," being hidden because of the smoke-encumbered atmosphere. The moon viewed through the smoke appeared as the color of blood. All this took place **before** the preaching of the first gospel sermon; the preaching of this message of redemption made this day of Pentecost "the day of the Lord." And then it could be said that "Whosoever shall call upon the name of the Lord shall be saved." How this "calling" upon the name of the Lord took place may best be understood by reading the rest of the chapter.

Peter's answer to the accusation of the drunkenness formed a springboard for the rest of his message. Having shown that the events happening were in fulfillment of the prophet's words, he now continues his message, and immediately brings forward the burden of his inspired utterance. Those who stood before him must have now understood that he and the eleven were indeed inspired, and the message they proclaimed was one from God. There must have been but one question in the mind of every thoughtful Jew: "We must indeed confess that these men are speaking under divine leadership, but **what is the purpose?** What is the reason behind all this? Surely there must be more to this occasion than a mere declaration unto various nations in their various languages 'the mighty works of God'." This question is now answered by the apostle Peter. We might say in our own words that the intent of this divine splendor was to prepare the way for the declaration of Jesus as Christ and Lord.

22-24 These verses contain the theme and proposition of the message. Verses 25-36 are but a development and enlargement of the facts stated in verses 22-24. Consider the facts in these verses: "Ye men of Israel, hear these words." A preparatory remark which called attention to the importance of what was to follow: This Jesus of Nazareth was a man approved of God by mighty works and wonders and signs, which were performed through the power of

57. Where were the wonders and signs, spoken of in prophecy, fulfilled?
58. From your open Bible read the 19th and 20th verses and then from memory show how these things were fulfilled on the day of Pentecost, with special note concerning "the day of the Lord."
59. Following the answer of the charge of drunkenness, what natural question would be in the mind of every thinking Jew?
60. What was the real purpose behind all of this divine splendor?
61. In which verses do we have the theme and proposition for the message of Peter? What would you say the theme is? The proposition?

God, in their very midst. They who stood before Peter, especially those "dwellers in Judea," had witnessed many of the miracles wrought by Jesus, and therefore well knew the words of Peter were the truth. The real purpose of these works, wonders and signs had evidently escaped the perception of those who beheld them, for Peter now gives to those acts of power their full meaning. These things were done that they might believe and know that God's approval was upon this man; that God had singled Him out above others, upon whom to place His sanction and seal. This to the mind of the Jew could be nothing else than a description of the Messiah, or Christ.

Next come the words that struck conviction and intense personal guilt to the hearts of all who heard. That this Nazarene was One who was mighty in word and deed could hardly be denied; but what had happened to Him? Yes, that was the question; and all those on that day **knew** what had happened. It must have been a much talked of fact, that this Jesus of Nazareth had been crucified outside the city of Zion a few short weeks ago. But none had thought of its terrible import until these words spoken by God's direction fell upon their understanding. Peter now says that God Himself had directed the death of this one, and yet they (the Jews) were personally responsible for the despicable deed. More than this "God raised Him from the dead." Such a one could not be held by the bonds of death; through the power of God, He tore away the bonds of death and came forth the triumphant victor over death and the grave. What shocking news, they had crucified **the Messiah!** And yet God had foreordained it to be so. Still more astounding, He is now raised from the dead.

There were four facts stated by Peter in the opening words of his message: (1) Jesus was approved of God by mighty works, wonders and signs. (2) He was crucified by the Jews, using the "lawless hands" of the Romans. (3) God had predetermined this. (4) God raised this Holy One from the dead. Of these four facts, the first two needed no proof for they could not be gainsayed; the last two needed further evidence for verification.

25-32 Verses 25-32 contain scriptural proof for facts three and four. The easiest way to convince any Jew God had predetermined an event was to refer to the Old Testament scriptures and there show a prophetic word that would apply to the point under dispute.

62. Why would the words of Peter as found in verses 22-24 strike conviction to the hearts of those that heard?
63. State from memory in your own words, the four facts that Peter gave in the opening words of his message.
64. What purpose can be assigned to verses 25-32?
65. What is the procedure used by Peter in convincing the Jews of points 3 and 4?

This procedure is here used by Peter. The Psalmist David is called in to witness that God had previously determined that a certain person would be raised from the dead. Verses 25-27 contain the words of David written prophetically some five hundred to seven hundred years before Christ. In this quotation from this Psalm of David we note in verses 25, 26 introductory remarks to the real point of the prophecy contained in verse 27. The first person is here used by David in referring to the Christ. Note his words:

"I beheld the Lord always before my face; for he is on my right hand, that I should not be moved: Therefore my heart was glad, and my tongue rejoiced; moreover my flesh also shall dwell in hope."

Since the person spoken of is the Christ, we can say that the words of these verses have to do with His pre-existence. While in this state, He "beheld the Lord always before His face," for Jehovah was very near to Him, and was His strength. This nearness, and harmony caused His heart to be glad and also resulted in words of rejoicing. Then looking forward to His earthly advent He could say, because of His previous perfect harmony with the Father, that when He became flesh that He could live or dwell "in hope." This leads us to the theme of the prophecy: That although the spirit of the Christ would depart from the body, yet it would not remain in the place of the departed spirits, i.e. in "Hades"; neither would the flesh or body of the Holy One of God see corruption. This is speaking of a resurrection, of a return of the spirit to the body ere the body could decay. **Thus were the two facts of the pre-determination of God and the resurrection of the Christ established in one concerted effort.**

Peter has yet to make the direct application of this proof to Jesus of Nazareth.

Verse 28 refers to the fact that the ways of the life of the Christ while on earth were directed by Jehovah . . . because He thus allowed Himself to be directed, He could look forward to the gladness of beholding His Father's face in glory.

The thought that in this prophecy David was describing a resurrection from the dead was undeniable. The only question remaining in the mind of the Jewish multitude was "Of whom speaketh the prophet, of himself, or of some other?" Since the Psalmist had used the first person, it was necessary to first show that this prophecy did not refer to David. Of this Peter now speaks: It was a well known fact that David both died and was buried, and his tomb could be witnessed by any interested. So it could never be said the resurrec-

66. Explain in your own words the application of verse 25, 26 to the Christ.
67. Show how the two points, three and four, are established in one concerted effort.
68. Explain verse 28.

tion prophecy found its fulfillment in the prophet. The solution is found in the prophetic office David held; he being a prophet could speak accurately of future events. David knew that God had made a promise to him, and in this promise God had said that from his loins there would come One who would occupy the eternal throne in heaven. He knowing these facts, then spoke as he did in Psalm Sixteen. In this Psalm David spoke of the resurrection of the Christ; that neither was He left in Hades, nor did His flesh see corruption. To what purpose was the resurrection here spoken of? The answer is very evident; because only such a resurrected, glorified being could occupy this promised throne.

It now begins to be more and more manifest to those listening that it was predicted of the Christ:

(1) He would die. (2) Yet His spirit would not remain in Hades. (3) Nor would His body decay. (4) Furthermore, He was to be raised to sit on the heavenly throne at the right hand of God.

33 The ultimate conclusion has been reached and Peter now enforces the thought that must have been in the mind of every thinking Jew. Jesus had fulfilled every other qualification of the Christ, there only remains the exaltation at the right hand of the Father. This, Peter says of Jesus in no uncertain terms, note:

"Being therefore by the right hand of God exalted," and then in connection with His exalted position and in direct relation to the present circumstances of the day of Pentecost, Peter states that upon being thus enthroned Jesus received the promise of the Father, the Holy Spirit. The demonstration of the Holy Spirit's action on the day of Pentecost was a result of the sending forth of this promised Comforter by none other than Jesus of Nazareth, who is the Christ.

The following have a fulfillment in only **one person,** Jesus of Nazareth, for:

(1) He was crucified. (2) His body did not decay in the tomb. (3) His spirit did not remain in Hades. (4) He is spoken of as raised by God from the dead.

Then indeed this one must be the Christ of God. He now is at the right hand of the Father. This conclusion Peter drives home in these words filled with meaning:

"This Jesus did God raise up, whereof we all are witnesses."

Peter had said previously that God had raised Jesus from the dead (24) but in the intervening verses He tells us **why** He was raised from the dead. He here gives to us the proof of His resurrection. "We know God raised Him from the dead," says Peter, "for we all (we apostles) are witnesses of His resurrection."

69. What relation does verse 29 have to the prophecy of David?
70. What connection is there between the promise God made to David and the resurrection of the Christ?
71. Show how what was predicted of the Christ found its fulfillment in Jesus.

34-35 The final word of prophetic proof is found in verses thirty-four and thirty-five. Peter here shows that what he had said of the Christ could never have been said of David, for he never made an ascent into heaven. Further than that, David denied any thought of himself ascending into heaven when he said (in Psalm 110:1) that Jehovah was speaking to David's Lord (which could be none other than the Christ), when He invited Him to sit at His right hand till His enemies were subdued. This word from the Psalmist of the exaltation of the Christ and the evident application of it to the experience of Jesus gives a mighty background and foundation of power, for the words of Peter's climactic conclusion. Hear him:

36 "Let all the house of Israel therefore know assuredly that God hath made him both Lord and Christ, this Jesus whom ye crucified."

The impact of these words can hardly be imagined by you and me. The one for whom all the Jews of ages past had longed and prayed had now arrived, only to be crucified by the very ones for whom He came.

Now, shall we rethink Peter's sermon in outline form? Notice:

Introduction of the sermon. 2:14-21. Peter's answer to the drunken charge:

1. A call to attention as to the import of what is to be said. 14.
2. Peter's first answer based upon the time of the day. 15.
3. Peter's second answer, based upon the fact that the events of the day were happening in fulfillment of Joel's prophecy. 16-21.

Theme of the sermon: . . . A demonstration of Jesus as the Christ.

Development of the sermon. 2:22-35.

1. The mighty works, wonders, and signs of Jesus demonstrate God's approval. 22.
2. His death was predetermined by Jehovah and carried out through the lawless hands of the Romans, prompted by the hate of the Jews. 23.
3. God raised Him from the dead. 24.
4. David spoke in great detail of the resurrection and exaltation of the Christ, which finds its fulfillment not in David, but only in Jesus. 25-31.
5. Jesus was raised from the dead. This fact was attested by eye-witnesses. 32.
6. Jesus was exalted for the express purpose of receiving the Holy Spirit. Jesus in this exalted position now gives the Holy Spirit to the apostles in this special manifestation. 33.
7. David spoke of this exaltation in another Psalm (110:1) when

72. What connection does the manifestation of the Holy Spirit on Pentecost have with the exaltation of the Christ?
73. Explain verses 34 and 35.
74. Show how verses 34 and 35 form a background for the thought of verse 36.

he himself had not ascended into heaven but referred to "his Lord" as being asked by "the Lord" to sit at His right hand till all his enemies were subdued. 34.

Conclusion of the sermon. 2:36. "Let all the house of Israel therefore know assuredly," i.e. because:

1. Jesus was approved of God. 22
2. The prediction of the death of the Christ finds an exact fulfillment in Him. 23.
3. God has raised Him from the dead, even as David said of the Christ. 24-28.
4. More than this, Jesus is now exalted even as David spoke of the Christ. 29-31.
5. We apostles are eye-witnesses of the resurrected Jesus. 32.
6. The out-pouring of the Holy Spirit here on the day of Pentecost, comes from this Jesus because of His exaltation. 33.
7. Finally, David spoke not of himself when he described "the Lord" (Jehovah), speaking to "my Lord" (the Christ) asking Him to sit at His right hand till all His enemies were subdued, but rather of the Christ which finds its fulfillment in Jesus of Nazareth. 34.

We say then, in view of all this, "that God hath made him both Lord and Christ, this Jesus whom ye crucified."

d. The results of the sermon. 37-42.

37 Now when they heard this, they were pricked in their heart, and said unto Peter and the rest of the apostles, Brethren, what shall we do?

38 And Peter said unto them, Repent ye, and be baptized every one of you in the name of Jesus Christ unto the remission of your sins; and ye shall receive the gift of the Holy Spirit.

39 For to you is the promise, and to your children, and to all that are afar off, even as many as the Lord our God shall call unto him.

40. And with many other words he testified, and exhorted them, saying, Save yourselves from this crooked generation.

41 They then that received his word were baptized: and there were added unto them in that day about three thousand souls.

42 And they continued stedfastly in the apostles' teaching and fellowship, in the breaking of bread and the prayers.

75. Why did the words of verse 36 cause such an impact on those who heard?
76. From memory give the outline of Peter's message.

37-41 "The immediate results were: first, conviction and inquiry; secondly, instruction and exhortation; and finally obedience, and the addition of those who received the Spirit" (G. Campbell Morgan. **Acts Of The Apostles,** page 87). These words give us a very fine outline of the results of Peter's message. Let us notice the outline in detail.

The last words of Peter were "Whom ye crucified," now they knew in truth whom they had crucified. Can we not attempt to stand in the place of the persons who heard these words? They crucified the Messiah. And yet it had been predicted by God that the Christ would thus suffer. This did not lessen their personal guilt. To whom should they turn? Could they dare now to look to God, seeing that the blood of His only begotten Son was upon their hands? They were in desperate need of forgiveness, but how to obtain it was the question unanswered in their burdened hearts. It is natural then to hear that cry rising spontaneously from the multitude: "Brethren, what shall we do?" What should they do for what? What was their conscious need? It was for **forgiveness** that they cried.

We now notice the instruction and exhortation given by Peter in answer to the conviction and inquiry of the Jews.

Peter makes a direct and unhesitating answer to the question. He tells them exactly what they "must do" to be forgiven or to secure the remission of their sins. Says the apostle, "Repent ye, and be baptized every one of you in the name of Jesus Christ unto the remission of your sins." How can it be thought that baptism has no connection with the forgiveness of sins when Peter answers the question of forgiveness after this fashion?

(A complete study on the connection of baptism with the remission of sins is given by J. W. McGarvey in his **New Commentary On Acts,** Vol. I, pages 243-262).

Peter informs the guilty multitude that in addition to the boon of forgiveness by repentance and baptism they were to receive a gift from God, nothing less than the "Holy Spirit." He further tells them that this promise of remission and the gift of the Holy Spirit was expressly provided for them, for their children, and to all that were afar off (doubtless referring to the Gentiles), even as many as the Lord our God shall unto Him. As to how God thus called these persons unto Himself we can best answer by reading the rest of

77. Give in outline form the three results of Peter's sermon.
78. Describe the causes behind the cry "Brethren, what shall we do?"
79. For what were they inquiring when they asked the question "What shall we do?"
80. What is the first thought presented in Peter's instruction to these men?
81. What is meant by the expression, "the gift of the Holy Spirit?"
82. Explain in your own words verse 39.

the book and noting that God called Jew and Gentile unto Himself through the preaching of the gospel. (Cf. II Thess. 2:14).

We have just noted the words of instruction in verses thirty-eight and thirty-nine; we now note the words of exhortation in verse forty. It was not enough to simply state in so many words the terms of pardon, for those listening had no previous knowledge of this plan of salvation by the grace of God. Hence, we find in verse forty the thought that Peter spent no little time, and no small amount of words, "testifying and exhorting" concerning this great salvation. Without doubt he outlined the plan of redemption through the death of Christ. His words on this portion of the message could be considered words of testimony or a logical presentation of the soul saving facts of the gospel. Then in words of exhortation, or earnest appeal, he urged them to repent and be baptized and thus appropriate the blood of Christ. By saying "Save yourselves from this crooked generation" Peter no doubt was referring to what he said in verse thirty-eight when he demanded action of them in the form of repentance and baptism. As to being saved "from this crooked generation" it evidently points to the fact that the generation as a whole was eternally lost, and that they should save themselves from it, as from a "sinking ship."

And finally, the obedience and addition of those who received the word. The "receiving of the word" can be understood in the sense that they determined to follow his word and comply with its demands, hence we find them being baptized.

That 3,000 souls were baptized upon this occasion has posed to some a problem as to the sufficiency of water, time, etc. All of these difficulties are set aside, however, through a careful consideration of certain historical facts of the city of Jerusalem.

As to the latter portion of the forty-first verse, we can say in the words of Adam Adcock:

"When nothing exists, only God can originate it by creation. To form the human race out of nothing, God had to **make** the first man and the first woman. To bring the church of Christ into being, the Lord **created** the first Christians on Pentecost by the supernatural power of the Holy Spirit. It is no wonder that 'the multitudes were confounded' and 'were all amazed and marveled' and 'were perplexed.' Nothing like this occasion ever happened before or again since God rolled the world into space. To speak of Pentecost as the 'birthday' of the church is a misnomer, improper, nothing can be born without antecedents or precedents in kind. Adam and Eve had no

83. What is the difference between "words of testimony," and "words of exhortation?"
84. What association with what had already been said, do the words "save yourselves" have?
85. What is meant by the expression, "as many as received his word?"

antecedents in kind; neither had the church. The church is the new creation. The human race was **originated** in the first pair; the church was **created** in the first Christians, the original twelve apostles. To say that the church was 'born' on Pentecost is to use an inadequate figure; to say that the church was **created** is to give a proper description of its origin. But the Lord creates only when it is necessary. Creation in process is not identical with birth. There is no indication that the Twelve ever had any baptism in water but John's. The first father and the first mother had to be **created;** all other human beings are **born.** The church was created in the apostles as the first Christians; all other Christians come into being by the **new birth.** Creation is essentially miraculous; **birth,** old or new, is always by operation of law." (**Acts Analyzed,** pages 28, 29).

And thus the 3,000 were added to the church created. They were born into the family of God "by the water and the spirit", in contrast the apostles were created as the first members of God's family.

42 The final word as to the results of Peter's sermon can be found in the fruit of faithfulness. The gospel so took hold of the lives of those first converts that they continued steadfastly in worship to God. This worship was expressed in the four items of: (1) the apostles' teaching, (2) the fellowship, or partnership with one another in the common cause, (3) the breaking of bread, or the Lord's Supper, and (4) the prayers.

e. The unity of the church. 43-47.

43 And fear came upon every soul: and many wonders and signs were done through the apostles.

44 And all that believed were together, and had all things common;

45 and they sold their possessions and goods, and parted them to all, according as any man had need.

46. And day by day, continuing stedfastly with one accord in the temple, and breaking bread at home, they took their food with gladness and singleness of heart,

47 praising God, and having favor with all the people. And the Lord added to them day by day those that were saved.

43-47 The **cause** of unity can be found in the first portion of the forty-third verse.

"And fear came upon every soul."

The fear of the Lord is not only "the beginning of wisdom" but is also the beginning of unity among brethren. When Jehovah is held in great reverence and honor, when He is loved better than any

86. How can we explain that the 3,000 were added to the church when the 3,000 were the first members of the church?

87. What connection do the four items mentioned in verse 42 have to worship?

88. What was the cause of the unity described in verses 43-47?

earthly possession or position by His children, then can there be unity. For there is then one common standard, each counts himself as personally responsible to God; when all do this all are one.

The **results** of the unity can be found in verses 43b-47. Note them:

1. The apostles were enabled to work more effectively. This would not have been possible had there been division. 43.
2. All that believed were together, and unselfishness prevailed. 44.
3. They not only had a spiritual sense of oneness, but they worked it out in a practical demonstration. 45.
4. This unity with God and one another caused them to daily worship God, not only in the temple, but also at home. Their reverence for God made the common tasks of the day a joy to perform. 46.
5. The final and inevitable result of this divine oneness was the salvation of souls. Because they praised God with their lips and lives, they grew in favor with the common folk. And God was adding to their number each day those that were being saved. Their names were written down in the Lamb's book of life at the time of their salvation. When Jehovah looks over that mightly list of names, He must say, "these are my 'called out ones,' 'my church'." 47.

ACTS EXAMINATION OVER CHAPTERS ONE AND TWO

1. What do you think of the title of the book?
2. Give two reasons for saying Luke wrote the book.
3. What does Nero have to do with the book of Acts?
4. How many years are covered in this narrative?
5. How do I know that gospel preaching began in this book?
6. Do you say the church has the record of its beginning in this book? Prove it.
7. What four cities appear most often in this book?
8. What is meant by "the divine execution of the great commission?"
9. What is a treatise?
10. Is everything Jesus taught recorded in the New Testament?
11. What is "The commandment" spoken of in verse two?
12. In what places was the great commission given?
13. What question did the apostles ask Jesus on His last day on earth?
14. What is strange about the above question?

89. With an open Bible outline the five results of the unity.
90. Should the community of goods described in these verses be practiced today? If not, why not?
91. Why would it be logical to imagine Jehovah saying while looking over the list of names in the Lamb's book of life "these are my called out ones, my church?"

15. How did the promise of the power answer the question of the apostles?
16. How will Jesus come "in like manner as He went?"
17. What comparison can we make in verse 12 to our lives? (Read the text).
18. How did the apostles secure the upper room as place for their living?
19. Name the twelve apostles.
20. Was there a ten day prayer meeting? If not, what was there?

True or False

_____ 1. There was a lapse of time between the prayer meeting and the filling of the office of Judas.

_____ 2. The filling of the office of Judas happened while there were 120 present in the large upper room.

_____ 3. The filling of the office of Judas lends no particular force to the thought that only the apostles were baptized in the Holy Spirit.

_____ 4. Isaiah said: "Let his habitation be made desolate, and let no man dwell therein and, his office let another take."

_____ 5. It was 700 years between the prophecy and its fulfillment.

_____ 6. Judas pointed Jesus out to His enemies by kissing Him.

_____ 7. Jesus never really called Judas.

_____ 8. Judas did not himself buy the field in which he fell. (i.e. personally).

_____ 9. Judas was slaughtered in this field.

_____ 10. It was a "potter's field."

_____ 11. The field came to be called by strangers: "The field of blood."

_____ 12. There was only one direct qualification given for an apostle.

_____ 13. The apostles knew even before Pentecost that they were to preach the resurrection of Christ.

_____ 14. The place to which Judas fell was the "paupers' field."

_____ 15. God was the one who chose Matthias.

Fill in the Blanks

1. The five steps in discovering God's will in matters that are not spoken of in God's word are:
Know that _____ _____ _____ _____ _____
_____ Second. Know that _____ _____ _____ _____
_____ _____ _____. Third. To have _____
_____ _____ _____ _____ _____ _____
Fourth. To pray _____ _____ _____ _____·
Fifth. Make _____ _____ _____ _____ _____

....
....

2. The day of Pentecost was the day toward which the whole
_____ and _____ of Jesus pointed.
3. On this day Jesus' words in Caesarea Philippi were fulfilled when He said: _____ _____ _____ _____
_____. Matt. 16:18
4. The hand of God can be seen in the selection of the day of
Pentecost as the day for the establishment of the church for
the proper _____ were present, the proper _____ was
present, and the proper _____ was present to accomplish
this wonderful work.
5. The apostles were all together in an _____ in
the temple for the Holy Spirit baptism.
6. The day of Pentecost was also called the feast of the _____
_____ because:
7. The reason for the sound as of a rushing wind and the tongues
like as of fire was to attract _____ and _____
from the crowd.
8. We can know for a certainty that verse _____ of the
second chapter is a fulfillment of verse _____ of the first chapter.
9. The _____ of the apostles was that portion of their
beings baptized in the Holy Spirit.
10. There was devout Jews from _____ (give the number) nations present in Jerusalem for Pentecost.

Can you find TEN MISTAKES in this paragraph?
(Cross out the mistakes)

All the crowd said: "They are filled with new wine." But Peter
standing up with the twelve lifted up his voice and spake forth unto them and said: "Ye men of Judea and all ye that dwell at Jerusalem" . . . then it was that he said it was only the ninth hour of
the day and therefore these men could not be drunk. He further
said that this was a fulfillment of Jacob's prophecy. The last days
mentioned are the last days of Israel and Jacob. The pouring forth
of His spirit upon "all flesh" was not accomplished on that day in
any form. The statements in verses seventeen and eighteen relative
to the prophesying and visions (read them if you like) can be understood as the baptism in the Holy Spirit of such persons. The
proposition of Peter's sermon was: "A demonstration of Jesus as
the Christ." His sermon was addressed directly to the men present
and brought great conviction to them. There were five points in
the sermon's development. David spoke of the death, burial and
resurrection of the Messiah. These facts Peter's sermon demonstrated occurred in the life of the Christ. There were two results to
Peter's sermon. The three thousand were baptized in a day or two
and thus on the coming Lord's day they continued in the breaking
of the bread.

4. AT THE GATE BEAUTIFUL 3:1-10.

1 Now Peter and John were going up into the temple at the hour of prayer, being the ninth hour.
2 And a certain man that was lame from his mother's womb was carried, whom they laid daily at the door of the temple which is called Beautiful, to ask alms of them that entered into the temple;
3 who seeing Peter and John about to go into the temple, asked to receive an alms.
4 And Peter, fastening his eyes upon him, with John, said, Look on us.
5 And he gave heed unto them, expecting to receive something from them.
6 But Peter said, Silver and gold have I none; but what I have, that give I thee. In the name of Jesus Christ of Nazareth, walk.
7 And he took him by the right hand, and raised him up: and immediately his feet and his ankle-bones received strength.
8 And leaping up, he stood, and began to walk; and he entered with them into the temple, walking, and leaping, and praising God.
9 And all the people saw him walking and praising God:
10 and they took knowledge of him, that it was he that sat for alms at the Beautiful Gate of the temple; and they were filled with wonder and amazement at that which had happened unto him.

1 The great day of Pentecost had passed but its power yet remained. This is as it should be in all true religious experience. We see now the power of Pentecost in action in the everyday life of God's servants. Being Jews, Peter and John observed the three Jewish hours of prayer; nine in the morning, at noon, and at three in the afternoon.
2 The temple in Jerusalem was the place of prayer and public meeting for all Jews in the city. It happened on a certain day at the afternoon hour of prayer that two of the apostles were ascending the steps into the temple. These steps led them through a particular gate of the temple called the Gate Beautiful, doubtless because of its beauty of construction. To this particular gate a beggar was carried daily and there was laid that he might ask a pittance of those who entered the temple. Luke describes the man's physical condition as being lame from his mother's womb.

92. Why could we say that the power of Pentecost was manifested at the gate beautiful?
93. Name the three hours of prayer, both in the Jewish time and our time.

3 Why the eyes of this poor lame man fell upon Peter and John, and why he should ask alms of them among all the rest of the multitude that was going into the temple, only He who marks the fall of the sparrow can know. Hearing the pitiable mumbled words of the prostrate beggar the hearts of Peter and John were stirred by the same Spirit that filled their lives on the great day of the first fruits; they knew that here was a man among men, whom God was going to now use to glorify His Servant Jesus.

Ah, friends, let us see that we are like this poor stricken soul just outside the Beautiful Gate, **we** have utterly nothing to recommend us as a means of God's glory, but through us He does make His glory known. How wonderful! "Where then is the glorying? It is excluded." How completely left out of salvation is the boasting of men.

4-6 The man looked up from his reclining position into the piercing yet compassionate eyes of these two strangers. The look of the man was one of hopeful expectancy, but not different from the gaze he had turned on many a benevolent Jew. Disappointment and curiosity fleeted across the mind of this unfortunate Jew as the words: "Silver and gold have I none," fell from the lips of Peter. "No money? Why then arrest my attention? Why bother? I am only here for one purpose. I want nothing else." Then, the words "But what I have, that give I thee" . . . "What you have? I do not see you reach under the folds of your robe. I see nothing in your outstretched hand." All of these thoughts could have flashed over the mind of this man.

Perhaps not even expressed in the mind but only felt in the heart were these thoughts. And then it happened. The unforgettable words of power and life:

"In the name of Jesus Christ of Nazareth, **walk**."

The firm grasp of Peter's hand upon his, the strength, the joy that literally flooded his soul, the experience of ecstasy in leaping up, standing, walking!

7-10 Luke with his customary medical exactness describes the action of the healing as being immediate in his feet and his ankle bones. What shouts of joy and praise rang through the halls of the temple. "Was this any way for a man to act in such a place as a temple "walking and leaping and praising God." What amazement passed over the faces of the reverent multitude on their ways into

94. What two characteristics of the beggar's physical condition are given to us by Dr. Luke?
95. Show the comparison of the beggar with you and me as sinners.
96. Describe the healing of the lame man from the first words of Peter to the entering into the temple.

the temple. "Was this any way for a man to act in such a place and at such a time?" But then upon looking more closely they recognized something familiar about this exuberant one. "Why, it is none other than the beggar whom we have seen and passed every day at the Gate Beautiful. Can this be that one who but a few moments before was appealing to us for alms? It is indeed." Then were they in truth filled with wonder and amazement at that which had happened unto him.

5. ON SOLOMON'S PORCH 3:11-26.

11 And as he held Peter and John, all the people ran together unto them in the porch that is called Solomon's, greatly wondering.

12 And when Peter saw it, he answered unto the people, Ye men of Israel, why marvel ye at this man? or why fasten ye your eyes on us, as though by our own power or godliness we had made him to walk?

13 The God of Abraham, and of Isaac, and of Jacob, the God of our fathers, hath glorified his Servant Jesus; whom ye delivered up, and denied before the face of Pilate, when he had determined to release him.

14 But ye denied the Holy and Righteous One, and asked for a murderer to be granted unto you,

15 and killed the Prince of life; whom God raised from the dead; whereof we are witnesses.

16 And by faith in his name hath his name made this man strong, whom ye behold and know: yea, the faith which is through him hath given him this perfect soundness in the presence of you all.

17 And now, brethren, I know that in ignorance ye did it, as did also your rulers.

18 But the things which God foreshowed by the mouth of all the prophets, that his Christ should suffer, he thus fulfilled.

19 Repent ye therefore, and turn again, that your sins may be blotted out, that so there may come seasons of refreshing from the presence of the Lord;

20 and that he may send the Christ who hath been appointed for you, even Jesus:

21 whom the heaven must receive until the times of restoration of all things, whereof God spake by the mouth of his holy prophets that have been from of old.

22 Moses indeed said, A prophet shall the Lord God raise up unto you from among your brethren, like

97. Is there any reason to believe that the lame man was well known among the Jews?

unto me; to him shall ye hearken in all things whatsoever he shall speak unto you.

23   And it shall be, that every soul that shall not hearken
to that prophet, shall be utterly destroyed from among
the people.

24   Yea and all the prophets from Samuel and them that
followed after, as many as have spoken, they also
told of these days.

25   Ye are the sons of the prophets, and of the covenant
which God made with your fathers, saying unto Abraham, And in thy seed shall all the families of the
earth be blessed.

26   Unto you first God, having raised up his Servant, sent
him to bless you, in turning away every one of you
from your iniquities.

11 It will be noted that the healing of the lame man occurred at
the entrance of the temple proper, the gate which opened into the
court of the women being the exact spot. The incident to be described under the above heading occurs on Solomon's portico or porch,
located on the outside of the Jewish portion of the temple.

It must be concluded from the text that upon being healed the
lame man went into the temple with Peter and John (cf. 8). The
apostles then came out of the sacred enclosure, doubtless because
of the tumult caused by the miracle, and while they stood in Solomon's portico the lame man embraced them. The lame man might
have called out to the crowd and thus gathered them, but it is not
here mentioned.

12-13a Peter, upon witnessing the circumstances, noticed that the
wonder of the people was centered upon them and not in the God
they served. Peter's boldness, wisdom and humility are seen in the
next four verses. His boldness is portrayed in the fact that in spite
of the unlikely circumstances he took this occasion to preach a gospel message. His wisdom is shown in the manner of development,
and his humility is found in the introduction of the message. Peter
in introducing his sermon gives credit to God for the miracle:

"It was not power or godliness of ours that made this one to
walk . . . look to the God of your fathers, the God of Abraham,
Isaac and Jacob," says Peter.

98. Where did Peter preach his second sermon?
99. Had Peter, John, and the man who was healed been in the temple? Why
did they come out?
100. Why do you suppose the beggar "held Peter and John?"
101. What elements of Peter's character are brought out in his sermon and
its delivery?

13b-19 Then follows the body of the sermon. Why was this thing done? The answer comes: "To glorify Jesus," God's Servant or "Child." Peter again reminds these Jews of whom he is speaking . . . God's Servant is Jesus.

"Jehovah is glorifying in this act just performed none other than the very one whom you Jews delivered up and denied. You preferred a murderer. You killed this one and in so doing you slew the very Prince or Author of Life. God, however, raised Him from the dead. Of this fact we apostles can all witness."

The question of **how** the healing of the lame man glorifies Jesus yet remains to be answered. The answer is found in the words of the sixteenth verse. The thought is that when the beggar was made whole, glory went to Jesus because it was only through faith in His name that this miracle could occur. The question naturally arises, Who exercised this faith? A moment's consideration of the facts will teach us that the beggar knew nothing of Jesus and as Luke tells us, was concerned with nothing but alms.

The faith of Peter and John in Jesus is the only logical answer to this question. This is in perfect accord with Mark 16:14-20 in which Jesus upbraids the apostles for their unbelief and then promises that signs would follow their work if they would believe. The power of performing miracles was given to the apostles by virtue of the baptism in the Holy Spirit, but they needed to exercise faith before this power could be used.

Peter follows this thought with the second point of his message. He speaks of the **predetermined death of Jesus.** This same truth was presented before by Peter on the day of Pentecost. It had great effect upon the Jew whenever given because it presented to his mind the strongest proof that the things being spoken of were true. Tempering his message just a little he says: "And now, brethren, I know that in ignorance ye did it, as did also your rulers." To show in their act the fulfillment of prophecy he says that the prophets spoke of the suffering Christ and thus were these prophecies fulfilled. The Jews were convinced that Jesus was the Christ from what had been said previously and even more so now by what was said concerning His resurrection and power to heal. They were convicted of sin through the words of Peter describing the tragedy of delivering up the Messiah to a heathen governor, of denying the very Christ of God and preferring a murderer; of killing the "Author"

102. What purpose does Peter assign to this miracle?
103. Name three things Peter said the Jews did with Jesus.
104. How did the healing of the lame man bring glory to Jesus?
105. Explain how this miracle was accomplished by faith. How does the Holy Spirit baptism enter this incident?
106. What is the second thought of Peter's sermon?

of Life. In light of this Peter could with great power call them to repentance and obedience. Note his words: "Repent ye therefore, and turn again, that your sins may be blotted out so that there may come seasons of refreshing from the presence of the Lord."

We need not ask as to the meaning of the first words of this charge for all know with at least some degree of completeness the meaning of the word repentance (the word signifying a change of mind, which works a complete change of conduct). But for what is Peter asking when he calls upon these Jews to "turn again?" To begin with note that in repenting and turning again, they were to receive exactly what was promised in the second chapter for "repentance and baptism." Mark the parallel: in Acts 2:38 they were told to repent and be baptized for **the remission of their sins** to receive the gift of the Holy Spirit. In Acts 3:19 they are told to repent and turn again **that their sins might be blotted out** and that they might receive seasons of refreshings from the presence of the Lord. Does it seem logical that Peter would require repentance and baptism on the day of Pentecost for the forgiveness of sins and here on Solomon's porch, while speaking to the same type of persons, require something else for the same result? We say then that the thought behind the words "turn again" was nothing short of baptism. The Jews had no doubt witnessed the baptism of persons every day (cf. 2:47) and thus when Peter called upon them to "repent and turn again" they knew exactly what he inferred. A complete discussion of this text is found in J. W. McGarvey's **New Commentary** on pages 58-63.

20-21 Still another result was to follow. Upon their repentance and "turning again" their sins were to be blotted out. They were to receive the times or seasons of refreshing from the gift of God's Spirit, sent as he was from His presence. But also upon their obedience to this charge they were promised that God would send to them "the Christ." What is the meaning of this expression? It could have no reference to the first advent of Jesus for He had already come; nor could it refer to the presence of Christ through His Spirit, for the gift of the Holy Spirit had already been spoken of. It could only refer to the second coming of Christ. Every Jew looked forward to the Christ coming as a great king in his kingdom. He was to come to conquer and subdue all kingdoms. This indeed He will do when He comes again; hence, we have the words of Peter to these Jews that their hopes will be realized in the second coming of the Christ. Not in a temporal, earthly, kingdom, but in the trium-

107. Why was it appropriate for Peter to call the Jews to repentance and obedience at the time that he did?
108. What is the meaning of the word "repentance?"
109. What is the meaning of the expression "turn again"? Prove your answer.
110. What is the meaning of the phrase: "seasons of refreshing?"

phant glory of the eternal conquering king in His kingdom. When He does come it will be none other than the same Jesus whom they had crucified.

But says Peter, "The heavens will hold Him until a certain time, then He will come." The time being set as "the times of the restoration of all things whereof God spake by the mouth of the holy prophets that have been from of old." Upon this point we say with J. W. McGarvey:

"It is difficult to determine the exact meaning of the word restoration in this place; but it is limited by the expression, "all things whereof God spake by the holy prophets" . . . and consequently it consists in the fulfillment of the Old Testament predictions; and the remark gives assurance that Jesus will not return again till all these predictions shall have been fulfilled" (ibid. p. 63).

What these predictions are and what they entail it is not our purpose to discuss in these notes.

22-26 Peter ends as he began; with proof from the Old Testament that this Jesus was the Christ. The prediction made by Moses and read by the Jews for these hundreds of years now finds its fulfillment. Moses said:

1. The Lord God would raise up a prophet; which thing God did in Jesus.
2. That this prophet would be raised up to be sent to the Israelites; which thing was fulfilled in Jesus.
3. That the prophet would be from among their brethren; Jesus was of the tribe of Judah.
4. That he would be like unto Moses. The comparisons of Jesus and Moses are too numerous to mention. Moses also predicted the dire results that would follow upon not harkening unto this prophet.

Peter climaxes his message by making the sweeping statement that all the prophets from the first one, Samuel, down to the very last one foretold of the days of the Son of man.

Then the appeal of the apostle. He strikes at the very heart of the Jew when he reminds him of the treasured truth that they are the sons of the prophets and of the covenant God made with their fathers; saying unto Abraham, "And in thy seed shall all the families of the earth be blessed." The strong inference is that the blessing which God promised to the world through them was nothing short of Jesus Christ. He had come through them, i.e. through their seed, and now He was to bless the families of the earth through

111. What is the meaning of, "the times of the restoration of all things?"
112. How did Peter conclude his message?
113. What appeal is made by the apostle in the close of this message? What is the strong inference?

His work of redemption. They were indeed honored and blessed, for God had now sent this one first **to** them, even as He came **through** them, to turn every one of them away from his iniquities; to give them that balm for which their hearts longed, the blotting out of their sins.

Shall we now note an outline of Peter's message?

The circumstances of preaching. 11.

Theme: "The glorification of God's Servant Jesus."

Introduction: The question of Peter framed as it was to point away from the apostles as a source for the healing. 12.

    I — God, your Father, has done this through Jesus. 13-16.
        1. But you have delivered up this one, you have denied Him. 13.
        2. You asked for a murderer instead. 14.
        3. You have killed the very Prince of life. 15a.
        4. But God has raised Him from the dead and we are witnesses of this fact. 15b.
        5. It is our faith in Jesus that has performed this miracle. 16.

    II — He was put to death in ignorance but in fulfillment of prophecy. 17-18.

    III — A call to repentance and obedience for the blotting out of sins and the gift of the Holy Spirit. 19.

    IV — If obedience is forthcoming the promise of the blessings of the second advent will be yours. Christ must needs remain in heaven until all things which are spoken of Him in the Old Testament have been fulfilled. 20, 21.

    V — Further prophetic proof that Jesus is the Christ. 22, 24.
        1. Moses and what he said concerning Him. 22, 23.
        2. All the prophets have spoken of His days. 24.

    VI — A call to the Jews, as sons of the prophets and covenants, to accept Christ and thus enter into all the promises of the prophets and the covenants. 25, 26.

Luke only gives us a brief resume of the words of Peter. No doubt Peter developed each of these points at great length, and with much application.

6. IN THE PRISON 4:1-4.

    1 And as they spake unto the people, the priests and the captain of the temple and the Sadducees came upon them,
    2 being sore troubled because they taught the people, and proclaimed in Jesus the resurrection from the dead.

114. What is the theme of Peter's sermon?
115. Write from memory the main outline of Peter's message.

3 And they laid hands on them, and put them in ward unto the morrow: for it was now eventide.

4 But many of them that heard the word believed;
and the number of the men came to be about five thousand.

1-3 The sermon is not complete, there yet remains the final exhortation; there yet remains the response to the call. But the final
words are fated never to be spoken. The hands of the apostles are
not to immerse those who might have responded. For, while the
words were still falling from the lips of Peter, the crowd was burst
asunder by a body of armed men, who rushing through the midst of
the multitude seized Peter and John and hurried them off to the
public ward or jail.

Who were these men who came so boldly and acted so brash-
ly? Luke tells us they were "the priests and the captain of the
temple and the Sadducees." The Sadducees were the leaders in
this opposition; they were stirred up against the apostles because
they proclaimed in Jesus the resurrection from the dead. This
fact cut straight across their teaching of no resurrection. The high
priest Annas was a Sadducee and hence the action of these men
was either directed by him or would be supported in trial before
him. The popularity of the "good news" attracting as it was, multitudes of those in Jerusalem was another evident reason for the opposition of the Sadducees, they were filled with jealousy. We are not
told whether the priests spoken of in this arrest were Sadducees or
not. The immediate cause of this arrest was probably the disturbance
of the hour of prayer. The healing of the lame man caused "no
small stir" in the temple and temple area. The captain of the temple had been appointed for the express purpose of maintaining order
in the temple and its area; hence, when this miracle occurred it
evidently so disrupted the temple service that the captain deemed it
necessary to call the priests and the Sadducees to put down this excitement. (But since the healing of the lame man took place at
three o'clock and it was not until sundown that the apostles were
arrested, they were thus given some two or more hours to
preach. It does seem that the captain of the temple might have known
ahead of time of the hatred of the Sadducees. He could have known
that they were but waiting for some pretext by which they might

116. Who were the leaders in the arrest of Peter and John?

117. Why could the apostles be thus arrested? What had they done worthy
of arrest?

118. Why were the Sadducees troubled about the preaching of the resurrection from the dead? Who was the captain of the temple?

119. Do you believe the captain of the temple knew of the antagonism
of the Sadducees before he arrested Peter and John? If so, why?

lay hands on the apostles, therefore he seized upon this opportunity and went to them for that very purpose).

4 Luke adds an encouraging word in the fourth verse. Although Peter and John were not there to rejoice with the others, there were many that heard their word and believed—and that the number of men in Jerusalem came to be about five thousand. This is a wonderful word of victory for many of those baptized on Pentecost must have returned to their native homes. In spite of this fact, the number of men (to say nothing of the women) was now about five thousand.

7. **BEFORE THE SANHEDRIN.** 4:5-22.

5 And it came to pass on the morrow, that their rulers and elders and scribes were gathered together in Jerusalem;

6 and Annas the high priest was there, and Caiaphas, and John, and Alexander, and as many as were of the kindred of the high priest.

7 And when they had set them in the midst, they inquired, By what power, or in what name, have ye done this?

8 Then Peter, filled with the Holy Spirit, said unto them, Ye rulers of the people, and elders,

9 if we this day are examined concerning a good deed done to an impotent man, by what means this man is made whole;

10 be it known unto you all, and to all the people of Israel, that in the name of Jesus Christ of Nazareth, whom ye crucified, whom God raised from the dead, even in him doth this man stand here before you whole.

11 He is the stone which was set at nought of you the builders, which was made the head of the corner.

12 And in none other is there salvation: for neither is there any other name under heaven, that is given among men, wherein we must be saved.

13 Now when they beheld the boldness of Peter and John, and had perceived that they were unlearned and ignorant men, they marvelled; and they took knowledge of them, that they had been with Jesus.

14 And seeing the man that was healed standing with them, they could say nothing against it.

15 But when they had commanded them to go aside out of the council, they conferred among themselves,

16 saying, What shall we do to these men? for that indeed a notable miracle hath been wrought through them, is manifest to all that dwell in Jerusalem; and we cannot deny it.

120. Why is the statement made in verse 4 of particular encouragement?

17 But that it spread no further among the people, let us
    threaten them, that they speak henceforth to no man
    in this name.
18 And they called them, and charged them not to speak
    at all nor teach in the name of Jesus.
19 But Peter and John answered and said unto them,
    Whether it is right in the sight of God to hearken un-
    to you rather than unto God, judge ye:
20 for we cannot but speak the things which we saw and
    heard.
21 And they, when they had further threatened them, let
    them go, finding nothing how they might punish them,
    because of the people; for all men glorified God for that
    which was done.
22 For the man was more than forty years old, on whom
    this miracle of healing was wrought.

5-6 The night passed. In the public ward there ascended, no doubt,
prayers, songs and supplications from the hearts of Peter and
John. The other apostles and the church in Jerusalem were probably also gathered to petition the "throne of grace" on behalf of
Peter and John.

The morning came and at about ten o'clock, as was the custom,
the Sanhedrin was called to assemble. Luke is very explicit as to
who were present as authorities in this trial. He first describes the
assembly in a general statement, "the rulers and the elders and
scribes;" then explicitly, when he tells us there were present: "Annas the high priest and Caiaphas, and John, and Alexander, and
as many as were of the kindred of the high priest." Annas and
Caiaphas were related, Caiaphas being the son-in-law of Annas.
The predecessor of Pilate had deposed Annas of his rightful position as high priest and had put his son-in-law in his place. The
people, however, did not recognize this unlawful procedure and
considered Annas as the high priest as did Luke when he recorded
this word. There is no historical information as to who John and
Alexander were. We can only know that they were men of position
and authority in the Sanhedrin. As many as were kindred of the
high priest came out to see and hear what they could of this strange
trial. And they were not to be disappointed.

The Sanhedrin before whom the apostles were arraigned consisted of seventy men (or seventy-one—seventy members plus Moses.
Num. 11:16). The Sanhedrin was composed of twenty-four priests,
twenty-two lawyers (not "lawyers" as we understand that term) and

121. What relation to the assembled council do the words "rulers and elders
     and scribes" have?
122. Tell of the relationship of Caiaphas and Annas.

twenty-four elders. These were the "rulers and elders" spoken of earlier. This council was the highest court in the Jewish state. They had no power to pass the death sentence but their recommendation to Herod carried real weight. The cases before this court were all of a religious nature. (Suffice to say here that this Sanhedrin gathered in a semicircle and set the apostles before them to be tried).

7. Note carefully that there was no charge made by the council. In a move of subtle strategy they framed a question, the answer of which they hoped would contain a basis for a charge. Here is the question:

"By what power, or in what name, have ye done this?"

Done what? Yes, so it was, that if the apostles had broken any law they would, in their answer to this question, confess their guilt and try to defend themselves.

8-12 However, the time had come for the words of Jesus to find fulfillment—"But when they deliver you up, be not anxious how or what ye shall speak: for it shall be given you in that hour what ye shall speak. For it is not ye that speak, but the Spirit of your Father that speaketh in you." (Matt. 10:19, 20.)

And so it was that Peter, full of the Holy Spirit, said the very thing that would offer to the Sanhedrin a defense that had no answer. Here are the thoughts of his defense. "What have we done? We have healed a poor impotent man. This we would consider a good deed. Now if we this day are to be examined concerning this deed, I am perfectly willing to face the charge. In what power was this miracle wrought? Why, be it known to you and to all the children of Israel that in the name of Jesus of Nazareth, whom you crucified, whom God also raised from the dead, even in Him does this man stand before you whole. He is the stone which was set at nought of you, the builders, who was made the head of the corner; and in none other is there salvation, for neither is there any other name under heaven given among men wherein we must be saved."

What a marvelous progression of thoughts. Note them: (1) He calls attention to the man who was healed, he was standing with them. How did he come to be thus? (2) Through Jesus of Nazareth. Who is He? You know. He is the one whom you crucified. He is the one God raised from the dead; yea, He is the very stone which was set at nought of you, the builders.

This last statement was full of meaning to these rulers. Peter pictures the rulers as the builders of the temple of God and then

123. What was the Sanhedrin? What cases did they try?
124. What subtle strategy does the question of the council reveal?
125. What words of Jesus were fulfilled upon this occasion?
126. How did Peter answer the question of the Sanhedrin?
127. Give a brief outline of Peter's defense.

points out to them that they are like the builders of a temple who, coming upon the rock that has been hewn out to be the cornerstone, fail somehow to recognize it as such and set it aside to go ahead with the construction of the building without it. The fact that Jesus came as the prophets had foretold, as "a root out of a dry ground," as a servant and not as a Lord, no doubt had to do with the failure of the rulers of Israel to see in Him the "chief cornerstone."

But more especially had their greed, pride, lust and covetousness blinded their eyes to this wonderful truth. If Jesus was indeed the Christ, if He had been raised from the dead, if He was the chief cornerstone, then Peter could say with force and truth that: "In none other is there salvation," that God had not provided any other means or person under heaven wherein salvation could be found.

13-18 Whatever else the rulers beheld or understood on that day, one thing they did not miss, and that was "the boldness of Peter and John." In the face of judgment and death, they were unafraid to lay the charge of the death of Jesus at the feet of the very ones who were judging them. They were unafraid to call upon the leaders in Israel to find salvation in the name of the very one they had slain.

There could not but arise both admiration and wonder for these men, and especially so when they knew that they were "unlearned and ignorant men," i.e., unlearned in the learning of the Rabbinical school; ignorant of the various intricate points of the law and tradition. Some men are prone to "set at nought all others" as ignorant and unlearned, who have not been trained in just the way and manner they have. (From all of these things, dear Lord, deliver us).

There could be but one answer to the bold logic and appeal of the words of Peter and John—"they had been with Jesus." The wisdom of Jesus was admitted by them and now all they could say was that they must have been with Jesus and from Him imbibed His spirit and wisdom. The one fact they failed to realize was that not only had they been **with** Jesus but that Jesus was now **in** them.

These rulers were placed in a position of great embarrassment for

128. Why did the words of the apostles concerning the cornerstone have particular application to those who heard?
129. What reasons could you give for the failure of the Jews to see in Jesus the chief cornerstone?
130. Why were the words in verse 12 especially appropriate?
131. Why could the defense of Peter and John be called a bold defense?
132. What is meant by the thought that Peter and John were unlearned and ignorant men?
133. What reason did the rulers assign for their boldness? What was right about it? What had they failed to see?

they had no charge to begin with and they could find no flaw in the defense of Peter; and finally, they could say no word against what had been done—for the man who was healed stood in their very midst and the people were highly in favor of what had occurred. The name of God was being exalted as a result of this incident. What could they do? And so it is with all attempts to cover up hypocrisy and sin with a cloak of apparent righteousness.

The council did the only thing they could—they stalled for time that they might consider their dilemma. So, commanding the apostles to go outside of their council, they conferred among themselves. But their private conversation only brought to light the facts of the case which they all knew to be so. Here were the points in the case:

1. A notable miracle had been wrought through the apostles.
2. It was manifest unto all those of Jerusalem.
3. There would be no need to deny it.

What will be done with these men?

No punishment beyond a mere charge could be given. And in this charge, they could give no reason for not "speaking any more in this name." The real reason, of course, was the desire of the Sadducees to stop this teaching and to put down this movement that was offering so much competition by way of popularity and influence. But these things could not be spoken of in a gathering of the mighty Sanhedrin. So they called in the apostles and gave them the simple charge, backed by the Sanhedrin:

"Not to speak at all nor teach in the name of Jesus."

19-20 If this council expected the apostles to cower because of their power and position they were sadly disappointed, for Peter and John immediately answered that it was not a matter of obeying men, even though it was the Sanhedrin. What they were speaking and doing was in obedience unto God Himself. The statement of Peter and John was formed in such a way as to appeal to the judgment of those present; to appeal to their honesty before God. Their words were in essence:

"Put yourselves in our place; suppose God told you to do one thing and man told you not to do it—which one would you obey?

134. Show how the defense of Peter placed the Sanhedrin in a dilemma.
135. What was the immediate action of the council? What were the facts of the case brought to their attention from the private conference?
136. What was lacking in the charge given as punishment?
137. What was the real reason back of the charge?
138. Why did not Peter and John keep quiet and then go on preaching in spite of the charge?
139. What was the answer of Peter to the request of the Sanhedrin? To what did it appeal?

Well, that is exactly our situation—Jesus Christ whom we beheld
risen from the dead, commissioned us to tell of His resurrection
and saving power; now you tell us not to speak of the very thing the
risen Christ has told us to speak. You be the judge; to whom should
we hearken?"

21-22 But the council had made a decision and to it they must be
true; hence, we see them further threatening the apostles (they promised them punishment if they disobeyed this charge). But they let
them go with no punishment, not because they wanted to, but because they "feared the people." The common folk, who had no
position to maintain, no name to uphold, were glad to behold
the power of God and to give Him the glory. Luke gives us one
more fact about this man who started all this chain of events—
"He was," says Luke, "more than forty years old."

8. IN THE UPPER ROOM. 4:28—5:11.
a. The Prayer Service. 23-21.

23 And being let go, they came to their own company,
and reported all that the chief priests and the elders
had said unto them.

24 And they, when they heard it, lifted up their voice to
God with one accord, and said, O Lord thou that
didst make the heaven and the earth and the sea,
and all that in them is:

25 who by the Holy Spirit, by the mouth of our father
David thy servant, didst say,
Why did the Gentiles rage,
And the peoples imagine vain things?

26 The kings of the earth set themselves in array,
And the rulers were gathered together,
Against the Lord, and against his Anointed:

27 for of a truth in this city against thy holy Servant Jesus,
whom thou didst anoint, both Herod and Pontius Pilate,
with the Gentiles and the peoples of Israel, were gathered together,

28 to do whatsoever thy hand and thy counsel foreordained to come to pass.

29 And now, Lord, look upon their threatenings: and grant
unto thy servants to speak thy word with all boldness,

30 while thou stretchest forth thy hand to heal; and
that signs and wonders may be done through the name
of thy holy Servant Jesus.

31 And when they had prayed, the place was shaken wherein they were gathered together; and they were all filled with the Holy Spirit, and they spake the word of
God with boldness.

140. Why weren't the apostles given a severe punishment?

23-30 The apostles left the assembly in triumphant joy but with no pride. Being let go "they came to their own company." Who was this company and where were they gathered?

We are inclined to the opinion that the term refers to the other apostles and those who were their close friends and associates.

The upper room was the abode of the apostles (Acts 1:13) so it does seem reasonable that this was the place to which Peter and John returned upon this occasion.

Can we not imagine them entering the room and hurrying into the presence of their friends to tell with mingled joy and apprehension all that had been said and done?

Immediately upon hearing the news the whole assembly cried out in a united prayer to God. Note the appropriativeness of this prayer—

(1) They were in need of protection and guidance and in their prayer they addressed God as the one who "didst make the heaven and earth and sea and all that in them is." If He was indeed so great He could afford them protection and direction..(2) Then the second Psalm is quoted in which we have a description given by David hundreds of years before. The prophetic picture found its fulfillment in the trial and crucifixion of Jesus. What Herod, Pontius Pilate, the Gentiles and the people of Israel did to Jesus was only in fulfillment of God's purposes. Since, then, God had thus delivered in the terrible days of His Son's adversity, He could now do the same for His chosen children. (3) The one petition made in this whole prayer was that God would consider the threatenings of His enemies and grant boldness to His servants as they spoke His word, that He would continue to accompany the words of the apostles with the signs and wonders that were already in evidence with their work. These supernatural demonstrations were to place the stamp of divine approval upon the words spoken by the apostles.

31 Almost before the last word of the prayer had been uttered the answer arrived. Notice please how the petitions of their prayer were answered:

1) They prayed that God would consider the opposition and would in the face of it grant boldness. The answer: The place where they were meeting was shaken as a reed in the wind. This was the answer of the Lord reminding them that He had heard and was in-

141. Who composed "the company" to whom the Apostles went following their trial?

142. Where was "the company" gathered? How do you know?

142. Give the three points of appropriativeness in the prayer of the "company."

144. Give the requests of the prayer and show how they were immediately answered.

terested enough to let them know His concern. They, knowing His character, would realize that He would not thus answer them unless He was in agreement with their request. This gave them great boldness. 2) They prayed that God would continue to manifest His supernatural power; here in this earthquake He stamped an affirmative answer on the request.

And so they were indeed in accord with the Holy Spirit and He could thus literally fill their hearts and lives. The closer in accord our spirit is to the Holy Spirit, the more completely does He fill our lives. Following this experience the little company could go forth into the city with God's own assurance. They could truly speak the work of God with boldness.

b. The Unity of Believers. 32-37.

32 And the multitude of them that believed were of one heart and soul: and not one of them said that aught of the things which he possessed was his own; but they had all things common.

33 And with great power gave the apostles their witness of the resurrection of the Lord Jesus: and great grace was upon them all.

34 For neither was there among them any that lacked: for as many as were possessors of lands or houses sold them, and brought the prices of the things that were sold,

35 and laid them at the apostles' feet: and distribution was made unto each, according as any one had need.

36 And Joseph, who by the apostles was surnamed Barnabas (which is, being interpreted, Son of exhortation), a Levite, a man of Cyprus by race,

37 having a field, sold it, and brought the money and laid it at the apostles' feet.

32-35 Since Pentecost, the creation day of the church, our attention has been centered upon the work of Christ in the lives of but two of His servants. Luke now opens the door of information to let us behold something of the work of the Master in the life of the whole church. Observe the wonderful power of Christ in "the multitude of them that believed:"

1) They were of one heart and one soul. There was total unity of love and faith.

2) They knew that they had been "bought with a price" and therefore "they were not their own." But this unselfishness

145. The earthquake had what relationship to all being filled with the Holy Spirit?

146. What change of thought is found beginning with 4:32?

reached right into their material posessions and caused them to seek the common good of all. We have much talk of this unselfish attitude today but not much of its fruits.

3) This actual and practical unity afforded a bulwark of strength for the testimony of the apostles. The apostles could point to a group of living examples of the power of their resurrection message. Hence could they give with great power their witness of the resurrection of the Lord Jesus.

4) "Great grace was upon them all." Because of the aforementioned virtues proceeding from the surrendered lives God's favor and approval rested upon them.

Luke tells us why God's favor and approval rested upon them. He says it was because of the utterly selfless attitude and life of the believers. There was none that lacked "for as many as were possessors of lands or houses sold them, and brought the prices of the things that were sold, and laid them at the apostles' feet: and distribution was made unto each, according as any one had need."

36-37 An example is given of one who portrayed the spirit and work of the united Jerusalem church. "Joseph, who by the apostles was surnamed Barnabas" did like many others, sold his own field that his brethren might not be in want.

c. The First Church Discipline. 5:1-11.

1 But a certain man named Ananias, with Sapphira his wife, sold a possession,

2 and kept back part of the price, his wife also being privy to it, and brought a certain part, and laid it at the apostles' feet.

3 But Peter said, Ananias, why hath Satan filled thy heart to lie to the Holy Spirit, and to keep back part of the price of the land?

4 While it remained, did it not remain thine own? and after it was sold, was it not in thy power? How is it that thou hast conceived this thing in thy heart? thou hast not lied unto men, but unto God.

5 And Ananias hearing these words fell down and gave up the ghost: and great fear came upon all that heard it.

6 And the young men arose and wrapped him round, and they carried him out and buried him.

147. Give the four points in verses 32-37 which manifests the power of Christ in the lives of "those that believed."

148. How did the unity of the church afford to the apostles opportunity to give with greater power their witness of the resurrection?

149. What is the meaning of the statement "great grace was upon them all?"

150. Who was given as an example of the unity of the Jerusalem church? What did he do?

7 And it was about the space of three hours after, when his wife, not knowing what was done, came in.

8 And Peter answered unto her, Tell me whether ye sold the land for so much. And she said, Yea, for so much.

9 But Peter said unto her, How is it that ye have agreed together to try the Spirit of the Lord? behold, the feet of them that have buried thy husband are at the door, and they shall carry thee out.

10 And she fell down immediately at his feet, and gave up the ghost: and the young men came in and found her dead, and they carried her out and buried her by her husband.

11 And great fear came upon the whole church, and upon all that heard these things.

1-2 There is a little three lettered word that can be set up most anywhere in the chain of narrated events to serve as a stop sign. That word is "but." Here in the midst of the history of the onward march of the church Luke must set up this stop sign. There was a great unity of belief, of possessions, and great were the results of this unity—"but." It is here we have the first effort of Satan from within the body. We have witnessed in the past record the evil forces from without, but this chapter opens with the account of the first marks of the evil one within the fold. Let us notice the first church discipline.

Two members of the Jerusalem congregation, two members "in good standing" as far as those of Jerusalem knew, were Ananias and Sapphira, his wife.

Someone might say that the possession of land was their trouble, that if they had not the possession they would have had no sin. This is not so for their sin was located in their heart and not in their field.

The sin was twofold: the love of the praise of men and the love of money. No doubt those noble souls who sold that which was theirs for the help of others were admired by those of the church. This was what Ananias and Sapphira wanted, but they were not willing to obtain it through unselfish effort. Their difficulty lay in that "root" in their heart which is the source of all kinds of evil—"the love of money."

3-10 According to Peter they were guilty of the sin of hypocrisy,

151. What is peculiar about the efforts of Satan in the case of Ananias and Sapphira?

152. If Ananias and Sapphira had not owned the field would they have escaped the sin they committed?

153. What was the two-fold sin of Ananias and Sapphira?

of **pretending,** which amounted to nothing short of lying. Yes, of lying to the Holy Spirit. Peter also says that Satan was the **one who suggested** the decision of these two. How the words of Peter must have cut the heart of Ananias when he reminded him that he need not lay the blame upon the land, or by saying that if he had never had the land he would never have sinned (as we are so wont to do). Peter reminded him that it was purely a matter of his own choice, that he, in league with the Devil, decided to try to deceive God with a lie, to deceive not man, but **God!**

The congregation was no doubt greatly surprised when the sin of Ananias was brought to light before them all. But we are persuaded that even Peter himself was not prepared for the results of his rebuke. Here are the words of Luke which describe the startling incident.

"Ananias hearing these words fell down and gave up the spirit."

We quote the fine expression of J. W. McGarvey as to the reason for such a stringent measure:

"There is no evidence that Peter had any will of his own in this sudden death. It seems to have been a sudden stroke of the divine will, the responsibility for which attached not to Peter as an officer of the church, but to God as the moral governor of men. The propriety of it may be appreciated if we suppose Ananias to have succeeded in his undertaking. His success would have been but temporary for the fraud, like all other frauds, would have been detected sooner or later, and when detection came it would have brought with it a serious discount in the minds of the people on the powers of the Holy Spirit dwelling in the apostles. To learn that the Spirit could be deceived would have undermined the whole fabric of apostolic authority and might have overthrown the faith of many, if not all. The attempt brought on a crisis of vital importance and demanded such a vindication of the power of the Spirit as could be neither mistaken nor forgotten."

"The immediate effect was precisely the effect desired: 'Great fear (or awe) came upon the whole church and upon all who heard these things'."

"The scene was too awe-inspiring for lamentation." Hence, there was no delay in the burial of this one. Such a one did not deserve anything more than a hasty burial of the "Achan in the camp." The young men who acted as "pall bearers" were probably direct-

154. According to this incident what definition does Peter give for hypocrisy?
155. What portion of Peter's rebuke must have cut Ananias the deepest?
156. How was this sin originated?
157. What two surprises are present in this incident?
158. Why was so stringent a punishment necessary?
159. What was the immediate result of the discipline?

ed to do so by Peter. The whole congregation, the young men included, were also evidently explicitly told not to carry the sad news to Sapphira.

And so it came to pass that three hours had passed, probably spent in prayer and heart searching, when into the assembly stepped the wife of the deceased. With the discernment of spirits (I Cor. 12:10) that was Peter's he knew the moment Sapphira faced him that she was as guilty as her husband. But to bring before the minds of all present the complete evidence on the case and to allow Sapphira with her own mouth to condemn herself (knowing how much Ananias had laid at his feet as a full price for the land), he framed the question in the manner he did:

"Tell me whether ye sold the land for so much" (naming the price Ananias had given).

Sapphira was all ready to carry out her part of the act and she answered, "Yea, for so much." Peter gives to her the same rebuke he delivered to Ananias but adds the punishment to her rebuke which he did not do in Ananias' case. Peter says in essence: "Your husband was struck dead for his part in this sin—he has just been buried; the feet of them that carried him to his grave are at the door to do the same for you." What a thought! Sapphira like her conspirator fell down under the hand of God and died at the very feet of the apostle. The young men who were about to enter came in and knowing the circumstances, finding Sapphira dead carried her out and laid her by her husband.

11 "The failure of the plot proved as propitious to the cause of Christ as its success would have been disastrous. 'And great fear came upon the whole church, and upon all that heard these things.' This fear was excited not merely by the sudden and awful fate of the guilty pair; but also by the evidence which the incident furnished of the heartsearching power which dwelt in the apostles. The disciples now had a better conception of the nature of apostolic inspiration and the unbelieving masses were awed into respect and reverence." (Ibid. p. 87).

9. ON SOLOMON'S PORCH. 5:12-16.

12 And by the hands of the apostles were many signs and wonders wrought among the people; and they were all with one accord in Solomon's porch.

13 But of the rest durst no man join himself to them: howbeit the people magnified them;

160. Why was there such an immediate burial?

161. How it is that Sapphira did not know of the death of her husband?

162. How did Peter detect the guilt of the pair?

163. What did Peter add to the rebuke of Sapphira that he did not include in the rebuke of Ananias?

14 and believers were the more added to the Lord,
multitudes both men and women.

15 insomuch that they even carried out the sick into the
streets, and laid them on beds and couches, that, as
Peter came by, at the least his shadow might overshadow some one of them.

16 And there also came together the multitude from the
cities round about Jerusalem, bringing sick folk, and
them that were vexed with unclean spirits: and they
were healed every one.

12 The outcome of the purity produced by the discipline.

1) It has already been noted that fear or holy awe was one result.

2) We must consider also that **power** was a fruit of the cleansing.
The leaders of the church could effectively carry forth their work.
The power by which they performed their work was vindicated. These
men could not be deceived. They were "God's Ambassadors." When
the apostles went forth into the temple area not just one sign or
wonder was performed as with the lame man, but many signs and
wonders were wrought among the people by the hands of the
apostles. Solomon's portico continued to be the place of meeting,
but now not only the saints, but also many sinners came to see, and
hear, and to be healed.

13 3) "But of the rest durst no man join himself to them: howbeit the people magnified them." Here is another result of this purity.
We understand this passage to carry this meaning: That of
the multitude of the unsaved (in contradistinction to the apostles
in this case) none who might have some of the tendencies of Ananias
and his wife dared join himself to these holy believers, lest there
should fall upon him the same fate. But in it all the people magnified
them. The people admired the straight and holy position of the
apostles and the Jerusalem church. The world will always magnify
a church that will stand uncompromisingly for holiness of life and
word. It is only when the lives of the saints are diluted by worldly compromise that the church ceases to be a power and the world
begins to laugh.

14 4) As we have said, the immediate result of holiness and
preaching is the conversion of souls. In verse fourteen we have the
statement that "believers were the more added to the Lord; multitudes
both of men and women." What is the meaning of the expression

164. What did the death of these two add to the conception of the disciples?
165. What is meant by the statement that, "power was a fruit of the cleansing"?
166. What is meant by: "But of the rest durst not any man join himself to
them?"

"added to the Lord?" When we refer to Eph. 1:22, 23 (and other passages) we find the church is referred to as "the body of Christ," thus we can draw the logical conclusion that the thought of being "added to the Lord" was in reference to the action of being added by their conversion and baptism into the **Lord's body, His** church. (Compare 2:41 and 47.)

15 The intimation of verse fifteen is that many of these persons who became members of Christ's body did so as a result of the miraculous deeds of the apostles, accompanied as they were with the word of truth, so that now we see the believers and others carrying the sick folk out into the streets, laying them on beds and couches, that as Peter came by "at the least his shadow might overshadow some one of them." The thought of healing power in Peter's shadow was an Oriental superstition that attributed virtue to the shadow of a righteous man and evil to the shadow of a wicked man.

The text does **not** say that anyone was healed from Peter's shadow, but only that this was the belief of the people.

16 5) Verse sixteen speaks of the far reaching effects of the power of the Jerusalem church. The word of the apostles' miraculous ministry soon was carried to the cities round about Jerusalem and they brought their sick folk and those that were vexed with unclean spirits. They were not disappointed for "they were healed **every one.**" (Somewhat different than cases of healing today by those who claim the same power of the apostles.) Doubtless many of these same persons became Christians and thus caused churches to spring up in the cities round about Jerusalem. This probably accounts for the origin of the church visited by Peter at a later time. (Cf. 9:31, 32.)

When Peter and John stood before the high priest they had faithfully promised to disobey the charge given them: "Not to preach nor teach any more in this name. They had taught and preached in this name with outstanding success. Note the progression of events:

1) They returned from the Sanhedrin to their own company; they prayed and the Lord answered with great encouragement.

2) Sin entered the fold but God turned it into a triumph for His cause.

3) The apostles continued to preach on Solomon's porch. The power of the apostles manifest in the punishment of Ananias and

167. What is the meaning of the expression "added to the Lord?"
168. What connection did the miracles have with the conversions?
169. Was there any healing power in Peter's shadow? Explain your answer.
170. What comment in verses 5:12-16 speaks of the far reaching effects of the miraculous ministry of the apostles?
171. What difference can be noted between the healing of the apostles and of those of today who claim this power?
172. What relation does Acts 9:31-22 have with these miracles?

Sapphira greatly strengthened their position in the eyes of the common folk. The apostles were almost worshiped by those of the city. Every day their message and popularity grew.

10. IN THE PRISON. 5:17-20

17 But the high priest rose up, and all they that were with him (which is the sect of the Sadducees), and they were filled with jealousy,

18 and laid hands on the apostles, and put them in public ward.

19 But an angel of the Lord by night opened the prison doors, and brought them out, and said,

20 Go ye, and stand and speak in the temple to the people all the words of this Life.

17 This was too much for the high priest and the Sadducees. They could bear it no longer. Luke gives a picturesque word respecting the anger of the high priest and the Sadducees. He says . . . "The high priest **rose up**, and all that were with him." As if they could sit still no longer. They could no longer witness this flagrant disobedience to their command. If the disobedience of these men had not caused such an interest among the people the high priest might have overlooked it, but how he was "filled with jealousy."

18 These authorities came much as they had before, and laid hands upon the apostles and put them in the public ward. It will be of import to realize that **all twelve** of the apostles were jailed upon this occasion.

When man has reached his extremity, then it is that there is afforded to God an opportunity. The extremity had been reached. An emergency had arisen. What would have happened to the cause if all twelve of the apostles had been tried and condemned? This was exactly the plan of the Sanhedrin, not to stop with two of them, but to silence all twelve once and for all.

19 Heb. 1:14 states that the angels are "ministering spirits, sent forth to do service for the sake of them that shall inherit salvation." Upon this occasion God gave to one of these "ministers" a special task . . . the task of opening those doors that were only shut to the power of men. And so it was that the apostles had an angelic visitor in the quiet of the early morning hours. To their unspeakable amazement the angel opened the prison doors and lead them out. Why were they thus delivered? The angel answered this question when he had led them out under the stars of the Syrian sky.

173. What events had transpired that incited the wrath of the high priest?

174. What is the picturesque statement Luke gives that describes the wrath of the high priest?

175. What is there about the second arrest that is different from the first?

176. What was the purpose in the arrest of all twelve apostles?

20 Can you imagine the apostles with incredulous gaze searching the face of the angel for a reason for their freedom? Perchance
the hearts of the apostles were troubled as they communed together
in the dark of the prison: "Why has God permitted this? "Why has
God thus dealt with us? If our message is what He wants preached
why has He thus permitted us to be confined? Maybe He does not
intend that we should speak any more in His name." All of these
questions were answered, all of their fears were dispelled when
the angel said: "Go ye, and stand and speak in the temple to the
people all the words of this Life."

11. ON SOLOMON'S PORCH. 5:21a
21 And when they heard this, they entered into the temple
about daybreak, and taught.

21a As the sun broke over the eastern horizon of the hills of Judea
the apostles entered the familiar portico of the temple to take up
their message where it had been interrupted the day before. Who
would be in the temple at this hour? Perhaps a few of the disciples
who because of anxiety and prayer did not sleep that night. They
were here in this hallowed spot where they had heard the words of
"this Life." Here they could worship and pray. But here too they
were to bet met by the twelve. How the faces of God's servants
must have been aglow with the inner joy of their victorious faith.
How they must have preached as never before. In but a few moments
the few who were present ran to carry the news to others and in a
short while a multitude had gathered to listen.

12. BEFORE THE SANHEDRIN. 5:21b-41.
a. The assembling of the council and the apostle's trial.
21b-28.
But the high priest came, and they that were with him,
and called the council together, and all the senate of
the children of Israel, and sent to the prison-house to
have them brought.
22 But the officers that came found them not in the prison;
and they returned, and told,
23 saying, The prison-house we found shut in all safety,
and the keepers standing at the doors: but when we had
opened, we found no man within.
24 Now when the captain of the temple and the chief priests
heard these words, they were much perplexed concerning them whereunto this would grow.

177. What question do you imagine was in the minds of the apostles upon
their release by the angel? How was it answered?
178. Who would be in the temple at the break of dawn?
179. How do you suppose the apostles obtained an audience?

25 And there came one and told them, Behold, the men
   whom ye put in the prison are in the temple standing
   and teaching the people.
26 Then went the captain with the officers, and brought
   them, but without violence; for they feared the people,
   lest they should be stoned.
27 And when they had brought them, they set them before the council. And the high priest asked them,
28 saying, We strictly charged you not to teach in this
   name: and behold, ye have filled Jerusalem with your
   teaching, and intend to bring this man's blood upon us.

21b-23 A few short hours later, in another part of the temple, the
high priest called the council together. Luke says that the high
priest in assembling the council called "all the senate of the children
of Israel." This reference to "the senate" has to do with the Sanhedrin proper, the term "senate" comes from the word meaning
"older" so it doubtless has reference to the official capacity of the
Sanhedrin, or the "elders." While this "august assembly" waited,
the officers were sent to have the apostles brought. A few moments
later the council members looked up to behold the officers returning but they were without their prisoners. They brought the astounding news that, although they found the prison locked and the guards
at their stations, when the doors were opened they found "no man
within." The officers probably also questioned the keepers of the
prison who could give no explanation of the disappearance of the
apostles.

24-28 The captain of the temple and the priests had dealt with
these men before and had been defeated in their efforts to oppose
them, but when they heard the message of the officers they began to
wonder **what** would be the result if the news of **this** event became common knowledge. While they were thus thinking, a certain man
hurried into their midst to tell them that the very ones whom they
had publicly apprehended and jailed were now in another part of
the temple doing the very thing for which they had been twice arrested: "Standing and teaching the people."

The captain of the temple went off to a mission he had performed
before: to "lay hands on the apostles" and bring them before the
council. But as he and the officers went to their task he must have
felt somewhat different toward these men they were about to ar-

180. How could the council gather in the temple without observing the
     preaching of the apostles?
181. What is the meaning of the term "Senate" as it is used here?
182. What was the message of the soldiers upon their return from prison?
183. Do you suppose this incident of the release of the apostles caused the
     council to think about their former experience with these men? Where
     is this suggested in the text?

rest than he did on the first occasion. The authorities knew that no violence could be exercised lest the people stone them.

b. The answer of the apostles. 29-32.

29 But Peter and the apostles answered and said, We must obey God rather than men.

30 The God of our fathers raised up Jesus, whom ye slew, hanging him on a tree.

31 Him did God exalt with his right hand to be a Prince and a Saviour, to give repentance to Israel, and remission of sins.

32 And we are witnesses of these things; and so is the Holy Spirit, whom God hath given to them that obey him.

29-32 Having been ushered in before the council the high priest immediately laid before them the two charges against them:

First, that they had violated the charge of the Sanhedrin;

Second, that in their teaching they were seeking to place the blame of the death of Jesus upon the rulers of the Sanhedrin.

The response of the apostles was straight to the point. With Peter as their spokesman they pleaded **"guilty"** to both charges.

Notice:

1) We have disobeyed your charge; "We **must** obey God rather than men."

2) We **intended** to convey the thought that the blood of Jesus is upon your heads for you **have** slain Him and hung Him upon a tree. But God has raised Him up; indeed He has been exalted at the right hand of God. He is thus exalted and has gone through His suffering to be a "Prince and a Saviour, to give repentence to Israel, and remission of sins."

3) The apostles added one more thrust to this bold rebuke. They said in thought "Concerning all these facts regarding Jesus we are personal witnesses, and so is the Holy Spirit whom God hath given to them that obey Him." The apostles witnessed the earthly work and triumph of Jesus whereas the Holy Spirit beheld not only this, but also His heavenly coronation at the right hand of the Father.

c. The result of the defense and the advice of Gamaliel. The release. 38-41.

33 But they, when they heard this, were cut to the heart, and were minded to slay them.

184. What two charges were made against the apostles?

185. What response did the apostles make to these charges?

186. What was the additional remark the apostles made following their answer to the charges?

187. What is the meaning of 32b?

34 But there stood up one in the council, a Pharisee, named Gamaliel, a doctor of the law, had in honor of all the people, and commanded to put the men forth a little while.

35 And he said unto them, Ye men of Israel, take heed to yourselves as touching these men, what ye are about to do.

36 For before these days rose up Theudas, giving himself out to be somebody; to whom a number of men, about four hundred, joined themselves: who was slain; and all, as many as obeyed him, were dispersed, and came to nought.

37 After this man rose up Judas of Galilee in the days of the enrolment, and drew away some of the people after him: he also perished; and all, as many as obeyed him, were scattered abroad.

38 And now I say unto you, Refrain from these men, and let them alone: for if this counsel or this work be of men, it will be overthrown:

39 but if it is of God, ye will not be able to overthrow them; lest haply ye be found even to be fighting against God.

40 And to him they agreed: and when they had called the apostles unto them, they beat them and charged them not to speak in the name of Jesus, and let them go.

41 They therefore departed from the presence of the council, rejoicing that they were counted worthy to suffer dishonor for the Name.

33 Ere the last words of the apostles died out on the air an angry rumble was heard among the council. The words struck home like a knife and they had to make a decision. The truth concerning sin applied to man's conscience will either make him angry or cause godly sorrow for his sin. In the case of Pentecost godly sorrow was the result, here anger was manifest. The anger was growing in such intensity that it seemed inevitable that it would soon burst forth in a sentence of death.

34-41 When the storm was just about to break, there stood up one in the council and averted the terrible crisis. It is refreshing to meet here one who in the midst of the storm of emotion is governed by judgment rather than by hatred and pride.

"Gamaliel, a Pharisee, a doctor of the law, had in honor of all the people." The same man from whom Paul was taught the law,

188. State the two results of the truth applied to the heart and give an illustration of each.

189. Name three facts about Gamaliel.

190. Did the apostles hear the words of Gamaliel?

(22:3). What had this man to say? Whatever it was, it was to be addressed to the Sandhedrin. There was much that could be heard by the apostles. The twelve were commanded by Gamaliel to step out of the presence of the Sanhedrin.

Speaking to the council, Gamaliel gave the following advice: "Consider yourselves in the action you are about to take." He suggested that if they were to condemn these men to death and then it be found that evidence was wanting, it would go hard with them. His advice was, in light of this, "let them alone." He gave substantial reasons for so acting. Two illustrations were used of movements that at their inception caused quite a stir but later came to nothing. The inference was made in the use of these illustrations, that the excitement concerning Jesus was probably of the same nature and would come to the same end. By leaving these men alone the Sanhedrin would be acting wisely, for then they could determine the origin of this movement by its fruit. It if was not of God it would come to nought. But if it indeed was of God it could not be overthrown with opposition, and if they did oppose it they would be fighting against God. This was sound advice and they could not help but see its wisdom. "To him," in spite of their injured pride, "they agreed." But they could not bear to let these men go without some punishment; so calling the apostles in they caused the apostles to be beaten with the 39 stripes of the Jewish law. This beating was just in the eyes of the council for they had disobeyed their charge.

41 The stripes laid upon their backs by the council were such as would cause their flesh to be torn and bleeding, and yet they left this meeting with a heart of rejoicing, not with the burdened spirit of a martyr but with joy "that they were counted worthy to suffer dishonor for the Name." This was not a cross to be borne but a privilege to enjoy.

13. THE SPREAD OF THE WORD. 5:42.

42 And every day, in the temple and at home, they ceased
   not to teach and to preach Jesus as the Christ.

42 How lightly they considered the marks of the Jewish rods can be seen when we read that they went right back to the same place where they had been thrice arrested and "ceased not to teach and to preach Jesus as the Christ." Not content with this, they brought the same glad tidings to the neighborhood in which they lived.

191. Why did Gamaliel say, "Take heed unto yourselves as touching these men, what ye are about to do?"
192. State in three words the advice of Gamaliel and then give the reasons for so acting.
193. Of what did the "beating" consist?
194. What is wrong with "the martyr complex or spirit?"
195. What manifests the utter disregard of the Apostles for the punishment of the council?

14. ON SOLOMON'S PORCH. 6:1-6.

1 Now in these days, when the number of the disciples was multiplying, there arose a murmuring of the Grecian Jews against the Hebrews, because their widows were neglected in the daily ministration.

2 And the twelve called the multitude of the disciples unto them, and said, It is not fit that we should forsake the word of God, and serve tables.

3 Look ye out therefore, brethren, from among you seven men of good report, full of the Spirit and of wisdom, whom we may appoint over this business.

4 But we will continue stedfastly in prayer, and in the ministry of the word.

5 And the saying pleased the whole multitude: and they chose Stephen, a man full of faith and of the Holy Spirit, and Philip, and Prochorus, and Nicanor, and Timon, and Parmenas, and Nicolaüs a proselyte of Antioch;

6 whom they set before the apostles: and when they had prayed, they laid their hands upon them.

a. The murmuring of the Grecian Jews. 1.

1 While Luke gives us the glad news that the number of disciples was multiplying exceedingly, he wants us to see something of the personal life and the working of the "called out body." So he records here the problem and incident out of which grew the work of the deacon. Luke has already told us of the distribution of goods so it is not at all strange to read of this same action again here in the sixth chapter. It might be well to point out that this distribution was a "daily ministration," not just once or twice a year as we are so wont to do. The church was progressing wonderfully until someone was neglected. Somehow in the feeding and caring for the many widows of this church, some of the women of the Grecian Jews were overlooked. These Jews were those who were either born and reared in Greece or had come under the sway of Grecian culture. No one carried the news of this neglect to the apostles, no word was spoken directly of the trouble, they just "murmured." How murmuring can and has stopped the progress of the children of God through the centuries.

b. The action of the twelve and the church. 2-6.

2-6 The murmuring had not continued long until it reached the

196. What is the difference between the ministration of the church today and that of the Jerusalem church?
197. What is meant by "Grecian Jews?"
198. Why were the seven appointed?
199. How was this difficulty alleviated?

ears of the apostles. They did the only wise thing that could be done; they called together all those concerned, and by this time the whole church knew about the trouble, and presented to them a plan of action that would alleviate the difficulty. First they presented the thought that although they were the leaders in the church, yet this work was not theirs to do, for they had been called to "prayer and the ministry of the word," not to "serving tables. If the apostles were to take up this added responsibility it would cause them to neglect their God-given work. The solution lay in selecting seven men from among the church who would be qualified according to the divinely given qualifications, i.e. (1) "of good report, (2) full of the Spirit and (3) of wisdom."

Having done this, the disciples were to bring these men before the apostles who were then to set them aside to this work by the laying on of hands. If this would be done, the need would be met, and the twelve could go on unhampered in giving themselves to prayer and the ministry of the word.

This saying pleased the whole multitude and they chose seven men who met the qualifications. It is interesting to note that all of the seven bear Grecian names. In this selection we see both the wisdom and love of the believers in the Jerusalem church. These men were set into this work by the laying on of the apostles' hands. Since these men were to care for the daily "diaconia" or ministrations (the word from which "deacon" is derived), we could say that they were indeed "deacons" of the church. We then also know the formal setting apart was the placing of these men into this office.

15. THE INCREASE OF THE WORD OF GOD. 6:7, 8.

7 And the word of God increased; and the number of the disciples multiplied in Jerusalem exceedingly; and a great company of the priests were obedient to the faith.

8 And Stephen, full of grace and power, wrought great wonders and signs among the people.

7 Each time the writer of the book of Acts mentions some difficulty that arose in the church he always concludes the incident with the heartening word that this difficulty was used by God to resound unto His glory, and that through it all there was even a greater turning to Christ. So it is here that after the murmuring ceased "the Word of God increased" i.e. the words of the apostles which

200. What two-fold task did the Apostles have in the Jerusalem church?
201. Who was to select the seven? How was it to be done?
202. What was the purpose of the laying on of hands?
203. How is the love and wisdom of the believers shown in the selection?
204. Would it be proper to call these men "deacons?"
205. What is meant by the expression "the Word of God increased?"

were veritably the "words of God" made entrance into many hearts, this resulted in the multiplying of the disciples "exceedingly."

We have often thought while reading the account of the association of the twelve with the Sanhedrin: "Why was there not some among that group of intelligent, sincere men, who would come to a belief in Jesus as the Christ?" So it is with great joy that we read here in 6:7 that "a great company of the priests were obedient to the faith." We do not know it as a fact, but we like to think that at least some of these men were priests of the Sanhedrin. We must not overlook the expression "obedient to the faith." There was something more to their faith than mere mental assent, there was something in it that demanded obedience.

We hold to the position that "the faith" spoken of was the same as "the faith" mentioned in Jude 3; i.e. that scheme of God for man's redemption. The apostles preached "the faith" and men became obedient to it. When we examine 2:38 and 3:19 we must conclude that their obedience entailed repentance and baptism for the "blotting out of" or "remission of sins."

8 Associated with and a part of the spreading of the word was the work of this Jerusalem deacon, Stephen. When the hands of the apostles were placed upon his head, there must have coexisted with the act of setting him into the office, the impartation of one or more of the special spiritual gifts. (See the notes on the special study of the Holy Spirit.) This is suggested in the fact that Stephen, "full of grace and power, wrought great wonders and signs among the people." These were performed to confirm the truthfulness of his words. This we can observe in the following verses.

16. **AT THE SYNAGOGUE OF THE LIBERTINES.** 6:9-12.

9 But there arose certain of them that were of the synagogue called the synagogue of the Libertines, and of the Cyrenians, and of the Alexandrians, and of them of Cilicia and Asia, disputing with Stephen.

10 And they were not able to withstand the wisdom and the Spirit by which he spake.

11 Then they suborned men, who said, We have heard him speak blasphemous words against Moses, and against God.

12 And they stirred up the people, and the elders, and the scribes, and came upon him, and seized him, and brought him into the council,

a. Those who opposed. 9

9 To whom did Stephen preach? To those of Jerusalem to be sure,

206. What in verse 7 is suggestive of a victory for Christ in the Sanhedrin?
207. What is the thought of "obedient to the faith?"
208. What is the meaning of the term "faith" as it is used in 6:7?
209. What two purposes were involved in the laying on of the apostles' hands?   86

but can we be any more specific than that? In looking into these verses we can secure at least a little suggestion of the persons to whom Stephen addressed his message. As we have mentioned, Stephen was doubtless a Grecian Jew. With whom would it be more logical to imagine Stephen laboring than with those of his own background? This thought finds support when we are told that those of the Grecian provinces of Cyrene, Alexandria, Cilicia, and Asia disputed with Stephen. The ones who opposed Stephen's work were evidently all members of one synagogue called "The Synagogue of the Libertines." It is to be concluded from the use of the word "Libertines" that these Grecian Jews were at one time slaves but now were "Libertines" or "Freedmen." They either purchased or earned their freedom.

b. The evil means used by those who refused. 10-12.

10-12 These disputants although they strongly opposed the position of their countrymen, could not withstand the logical conclusion to which he led them. Rather than yield their hearts to the Lordship of Jesus, they stiffened their necks. Not only were they stubborn but also dishonest. Deceit is the first step in defending a position maintained only because of stubborness. Men can be found almost anywhere who will do almost anything for a price. In this case money was paid to twist the truth. By this twisting Stephen was to be implicated in blasphemy. These "suborned" men were very zealous in their efforts. They spread the word throughout the city that this man had spoken against both God and Moses. Since the minds of the populace were filled with the thought of God through the message and miracles of the apostles, this was a serious charge.

It was not long until this malicious lie had done its work. Word reached the Sanhedrin that there was a great stir among the people; that a certain man was accused of blasphemy. This was a charge to be investigated. Especially so since the one accused was a member of the movement the Sanhedrin hated.

The elders and scribes came upon Stephen as they had upon the apostles and brought him into the council. This charge was punishable by death. It was the one for which Jesus was tried. (Matt. 26:65; Mark 14:58).

210. To whom did Stephen preach? Prove your answer.
211. What is the meaning of the term "Synagogue of the Libertines?" How is it used here?
212. What was the response of the Libertines?
213. What is the first step in supporting a position maintained only through stubbornness? How is it shown here?
214. What was the work of these suborned men? How did they carry it out?
215. Why did this false accusation receive such a ready response?
216. Why would the Sanhedrin be especially interested in the charge against Stephen?
217. What do you know about the importance of the charge?

17. STEPHEN BEFORE THE SANHEDRIN. 6:13—7:57.
a. The testimony of the false witnesses. 6:13, 14.

13 and set up false witnesses, who said, This man ceaseth
not to speak words against this holy place, and the law:
14 for we have heard him say, that this Jesus of Nazareth
shall destroy this place, and shall change the customs
which Moses delivered unto us.

13-14 With Stephen before the council the false witnesses came
forward with their **specific** charge:
"This man ceaseth not to speak words against this holy place,
and the law: **For we have heard him say, that this Jesus of Nazareth
shall destroy this place, and shall change the customs which Moses delivered unto us.**"

The general charge of blasphemy is now made specific. The
accusation prior to this time was general; these men had hurled the
charge of blasphemy with no explanation; now we hear their explanation. They said:

"He blasphemed because he said Jesus of Nazareth would destroy this place, and in so doing the customs of worship which
Moses gave would perish with the temple."

This accusation was nothing but a black lie concocted by twisting Stephen's words. Stephen had probably in his preaching spoken
of the destruction of the temple as Jesus had prophesied (Matt.
24:1, 2) and he may have also given the words of the Master as to
the destruction of His body (John 2:19-22). By accommodating
these words to their own evil purpose and they formulated the charge.

b. The glowing face of Stephen. 15.

15 And all that sat in the council, fastening their eyes on
him, saw his face as it had been the face of an angel.

15 We like the words of McGarvey upon this verse, we quote here
from his commentary upon this verse:

"There is no need to suppose anything supernatural in his appearance. He was standing just where his Master had stood when
condemned to die; he was arraigned on a similar charge; he had
the same judges; and he knew perfectly well that the court had come
together not to try him, but to condemn him. He knew that the
supreme hour of his life had come; and the emotions which stirred
his soul as he thought of the past, of death, of heaven, of the cause
which he had pleaded, and of the foul murder about to be per-

218. State in your own words the specific objection urged by the false witnesses.
219. How had these charges been formulated?
220. Why did the face of Stephen glow as he stood before the council?

petrated, necessarily lit up his countenance with a glow almost supernatural." (Page 115.)

    c. Stephen's defence. 7:1-53.

1 And the high priest said, Are these things so?

2 And he said,
Brethren and fathers, hearken: The God of glory appeared unto our father Abraham, when he was in Mesopotamia, before he dwelt in Haran,

3 and said unto him, Get thee out of thy land, and from thy kindred, and come into the land which I shall show thee.

4 Then came he out of the land of the Chaldaeans, and dwelt in Haran: and from thence, when his father was dead, God removed him into this land, wherein ye now dwell:

5 and he gave him none inheritance in it, no, not so much as to set his foot on: and he promised that he would give it to him in possession, and to his seed after him, when as yet he had no child.

6 And God spake on this wise, that his seed should sojourn in a strange land, and that they should bring them into bondage, and treat them ill, four hundred years.

7 And the nation to which they shall be in bondage will I judge, said God: and after that shall they come forth, and serve me in this place.

8 And he gave him the covenant of circumcision: and so Abraham begat Isaac, and circumcised him the eighth day; and Isaac begat Jacob, and Jacob the twelve patriarchs.

9 And the patriarchs, moved with jealousy against Joseph, sold him into Egypt; and God was with him,

10 and delivered him out of all his afflictions, and gave him favor and wisdom before Pharaoh king of Egypt; and he made him governor over Egypt and all his house.

11 Now there came a famine over all Egypt and Canaan, and great affliction: and our fathers found no sustenance.

12 But when Jacob heard that there was grain in Egypt, he sent forth our fathers the first time.

13 And at the second time Joseph was made known to his brethren; and Joseph's race became manifest unto Pharaoh.

14 And Joseph sent, and called to him Jacob his father, and all his kindred, three score and fifteen souls.

15 And Jacob went down into Egypt; and he died, himself and our fathers;

16 and they were carried over unto Shechem, and laid in the tomb that Abraham bought for a price in silver of the sons of Hamor in Shechem.

17 But as the time of the promise drew nigh which God vouchsafed unto Abraham, the people grew and multiplied in Egypt,

18 till there arose another king over Egypt, who knew not Joseph.

19 The same dealt craftily with our race, and ill-treated our fathers, that they should cast out their babes to the end they might not live.

20 At which season Moses was born, and was exceeding fair; and he was nourished three months in his father's house:

21 and when he was cast out, Pharaoh's daughter took him up, and nourished him for her own son.

22 And Moses was instructed in all the wisdom of the Egyptians; and he was mighty in his words and works.

23 But when he was well-nigh forty years old, it came into his heart to visit his brethren the children of Israel.

24 And seeing one of them suffer wrong, he defended him, and avenged him that was oppressed, smiting the Egyptian:

25 and he supposed that his brethren understood that God by his hand was giving them deliverance; but they understood not.

26 And the day following he appeared unto them as they strove, and would have set them at one again, saying, Sirs, ye are brethren; why do ye wrong one to another?

27 But he that did his neighbor wrong thrust him away, saying, Who made thee a ruler and a judge over us?

28 Wouldest thou kill me, as thou killedst the Egyptian yesterday?

29 And Moses fled at this saying, and became a sojourner in the land of Midian, where he begat two sons.

30 And when forty years were fulfilled, an angel appeared to him in the wilderness of mount Sinai, in a flame of fire in a bush.

31 And when Moses saw it, he wondered at the sight: and as he drew near to behold, there came a voice of the Lord,

32 I am the God of thy fathers, the God of Abraham, and of Isaac, and of Jacob. And Moses trembled, and durst not behold.

33 And the Lord said unto him, Loose the shoes from thy feet: for the place whereon thou standest is holy ground.

34 I have surely seen the affliction of my people that is in

THE DAMASCUS GATE—BAB EL AMUD (GATE OF THE COLUMN).

The northern entrance to Jerusalem.

Out of the northern gate of the ancient city of Jerusalem went the proud Pharisee on his way to Damascus to bring back bound to Jerusalem all those of the Way. But he himself came back through the same gate bound to the one he went to persecute. There are multitudes of persons who go in and out of glory than Saul of Tarsus gate with no more thought of the king of glory than Saul of Tarsus in the long ago. Through the northern entrance came Paul and Barnabas with the offering for the poor saints in Jerusalem. (Acts 11:27-30) Once again they must have come with an offering for the poor. (Acts 21:17) As Paul returned to the city of Zion from time to time did these familiar places call to his heart the events associated with them? Have you traveled the Damascus road? Have you gone through the northern gate?

91

Egypt, and have heard their groaning, and I am come down to deliver them: and now come, I will send thee into Egypt.

35 This Moses whom they refused, saying, Who made thee a ruler and a judge? him hath God sent to be both a ruler and a deliverer with the hand of the angel that appeared to him in the bush.

36 This man led them forth, having wrought wonders and signs in Egypt, and in the Red sea, and in the wilderness forty years.

37 This is that Moses, who said unto the children of Israel, A prophet shall God raise up unto you from among your brethren, like unto me.

38 This is he that was in the church in the wilderness with the angel that spake to him in the mount Sinai, and with our fathers: who received living oracles to give unto us:

39 to whom our fathers would not be obedient, but thrust him from them, and turned back in their hearts unto Egypt,

40 saying unto Aaron, Make us gods that shall go before us: for as for this Moses, who led us forth out of the land of Egypt, we know not what is become of him.

41 And they made a calf in those days, and brought a sacrifice unto the idol, and rejoiced in the works of their hands.

42 But God turned, and gave them up to serve the host of heaven; as it is written in the book of the prophets,
Did ye offer unto me slain beasts and sacrifices
Forty years in the wilderness, O house of Israel?

43 And ye took up the tabernacle of Moloch,
And the star of the god Rephan,
The figures which ye made to worship them:
And I will carry you away beyond Babylon.

44 Our fathers had the tabernacle of the testimony in the wilderness, even as he appointed who spake unto Moses, that he should make it according to the figure that he had seen.

45 Which also our fathers, in their turn, brought in with Joshua when they entered on the possession of the nations, that God thrust out before the face of our fathers, unto the days of David;

46 who found favor in the sight of God, and asked to find a habitation for the God of Jacob.

47 But Solomon built him a house.

48 Howbeit the Most High dwelleth not in houses made with hands; as saith the prophet,

49 The heaven is my throne,
And the earth the footstool of my feet:
What manner of house will ye build me? saith the Lord:
Or what is the place of my rest?

50 Did not my hand make all these things?

51 Ye stiffnecked and uncircumcised in heart and ears,
ye do always resist the Holy Spirit: as your fathers did,
so do ye.

52 Which of the prophets did not your fathers persecute?
and they killed them that showed before of the coming
of the Righteous One; of whom ye have now become
betrayers and murderers;

53 ye who received the law as it was ordained by angels,
and kept it not.

1-57 Remember as we consider this defense that Stephen stood
before the Sanhedrin to answer the charge of blasphemy. He evidently
thought it would be best to approach this charge in an indirect manner. He did this because of the terrible antagonism against Jesus
already existing in the Sanhedrin.

Thus this Grecian Jew who was "full of wisdom" evidently felt
that if he used an analogy the rulers would see the evident application and yet would not be offended, thus giving them the greatest opportunity to accept the Messiahship of Jesus. With this
thought in mind Stephen devoted his discourse to a review of Jewish
history. He could not have selected a more appropriate subject,
for these men were exceedingly proud of their heritage. Note this:
**Throughout the entire history of the Jews he weaves the thought
that every man whom God sent to the nation of Israel was rejected and mistreated; that there was not one man sent from God
who was accepted for what he was.** In the case of Joseph, the Patriarchs refused him and sold him into Egypt. Moses was twice rejected. The application of this narrative should have been self-evident.
The application that fairly shouts from Stephen's account is that **the
rulers of the Jews in his day were doing with Jesus exactly what their
fathers did with Joseph, Moses and all the prophets.**

While the above comments contain a brief resume of Stephen's
message it is well to point out here that Stephen did not close his
sermon without giving a direct answer to the charge of speaking
against the temple. He answered the accusation by saying that God
did not dwell in temples made with hands. It was even as Isaiah

221. In what manner did Stephen approach the charge of the blasphemy?
222. How did the method used by Stephen give to the Sanhedrin the greatest opportunity to accept Jesus as the Christ.
223. What thought is interwoven throughout the entire message of Stephen?
224. What is the self-evident application of Stephen's sermon?

had said: "The heaven is my throne, for all these things hath my hands made. The earth is the footstool of my feet. What manner of house will ye build me? saith the Lord. Or what is the place of my rest? Did not my hands make all of these things?" So, if the temple was to be destroyed (and it was), this would **not** destroy the dwelling place of Jehovah.

As the young Grecian Jew looked into the faces of those before him, he saw as he drew near the end of his narrative that all of his wisdom and earnestness was not going to avail in convincing these Jews that they should accept Jesus as the Messiah. There was nothing they could say against it but they were not going to accept it. The response of those before him must have been one of cool indifference mingled with self-righteous judgment. To see this expression upon the faces of those before whom you were pleading for life would have filled with icy fear the heart of one less brave than Stephen. In the heart of this noble soul there was aroused nothing but a great passionate indignation that these men could face the truth and yet refuse it, these who above all others were to be devoted to a search for and acceptance of the truth. Stephen could no longer forebear. If these men would make the application he would make it for them. It was not that they did not see, nor that they did not understand, it was only that they **would not.** From his pent-up heart there burst forth these words:

"Ye stiffnecked and uncircumcised in heart and ears, ye do **always** resist the Holy Spirit: as your fathers did, so do ye. Which of the prophets did not your fathers persecute? And they killed them that showed before the coming of the Righteous One; of whom ye have now become betrayers and murderers; ye who received the law as it was ordained by angels and kept it not."

We do not deem it necessary to give an extended explanation of each of the verses contained in Stephen's address. Most of these verse are self-explanatory.

Here is an outline of Stephen's defense for careful study:
Introduction:
   The life of Abraham. 2-8.
   1) First called by God in Ur of the Chaldees. 2, 3.
   2) Removed to Canaan from Haran following the death of his father. 4, 5.
   3) His seed to be in bondage four hundred years. 6.

225. How did Stephen answer the charge of blasphemy?
226. What must Stephen have perceived in the faces of those to whom he spoke? What was the result?
227. Why would it have been reasonable for Stephen to expect these men to accept Jesus as the Messiah? Why didn't they do so?
228. What did Stephen do for these men that they would not do for themselves?

4) The judgment of Egypt and the return to Canaan. 7.
5) The covenant of circumcision and the birth of Isaac, Jacob and the twelve patriarchs. 8.

I—The case of Joseph. 9-19.
  1. The rejection and ill treatment of Joseph. 9.
  2. God was with Joseph and gave him favor in the sight of Pharaoh. 10.
  3. The famine resulting in the ending of the fathers. 11, 12.
  4. At their second visit Joseph manifests himself to his brethren. 13.
  5. Joseph sends for his father and all his kindred. 14.
  6. Jacob dies in Egypt. The Patriarchs also die and are carried over into Shechem and buried in the tomb which Jacob purchased from the sons of Hamor in Shechem. 15, 16.

II—The case of Moses. 20-43.
  1. Moses born at the time of the slaying of the infants; was nourished three months at home, when put out was found by the daughter of Pharaoh and reared in her court. 20, 21.
  2. He was instructed in all the wisdom of Egypt and became mighty in word and work. 22.
  3. At forty years of age he attempted to deliver his people from bondage but was rejected. 23-28.
  4. Killed an Egyptian in his zeal for his people; lest he be found out he fled to Midian. 29.
  5. Having been in Midian forty years and having begotten two sons he was called by God through the burning bush to deliver the children of Israel. 30-34.
  6. The very Moses whom they rejected at first was now the one to perform wonders and signs and to lead them out of Egypt through the Red Sea into the Wilderness. 35, 36.
  7. This was the Moses who spoke of the prophet to come who would be like unto him; this was the man who was in the wilderness and with the angel that spoke to him in the mount and with the fathers who received the living oracles. 37, 38.
  8. But the fathers were not obedient but longed for Egypt and asked for a Golden Calf while Moses was in the mount. 39, 40.
  9. The calf was made and they worshiped it. God gave them up to fulfill the prophesy of Amos. 41-43.

III—The direct answer of Stephen to the blasphemy charge. 44-50.
  1. The tabernacle was movable and perishable in nature. 44, 45.
  2. The temple was built through David and Solomon but the prophet Isaiah said that even it was infinitely too small to contain the living God. 46-50.

229. What were the thoughts of Stephen's introduction and first divisions?
230. Give from memory three facts about Moses.

3. Hence, it would not be blasphemy to say that this temple was yet to be set aside and destroyed.

Conclusion:

Stephen makes the application of his message. 51-53.

1. Considering the manner in which they received his message they are called "stiffnecked" like an ox that would not bow its head to receive the yoke. "Uncircumcised in heart and ears": this was as much as to say that their hearts and ears were "unclean." (cf. Lev. 26:41; I Sam. 17:26; Jer. 6:10).

2. He states the evident application of his message. 52.

3. Another privilege that was theirs: they had "received the law as it was ordained (or given) by angels." But they kept it not. This only added to their guilt. 53 (cf. Heb. 2:2; Gal. 3:19).

d. The results. 54-57.

54 Now when they heard these things, they were cut to the heart, and they gnashed on him with their teeth.

55 But he, being full of the Holy Spirit, looked up stedfastly into heaven, and saw the glory of God, and Jesus standing on the right hand of God,

56 and said, Behold, I see the heavens opened, and the Son of man standing on the right hand of God.

57 But they cried out with a loud voice, and stopped their ears, and rushed upon him with one accord;

Stephen reached the hearts of his listeners but they were hearts of stone. There was not the spirit of inquiry and honesty that would allow them to receive the word with meekness. There was only the spirit of pride and self-righteousness. Hence, when Stephen let them see themselves as God did they were full of anger and literally ground their teeth at him. They bared their teeth in rage as a dog or any other carnivorous animal.

God gave to Stephen in this hour a vision of his home. Jehovah drew aside the curtain and let Stephen look for this fleeting moment into His very presence. The scripture here paints a beautiful scene. There in front of that angry mob stands Stephen with his face uplifted to God. The Holy Spirit floods his soul, his spirit is totally yielded to the spirit of God. There, as he gazes into the heavens the limitations of material sight are removed and he looks into that spiritual realm. As he looks into the glory that surrounds God he sees Jesus "standing on the right hand of God." Luke has told us that Jesus "sat down at the right hand of God," but here He

231. What two points did Stephen give in answer to the charge of blasphemy?
232. How could their ears be uncircumcised?
233. What is the meaning of the phrase "gnashed on him with their teeth?"
234. What thought is given as to why Jesus was "standing on the right hand of God?"

stands to welcome home the first martyr to His cause. Speaking under the ecstasy of the vision Stephen cries out to his would-be murderers, "Behold, I see the heavens opened, and the Son of man standing on the right hand of God." Surely this touching word should stop them in their purpose.

But when pride is injured there is no reason in the actions. They did the only thing they could do; they would hear no more of this, so "they cried out with a loud voice, and stopped their ears" so as to drown out and hold out these words of truth that were cutting so deeply their stubborn ego, "and rushed upon him with one accord." We might observe that this was not a very dignified way for seventy pious elders, lawyers and priests to act.

18. OUTSIDE THE CITY WALL. 7:58-60.

58 and they cast him out of the city, and stoned him: and the witnesses laid down their garments at the feet of a young man named Saul.

59 And they stoned Stephen, calling upon the Lord, and saying, Lord Jesus, receive my spirit.

60 And he kneeled down, and cried with a loud voice, Lord, lay not this sin to their charge. And when he had said this, he fell asleep.

58-60 As full of rage as were these men, they would not break the tradition of the elders and stone a man inside the city gates. Stephen was "cast out of the city," probably dragged hastily out by the very ones who sat as his judges. It was also a law that the witnesses against the man were to be the first to cast the stones at the condemned. The false witnesses surely took upon their hearts and souls a weighty responsibility when they accepted money to give a false testimony against this man.

Here outside the city wall these men must lay aside their outer garments and pick up stones to be the executioners of this innocent man.

In this account we have the first mention of Saul. The garments of the witnesses were laid at his feet. Whether he was a member of the Sanhedrin or just an observer we have no way of knowing. We do know that he was witnessing the death of Stephen with approval (8:4). It is difficult to find words to tell of the tragic, yet victorious death of this gallant young man. While the stones tore his flesh and bruised and broke his body, he cried out in imitation of his Master, "Lord, lay not this sin to their charge," and "Lord Jesus, receive my spirit. " "And when he had said this, he fell asleep."

235. What two customs were observed in the stoning of Stephen?

EXAMINATION OVER CHAPTERS THREE THROUGH SEVEN

True or False

_____ 1. We see the power of Pentecost in action at the gate beautiful.

_____ 2. The lame man was healed at the third hour.

_____ 3. This healing took place at the temple beautiful.

_____ 4. The lame man spoke to Peter and John before they spoke to him.

_____ 5. The lame man had no feet before he was healed.

_____ 6. The lame man was healed instantaneously.

_____ 7. Peter told him to "arise and walk."

_____ 8. The people of the temple recognized the beggar after he was healed.

_____ 9. The people immediately began to praise God for that which was done.

_____ 10. The theme of Peter's sermon was the glorification of God's servant Jesus.

_____ 11. The lame man was healed "by faith."

_____ 12. Peter discusses both the free will of man and the foreknowledge of God in his second sermon.

_____ 13. Acts 3:19 and 2:38 are very favorably compared.

_____ 14. The "season of refreshing" doubtless refers to the reception of the Holy Spirit.

_____ 15. The promise of the second coming of Christ is dependent on the conversion of the Jews.

Multiple Choice

1. "The times of the restoration of all things" refers to: 1) The end of the world. 2) The fulfillment of all the prophesies of the O.T. 3) The restoration of the ancient order of Israel.

2. Moses said that: 1) God would one day raise up the Messiah. 2) God would one day raise up a prophet like unto Himself. 3) God would one day restore Israel.

3. Peter appealed to the heart of the Jew in the conclusion of his sermon by telling them of: 1) The advantages in being a Christain. 2) The terrible death of their Messiah. 3) The blessing that God promised them through Abraham that was now to be found in Christ.

4. Peter and John were arrested at: 1) twelve o'clock. 2) Three o'clock. 3) Sundown.

5. Peter and John were arrested by: 1) The high priest and captain of the temple. 2) The Pharisees and Sadducees, with the captain of the temple. 3) The captain of the temple, the priests and the Sadducees.

6. The real reason for their arrest was: 1) They taught the people and proclaimed in Jesus the resurrection from the dead. 2) They disturbed the peace. 3) They had too large a crowd.

7. About this time Luke says: 1) There were 6,000 members in the Jerusalem church. 2) The number of men came to be about 5,000. 3)There were 8,000 members in the church.
8. 1) Ananias was the official or appointed high priest. 2) Caiphas was the official or appointed high priest. 3) Annas was the official or appointed high priest.
9. There were 1) seventy or seventy-one. 2) Seventy-one or seventy-two. 3) Sixty-nine or seventy men in the Sanhedrin.
10. The Sanhedrin asked the following question of Peter and John: 1) What have ye done? 2) By what power or in what name have ye done this? 3) By what authority have ye done this?

Fill in The Blanks

1. "Now when they beheld the _____ of Peter and John, and had perceived that they were _____ and _____ men, they _____ and took knowledge of them that they had been with Jesus." Acts 4:13.
2. "He is the _____ which was set at nought of you the builders but was made the _____ of the corner." Acts 4:11.
3. Peter said: "We cannot but speak the things which we _____ and _____." Acts 4:20.
4. "Being let go they came to their own _____ and _____ all that the chief priests and elders had said unto them." Acts 4:23.
5. "And now Lord _____ upon their threatenings and grant unto thy servants to speak thy word with all _____." Acts 4:29.
6. "And the multitude of them that believed were of one heart and soul: and not one of them said that aught of the things which he possessed was his own but they had _____ _____ _____ _____." Acts 4:32.

Can you find TEN MISTAKES in these sentences?

1. The apostles were enabled by the unity of the believers to give their witness of the resurrection with greater power.
2. Everyone sold everything so all could have some.
3. Jacob called Barnabas, having a field sold it and brought the money and laid it at the apostle's feet.
4. Ananias and Sapphira said they gave all when they only gave a part.
5. The sin of these two was two-fold; namely, the love of self and the love of money.
6. Peter attributed the sin to both Ananias and Satan.
7. It was one hour later that his wife came in and met her death.
8. "But of the rest durst no man join himself to them" refers to the rest of the members of the Jerusalem church.
9. Being "added to the Lord" is the same as being added to the church.
10. Peter's shadow is said to have healed some.

11. The high priest and Sadducees led in the arrest of the eleven apostles.
12. The angel opened the prison door near the break of day.
13. The Sanhedrin had a branch it called "the Senate."
14. The Holy Spirit was said to be a witness of the crucifixion, resurrection and coronation of Jesus.
15. The advice of Gamaliel was to refuse further opportunity to speak but not to mistreat the apostles.

Can You Put The Two Together?

1. Which of the following do you associate with Olivet? 1) Jerusalem. 2) Hope. 3) Ascension.
2. Which of the following do you associate with Judas? 1) Field of blood. 2) Apostle. 3) Servant.
3. Which of the following do you associate with Pentecost? 1) Celebration. 2) Many people. 3) Tongues of fire.
4. Which of the following do you associate with healing? 1) Miracles. 2) Powers. 3) The hands of the apostles.
5. With which of the following do you associate the break of day? 1) Solomon's Porch. 2) Prayer. 3) Work for Christ.
6. What scripture reference do you associate with the second trial before the Sanhedrin? (Supply yourself).

THE CHURCH IN JUDEA AND SAMARIA
8:1 — 12:25

THE DISPERSION   THE WORK OF PHILIP   THE WORK OF PETER AND JOHN. 8:1-40.

A. THE DISPERSION. 8:1-4.

1 And Saul was consenting unto his death.
   And there arose on that day a great persecution against the church which was in Jerusalem; and they were all scattered abroad throughout the regions of Judaea and Samaria, except the apostles.
2 And devout men buried Stephen, and made great lamentation over him.
3 But Saul laid waste the church, entering into every house, and dragging men and women committed them to prison.
4 They therefore that were scattered abroad went about preaching the word.

It might be well to say at the beginning of this section that the numbers which appear under the headings such as the one above **correspond to the numbers found upon the following chart.** All the events that took place in Jerusalem will be discussed under number one (1); all the events that took place in Samaria, under point two (2), etc.

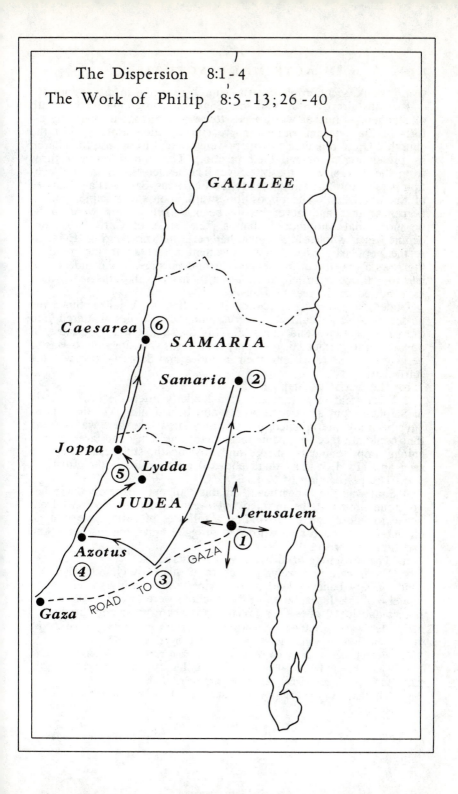

The Dispersion   8:1-4
The Work of Philip   8:5-13; 26-40

GALILEE

Caesarea ⑥   SAMARIA

Samaria ● ②

Joppa ●
⑤   Lydda ●

JUDEA

Jerusalem ●
①

Azotus ●
④   ③   GAZA

Gaza ●   ROAD TO

a. The persecution against the church resulting in dispersion. 1.

1 It has already been said that Saul was consenting to the death of Stephen. A further word needs to be added; that through the efforts of this one and others "a great persecution arose against the church." Up to this time the rulers were content to oppose the church by pretending to defend their position. The opposition now turns from the defensive to the offensive. The leadership of the persecution passes from the Sadducees to the Pharisees. Saul was a "Pharisee of the Pharisees." The opposition swept upon the disciples with a fierceness that had never before been known. There were to be no more trials, no more defenses. The cause of Christ was condemned in a wholesale manner that permitted no hearing. Evidently the popularity of the new movement presented to the mind of the Jews a real threat to their power and prestige. It did indeed, for had the church been left to continue its march, all Jerusalem would have bowed at the feet of Jesus.

Under the general persecution it was flee or be jailed. Since the persecution was localized in Jerusalem the disciples scattered into the parts of Judea and Samaria. This dispersion was God's use of opposition to further His own purposes. Jesus said the witness was to be given first at Jerusalem, then in Judea and Samaria; this was the start of it.

b. The burial of Stephen. 2.

2 With great sorrow devout men tenderly lifted the broken body of Stephen from amidst the stones and buried him. Yet there must have been joy intermingled, for now they knew that there was nothing they could not face, and come forth victorious. They had faced threatenings, imprisonments, stripes and now death; still Jesus could be seen and heard, leading them above it all to still greater efforts.

c. The persecution of Saul. 3.

3 Saul was the "spearhead" in this "all out" campaign. He left no stone unturned, he ferreted out every Christian. He went from house to house and upon finding a follower of Jesus gave him no chance for so much as a word, but dragged him from his home and cast him into prison.

d. The preaching of all who were scattered. 4.

4 There were not twelve preachers in this early church but thousands. Every believer held it his divine responsibility to tell someone else of this Jesus. So when the disciples were forced to leave their homes and loved ones they "Went everywhere preaching the word."

236. What was the difference between the persons persecuted in the earlier persecution and the ones described in the eighth chapter?

237. What change of party do we find in the leadership of the persecution?

238. What threat did the Pharisees see in this new movement?

239. How did this persecution fulfill the purpose of Christ?

240. Tell of the sorrow and joy that must have been present at the burial of Stephen.

**PART OF THE COLONNADE WHICH ONCE ENCIRCLED
SAMARIA.**

On the south side, near to the west end, a great number of columns
are still standing.

Could it be that Philip looked upon some of these same pillars?
Samaria stood upon a hill about three hundred feet high, in a wide
basin formed by the valley which runs from Shechem to the coast—
Here, on this hill, overlooked by still higher hills beyond the valley,
Omri built the new city which became the permanent capital of
the kingdom of the northern tribes. The city was almost impregnable.
Two sieges it sustained without yielding—one in 901 B.C. (I Kings
20:1) and one nine years later. (II Kings 6:24—7:20).

B. THE FIRST WORK OF PHILIP. 8:5-13.

5 And Philip went down to the city of Samaria, and proclaimed unto them the Christ.

6 And the multitudes gave heed with one accord unto the things that were spoken by Philip, when they heard, and saw the signs which he did.

7 For from many of those that had unclean spirits, they came out, crying with a loud voice: and many that were palsied, and that were lame, were healed.

8 And there was much joy in that city.

9 But there was a certain man, Simon by name, who beforetime in the city used sorcery, and amazed the people of Samaria, giving out that himself was some great one:

10 to whom they all gave heed, from the least to the greatest, saying, This man is that power of God which is called Great.

11 And they gave heed to him, because that of long time he had amazed them with his sorceries.

12 But when they believed Philip preaching good tidings concerning the kingdom of God and the name of Jesus Christ, they were baptized, both men and women.

13 And Simon also himself believed: and being baptized, he continued with Philip; and beholding signs and great miracles wrought, he was amazed.

5-8 The Bible is geographically accurate for when we read in 8:5 that "Philip went **down** to Samaria" although he journeyed northward we know by the topography of the land that he was making a descent. Who was this man who is here introduced as a special case among the many who scattered? It is not Philip the apostle, but rather Philip the deacon "one of the seven" (cp. 21:8). By the press of circumstances he became an evangelist of Christ Jesus. Philip's work was like that of all others who fled the city of David "to preach the word."

Coming in his journey to the city of Samaria he "proclaimed unto them the Christ." This preacher was not without divine evidence to confirm his word. The Samaritans not only heard his word but also beheld signs and great miracles performed to show the divine approval of his message. Luke, with his customary precision, tells us that the signs consisted in the healing of those possessed, the

241. How did Saul go about his efforts of persecution—his attitude and method?

242. What is the meaning of the term "word" as used in 8:4?

243. What do you know of Philip previous to his mention in 8:5a?

244. What relation did the signs and wonders performed by Philip have to do with his preaching?

palsied and the lame. The first response was one of intense interest, then of great joy as a result of both the healing and the good news.

9-12 In verse nine Luke refers to an incident that must have confronted Philip upon entering the city. He says that in this city there was a certain man named Simon. This one had for a long period of time carried out a program of deception. Through the means of sorcery he had amazed and confounded the people. This deception was believed by both the small and the great. All had accepted him as the fulfillment of a superstitious idea that one was to come who would be an offshoot of deity. His position was so generally recognized because he had carried out this practice over such a long period of time.

But in spite of this condition in the city "they believed Philip preaching good tidings concerning the kingdom of God and the name of Jesus Christ." It would seem that the more they thought of the message of the kingdom of God the less they thought of the words of Simon. The more they considered the signs of Philip the less they thought of the tricks of the sorcerer. Philip probably told them that there was but **one** manifestation of God's power and person and that was in and through Jesus Christ. Thus it came to pass that "they believed Philip" and "they were baptized, both men and women." (Note the obvious fulfillment of Mark 16:15, 16).

13 The most astounding part of this whole event is that the very ringleader of the opposition "Simon himself" was taken as a trophy for King Jesus. The account of the conversion of Simon is an exact counterpart of the Great Commission as given by Mark, "He that believeth and is baptized shall be saved" . . . (Mark 16:15, 16). Whatever else could be said of this man Simon we must say that at this time he evidenced honesty and humility; for it must have taken real humility and honesty to make this public profession of his acceptance.

There has been no little discussion as to whether Simon was truly converted or only made a pretense of faith. It seems to the writer that all hesitancy of accepting Simon's conversion as genuine would be removed if we could but remember that Luke is writing the account quite some time after the events, and with a personal contact with those who were eye-witnesses of the events. If Simon were pretending then would not Luke have so stated it when he record-

245. What was the first problem to face Philip upon entering Samaria?
246. Why was the deception of Simon the sorcerer so readily accepted?
247. How do you imagine it came to pass that the people turned from Simon to Philip?
248. What scripture did the conversion of Simon and the Samaritans fulfill?
249. Do you believe the conversion of Simon was genuine? Why yes or no?

THE APPROACH TO NABLUS, THE ANCIENT SHECHEM

Through the olive groves on the eastern side of the city the gate is shown beneath the minaret.

Here is a town in the country of Samaria to which Philip went to preach unto them Jesus. "After Vespasian destroyed the Samaritan temple on Mt. Gerizim, he built his new city ("Neapolis") farther up the valley, leaving the ancient Shechem in ruins. Archaeology has shown that Shechem was Tell Balatah, not the site of the later Roman city Neapolis or Nablus, which was considered for a long time to be Shechem, but is N.W. of it." **Unger's Bible Dictionary** p. 1008. It was near this town that Jesus taught the Samaritan woman of the water that was not in the well.

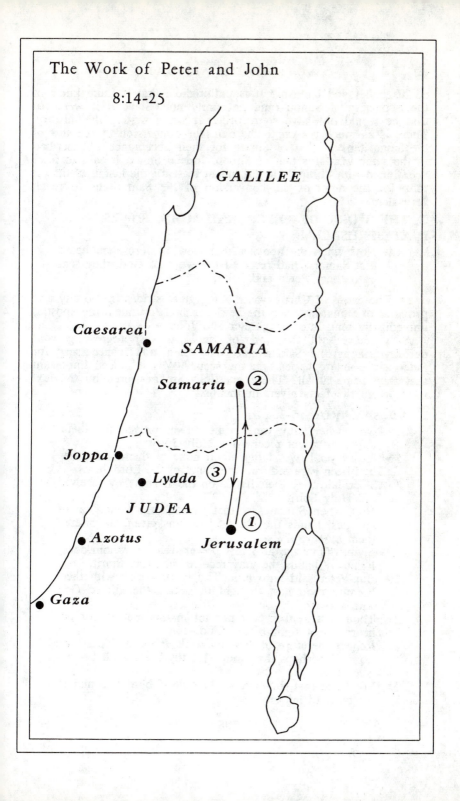

The Work of Peter and John
8:14-25

GALILEE

Caesarea

SAMARIA

Samaria ②

Joppa

③

Lydda

JUDEA

Azotus

①

Jerusalem

Gaza

ed his belief and baptism? It is unthinkable that if Luke knew of the hypocrisy of Simon (and he surely must have if it were so) that he would not have so recorded it when writing this history. There is as much reason to discount the conversion of the rest of the Samaritans as that of Simon for their acceptance is described in the same words as that of Simon. Indeed Simon is said to have **"continued with Philip."** He did this at least for the length of time it took for the news of the conversion of the Samaritans to reach Jerusalem.

C. THE WORK OF PETER AND JOHN. 8:14-25.

I. AT JERUSALEM. 14

14 Now when the apostles that were at Jerusalem heard that Samaria had received the word of God, they sent unto them Peter and John:

14 The cause of Christ was making great strides in the city and province of Samaria. When the news reached Jerusalem the apostles immediately sent unto them Peter and John.

As we have said, the work of the Lord was progressing wonderfully among the Samaritans. Why then was it necessary for Peter and John to appear on the scene? Was it indeed important that they come at all? These questions are answered by the text itself. Note the facts given in the text:

2. AT SAMARIA. 15-25a

15 who, when they were come down, prayed for them, that they might receive the Holy Spirit:

16 for as yet it was fallen upon none of them: only they had been baptized into the name of the Lord Jesus.

17 Then laid they their hands on them, and they received the Holy Spirit.

18 Now when Simon saw that through the laying on of apostles' hands the Holy Spirit was given, he offered them money,

19 saying, Give me also this power, that on whomsoever I lay my hands, he may receive the Holy Spirit.

20 But Peter said unto him, Thy silver perish with thee, because thou hast thought to obtain the gift of God with money.

21 Thou hast neither part nor lot in this matter: for thy heart is not right before God.

22 Repent therefore of this thy wickedness, and pray the Lord, if perhaps the thought of thy heart shall be forgiven thee.

23 For I see that thou art in the gall of bitterness and in the bond of iniquity.

24 And Simon answered and said, Pray ye for me to the Lord, that none of these things which ye have spoken come upon me.

25 They therefore, when they had testified and spoken the word of the Lord, returned to Jerusalem, and preached the gospel to many villages of the Samaritans.

15-17 As soon as the apostles heard of Philip's good work in Samaria they sent Peter and John. But we ask "for what purpose?" **What they did when they arrived would determine why they were sent.**

1) When they arrived they prayed and laid hands upon the Samaritans; through this means these received the special gifts of the Holy Spirit.

2) This action was necessary because the Samaritans had only been baptized in water into Christ. They had then consequently only received the "gift of the Holy Spirit" (2:38) or the (indwelling personality of the Holy Spirit.) The Holy Spirit in His miraculous powers had not **"fallen upon"** any of them. Luke uses the term "fallen upon" to describe the reception of the special powers. He uses this terminology in speaking of "fear" also (Luke 1:12; Acts 19:17). It carries the idea of "obtaining" or "acquiring." From what we should already have concluded concerning the special spiritual gifts (see special study on the Holy Spirit,) we must say the use of the term "Holy Spirit" in 15b is synonymous with "spiritual gifts." Nor is this unusual for there are other examples where the cause is placed for the effect.

18-24 In contrast to the wonderful impartation of the Holy Spirit we are brought to face the sin of Simon. This record should teach us that holy company and religious activities do not exclude temptation and sin. Luke is very brief in this account. So brief that we are constrained to believe that there must have been a lapse of time between verse seventeen and eighteen. It does not seem reasonable that Simon would immediately sin in the way he did. The rebuke of Peter shows that there must have been a premeditation on his part. It was no impulsive statement that was said one moment and repented of the next. Peter says in describing his sin, that he was held in "the bond of iniquity" i.e. his sin had so grown within him as to be a fetter upon his very soul. Simon had allowed this

250. Give the purpose of the coming of Peter and John to Samaria; prove your answer.

251. How is the term "Holy Spirit" used in 15b? Explain.

252. What lesson can be found in the wicked proposal of Simon?

253. Does the briefness of this account concerning the wicked proposal of Simon force us to any conclusion on the matter? If so, what?

254. What does the rebuke of Peter reveal about the heart condition of Simon?

thought to brood within his bosom so that the bitterness of hypocrisy had filled his heart.

He wanted this power of imparting the Holy Spirit by the laying on of his hands. The offer of money was not prompted by impetuousness nor was it probably offered in the public gathering, but rather at some opportune moment when Simon thought Peter would be most easily approached.

Peter did not hesitate a moment. We can think of a time in Peter's life when he would have hesitated and possibly yielded. But that was before Pentecost; that was before Peter was emptied of self and filled with the Holy Spirit. The apostle with the discernment of spirits that was his (I Cor. 12:10) knew Simon's exact predicament. This he revealed to Simon in the sternest of rebukes. He said in essence, "You are lost and your silver will be lost with you. This is true because you seek to put a price upon that which is priceless. You have sought to bring down into your carnal sphere the power of Almighty God. You cannot buy with your money any part of God or His power. Your heart is not right before God." Peter did not close this rebuke in a thunder of final anathema but with the hope of restoration. "Repent therefore of this thy wickedness and pray the Lord, if perhaps the thought of thy heart shall be forgiven thee."

Then, as we have already remarked, Peter spoke to Simon of what he "saw" in Simon's heart. The "gall of bitterness" bespeaks of the heart condition or Simon's personal feelings. The "bond of iniquity" describes the hold or power his sin had upon him.

It is not our intention to decide motives, but from the words of Simon we seem to catch something of the meaning of the word "perhaps" in Peter's rebuke. Peter had suggested that the thought of this man's heart might not be forgiven. Why?

It would appear from what Simon here says, that Peter, looking into the purposes of the soul, could see that he was not yet ready or willing to follow his request for repentance. Even as the apostle spoke the words he knew the heart of Simon and so said "if perhaps." The thought of verse twenty-four is an indication of Simon's unwillingness to do what was demanded of him. He was doubtless afraid and remorseful but not willing to forsake sin. Because of his fear he asked that Peter and John would pray for him. Note that he did not ask them to pray for him that he might have the courage to follow out the instructions given, but only that he might not be lost. He has many counterparts in our modern day.

255. How do you suppose the offer of money was made?

256. How did Peter know of the exact condition of Simon's heart?

257. What reason does the response of Simon give for Peter's use of the word "perhaps?"

258. If Simon was not willing to repent why did he ask Peter and John to pray for him?

25 Peter and John came to Samaria for one primary purpose; i.e. the installing of spiritually equipped leaders in the new congregation. This being accomplished they also "testified and spoke the word of the Lord" to the Samaritans. Following this they turned their faces toward Jerusalem. On their return journey they paused at numerous villages and preached the gospel among the "despised" Samaritans. It is interesting to notice the change in John's attitude toward these people. Read Luke 9:51-55.

D. THE LATER WORK OF PHILIP. 26-40.

1. ON THE ROAD FROM JERUSALEM TO GAZA. 26-39.

26 But an angel of the Lord spake unto Philip, saying, Arise, and go toward the south unto the way that goeth down from Jerusalem unto Gaza: the same is desert.

27 And he arose and went: and behold, a man of Ethiopia, a eunuch of great authority under Candace, queen of the Ethiopians, who was over all her treasure, who had come to Jerusalem to worship;

28 and he was returning and sitting in his chariot, and was reading the prophet Isaiah.

29 And the Spirit said unto Philip, Go near, and join thyself to this chariot.

30 And Philip ran to him, and heard him reading Isaiah the prophet, and said, Understandest thou what thou readest?

31 And he said, How can I, except some one shall guide me? And he besought Philip to come up and sit with him.

32 Now the passage of the scripture which he was reading was this,
He was led as a sheep to the slaughter;
And as a lamb before his shearer is dumb,
So he openeth not his mouth:

33 In his humiliation his judgment was taken away:
His generation who shall declare?
For his life is taken from the earth?

34 And the eunuch answered Philip, and said, I pray thee, of whom speaketh the prophet this? of himself, or of some other?

35 And Philip opened his mouth, and beginning from this scripture, preached unto him Jesus.

36 And as they went on the way, they came unto a certain water; and the eunuch saith, Behold, here is water; what doth hinder me to be baptized?

259. What interesting detail is given in the "former treatise" concerning John and Samaria?

38 And he commanded the chariot to stand still: and they
both went down into the water, both Philip and the
eunuch; and he baptized him.

39 And when they came up out of the water, the Spirit
of the Lord caught away Philip; and the eunuch saw
him no more, for he went on his way rejoicing.

26 In verse twenty-six we again encounter the much used word
"but." This time it is a stop sign designating a halt in our consideration of the work of Peter and John; indeed it is the last mention of
John in the historical record. We are now to turn our attention to
Philip the evangelist. Right in the midst of the most encouraging of
evangelistic efforts, when it would seem that surely one could stay
a long while and reap many souls an angel of the Lord spake unto Philip, saying "Arise and go toward the south unto the way that
goeth down from Jerusalem unto Gaza; the same is desert." Philip's
faith was the kind that caused him to know that "God's way is always the best way." Since God had started him on this work he
knew that however strange and inexplainable the directions, there
was one directing who could see the whole pattern and that he was
but an instrument in performing God's work. So "he arose and
went."

It is such a well known fact that it hardly merits mention but to
someone it might be helpful to state that the word "desert" as used
in 26b means "uninhabitable." The word does not carry the same
thought that is commonly associated with it in the English. There
has never been anything but a fertile plain called the plain of
Philistia in the district where Philip met the eunuch. For comparative references as to the use of this word see Matt. 14:15, 19;
Mark 6:35, 39; John 6:10.

27-28 What was Philip to find in this uninhabited territory? Luke
does not mention any of the events that might have occurred on
the fifty mile journey from Samaria to this road. In Philip's day
the road that led from Jerusalem to Gaza was a fine paved Roman
thoroughfare. Perchance Philip encountered several persons upon this highway, but there was but one person on this road in the
plan of God for Philip. There traveled in this way a certain Ethiopian
eunuch of great authority. He was the treasurer of queen Candace,

260. Show how the request of the angel to Philip was strange and why he
immediately obeyed.
261. How is the word "desert" used in 26b?
262. How far was it from Samaria to the road from Jerusalem to Gaza?
263. Was the Ethiopian a Gentile? Why so, or why not?
264. How did Philip know the eunuch was reading from Isaiah?

queen of the Ethiopians. This man had been to Jerusalem to worship and was now on his way home. He was evidently either an Ethiopian Jew or a proselyte. At this time we find him reading aloud from Isaiah the prophet.

29-30 As Philip beheld the chariot and its retinue he had no reason to be particularly interested. Then it happened, the question of Philip's heart was answered; "the Spirit said to Philip go near and join thyself to **this** chariot." Philip did not hesitate a moment but "ran" to carry out the divine request. As his swift steps carried him close to the chariot, familiar words fell upon his ears, for he heard the occupant of the chariot reading from Isaiah the prophet. Probably this very passage he heard had formed a basis for many a sermon to Philip's Jewish friends. There is no plainer prophecy of the "suffering Servant."

It was natural for Philip to inquire of this one as he did. Philip came up alongside of the chariot and asked informally: "Understandest what thou readest?"

31-32 The eunuch, seeing in the words of Philip an invitation to learning, immediately spoke of his own inability and asked Philip to come up and ride with him that he might instruct him. This surely manifested "a good and honest heart" on the part of the eunuch. Now the passage of scripture he was reading was this: "He was led as a sheep to the slaughter; and as a lamb before his shearer is dumb, so he openeth not his mouth. In his humiliation his judgment was taken away: for his life is taken from the earth." "Philip . . . beginning from this scripture, preached unto him Jesus." Yes, yes, and where Philip began we must all begin if we are going to truly preach Jesus. To leave out the vicarious suffering of Jesus is to leave out the gospel from our preaching. Repentance, confession and baptism mean very little, if anything, without a deepseated knowledge and faith in Jesus as the Lamb of God slain for the sins of the world.

33-38 Verse thirty-three speaks of the fact that because of the manner of Christ's trial He was given no "judgment." This we hold to be the meaning of the word "humiliation." In the latter portion of the verse there is likewise an allusion to the humiliation of Jesus; in His trial and death He was to be like a man who was the last of his family; that being taken by death there would be no one to carry on the generation.

What did Philip preach when he opened his mouth and preached unto him Jesus? This can be answered by turning to the sermons of Peter and Stephen, for the same Spirit that spoke through these men

265. What do you think of the approach of Philip to the eunuch?
266. What real lesson in preaching can we learn from Philip?
267. Explain verse thirty-three.

ASHDOD (AZOTUS).

Ashdod was one of the five cities of the Philistines. These cities were famous in the days of Saul. Ashdod is between Lydda on the east and Joppa on the west. Into this ancient city the young evangelist Philip walked on his way to Caesarea. It was here that he was "found" preaching to the inhabitants the good news of Christ. What type of response do you suppose these people gave Philip? Was it easier for him to speak to these Philistines of Christ and his salvation than it is for you to speak to your next door neighbor? The ark of God was carried here in the long ago and placed in the temple of Dagon, an ancient Canaanite deity. Dagon was cast down and broken up by the power of God. What God's power did in the days of Saul (I Sam. 5:1-8) it did in the day of Philip. The gospel is the power of God **today** to the casting down of idols. We have the same power and the same opportunity for the salvation of souls today that Philip had in Azotus.

was now speaking through Philip. When Philip finished his message in Samaria he baptized both men and women. When Peter finished his sermon on the day of Pentecost 3,000 were added by baptism. So it is not at all strange to read here that "when they came to a certain water" the eunuch desired to be baptized. What water would be found in this "desert?" Geographical and historical surveys tell us that there were several bodies of water in this district that could have accommodated the baptism described. The mode of baptism is not before alluded to but here it is described, "And he commanded the chariot to stand still and they both went down into the water, both Philip and the eunuch; and he baptized him. And when they came up out of the water . . ." Could anything be more clearly descriptive of a "burial with Christ in baptism?" Is not immersion the inevitable conclusion of an open mind? The action of going down into the water and coming up out of the water would have been entirely superfluous had Philip only sprinkled or poured water upon the candidate.

39 Upon the completion of the baptism two events occurred.

1) The Spirit of the Lord caught away Philip. How this happened, whether the Spirit transported Philip bodily from the scene, or directed him suddenly to another field of service we have no way of knowing.

2) The eunuch saw Philip no more but went on his way rejoicing.

It might be well to note that "the remission of sins" (3:38), "the blotting out of sins" (3:19) and now the "rejoicing" (8:39) all occurred following belief, repentance and baptism. No doubt the eunuch went back to establish a work for Christ among his own people.

2. AT AZOTUS. 40a, 3. (LYDDA) 40b, 4. (JOPPA) 40c.

40 But Philip was found at Azotus: and passing through he preached the gospel to all the cities, till he came to Caesarea.

40 "But Philip was found at Azotus." This terminology would seem to indicate some sudden appearance by Philip in this city. "The Azotus at which Philip was found is the Ashdod of the Old Testament, one of the five cities of the Philistines. It stood a few miles from the seashore, nearly at a right angle to the line of the eunuch's travel

268. How can we know of the content of Philip's sermon? Name two ways.
269. What water could be found in this "desert place?" Give a full answer.
270. What inevitable conclusion do we find from the account of the baptism of the eunuch?
271. What two events occurred at the completion of the baptism? Explain each.
272. What do you know of Azotus mentioned in verse 40a?

"And they came to a certain water" . . . this is only one of the bodies of water in this district. There are several possible places where immersion could take place. "And they both went down into the water, both Philip and the eunuch; and he baptized him."

and probably fifteen miles distant." (McGarvey: **Commentary On Acts I**, p. 163).

The broad fertile plain of Philistia was thickly set with villages in Philip's time and offered a productive field for many years of evangelistic effort.

5. IN CAESAREA. 40d.

The distance from Azotus to Caesarea was about sixty miles. Caesarea was the northernmost city in the evangelistic tour of Philip. It is here with his family that we find him some five or six years later. (Cf. 21:7, 8.)

THE CONVERSION AND EARLY LABORS OF SAUL
9:1-30 Galatians 1:17-24

For a moment let us pause and look back over the pathway of the narrative. Luke has given the following events since the beginning of this section:

1. The city of Zion was our starting point. What was the first point mentioned in this new section? You will recall, it was the persecution that arose at the death of Stephen. And who was the leader in this persecution? Saul, the young man who looked on with cruel satisfaction while Stephen was crushed by the stones of his assassins. Why do we hear nothing more of this man?

2. The historian sees fit to follow the experiences of one of those who fled from Jerusalem and presents the life and work of Philip.

3. The success of Philip in Samaria suggests the part the apostles Peter and John played in this event.

4. Finally Luke outlines the conversion of the eunuch and the departure of Philip.

1. AT JERUSALEM. 9:1, 2.

1 But Saul, yet breathing threatening and slaughter against the disciples of the Lord, went unto the high priest,

2 and asked of him letters to Damascus unto the synagogues, that if he found any that were of the Way, whether men or women, he might bring them bound to Jerusalem.

1-2 Now we are back in Jerusalem. What is happening? Well, what was the condition of the city when we left? . . . The situation has not changed nor improved for Saul is "yet breathing threaten-

273. Tell two facts about Caesarea.
274. How does the death of Stephen relate to this section?
275. Where was Saul during the events of the life of Philip? What was he doing?
276. Why do we not hear any more of Saul after he is first mentioned in 7:58?

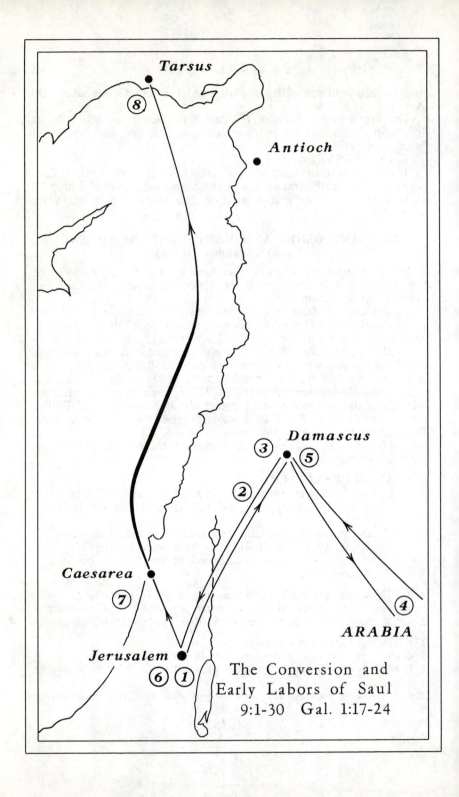

Tarsus

⑧

Antioch

Damascus

③ ⑤

②

Caesarea

⑦

① ④

ARABIA

Jerusalem

⑥ ①

The Conversion and
Early Labors of Saul
9:1-30 Gal. 1:17-24

ENTRANCE TO DAMASCUS

By the new French road through the Merj or meadow, west of the
city. The large building on the right, with its many domes and two
slender minarets, is the Tekiyeh, or hospital for pilgrims, built by
Sultan Selim I in A D 1516.

About 130 miles northeast of Jerusalem was the city of Damascus.
It is situated in a fertile plain at the foot of Mount Hermon. It was
at the head of the most important small state of ancient Syria, and
probably no other city of the present day can trace its history so
far back in the annals of the world. (**Historical Geography** p. 80.)
Paul entered this city with his eyes closed by the power of God. How
many cities do we enter with our eyes closed to the needs of the
people of its streets and shops? The world is doomed. The instability
of earthly things is apparent everywhere. Saving souls is the only
thing worth while. It ought to be the chief end of every man's life.
It was for Paul; is it for you?

ings and slaughter against the disciples of the Lord." Yea, he is not satisfied to wreck havoc only among the church in Jerusalem. He can not rest with this, his zeal in his mad opposition would take him to any and all places where Christians might be found. When Saul hears of Christians in Damascus he immediately takes steps to carry his persecution to this city.

The high priest of Jerusalem would, by virtue of his office, have jurisdiction over the Jews of all synagogues. Hence, Saul went to the high priest that he might secure letters that would grant him authority to go into the synagogues of Damascus and ferret out all the disciples of the Way, whether men or women. Saul intended to treat those of Damascus as criminals. He hoped to bring them bound in chains to Jerusalem. Such arrests were not ordinarily permitted in a foreign city. They could be carried out here because the governor of the district was in sympathy with such action. (Cf. II Cor. 11:32).

2. **ON THE ROAD TO DAMASCUS.** 9:3-8a.

3 And as he journeyed, it came to pass that he drew nigh unto Damascus: and suddenly there shone round about him a light out of heaven:

4 and he fell upon the earth, and heard a voice saying unto him, Saul, Saul, why persecutest thou me?

5 And he said, Who art thou, Lord? And he said, I am Jesus whom thou persecutest:

6 but rise, and enter into the city, and it shall be told thee what thou must do.

7 And the men that journeyed with him stood speechless, hearing the voice, but beholding no man.

8 And Saul arose from the earth; and when his eyes were opened he saw nothing;

3-8a What a prospect for conversion! There was nothing in the mind or attitude of Saul that would suggest the right-about-face that was to be made on this Damascus road. The distance from Jerusalem to Damascus was about 140 miles. If the company of Saul traveled twenty miles each day it would have been the noon of the seventh day that his conversion took place. While the walls of the city of Damascus loomed before him there suddenly "shone round about him a light out of heaven." Since the conversion of Saul is recorded in three places in the book of Acts, we deem it helpful to here present a harmony of these three records:

"And it came to pass (whereupon) as I made my journey (journeyed) to Damascus with the authority and commission of the chief

277. How could the high priest have influence in Damascus?

278. What is significant about the name used to describe the Christians of Damascus?

279. How far was the distance to Damascus from Jerusalem? How long do you suppose it took to make the trip?

priests, and I drew nigh unto Damascus about noon (midday) suddenly there shone (I saw on the way) from heaven a great light, above the brightness of the sun, shining round about me and them that journeyed with me.

And when we were all fallen (and I fell upon the earth) to the earth (ground), I heard a voice saying unto me in the Hebrew language, Saul, Saul, why persecutest thou me? It is hard for thee to kick against the goad. And I said (answered), "Who are thou, Lord? And he said (the Lord said), I am Jesus of Nazareth whom thou persecutest.

And the men that journeyed with me (were with me) stood **(evidently they had risen in the meantime)** speechless, hearing the voice (or "sound"), but they heard not **(understood not; I Cor. 14:2)** the voice of him that spake to me.

And I said, What shall I do, Lord? And the Lord said unto me, Arise, and stand upon thy feet, and go into Damascus (the city,) and there it shall be told thee of all things which are appointed for thee to do (what thou must do); for to this end have I appeared unto thee, to appoint thee a minister and a witness, both of the things wherein thou hast seen me, and of the things wherein I will appear to thee; delivering thee from the people, and from the Gentiles, unto whom I send thee, to open their eyes that they may turn from darkness to light and from the power of Satan to God, that they may receive remission of sins and an inheritance among them that are sanctified by faith in me.

And I (Saul) arose from the earth, and when my eyes were opened **(having been closed upon seeing the bright light and the Lord),** I saw nothing. And when I could not see for the glory of that light, they led me (being led) by the hand of them that were with me, and brought me (I came) into Damascus. And I was there three days without sight and did neither eat nor drink."

3. IN DAMASCUS. 9:8b-22.

8b and they led him by the hand, and brought him to Damascus.

9 And he was three days without sight, and did neither eat nor drink.

10 Now there was a certain disciple at Damascus, named Ananias; and the Lord said unto him in a vision, Ananias.
And he said, Behold, I am here, Lord.

11 And the Lord said unto him, Arise, and go to the street

280. What was the precise time of the conversion of Saul?
281. Read 9:7 and 22:9 and then explain the apparent contradiction.
282. Read 9:7 and 26:14 and explain the apparent contradiction.
283. Give in your own words the message Jesus spoke to Saul on the Damascus road.

which is called Straight, and inquire in the house of Judas for one named Saul, a man of Tarsus: for behold, he prayeth;

12 and he hath seen a man named Ananias coming in, and laying his hands on him, that he might receive his sight.

13 But Ananias answered, Lord, I have heard from many of this man, how much evil he did to thy saints at Jerusalem:

14 and here he hath authority from the chief priests to bind all that call upon thy name.

15 But the Lord said unto him, Go thy way: for he is a chosen vessel unto me, to bear my name before the Gentiles and kings, and the children of Israel:

16 for I will show him how many things he must suffer for my name's sake.

17 And Ananias departed, and entered into the house; and laying his hands on him said, Brother Saul, the Lord, even Jesus, who appeared unto thee in the way which thou camest, hath sent me, that thou mayest receive thy sight, and be filled with the Holy Spirit.

18 And straightway there fell from his eyes as it were scales, and he received his sight; and he arose and was baptized;

19 and he took food and was strengthened.
And he was certain days with the disciples that were at Damascus.

20 And straightway in the synagogues he proclaimed Jesus, that he is the Son of God.

21 And all that heard him were amazed, and said, Is not this he that in Jerusalem made havoc of them that called on this name? and he had come hither for this intent, that he might bring them bound before the chief priests.

22 But Saul increased the more in strength, and confounded the Jews that dwelt at Damascus, proving that this is the Christ.

10-16 "And one Ananias, a devout man according to the law, well reported of by all the Jews that dwelt there, departed, and entered into the house and came unto me, and standing by, and laying his hands on me said, Brother Saul, receive thy sight. And straightway there fell from my eyes as it were scales and in that very hour I received my sight and I looked upon him.

284. Tell what you know of the character and position of Ananias.
285. Why did Ananias call Saul "brother?"

And he said, The God of our fathers hath appointed thee to know His will, and to see the Righteous One, and to hear a voice from His mouth; the Lord, even Jesus, who appeared unto thee in the way which thou camest, hath sent me that thou mayest receive thy sight and be filled with the Holy Spirit. For thou shalt be a witness for him unto all men of what thou hast seen and heard. And now why tarriest thou? Arise, and be baptized, and wash away thy sins, calling on His name. And I arose and was baptized; and I took food and was strengthened." Acts 9:3-9, 17-19; 22:6-16; 26:12-18 are interwoven so as to make a complete narrative of all the facts stated in each account (Compiled by Wilbur Fields). Here are a few further points in this conversion.

1. Saul believed and repented and confessed Christ as "Lord." (This is the same word used in the epistles when referrings to Jesus as the Christ).

These events that occurred on the road accomplished a "conversion." The word conversion carries the thought of a complete change of mind and heart. But Saul was not forgiven of his sins until he had arisen and was baptized and "washed away his sins" (22:16).

Conversion takes place in the heart of the sinner but forgiveness occurs in the heart of God. Faith, repentance and confession completes the one, baptism completes the other.

2. Any effort exerted against the church is an effort directed against Christ. This thought is vividly portrayed in the fact that the church is "the body of Christ" (Eph. 1:22, 23). One cannot do injury to the body without affecting the head.

3. Jesus did **not** tell Saul what to do to be saved but rather directed him to a humble disciple in Damascus (9:6). The Lord never has and never will directly tell any soul what to do to be saved for He has ordained through the "foolishness of preaching to save them that believe" (I Cor. 1:21).

8b-9 When the light above the brightness of the Syrian sun fell upon Saul, Saul saw Jesus in all His effulgent glory. He could not, however, bear this intense brightness for long. Indeed he was blinded by it.

Following his conversation with Jesus, he lifted himself from the dust of the Damascus road and opened his eyes. The Lord had opened the eyes of Saul's understanding but had blinded the eyes of his body. (To say then that Ananias was sent to give Saul his spiritual sight is an absurdity, seeing that this was clearly given to him in what he saw and heard.)

286. What two things did Ananias mention as the purpose for his being sent to Saul?

287. What were the scales spoken of in verse eighteen? Was this not the receiving of his spiritual sight?

123

What a contrast do we behold in the humble penitent believer being led by the hand into Damascus from the maddened Pharisee who was to march through the gates of the city in a triumphant quest for "any that were of the Way." What thoughts of guilt and humiliation must have coursed through the mind of Saul as he followed in darkness the hand of him who led him.

Jesus had told Saul that it would be told him what he must do. But He did not say when Saul was to receive this information. Saul evidently felt that his sin was so great that he could only fast and pray. This he would do until his Lord would again speak to him. God knew what was best so He left Saul in this state for three days and nights.

The Master had said that it was "hard for him to kick against the goad." In this statement we have some indication of the thought that Saul in his heart of hearts was troubled concerning this Jesus of Nazareth. The death of Stephen had made a profound impression upon his mind (22:20). He must have been one of the synagogue of the Libertines since he was from Cilicia (6:9). If so he with others was not able to withstand the power and wisdom by which Stephen spake. The proof from the Old Testament that Jesus was the Christ must have been presented by Stephen. And then Saul was present when Stephen made his defense before the Sanhedrin (26:10). All of these influences were galling the conscience of this young man.

Saul's intense persecution was but a quenching of the voice of his conscience. When his heart was filled with anger and selfrighteousness and his life with activity he had no time nor inclination to listen to the call of his better self. But now in the house of Judas on the street called Straight, as he knelt in prayer, all of these pent up feelings and facts came all at once into focus. He saw clearly for the first time the dark picture of his evil work.

10 Sometime during the course of the three days there appeared in the mind of Saul the image of a man whom he had never seen. The vision was so clear, however, that he knew he would recognize him if he were to see him in person. As he meditated he saw in this vision this stranger come up to him and lay his hands upon him to give him his sight.

288. Explain the difference in the use and meaning of the words "conversion" and "salvation" as found in the case of Saul.

289. Did Jesus tell Saul what to do to be saved? What import does this have for us?

290. Did Saul see Jesus when he looked into the bright light?

291. What is the meaning of the phrase "it is hard for thee to kick against the goad?"

292. Do you believe that the intense zeal of Saul's opposition to Christ had anything to do with his conscience?

This man whom God had shown to Saul was a humble disciple of Jesus named Ananias. A short time after Christ appeared to Saul the Lord spoke to Ananias calling him by name. Ananias promptly answered with the statement that suggested a desire to hear and do the bidding of the Lord. "Behold I am here, Lord." The words of instruction were direct and explicit; he was told where to go and what to do. Ananias reacted like many of us would today. He asked "Why?" And then added the reason for his query. Hear him say: "Go and make a call on Saul of Tarsus? Why Lord when I think of what many fellow disciples have told me of the terrible cruelties of Saul in Jerusalem, then when I know that he is here armed with authority for the same purpose I cannot understand, I am filled with fear."

See the wonderful patience and love of our great God. Who is man to question the authority and word of Jehovah? And yet although the Lord insists on obedience He does not do so without reason. "Go thy way" or we might say "Arise and do my bidding." Then follows the explanation Ananias wanted "for he is a chosen vessel unto me, to bear my name before the Gentiles and kings and the children of Israel for I will show him how many things he must suffer for my name's sake."

17-19 We have already spoken of the events that took place upon the meeting of Saul and Ananias so it will not be necessary here to repeat them. The only word we would add is that Ananias must have given the Holy Spirit to Saul in the same way Peter gave the Holy Spirit to the three thousand, i.e. when Saul was baptized he received, as did those on Pentecost, the gift from God, the Holy Spirit.

How long did Saul remain in Damascus following his conversion? We have no way of knowing. But we do know that he began immediately to carry out the commission given him by Jesus.

20-22 He made no apology for his work or word but came out boldly with the message that Jesus of Nazareth was none other than the Son of God. (How could he call Him anything else after having seen Him as he did?) Saul's preaching was done in the very synagogues he had previously hoped to enter as a persecutor. Imagine the surprise of those who heard. There must have been present not only those disciples of the Lord but also those who were as zealous for the law as Saul had been. Despite both suspicion and unbelief Saul increased in strength and laid before the minds and

293. What was the response of Ananias to the call of God? What is revealed in the answer of God to his hesitancy?
294. Why would it be natural for us to imagine that Saul would declare that Jesus was the "Son of God?"
295. What is paradoxical about the place where Saul preached Jesus?
296. Tell of the reasons for the amazement on the part of those who heard Saul.

hearts of all present such proof that this Jesus was the Christ that the Jews who would not accept were at least "confounded." How alike was the response of these Jews to that of Saul with the message of Stephen (6:8-10).

4. IN ARABIA. 9:23a. Gal. 1:17a.

23 And when many days were fulfilled,

23a There is but a sentence to tell us of this period in the life of Saul. The construction of the sentences in Gal. 1:17, 18 would seem to indicate that the three year period spoken of had as its limitations the conversion of Saul and his return to Damascus; i.e. it was three years from his conversion to his return to Damascus from Arabia.

What Saul did while in Arabia has been the subject of no little discussion. It would seem to the writer in view of the commission given to him and of the immediate response to it in Damascus that Saul would have continued his preaching in the country of Arabia. The fact that there were numerous cities in the district of Arabia adjunct to Damascus, lends support to this contention. The governor of Damascus was under the authority of Aretas the king of Arabia (II Cor. 11:32). Indeed Damascus was but a city in the kingdom of Arabia. Hence, it would not be at all unusual to imagine Saul evangelizing this district. We agree with the thought that it would be inconsistent with the restless nature of the apostle to imagine him spending an extended period of time meditating in the desert of Arabia. Further than this such was not necessary in light of the fact that he received his message directly from God.

5. BACK IN DAMASCUS. 9:23b-25. Gal. 1:17b.

23b the Jews took counsel together to kill him:

24 but their plot became known to Saul. And they watched the gates also day and night that they might kill him:
25 but his disciples took him by night, and let him down through the wall, lowering him in a basket.

23b-24 Upon returning to Damascus Saul evidently became so earnestly insistent in his preaching that the Jews determined that the only solution to their embarrassment was the death of this heretic. A plot was laid for his life. Through someone the news leaked out and the word was quickly carried to Saul. It would seem

297. What one word describes the response of the Jews of Damascus to Saul's preaching?
298. Explain the meaning of the statement concerning the three year period
299. What did Saul do in Arabia? Why do you hold this opinion? What is spoken of in Galatians 1:18?

that the Jews knew of the fact that their plot had been discovered and so rather than to carry it out they watched carefully the city gates lest Saul should flee ere they could stay him. The guarding of the gates was with the sympathetic help of the governor.

25 The disciples soon knew of the guards at the gates and so came to Saul at night and effected his escape by letting him down over the wall in a basket (the same kind of basket spoken of in the feeding of the five thousand). Houses were built on the walls of many ancient cities. They were constructed in such a way that a portion of the house projected out over the edge of the wall. Such a construction would afford a perfect means of lowering a man as here described.

6. IN JERUSALEM. 9:26-29. Gal. 1:17b-19.

26 And when he was come to Jerusalem, he assayed to join himself to the disciples: and they were all afraid of him, not believing that he was a disciple.

27 But Barnabas took him, and brought him to the apostles, and declared unto them how he had seen the Lord in the way, and that he had spoken to him, and how at Damascus he had preached boldly in the name of Jesus.

28 And he was with them going in and going out at Jerusalem,

29 preaching boldly in the name of the Lord: and he spake and disputed against the Grecian Jews; but they were seeking to kill him.

26 Saul's destination when he climbed out of the basket in the dark shadows of the Damascus wall was the city of Zion. How vastly different was his return trip. How great a change had taken place in these past three years.

What were the thoughts of this humbled Pharisee as he approached the city of Jerusalem, as he looked upon the city wherein he had been trained, where he had so zealously labored for the Law? He would come face to face with many of his old friends. What would they think? But away with these thoughts of retrospect! He must make himself known to the disciples and above all he must meet the apostles.

How poignant must have been the feelings of Saul as he was re-

300. Explain the connection of the plot laid for Saul's life and the watching of the gates by the Jews.

301. How could it be possible that Saul was let down over the wall in a basket?

302. Explain the meaning of the terms "his disciples" as found in 25a.

303. What thoughts do you imagine passed through the mind of Saul as he returned to Jerusalem from Damascus?

304. What response did Saul receive in Jerusalem from the disciples?

Over the wall in a basket. A Rabbi, a teacher, and leader of men. How can this be the will of God? Did one of these thoughts flash through his mind on his way down? Read Phil. 3:7, 8 for an answer.

There is no joy equal to that of seeing lost souls turn from sin to righteousness. Earthly joys fade. The mirth and laughter of today may give place to the deepest sorrow ere another sun. But the joy of rescuing the lost endures.

HOUSES ON THE CITY WALL, DAMASCUS.

On the south-east side, belonging to the Jewish quarter. The Bab Kisan, which is not far from this spot, is a now disused and closed-up gate. It stands on the site of a much more ancient one.

pulsed in his efforts to join himself to the disciples. But when he thought upon this matter was not this just the natural response considering the circumstances? Evidently the only news the believers in Jerusalem received was, that their chief persecutor had embraced the faith, but no sooner had he done this than he disappeared into Arabia. And now it had been three years since any word had come. Under such conditions the disciples in Jerusalem had some reasons for being skeptical.

27-29 Luke says of Barnabas that "he was a good man" (11:24) and indeed his goodness is herein revealed. The heart of Barnabas was a heart of love for he "took not account" of evil. He believed when others doubted, he loved Saul with a love that expressed itself, while others were suspicious. Barnabas was willing not only to believe the story of Saul but was also willing himself to present him to the apostles, to plead before them that this man be accepted. Barnabas and Saul appeared before "the apostles." We know from Paul's account of this incident that they saw only Peter and James, the Lord's brother. The term **apostle** is here applied to the Lord's brother in the generic sense, i.e. "one sent." Any one who was sent could have been called an apostle (14:14) but only twelve were the ones sent from Jesus as witnesses. James was evidently considered as sent from the church in Jerusalem.

Three points in the defense made for Saul by Barnabas were: 1) Jesus had appeared to him. 2) Jesus had spoken to him. 3) In Damascus Saul had boldly preached Jesus. Saul was accepted and given acceptance by all the disciples and continued to labor for the space of fifteen days, speaking boldly in the name of Jesus. Saul went back to his own synagogue but received no better reception than he had given Stephen. As they had set a plot to kill Stephen, so they did with Saul.

7. AT CAESAREA. 9:30a.

30 And when the brethren knew it, they brought him down
     to Caesarea,

30a When the plan for Saul's death was known he was taken under the protection of the brethren from Jerusalem and boarded a ship at Caesarea. From here he sailed to the port of his home town, Tarsus in Cilicia.

8. IN TARSUS. 9:30b. Gal 1:21-24.

30b and sent him forth to Tarsus.

305. Who alleviated the situation? How did he do it?
306. Was James, the Lord's brother, one of the twelve? Why is he called an Apostle?
307. To what group did Saul preach in Jerusalem? Why?
308. How long did Saul stay in Jerusalem? When he left what did he do in Tarsus? Give proof.

30b What occurred at the meeting of Saul and his parents? We do not know but we cannot but wonder with a good deal of feeling. Whatever did occur it did not deter the apostle from evangelizing for we read that he "came into" the parts of both the provinces of Syria and Cilicia. From the future mention of disciples in these provinces we know he was preaching the Word.

THE WORK OF PETER
9:31 — 11:18

1. AT JERUSALEM. 9:31.

31 So the church throughout all Judea and Galilee and Samaria had peace, being edified; and, walking in the fear of the Lord and in the comfort of the Holy Spirit, was multiplied.

31 This is the intervening verse between the work of Saul and Peter. The historian gives us an insight into the state of the church in three provinces of Palestine. We have felt all the time that while we were following the labors of Philip, Peter and John, and Saul, that there were many others preaching the word and no doubt the events of their lives were just as interesting as were those of the men discussed. Luke here speaks of the church as one "ekklesia" called out body, located in the three above mentioned places. The coming of Saul, attended as it was by the intense persecution of the Jews, had interrupted the peace to some extent; now that he was gone the peace was restored. It is not to be concluded from this that the stirring caused by Saul was in any way harmful. Indeed it probably assisted in bringing peace, edification, and fear to the church. The "comfort of the Holy Spirit" spoken of in this verse is a subject worthy of some discussion.

2. IN LYDDA. 9:32-35.

32 And it came to pass, as Peter went throughout all parts, he came down also to the saints that dwelt at Lydda.

33 And there he found a certain man named Aeneas, who had kept his bed eight years; for he was palsied.

34 And Peter said unto him, Aeneas, Jesus Christ healeth thee: arise and make thy bed. And straightway he arose.

35 And all that dwelt at Lydda and in Sharon saw him, and they turned to the Lord.

32a The increase and health of the church in Canaan probably prompted Peter to attempt an evangelistic tour of this territory. For whatever reason we now are told that the apostle goes on a trip

309. Who brought the gospel to Lydda before Peter arrived?
310. How do we know that Aeneas was well known in the town?
311. We have said that whether faith was present or not healings could be performed. Prove it.

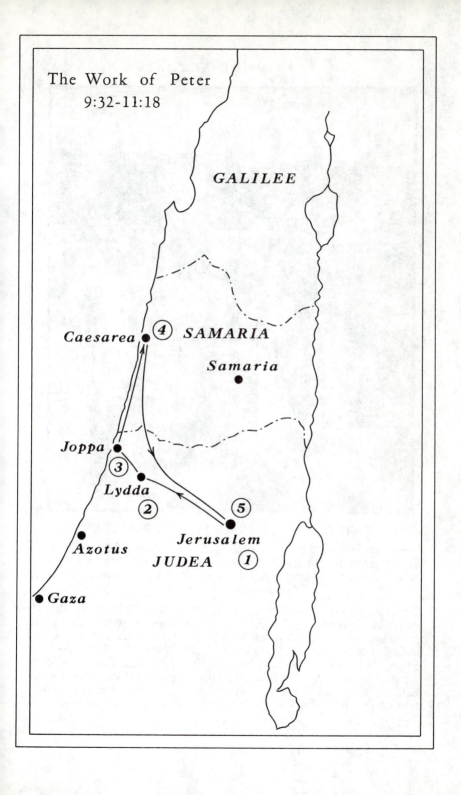

The Work of Peter
9:32-11:18

GALILEE

Caesarea ④ SAMARIA

Samaria

Joppa
③
Lydda
②

Azotus

Gaza

Jerusalem
⑤
①
JUDEA

VIEW OF THE ROCK-ENCIRCLED HARBOUR AT JAFFA.

From the roof of the house of Simon the Tanner. The building in the foreground, with its domes and perforated parapets, is a characteristic example of native domestic architecture in towns and cities of Southern Palestine.

This port, known today by its modern name of Jaffa or Yaffa, though having no harbor, is the chief port of Palestine. It was at this place the timber from Lebanon for both the first and second temples was landed. From this port Jonah sailed; and here also Peter had his vision. (II Chron. 2:16; Ezra 3:7; Jonah 1:3). Simon Peter was looking at the same sea of the Mediterranean which we can view in this picture when God spoke to him and told him to call no man common or unclean. Many of us have not learned this lesson yet.

through "all parts." This reference has to do with the three provinces mentioned in this verse.

32b In this trip Luke selects the incident that occurred among the saints at Lydda as the one most pertinent to his purpose. Who brought the gospel to Lydda before Peter arrived? Two answers seem to be suggested by the book; either "they . . . that were scattered" formed this work or Philip as he preached the gospel in all cities in this district.

33-35 In this city of Lydda there was a man well known by all those of the entire district. "Aeneas, who had kept his bed eight years; for he was palsied." The fact that he was well known is borne out in the great effect the healing had on the people. Peter, upon understanding the circumstances and evidently knowing what a wonderful witness for the power of Christ the healing of this one would be, said: "Aeneas, Jesus Christ healeth thee. Arise and make thy bed." In this case as in all others the man to be healed did not hesitate a moment. Whether faith was present or not did not have any influence on the healings. Immediately at the command of the apostle in the name of Jesus the lame were healed and the palsied were made whole. (3:1-10). The intended result was achieved . . . "all that dwelt at Lydda and in Sharon saw him, and they turned to the Lord." Indeed the word spoken by the apostles was confirmed by this sign which followed. (Mark 16:20).

3. AT JOPPA. 9:36-43.

36 Now there was at Joppa a certain disciple named Tabitha, which by interpretation is called Dorcas: this woman was full of good works and almsdeeds which she did.

37 And it came to pass in those days, that she fell sick, and died: and when they had washed her, they laid her in an upper chamber.

38 And as Lydda was nigh unto Joppa, the disciples, hearing that Peter was there, sent two men unto him, entreating him, Delay not to come on unto us.

39 And Peter arose and went with them. And when he was come, they brought him into the upper chamber: and all the widows stood by him weeping, and showing the coats and garments which Dorcas made, while she was with them.

40 But Peter put them all forth, and kneeled down, and prayed; and turning to the body, he said, Tabitha, arise. And she opened her eyes; and when she saw Peter, she sat up.

312. How is Mark 16:20 explained in this healing?

133

41 And he gave her his hand, and raised her up; and calling the saints and widows, he presented her alive.

42 And it became known throughout all Joppa: and many
believed on the Lord.

43 And it came to pass, that he abode many days in Joppa
with one Simon a tanner.

36-38 While Peter was healing the infirm among the saints at
Lydda there was one among the believers in the town of Joppa
who was near the door of death. Yea, before Peter finished his
work in Lydda she had departed this life. This woman was one of
the true saints of Joppa. Luke gives us her name in two languages.
In the Aramaic her name was Tabitha. In the Greek she was called Dorcas. Her name in English would be translated "Gazelle."

In her passing she had left the best memorial, the deeds of a Christian life. Luke very carefully describes the passing of Tabitha; he says
she was sick before her death, and that after she died her body was
washed and laid out in an upper chamber. The preparations for
burial were made as quickly as they were because of the warm climate.
The need for an immediate burial was the reason for the note of
urgency in the message of the two men that were sent for Peter.
After Dorcas had died why did the disciples of Joppa wish Peter
to visit them? It was possibly a desire for his understanding sympathy:
a feeling on their part that the man of God would have some word
of comfort or inspiration for them. When the text says that Lydda
was nigh unto Joppa we must understand this to mean about a
three or four hours' walk or about fifteen miles.

39-43 When the two returned with Peter they had no idea what
the apostle would say or do. But Peter knew. We are told of his
unhesitating action upon arriving. Peter was guided by the messengers up into the upper room where lay the body of Dorcas.
There in the room were a number of widows gathered around the
deceased. These women were in great sorrow as were the rest, but
the widows were, especially grief-stricken at the death of their beloved friend. Their actions tell why; we are told that they held up
to Peter the "coats and garments" or the tunics and the mantles,
which Dorcas had made for them. Evidently these women were
too poor to secure garments in any other way and if it had not been
for this unselfish soul they would have suffered. Peter gave direc-

313. Who was dying while Peter was healing?
314. Why the careful description of the death of this one?
315. Why the immediate preparations for burial?
316. Why did the saints of Joppa send for Peter?
317. How far from Lydda to Joppa?
318. Do you believe Peter knew what he was going to do when he arrived
in Joppa? If so, why?
319. Why were the widows especially grief stricken at the death of Dorcas?

tions that all should leave the room, to leave him and the body of the departed alone. What a beautiful scene is portrayed for us. Peter first kneels down and prays the prayer of faith, and then turning to the body he spoke but two words "Tabitha, arise." Once again life flowed into the body, the eyes were opened. Seeing Peter in the room she sat up. Without a word Peter gave her his hand and she stood up. Then came the glad call for the saints and the widows. What unspeakable joy there must have been in that upper chamber on that memorable day.

Word of this incident, like the healing in Lydda, soon spread and wherever news of it was taken it helped to create faith in the word and work of the apostles. "And many believed on the Lord."

Because of the good results from the raising of Dorcas, Peter stayed some number of days in this place. While remaining here he lived with "one Simon a tanner" whose house was by the seaside.

4. IN CAESAREA. 10:1-48.

a. Cornelius and his vision. 1-8.

1 Now there was a certain man in Caesarea, Cornelius by name, a centurion of the band called the Italian band,

2 a devout man, and one that feared God with all his house, who gave much alms to the people, and prayed to God always.

3 He saw in a vision openly, as it were about the ninth hour of the day, an angel of God coming in unto him, and saying to him, Cornelius.

4 And he, fastening his eyes upon him, and being affrighted, said, What is it Lord? And he said unto him, Thy prayers and thine alms are gone up for a memorial before God.

5 And now send men to Joppa, and fetch one Simon, who is surnamed Peter:

6 he lodgeth with one Simon a tanner, whose house is by the sea side.

7 And when the angel that spake unto him was departed, he called two of his household-servants, and a devout soldier that waited on him continually;

8 and having rehearsed all things unto them, he sent them to Joppa.

1-2 Beginning with the tenth chapter we have the introduction of the incident that opened the door of the kingdom for the Gentiles. The recording of this incident was in the mind of the inspired writer

320. Give in your own words an accurate account of the raising of Dorcas.
321. What incident do you believe was in the mind of Luke when he first began to describe the work of Peter?

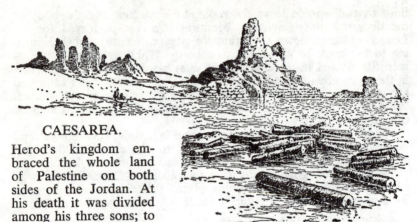

CAESAREA.

Herod's kingdom embraced the whole land of Palestine on both sides of the Jordan. At his death it was divided among his three sons; to Archelaus, with the title of king, fell Idumaea, Judaea, and Samaria; (Matt. 2:22) to Herod Antipas, Galilee and the territory between the Yarmuk and the Arnon called Peaea; and to Philip, the territory on the north of the river Yarmuk, embracing the small districts Ituraea, Trachonitus, Aurantitus, Gaulanatis, and Batanea. (Luke 3:1).

Archelaus had a troubled and inglorious reign of ten years, at the end of which on complaint of the Jews he was banished to Gaul. Judaea was then formed into a Roman province governed by a procurator. Procurators were for the most part appointed only in imperial provinces governed by a legate of the emperor. The duty of the procurator in such cases consisted of collecting the revenue and judging in causes appertaining to fiscal affairs. The procurator of Judaea, however, had a wider range of duties. There being no legate in the province he was charged with the general government and was invested with military and judicial authority. In some matters he was subordinate to the legate of Syria. He usually resided at Caesarea, but went to Jerusalem at the time of the feasts, taking with him a strong military force.

The taxes were of two kinds—the direct tax collected by imperial officers under the control of the procurator, and an impost tax which was farmed out to the highest bidder and again sold out to collectors. These collectors or publicans were of low social and moral standing and were looked upon with contempt. (Matt. 11:19; 21:31)

when he began to describe the work of Peter. Caesarea is the background setting for this incident. There lived in this town a certain man. This man was no ordinary person for he was to be the first Gentile in all the world to find forgiveness of his sins in the blood of Jesus. It would seem that Luke is trying to show us how religious a man could be and still be lost. Note a few facts about this Gentile:

a. His name was Cornelius.
b. He was an army captain or centurion.
c. He was an Italian, as was the cohort over which he had authority.
d. He was a devout man.
e. He feared or worshiped God as did his house.
f. He was very generous with his substance as he gave many gifts to the poor.

He evidently obtained his faith and devotion through close contact with the Jewish religion.

3-8 The devotion of Cornelius has been spoken of already; now see the result of this devotion. No devotion goes unrewarded that is given to Jehovah in complete sincerity.

While Cornelius was in the act of praying, God visited him. It is interesting to note that this was also true of the time He used in speaking to Peter, to Saul and many others. The vision of this devout Gentile was given to him "openly" at three o'clock in the afternoon. "He saw in a vision openly" suggests the idea that this angel "in bright apparel" was seen objectively by Cornelius. When such a heavenly visitor stood before this Roman officer he was quite naturally wide-eyed with fright. To him this man could be nothing short of God himself or a representative of deity. Hence, he cried out "What is it, Lord?" The angelic stranger let Cornelius know that his worship had not been in vain.

"Thy prayer is heard, and thine alms are had in remembrance in the sight of God" (10:31). "Thy prayers and thine alms are gone up for a memorial" (10:4).

In the mind of this Gentile there must have burned this question upon hearing these heartening words:

"If indeed my prayers have been heard what form will the answer take? I have prayed for acceptance and favor in the sight of

322. Give from memory four facts about Cornelius.
323. How did Cornelius obtain his faith?
324. What was the reward of the devotion of Cornelius and how does it apply today?
325. What is the meaning of the statement that the angel or vision appeared "openly?"
326. Do angels have bodies? If so, explain Heb. 1:14.

God. How can I find it? Can it be that I am already in the favor of Jehovah?"

The answer is forthcoming even while the question is forming. "And now, (i.e. because thy prayers have been heard) send men to Joppa and fetch one Simon who is surnamed Peter. He lodgeth with one Simon a tanner, whose house is by the sea side . . . who shall speak unto thee words, whereby thou shalt be saved, thou and all thy house" (cf. 11:14).

The prayer and devotion of Cornelius was all offered up by him that he might be saved. Now here is the opportunity for receiving God's answer to the petition. And so it is that God grants to all of a similar spirit a like opportunity.

The angel had no sooner vanished from his sight than Cornelius began immediately to obey the divine injunction. Two of his household servants and a devout soldier, these were some who were his personal attendants, were called in. These evidently made up a part of this man's house in whom he had instilled the fear of the Lord (2a). Even though the day was far spent these three were sent on their mission, after having been told in greatest detail of the vision that they might repeat it accurately to Peter. In the late afternoon the three started their walk to the seaport of Joppa.

b. Peter's vision. 9-16.

    9 Now on the morrow, as they were on their journey, and drew nigh unto the city, Peter went up upon the housetop to pray, about the sixth hour:

   10 and he became hungry, and desired to eat: but while they made ready, he fell into a trance;

   11 and he beholdeth the heaven opened, and a certain vessel descending, as it were a great sheet, let down by four corners upon the earth:

   12 wherein were all manner of fourfooted beasts and creeping things of the earth and birds of the heaven.

   13 And there came a voice to him, Rise, Peter; kill and eat.

   14 But Peter said, Not so, Lord; for I have never eaten anything that is common and unclean.

   15 And a voice came unto him again the second time, What God hath cleansed, make not thou common.

   16 And this was done thrice: and straightway the vessel was received up into heaven.

9 Since it is thirty miles from Caesarea to Joppa and from the fact that Luke states they arrived on the noon of the day following the vision in Caesarea, we might conclude these men walked all night.

327. What causes us to conclude that these men from Caesarea walked all night? Or, do you conclude this?

10-16 It would be delightfully refreshing if when we came to the homes of our friends we could know that at certain hours we would find them in prayer. It was so with the household of Simon.

While Peter awaited the preparations of the noon meal he retired to the housetop to observe the Jewish hour of prayer. While here his hunger reminded him that it was time to eat. As he waited and prayed God gave him some real "food for thought." The experience of Peter was somewhat different from that of Cornelius, for Peter's experience seems to be more subjective than objective. Before the mind of Peter there came a strange sight; he saw the expanse of heaven opened and a large receptacle let down through the opening. It seemed to be a great sheet suspended from the four corners. It came to rest directly before the astonished Peter. When Peter could view the content of this unusual vessel he saw upon it "all manner of four-footed beasts and creeping things of the earth and birds of the heaven." If Peter was astonished when the heaven-sent vessel began its descent, he must have been completely confounded when a voice spoke and calling him by name said:

"Arise, Peter; kill and eat."

At once Peter spoke the convictions of his heart in regard to the use of such animals. It would have been a two-fold sin, thought the apostle, the sin of sacrificing something unclean and the sin of eating something unclean. Both of these thoughts were repugnant to the Jewish mind, trained as it was in the law of Moses against such. Perhaps Peter thought the Lord was trying him; be that as it may, he impulsively replied:

"Not so, Lord; for I have never eaten anything that is common and unclean."

Again the voice of God; and this time it must have shaken the heart of Simon even as the same voice did melt the hearts of those on Sinai. Indeed this was the first and only revoking of the law of Sinai by the audible voice of Jehovah:

"What God hath cleansed, make not thou common."

This divine mandate was repeated three times and then the vessel was taken back to heaven out of the sight of the apostle.

c. The messengers arrive. God directs Peter. Messengers received. 17-23a.

17 Now while Peter was much perplexed in himself what the vision which he had seen might mean, behold,

328. What fine custom was observed in the house of Simon the tanner that we would do well to imitate?

329. What was the difference between the vision of Cornelius and that of Peter?

330. What two-fold sin would have been committed according to Peter if he were to have obeyed the divine injunction: "Arise, Peter, kill and eat?"

331. What was repeated three times?

the men that were sent by Cornelius, having made inquiry for Simon's house, stood before the gate,

18 and called and asked whether Simon, who was surnamed Peter, were lodging there.

19 And while Peter thought on the vision, the Spirit said
unto him, Behold, three men seek thee.

20 But arise, and get thee down, and go with them, nothing
doubting: for I have sent them.

21 And Peter went down to the men, and said, Behold,
I am he whom ye seek: what is the cause wherefore ye
are come?

22 And they said, Cornelius a centurion, a righteous man
and one that feareth God, and well reported of by all
the nation of the Jews, was warned of God by a holy
angel to send for thee into his house, and to hear words
from thee.

23 So he called them in and lodged them.

17-20 The perplexity of Peter can be more clearly understood
when we consider his Jewish background. "Why was it that God
had revoked the law of clean and unclean animals?" To Peter this
must have been the whole import of the vision. He may have wondered if the rest of the Mosaic law had been abrogated as well.

But even while he thought on these things there were men standing before the gate of the house who could give to him God's answer. The three messengers from Cornelius had inquired diligently for
the house of Simon the tanner; now having found it they stood at the
outer gate of the house and called to those inside in an inquiry as
to whether Simon Peter lodged there. The Lord had synchronized
perfectly the movements and thoughts of both Peter and the three.

Now it was time to bring them together; but they could not meet
as God wanted without a word of divine introduction. Hence, the
spirit introduced Peter to his visitors before he saw them.

"The Spirit said unto him, Behold, three men seek thee. But
arise, and get thee down, and go with them, nothing doubting, for
I have sent them."

Peter did not even wait for Simon the tanner to call him, but
immediately arose and descending the stairs came into the presence
of the three.

While on his way down, what type of men do you suppose Peter
expected to see? He probably expected something unusual, but he

332. What import do you suppose Peter put upon the vision?
333. Show how the Lord had perfectly synchronized the movements and
thoughts of Peter and the three.
334. What were the divine words of introduction Peter was given?
335. Show how all of this incident must have appeared strange to Peter.

would have hardly been prepared to find three **Gentiles.** But, obedient to the heavenly vision, he introduced himself and asked the question that was clamoring for an answer in his heart. It was in essence: "God has sent these men, I am to go with them, but to where? And for what?"

21-23a Strange indeed were the workings and messages of God. First a strange vision; next a stranger command; now the strangest of all, Peter is called to speak to an uncircumcised Gentile. Such must have been something of the feelings of the apostle on this matter.

The embassaries of Cornelius made the mission as attractive to the Jewish mind as possible. Peter was to come to speak words to a Gentile named Cornelius, a righteous man, one that feared God and had a fine reputation among the Jews for his devotion. None the less he was a Gentile. But Cornelius had been commanded by "a holy angel" to send and bring Peter. The three were invited into the house of Simon. As Peter thought on these things, he must have surely tied together the events with the truth God wanted him to receive. There yet remained the inherent hesitancy which was to be entirely removed when he arrived at his destination.

d. The trip and arrival at Caesarea. 23b-27.

23b And on the morrow he arose and went forth with them, and certain of the brethren from Joppa accompanied him.

24 And on the morrow they entered into Caesarea. And Cornelius was waiting for them, having called together his kinsmen and his near friends.

25 And when it came to pass that Peter entered, Cornelius met him, and fell down at his feet, and worshipped him.

26 But Peter raised him up, saying, Stand up; I myself also am a man.

27 And as he talked with him, he went in, and findeth many come together:

23b-27 The trip was started in the morning, probably because Peter felt that the thirty mile walk could best be made in two days. By starting in the morning they could time their arrival on the next day at an appropriate time for the work to be done. Six brethren from Joppa were taken on the journey to be witnesses of this unusual circumstance (11:12). On the morrow following their departure they entered, as planned, into the city of Caesarea.

336. Show how the servants of Cornelius made their request as attractive to the Jewish mind as possible.

337. Why start the journey on the morning after the arrival of the three men? Who was taken along?

Cornelius with his customary military efficiency had prepared carefully for their arrival. When Peter stepped into the house of Cornelius he had a waiting audience; this was made up of the friends and relatives of Cornelius. It would seem from the wording of the text that Cornelius was either waiting on the outside of the house or saw Peter coming, and left the house to meet him. There somewhere outside the house in the court of Cornelius there met for the first time a Jew and Gentile for the avowed purpose of worshiping God as one (although at this time Peter was not thoroughly convinced that it should be so).

Cornelius fell at the feet of Peter and paid homage to him as to one whom God had sent. The word "worshiped" indicates a type of reverence paid to those of superior rank. Peter did not know the mind of Cornelius and so imagined that he was worshiping him as deity, even as so many of the Gentiles were wont to do with great men. Hence, Peter reached down and lifted Cornelius to his feet with the words "Stand up. I myself also am a man."

From the court or patio surrounding Cornelius' house the two walked together into the house; as they did they talked. Perchance Cornelius explained the reason for his kneeling at Peter's feet and Peter made it evident to Cornelius that there was no distinction between them. There was nothing in God's will that would exalt Peter as divine.

e. Cornelius explains. 28-33.

28 and he said unto them, Ye yourselves know how it is an unlawful thing for a man that is a Jew to join himself or come unto one of another nation; and yet unto me hath God showed that I should not call any man common or unclean:

29 wherefore also I came without gainsaying, when I was sent for. I ask therefore with what intent ye sent for me.

30 And Cornelius said, Four days ago, until this hour, I was keeping the ninth hour of prayer in my house; and behold, a man stood before me in bright apparel,

31 and saith, Cornelius, thy prayer is heard, and thine alms are had in remembrance in the sight of God.

32 Send therefore to Joppa, and call unto thee Simon, who is surnamed Peter: he lodgeth in the house of Simon a tanner, by the sea side.

338. What preparations had Cornelius made for Peter's arrival? Where was Cornelius while awaiting Peter?

339. What is meant when Luke states that Cornelius "fell down at his feet and worshipped him?"

340. What construction did Peter put upon this worship?

341. What could have been the content of the conversation between Peter and Cornelius as they walked from the patio into the house?

33 Forthwith therefore I sent to thee; and thou hast well done that thou art come. Now therefore we are all here present in the sight of God, to hear all things that have been commanded thee of the Lord.

28-33 Upon coming into the room where all were assembled Peter addressed his remarks to the whole group. He came right to the point. Naturally the first question in the minds of all assembled was: "How is it that this Jew has been sent to us Gentiles?"

Peter removes this query by speaking of the divine hand in breaking down "the middle wall of partition." In the statements made by Peter we can see that God's efforts had not been in vain, but that Peter had drawn the conclusion the Lord wanted him to draw:

"God hath shown me that I should not call any man common or unclean." He said in essence:

"You want to know why I am here? It is because God broke down my prejudice and sent me to you."

Peter had heard from the messengers that he was to come and speak but now he wanted to know if there were any more particulars to this mission. He wanted to hear from Cornelius himself. Perhaps there was something more he should know concerning his words that he was to speak. Cornelius immediately came forward to answer for all; after all he was the "main-spring" in this whole circumstance. In the recital of Cornelius to Peter there are a number of points that we have not before considered that should be here mentioned:

1. Cornelius stated that it was four days to the very hour since he had seen the angel. Since the Jewish way of reckoning time was to count a part of a day as a whole day this would be true.
2. When Peter reiterated the message of Cornelius to him he said that the angel asked Cornelius to send for him that he might speak unto Cornelius things whereby he and his house might be saved.
3. Cornelius also informed Peter that they were gathered together "to hear all things that have been commanded him (thee) of the Lord."

f. Peter's sermon. 34-43.

34 And Peter opened his mouth, and said, Of a truth I perceive that God is no respecter of persons:

35 but in every nation he that feareth him, and worketh righteousness, is acceptable to him.

342. What was the natural question in the mind of all the Gentiles assembled? How answered?

343. Why did Peter ask the question, "I ask therefore with what intent you sent for me?"

36 The word which he sent unto the children of Israel,
   preaching good tidings of peace by Jesus Christ (he is
   Lord of all)—

37 that saying ye yourselves know, which was published
   throughout all Judaea, beginning from Galilee, after the
   baptism which John preached;

38 even Jesus of Nazareth, how God anointed him with the
   Holy Spirit and with power: who went about doing
   good, and healing all that were oppressed of the devil;
   for God was with him.

39 And we are witnesses of all things which he did both
   in the country of the Jews, and in Jerusalem; whom
   also they slew, hanging him on a tree.

40 Him God raised up the third day, and gave him to be
   made manifest,

41 not to all the people, but unto witnesses that were
   chosen before of God, even to us, who ate and drank
   with him after he rose from the dead.

42 And he charged us to preach unto the people, and to
   testify that this is he who is ordained of God to be the
   Judge of the living and the dead.

43 To him bear all the prophets witness, that through his
   name every one that believeth on him shall receive remission of sins.

34-35 With this request before the apostle there was only one
message he could bring. Neither the details of the Jewish law nor
the rite of circumcision were the need of these Gentiles.

God through the angel had asked Peter to tell these persons what
to do to obtain salvation, to speak to them those things the Lord had
commanded him. There was only one word for this occasion, the
message of Jesus Christ.

Peter prefaced his sermon with a bold statement of the fact
that he was now fully persuaded that "God is no respector of persons"; i.e. God does not consider the fact that a man is a Jew or
a Gentile has any part in His acceptance of him. "In every nation"
the emphasis is upon "nation" not on "he that feareth him, and
worketh righteousness." Those in any nation who were going to be
acceptable to God would have to fear Him under His Son and
work righteousness through Him. This is a discussion of man's
equality on a national or racial standing and not on a spiritual standing.

36-37 Now follows the body of the apostle's discourse. If salvation were the request, if the things commanded him of the Father
were to be heard, he could only tell of Jesus and His glad tidings. It

344. What does Peter mean by the statement in verses 34-35? What is meant
   by "acceptable?"

was in Jesus that salvation was to be found; it was Jesus who had commanded and empowered him to preach.

But then, these Gentiles knew something of the events of this beautiful life. God had sent His word to Israel that through Jesus Christ there was peace. Peter here injects a statement concerning this One in whom we have peace: "He is Lord of all" . . . that is, He not only offers reconciliation to God but is to be held as the Lord of our lives as well. Luke gives us a challenging historical word here, for he states that the word concerning the life and works of Jesus was common knowledge to many persons in that day. The household of Cornelius evidently had not only heard of Jesus but had also a deep respect for Him as a servant of God.

38-42 Of what these Gentiles were yet ignorant was how this message of peace applied to them. Incidentally, they were also told that Peter and his Jewish friends were witnesses of all these things of which they had heard. The meaning and power of the death of Christ was not yet known to them, to say nothing of His resurrection. Of these facts Peter now speaks; he tells of the humiliating death and then of the glorious resurrection and of His appearances to "witnesses that were chosen before of God." The witnesses were of course the apostles, who, as Peter said, "ate and drank with Him after He rose from the dead."

These men were not the only ones to whom Jesus appeared. The record speaks of others to whom He showed Himself alive after His passion. (Cf. Mark 16:9; Matt. 28:8-10; Luke 24:13-31; I Cor. 15:6). The eleven were to be His special witnesses of this fact . . . they were chosen before His death for this very purpose. What joy must have flooded the hearts of these Gentiles as they heard for the first time the glad news of the death of Christ for the sins of the world. Yea, and that they were included in this covering for sins. Peter's next and closing word was that after Jesus had suffered and arose He commissioned the eleven to preach the Lordship and judicial position of Christ. Jesus had said that "salvation is from the Jews" (John 4:22), of a truth the household of Cornelius could witness to this fact.

43 The last word spoken by Peter before the Holy Spirit fell upon these persons was that all the Jewish prophets testified or looked forward to one great promise in the coming Messiah: "the remission of sins." Peter could now say with real meaning that "through His name **everyone** that believeth on Him shall receive remission of sins."

345. What was the need to be met by Peter's sermon?
346. Give a brief outline of Peter's sermon to the household of Cornelius.
347. How did the words of the prophets come to have new meaning for Peter on this occasion?

g. The baptism in the Holy Spirit. 44-46.

44 While Peter yet spake these words, the Holy Spirit
   fell on all them that heard the word.

45 And they of the circumcision that believed were amazed,
   as many as came with Peter, because that on the Gentiles also was poured out the gift of the Holy Spirit.

46 For they heard them speak with tongues, and magnify
   God. Then answered Peter,

44-46 Here as previously on Solomon's porch Peter never finished
his discourse (cf. 4:1-2), but for a vastly different reason. In the previous instance man intervened, but in this case God himself steps in.
The purpose of the Holy Spirit baptism as given here is being discussed in our notes on the Holy Spirit. The special manifestations of the
Holy Spirit are sometimes spoken of as the "falling" of the Holy
Spirit; note 8:16; 11:15 and in 19:6 "came upon." We like the
pointed remarks of J. W. McGarvey on verses 45-46. He says:

"The ground of amazement to the Jewish brethren was not the
mere fact that these Gentiles received the Holy Spirit; for if Peter
had finished his discourse, promising them the Holy Spirit on the
terms which he had laid down on Pentecost, and had then baptized
them, these brethren would have taken it as a matter of course that
they received the Spirit. And if, after this, he had laid hands on
them and imparted the miraculous gift of the Spirit as in the case
of the Samaritans, they would not have been so greatly surprised.
The considerations which caused the amazement were, first, that
the Holy Spirit was 'poured out' upon them directly from God, as
it had never been before on any but the apostles; and second, that
this unusual gift was bestowed on Gentiles." (Page 213.)

h. Baptism in water. 47, 48.

47 Can any man forbid the water, that these should not be
   baptized, who have received the Holy Spirit as well as
   we?

48 And he commanded them to be baptized in the name
   of Jesus Christ. Then prayed they him to tarry certain
   days.

47-48 In verse 47a we have a glimpse of the thinking of Peter
on the whole incident. The question of this verse is evidently directed to the six Jewish brethren. "Can any man forbid the water that
these should not be baptized . . .? It would seem that up to this
point they were going to object to their baptism but now the direct

348. Show how the circumstances here are alike and unlike those that oc-
     curred on Soloman's porch.

349. What was the ground of the amazement of the Jewish brethren?

350. To whom were the words "can any man forbid water that these should
     not be baptized—" directed?

action of God in the case overrules any such hesitancy. Peter had commanded the first Jews to be baptized, and that "in the name of Jesus Christ." Here he commands the first Gentiles to do the same thing. In the command to the Jews he had told them what preceded baptism as well as the purpose of it (cf. 2:38). Here the same man commands the same thing. We are persuaded that in the message of Peter (which is only briefly outlined) he included the same prerequisites since this gospel was to be preached unto "all the nations, beginning from Jerusalem" (Luke 24:47).

5. AT JERUSALEM. 11:1-18.

a. News reaches Jerusalem; objection. 1-3.

1 Now the apostles and the brethren that were in Judaea heard that the Gentiles also had received the word of God.
2 And when Peter was come up to Jerusalem, they that were of the circumcision contended with him,
3 saying, Thou wentest in to men uncircumcised, and didst eat with them.

1-3 The news of Peter's work in Caesarea traveled faster than the apostle. The word of the preaching to the Gentiles had spread throughout the entire assembly by the time Peter arrived. Not only the apostles of Jerusalem heard, but also "the brethren that were in Judea."

The report of Peter's work was that "the Gentiles also had received the Word of God." But when Peter arrived, the point at issue was not the reception of the Word of God but rather the propriety of eating with the uncircumcised.

b. The answer of Peter. 4-18.

4 But Peter began, and expounded the matter unto them in order, saying,
5 I was in the city of Joppa praying: and in a trance I saw a vision, a certain vessel descending, as it were a great sheet let down from heaven by four corners; and it came even unto me:
6 upon which when I had fastened mine eyes, I considered, and saw the four-footed beasts of the earth, and wild beasts and creeping things and birds of the heaven.

351. What is familiar about the command of Peter that these be baptized in the name of Jesus Christ?
352. Name the two groups in Jerusalem that heard of Peter's work in Caesarea.
353. What was the point of issue when Peter returned to Jerusalem?

7 And I heard also a voice saying unto me, Rise, Peter; kill and eat.

8 But I said, Not so, Lord: for nothing common or unclean hath ever entered into my mouth.

9 But a voice answered the second time out of heaven, What God hath cleansed, make not thou common.

10 And this was done thrice: and all were drawn up again into heaven.

11 And behold, forthwith three men stood before the house in which we were, having been sent from Caesarea unto me.

12 And the Spirit bade me go with them, making no distinction. And these six brethren also accompanied me; and we entered into the man's house:

13 and he told us how he had seen the angel standing in his house, and saying, Send to Joppa, and fetch Simon, whose surname is Peter;

14 who shall speak unto thee words, whereby thou shalt be saved, thou and all thy house.

15 And as I began to speak, the Holy Spirit fell on them, even as on us at the beginning.

16 And I remembered the word of the Lord, how he said, John indeed baptized with water; but ye shall be baptized in the Holy Spirit.

17 If then God gave unto them the like gift as he did also unto us, when we believed on the Lord Jesus Christ, who was I, that I could withstand God?

18 And when they heard these things, they held their peace, and glorified God, saying, Then to the Gentiles also hath God granted repentance unto life.

4-17 There was no delay in raising the issue, probably because of the previous close association of Peter and these brethren. "They of the circumcision" gave voice to the objection. The terminology would seem to indicate these were the ones among the Jewish brethren who were special sticklers for the rite of circumcision. We are persuaded it came from some among "the brethren that were in Judea." The apostles all being Galileans and coming from the more humble walks of life would not be so ready to take up such an exclusive position. Especially would this be true in light of the fact that the apostles had been baptized with the Holy Spirit and thus would have a more complete knowledge of the will of the Lord.

What the brethren in Judea and Jerusalem wanted was an answer to their question and charge. Peter did not disappoint them. Peter

354. Who do you suppose voiced the objection?

was just as hesitant as were these other Jews to admit the Gentiles into the full favor of God. Peter thought that what convinced him and the other six Jewish brethren should convince his objectors. Hence, he rehearsed "in order" all that had happened to him beginning with his vision on the house-top of Simon the tanner and concluding with the baptism in the Holy Spirit of the household of Cornelius. The only word to be added to the account as it has already been given is the statement of Peter in verses fifteen to seventeen where we find the words of Jesus respecting John's baptism and the Holy Spirit baptism which lends emphasis to the Holy Spirit's work with the household of Cornelius. Peter says the Holy Spirit "fell on them, even as on us at the beginning." That is, God himself placed His stamp of acceptance upon these persons; and that, totally apart from any effort of Peter. This happened unto them even as it had happened to the apostles in the beginning or "creation" of the church. Then the words of Jesus immediately came to the mind of the apostle; those words which he had thought had exclusive application to him and the eleven. But now for some strange reason (he was not long in seeing) the same gift, "the baptism in the Holy Spirit," was given to these Gentiles as was given to the apostles.

18 Peter had been given two or three divinely directed reasons for bringing the gospel to the Gentiles; now he could see that the Lord intended that he hold no barriers at all but accept these persons into the full fellowship of the body of Christ. Peter felt that to do anything else would be resisting and refusing the will of God. The response of these Jewish brethren is wonderful. It is a beautiful pattern for all of us. When we have disagreed with a brother or sister over any matter of God's will and that person presents the will of God from His word, let us follow their example. Note:

1. When God speaks we are to keep quiet. "They held their peace." They were not stubborn and willful but ready to concede.
2. Then we are to thank God for new truth or light ("and they glorified God") rather than grudgingly admitting our inability to object.
3. Admit into full and unrestricted fellowship those you had once cut off. "Then to the Gentiles also hath God granted repentance unto life."

355. What method did Peter use in convincing the apostles and brethren of Judea?
356. What is the meaning of the term "beginning" as it appears in verse 15?
357. Why can we say that the response of these Jewish brethren was wonderful? How does it offer an example for today?

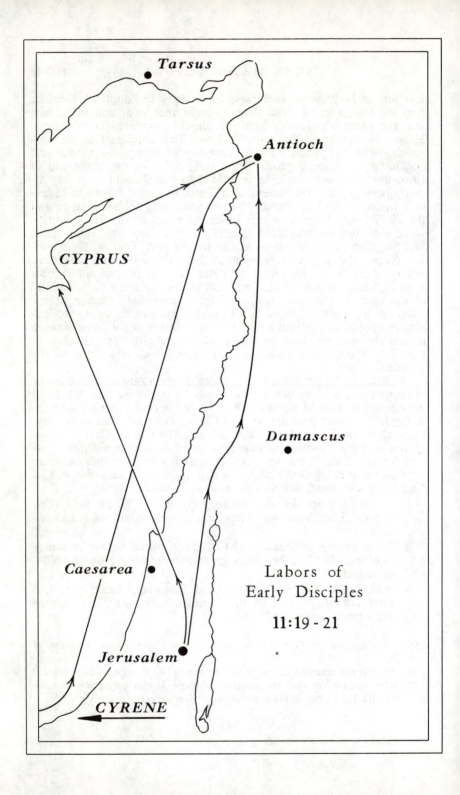

Tarsus

Antioch

CYPRUS

Damascus

Caesarea

Labors of
Early Disciples

11:19 - 21

Jerusalem

CYRENE

THE ESTABLISHMENT OF THE CHURCH
IN ANTIOCH.
11:19-21

19 They therefore that were scattered abroad upon the tribulation that arose about Stephen travelled as far as Phoenicia, and Cyprus, and Antioch, speaking the word to none save only to Jews.

20 But there were some of them, men of Cyprus and Cyrene, who, when they were come to Antioch, spake unto the Greeks also, preaching the Lord Jesus.

21 And the hand of the Lord was with them: and a great number that believed turned unto the Lord.

19-21 The work has begun. The line has been crossed. The household of the faith has been immeasurably enlarged. What then would be more natural for the historian Luke to record than the continuance of this work among the Gentiles?

The next step in the spread of the Word to "the Greeks also," as the Gentiles were so often called, was not carried out by way of the apostles but rather by "men from Cyprus and Cyrene." If the reader will grant us the privilege we will tell in our own words the way in which this came to pass. The story starts at the time of the stoning of Stephen. As all know, a great tribulation or persecution arose against the whole church at this time. Some of those who were scattered went not only into "Judea and Samaria," as Luke previously stated (8:1), but also into the country of Phoenicia, to the isle of Cyprus and to the metropolis of Antioch. To these places they brought the word of life but they were careful to preach only to the Jews. Then a change takes place. The men from Cyprus and Cyrene came to Antioch and preached the Lord Jesus unto "Greeks also." What prompted these Jews to do this? Could it not have been that the word of the work of Peter among the Gentiles reached these places and when this report came to them, they, in their zeal for the Lord, did not hesitate to take the gospel to the great Gentile center of Antioch? The preaching of Christ attracted much interest, many listened, many believed, and many of those who did believe "turned unto the Lord," i.e. were baptized (cf. McGarvey I pp. 224-225). Truly "the hand of the Lord was with them." Thus, was the first church established among the Gentiles.

358. Show how the persecution of the church by Saul started the work of Christ in Antioch.

359. What change takes place in the preaching of those that were scattered following the conversion of Cornelius?

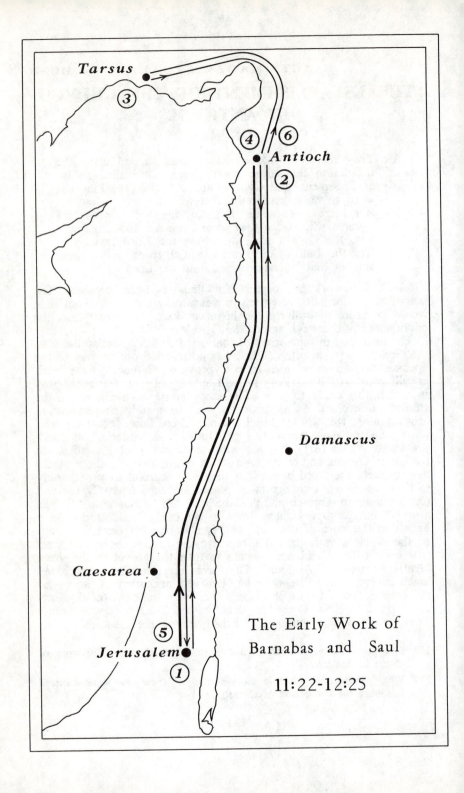

Tarsus

③

④ ⑥

Antioch

②

Damascus

Caesarea

⑤

Jerusalem

①

The Early Work of
Barnabas and Saul

11:22-12:25

THE EARLY LABORS OF BARNABAS AND SAUL.
11:22 — 12:25

1. IN JERUSALEM. 11:22.

22 And the report concerning them came to the ears of
the church which was in Jerusalem: and they sent forth
Barnabas as far as Antioch:

22 News of persons who are attempting to carry forth the same
type of work you are is always of great interest. Especially must this
have been true in the early years of the church when there were
but few Christians, and these were as foreigners in the midst of a
strange and hostile country. The report of the work among those
of Antioch must have been received with the greatest of interest
since it was concerning not only "their common work" but it was
carried out among the Gentiles.

The choice of Barnabas as the man to visit the work in Antioch
was surely a happy one; Barnabas "the son of exhortation." Barnabas
the one who had the faith and courage to believe in and defend one
for whom others had only suspicion and unbelief. Barnabas "was
a good man and full of the Holy Spirit and faith."

2. AT ANTIOCH. 11:23, 24.

23 who, when he was come, and had seen the grace of
God, was glad; and he exhorted them all, that with
purpose of heart they would cleave unto the Lord:

24 for he was a good man, and full of the Holy Spirit and
of faith: and much people was added unto the Lord.

23-24 When this man came to Antioch and was introduced to
converted men and women of this city, he looked upon them as a
manifestation of "the grace of God." His heart was glad, and true
to his name and reputation, "he exhorted them all, that with purpose of heart they would cleave unto the Lord."

What better word could the preacher give them? This thought is
so much neglected today; it is not enough that "a great number turn
to the Lord," it is just as important that "they with purpose of heart
cleave unto the Lord."

Because of the actions of Barnabas on this occasion, Luke could
say of him "for he was a good man, and full of the Holy Spirit and
faith." Barnabas was not content only to rejoice in the work of others
but to cast himself also into the effort. Through his preaching and

360. Why was the word of the work in Antioch of special interest to those
in Jerusalem?

361. Why was the choice of Barnabas a happy one?

362. Why could Luke say of Barnabas "he was a good man, and full of
the Holy Spirit?"

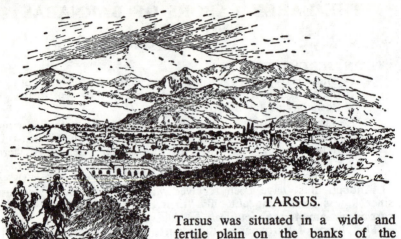

TARSUS.

Tarsus was situated in a wide and fertile plain on the banks of the Cydnus, which flowed through it; hence it is sometimes called Tarsoi. The founding of Tarsus in legendary. The Assyrians entered Cilicia in 850 B.C. and Shalmaneser III's Black Obelisk mentions the taking of the city. It appears in history in Xenophon's time, when it was a city of considerable importance. It was occupied by Cyrus and his troops for twenty days, and given over to plunder.

After Alexander's conquests had swept this way, and the Seleucid kingdom was established at Antioch, Tarsus usually belonged to that kingdom, though for a time it was under the Ptolemies. In the civil wars of Rome it took Caesar's side, and on the occasion of a visit from him had its name changed to Juliopolis. Augustus made it a "free city". It was renowned as a place of education under the early Roman emperors. Strabo compares it in this respect to Athens and Alexandria. Tarsus was also a place of much commerce. Both land and sea highways made Tarsus a famed ancient emporium. The famous Cilician Gates, one of antiquity's most famous mountain passes, is not far distant, and access by water to the Mediterranean made Tarsus a famous trading center. (**Unger's Bible Dictionary** p. 1071.) This was the town where Saul was born; think of his background with its advantages and disadvantages.

exhortation "much people were added unto the Lord." This terminology as we have said elsewhere refers to being added to the
body of Christ which is His church, Eph. 1:22, 23 and Acts 5:14.

3. AT TARSUS. 11:25-26a.

25 And he went forth to Tarsus to seek for Saul;
26 and when he had found him, he brought him unto Antioch. And it came to pass, that even for a whole year
   they were gathered together with the church, and taught
   much people;

25 It would seem that the number turning to the Lord grew to
such proportions that Barnabas needed a helper to assist him in the
work of an evangelist. Who would be better qualified to do this work
than Saul of Tarsus? Tarsus was but a few miles from Antioch. So
it happened that one day Barnabas said goodbye to those of the church
in Antioch and traveled as far as Seleucia and sailed across the short
span of the Mediterranean to Tarsus. To say what Saul had been doing since he arrived from Jerusalem would be pure speculation, but it
does seem highly probable since he was in "the regions of Syria
and Cilicia" (Gal. 1:21b), and since churches were established about
this time in these parts (Acts 15:41) that he was preaching the Word.
26a Luke suggests that Barnabas encountered a little difficulty in
finding Saul. But when he did find him what a meeting there must
have been. Saul looked upon the request of Barnabas for help as
the will of God. He hence returned with Barnabas to Antioch. The
work was increasing so rapidly that Saul and Barnabas continued
for a whole year unabated in their work in the church. The efforts
of these two men were to teach the people (cf. 13:1). There is a
real word of meaning in the work of Barnabas and Saul for the
ministers of today.

4. IN ANTIOCH. 11:26b-30.

26b and that the disciples were called Christians first in
    Antioch.
27 Now in these days there came down prophets from
   Jerusalem unto Antioch.
28 And there stood up one of them named Agabus, and
   signified by the Spirit that there should be a great famine over all the world: which came to pass in the days
   of Claudius.
29 And the disciples, every man according to his ability,

363. What was Saul doing in Tarsus?
364. Why was Saul willing to leave Tarsus and go with Barnabas?
365. What was the effort of these two men as they labored for a year in
     Antioch? (cp. 13:1)

determined to send relief unto the brethren that dwelt in
Judaea:
30 which also they did, sending it to the elders by the hand
of Barnabas and Saul.

a. The labors of Saul and Barnabas. 26b.

The name "Christian" is here used for the first time. The manner
of giving the name has been a subject of no little comment. It is
our contention that the use of the Greek word for "called" as used
here carries something of the thought of being "divinely called."
That is, God Himself selected this new name (Isa. 62:2) and here
called the disciples by their new name "Christians." It was especially appropriate at this time for now both Jews and Gentiles made
up the church and a name could be given by which all of them
could be known.

b. The coming and message of the prophets from Jerusalem. 27-28.

27-28 Following the year's fruitful work in Antioch the brethren
were visited by prophets from Jerusalem. They no doubt were glad
to receive them but wanted to know the intent of their visit. The
Spirit did not delay long in speaking through these men. As they
gathered in a group there stood up one of the prophets named Agabus, who, speaking under the impulse of the Holy Spirit, foretold a
great famine that was to affect the whole inhabited earth. Luke upon recording this scene sometime later states that this promised
famine did occur in the days of Claudius, the emperor of that time.

c. The free will offering taken and sent. 29-30.

29-30 Immediately the brethren in the church in Antioch thought
of others. How would **they** fare? How would **others** be affected? Always the first to suffer in a famine were "those of Judea." The
ground of the province of Judea was not productive enough to supply all the needs of the many who lived within its borders. This was
true in natural times; what then would be their condition in a famine?
Since the time for the celebration of the feast of the Passover was
near many of Judea would be in Jerusalem. They took up a free
will offering for the brethren of Judea and sent it by the hands of
Barnabas and Saul to the elders of the Jerusalem church. This is
the first mention of elders in the church.

366. Who gave the name "Christian" to the disciples? Why especially appropriate at this time?
367. How did Agabus and the others from Jerusalem become prophets?
368. Who was Claudius?
369. Why send relief to "those of Judea" since the famine was to affect
the whole world? Why at this particular time?

5. AT JERUSALEM. 12:1-24.

a. Persecution of Herod. James beheaded. Peter imprisoned. 1-5.

1 Now about that time Herod the king put forth his hands to afflict certain of the church.

2 And he killed James the brother of John with the sword.

3 And when he saw that it pleased the Jews, he proceeded to seize Peter also. And those were the days of unleavened bread.

4 And when he had taken him, he put him in prison, and delivered him to four quaternions of soldiers to guard him; intending after the Passover to bring him forth to the people.

5 Peter therefore was kept in the prison: but prayer was made earnestly of the church unto God for him.

1-2 Luke leaves the narrative of the two on their way to Jerusalem to travel ahead of them in his account to prepare our minds for the condition they were to face when they arrived. It was the year 44 A.D. and Herod Agrippa I had just been given his position as "king" over several provinces. (The history of the Herods as well as the emperors is of real interest and help to our study of this book). The king had the difficult task of ruling as a Roman and pleasing the Jews. The Christians or the church could very effectively serve the purpose of Herod; he could mistreat them and please the Jews and still give no offense to the Roman authorities. His plan of persecution was to "put forth his hands to afflict certain of the church." It would appear that his plan was to strike at the leaders. James, brother of John, was the first victim. There is no trial recorded; a mere statement that James was slain with the sword.

3-5 As we have said, Herod was carrying out this persecution purely for selfish ends, i.e. to seek the favor of the Jews. Since Herod was a part Jewish such actions would suggest to the Jews that he truly was in sympathy with their beliefs. The death of James was heralded as a victory for the cause of Judaism.

When word of this reached the ears of Herod he immediately went a step further and imprisoned Peter. But alas, no swift execution could take place for the "days of unleavened bread" had started. If he were to please the Jews he must lay aside the work of slaughter that they might observe the Passover Feast. There were

370. Why leave the two on the road and take up the narrative of the events in Jerusalem?

371. What was the date of the death of James?

372. How could the Christians serve the purpose of Herod?

373. Give a brief account of the life and rulership of Herod Agrippa I. (It will be necessary to use a Biblical encyclopedia for this answer.)

374. Why could not Peter be put to death as quickly as James?

seven days following the eating of the Passover called the "days of unleavened bread." In these days the spirit of the Passover was still present and they were made a vital part of the feast. (cf. Ex. 12:1-20).

Peter was made especially secure in the king's prison. Herod had doubtless heard of Peter's previous experience in being released from prison; this time he would not escape. To insure this he was delivered to four "quaternions of soldiers" that they might act as his guards. Four men made up a **"quaternion."**

While these sixteen soldiers set about their task of guarding Peter there were others who were looking to a higher and greater power than Herod the king, for Peter's release. "Prayer was made earnestly of the church unto God for him." This prayer meeting, as we shall observe later, was held in the home of Mary the mother of John Mark. The manner in which the soldiers guarded Peter is described in the sixth verse. It would seem that the four quaternions divided the hours up into four watches of three hours apiece every twelve hours. Thus Peter was chained between two men; half of the quaternion and the other two stood guard at the prison gates.

    b. The miraculous release. 6-11.

6 And when Herod was about to bring him forth, the same night Peter was sleeping between two soldiers, bound with two chains: and guards before the door kept the prison.

7 And behold, an angel of the Lord stood by him, and a light shined in the cell: and he smote Peter on the side, and awoke him, saying, Rise up quickly. And his chains fell off from his hands.

8 And the angel said unto him, Gird thyself, and bind on thy sandals. And he did so. And he saith unto him, Cast thy garment about thee, and follow me.

9 And he went out, and followed; and he knew not that it was true which was done by the angel, but thought he saw a vision.

10 And when they were past the first and the second guard, they came unto the iron gate that leadeth into the city; which opened to them of its own accord: and they went out, and passed on through one street; and straightway the angel departed from him.

11 And when Peter was come to himself, he said, Now I know of a truth, that the Lord hath sent forth his angel and delivered me out of the hand of Herod, and from all the expectation of the people of the Jews.

6-8 The seventh day of unleavened bread had come and gone and on the morrow Herod was to bring Peter and mock and slay him

375. How did Herod make special provisions in the imprisonment of Peter?

before the Jews. Peter was not anxious about the outcome of his imprisonment. His mind and heart were at rest in his Saviour. A few hours before he was scheduled to appear before a murderous assassin he was fast asleep in his cell. So sound asleep was the apostle that neither the appearance of the angel nor the light that shone into his cell awakened him.

Evidently the two guards were also fast asleep or else their eyes were holden. It was necessary for the angel to strike Peter to awaken him. When Peter finally opened his eyes he was greeted by his heavenly visitor with the words "Rise up quickly." He immediately arose from his sitting position; as he did, the shackles that had bound him to his guards clattered to the floor.

Peter was following the instructions of the angel with no comment, like one in a trance. We shall see later that he thought it was all a vision. "Gird thyself, and bind on thy sandals." The outer garment or cloak had been laid aside and Peter had removed his sandals to give him greater comfort for the night (what a manifestation of commitment to the will of God.) Peter followed the instruction of the angel. The final words of the angel were "Cast thy garment about thee and follow me." The first portion of this statement is given to emphasize the second. Peter had already dressed, now the angel says in essence "draw your clothes about you to prepare for departure and come follow me."

9-11 As we have said, Peter moved as one in a dream for although he was now following the angel he could not believe it was real. Probably the first and second guards spoken of in verse ten were half of the quaternion that was on guard at the time of the deliverance. The fact that they were enabled to pass by these men without detection bespeaks of some providential intervention. There was yet one barrier between Peter and the streets of Jerusalem, the iron gate which opened into the prison. Upon approaching this gate it began to move of its own accord and opened to permit the two to step out into the street. The angel stayed with Peter until they had "passed on through one street" (probably referring to a walk of a few blocks distance) until they reached the street on which Mary the mother of John Mark lived.

When the angel left him Peter "came to himself." Upon looking

376. Where was the prayer meeting for Peter held?
377. What did the angel do to awaken Peter?
378. How is the faith and humility of Peter shown in his imprisonment?
379. What were the three statements of the angel?
380. What was the first thought of Peter as to this incident?
381. Who are the first and second guards spoken of in verse ten?
382. How could Peter and the angel so easily pass these soldiers?
383. Why did the angel stay with Peter until they had passed on through one street?

about him he could truly lift his face to God and say from his heart "Now I know of a truth, that the Lord hath sent forth His angel and delivered me out of the hand of Herod, and from all the expectation of the people of the Jews." While the angel was with him it seemed too good to be true; but now he could rejoice in an unmistakable reality. The phrase "the people of the Jews" refers to the Sanhedrin or rulers who here are called "the people."

c. At the house of Mary. 12-17.

12 And when he had considered the thing, he came to the house of Mary the mother of John whose surname was Mark; where many were gathered together and were praying.

13 And when he knocked at the door of the gate, a maid came to answer, named Rhoda.

14 And when she knew Peter's voice, she opened not the gate for joy, but ran in, and told that Peter stood before the gate.

15 And they said unto her, Thou art mad. But she confidently affirmed that it was even so. And they said, It is his angel.

16 But Peter continued knocking: and when they had opened, they saw him, and were amazed.

17 But he, beckoning unto them with the hand to hold their peace, declared unto them how the Lord had brought him forth out of the prison. And he said, Tell these things unto James, and to the brethren. And he departed, and went to another place.

12-15 What would Peter do now that he was released? This was the thought of his mind as he stood in the darkness of the narrow streets of Jerusalem. He considered his actions well, as we shall discover in the ensuing events. He made his way to the house of Mary the mother of John Mark. Whether Peter knew or not that a prayer meeting for him was here being conducted we do not know.

It might be well to say a word about the manner of construction of the houses of that day. A proper understanding of verses 13-16 is dependant upon this knowledge. There was erected a high fence or barricade some few yards out from the house. This entirely surrounded the home. In this fence there was built a large gate. This was opened for use at times during the day; it was closed and locked at night. In this gate there was built a small door just large enough for the entrance of one person. It was at this small door

384. Memorize that wonderful statement of praise and thanks found in verse 11.

385. Describe in your own words the construction of the houses in that day and how it relates to the entrance of Peter into the house of Mary, the mother of John Mark.

in the gate that Peter knocked. The young maid named Rhoda who came to answer the knock heard Peter call out; she had probably heard that same voice many times in prayer and preaching and knew it was Peter. She was so full of ecstasy at the thought and sudden realization that she did not even open the gate but immediately turned and ran into the presence of the others bursting with the news that Peter was standing at the gate. We are struck with the strange unbelief of these early Christians, praying for the release of Peter and then when their prayers are answered they are unwilling to accept it. But to pause a moment in reflection will cause us to confess that we, too, have often prayed in the same type of unbelief. Perhaps it was not so much a surprise at the answer to their prayer but rather at the form the answer assumed.

They offered two explanations for the startling message of the maid: (1) "You are mad." She paid no heed to this but only more resolutely stood her ground; (2) "It is his angel." That angels are associated with the lives of the saints can be observed from Heb. 1:14. To this association the disciples alluded in their words to Rhoda.

16-17 All doubt as to who was right was removed when there came echoing into the room the loud knocks and cries of the apostle himself. Imagine the absolute dismay and astonishment that must have filled the hearts of those assembled. They went out to greet him. Before any of them could say a word, Peter motioned for quietness and quickly told them what had happened. He requested that those present tell James and the other brethren of Jerusalem. Then without saying where he was going he departed. The wisdom in not telling where he was going can be immediately seen in view of the fact that soldiers would doubtless be inquiring on the morrow and the disciples could say with all truthfulness that they knew not where he had gone. That James was singled out to be told of the news seems to indicate something of his position of leadership. The account of the 15th chapter and Gal. 1:17, 18 bears this thought out.

d. The death of the soldiers. 18, 19a.

18 Now as soon as it was day there was no small stir among the soldiers, what was become of Peter.

19 And when Herod had sought for him, and found him not, he examined the guards, and commanded that they should be put to death.

386. What was strange about the prayer meeting of these Christians?
387. What two explanations did the disciples give for Rhoda's strange words? Explain the second.
388. How were they convinced?
399. Show the wisdom in the words of Peter upon this occasion.
390. Why "tell James?"

TYRE.

About eighty-five miles north of Joppa and about thirty miles from Nazareth, Tyre stood originally on the mainland. It was strongly fortified and resisted the siege of Nebuchadnezzar for thirteen years. At a later period the city was built on a small island about half a mile from the shore. On the land side it was protected by a wall 150 ft. high. This new city was taken by Alexander the Great, after a siege of seven months.

Hiram, King of Tyre, was closely connected in business affairs, both with David and Solomon. The destruction of Tyre was in fulfillment of prophecy. Ezekiel the twenty-sixth chapter foretells in detail the destruction of the city by Alexander the Great. The present city of Tyre is not on the location of the ancient city. Jesus visited Tyre. (Matt. 15:21) Paul spent seven days here. Acts 21:3-7. A thriving congregation of Christians was established here in the early days of the church. We do not know who established this church. Every Christian in that first day of the church felt his responsibility to the lost world about him. If Christians today would go everywhere preaching the Word then there would be congregations of believers everywhere.

162

18-19a We can add nothing in this account to the graphic words of Luke: "Now as soon as it was day, there was no small stir among the soldiers, what was become of Peter?" All sixteen soldiers were involved in this incident and many and varied must have been the comments of these men. The guards knew that the inevitable request would be forthcoming. Sure enough it came: "Bring forth the prisoner." But he was not to be found. Where he went was a perfect mystery. If there were no prisoner to stand before Herod then the guards would stand in his place. This they did and after an examination in which they could only plead complete ignorance of the circumstances, they were led off to their death. Such treatment of those that displeased him was usual for Herod Agrippa I.

e. Herod's speech and death at Caesarea. 19b-23.

19b And he went down from Judaea to Caesarea, and tarried there.

20 Now he was highly displeased with them of Tyre and Sidon: and they came with one accord to him, and, having made Blastus the king's chamberlain their friend, they asked for peace, because their country was fed from the king's country.

21 And upon a set day Herod arrayed himself in royal apparel, and sat on the throne, and made an oration unto them.

22 And the people shouted, saying, The voice of a god, and not of a man.

23 And immediately an angel of the Lord smote him, because he gave not God the glory: and he was eaten of worms, and gave up the ghost.

24 But the word of God grew and multiplied.

19b-20 Maybe the humiliating experience with Peter caused Herod to leave the place of his embarrassment to find satisfaction for his deflated ego, in exerting his authority in Caesarea. Whatever were the motives back of his move, we find him in Caesarea. After a short time in the city he called for a trial of certain persons from the cities of Tyre and Sidon. For one reason or another they had incurred the wrath of Herod. It would not do, however, to seek to establish their position for they were greatly dependent upon the country over which the king ruled for their food. All they wanted was peace. These of the two cities of Phoenicia had a plan where-

391. What do you imagine were the words of the soldiers when they discovered the disappearance of Peter?
392. Should the guards have been put to death? Why were they?
393. What occasioned the trip of Herod to Caesarea?

by they could gain the favor and leniency of Herod. They had secured the friendship of the king's "chamberlain" or personal servant.

21-24 The day for the trial arrived and it was to be no common affair. Herod arrayed himself in his most gorgeous of royal apparel. He pompishly took his place upon the judgment seat. Josephus states that the judgment seat or throne was located in the open air and that Herod was dressed in a dazzling silver robe that reflected the light of the sun. The king had prepared an oration to impress the people with his position and authority. As he spoke, if tradition is to be depended upon, the sun reflecting as it was from his silver cloak, there was given to him an appearance almost supernatural. This accounted for the cry of the people "the voice of a god, and not of a man."

It is to be remembered that Herod was partly Jewish. From contemporary history we learn that he was thoroughly acquainted with the laws and customs of the Jews. From this we might say the hand of God was laid upon him because he acted directly against his own knowledge when he accepted the worship of those of Caesarea.

Josephus says that . . . "Herod was seized with violent pains in the bowels, and that he lingered in great torture for five days."

In spite of all these acts of violence and opposition the word found a place in more and more hearts, and each day saw a multiplying of the members of the body of Christ.

6. **BACK TO ANTIOCH.** 12:25.
> 25 And Barnabas and Saul returned from Jerusalem, when they had fulfilled their ministration, taking with them John whose surname was Mark.

A review of the events of Chapter Twelve:
When Barnabas and Saul arrived in Jerusalem to give their offering to those of Judea they found:
1. James had been beheaded. 12:1-2.
2. That Peter was imprisoned. They were present at his divine release. 12:3-17.
3. They no doubt heard of the death of the soldiers. 12:18-19a.
4. They probably also heard of the divine vengeance wrought on Herod. 12-19b-23.
5. They must have rejoiced with the others in the increase of the word. 12:24.

394. Why did the peoples of Tyre and Sidon have Blastus for their friend?
395. Tell of the traditional account of Herod's oration to those of Tyre and Sidon at Caesarea.
396. Why could we say that Herod acted contrary to his own conscience in accepting the worship of the people?
397. What is the meaning of "eaten of worms?"
398. Give from memory the five points in the outline of the twelfth chapter.

25 Now of two servants of Christ return to Antioch following the distribution of their bounty; taking the young man John Mark as their attendant. 25.

ACTS TEST OVER CHAPTERS EIGHT THROUGH TWELVE
True or False
8:1-4

.... 1. The opposition of the church takes a definite turn in procedure beginning with the eighth chapter.

.... 2. This change, or turn, was in the fact that the Sadducees now took up the persecution whereas it was formerly the Pharisees.

.... 3. The rulers really had nothing to fear for the Christians would have always been in the minority.

.... 4. This persecution was in reality providential.

.... 5. The book of Acts teaches us that this persecution was only confined to Jerusalem.

.... 6. Christians stayed in Jerusalem; there is record of their secret meetings.

.... 7. The death of Stephen was a great defeat.

.... 8. Only the men, of course, "went everywhere preaching the word."

.... 9. There is a record of the apostles hiding themselves in Jerusalem and thus were they enabled to stay in the city.

.... 10. "The word" they preached was preached everywhere.

Multiple Choice
8:5-12

1. Philip went to Samaria and proclaimed unto them: 1) The Messiah. 2) The Christ. 3) Jesus.

2. This Philip was: 1) Philip the apostle. 2) Philip the deacon. 3) Another Philip.

3. Philip became "an evangelist": 1) When he was ordained by the apostles. 2) When he started evangelizing. 3) Later in Caesarea.

4. They believed Philip when they saw: 1) His honest face. 2) The signs which he did. 3) His marvelous delivery.

5. Among those diseases healed by Philip was: 1) Demon possession. 2) Blindness. 3) Deafness.

6. As a result of the preaching and healing there was much: 1) Conviction. 2) Joy. 3) Conflict in the city.

7. The record states that Simon amazed the people by: 1) Sorcery. 2) Ventriloquism. 3) Both.

8. All believed Simon "from the least to the greatest" because: 1) He had been doing it for such a long time. 2) He was the mayor of the town. 3) He had an agreement with the leaders of the city.

9. They believed Philip instead of Simon because: 1) Not all heard Simon. 2) Some never did believe in Simon. 3) Philip's message and work were plainly superior to those of Simon.
10. Acts 8:12 compares very well with: 1) Acts 2:38. 2) 3:19. 3) Mark 16:15-16.

Fill in the Blanks
8:20-25

1. "But Peter said: Thy silver _____ with _____ for thou hast thought to obtain the gift of God with money."
2. ". . . and pray the Lord, if _____ the thought of thy heart shall be forgiven thee."
3. "For I see that thou art in the _____ of bitterness and the _____ of iniquity."
4. "They therefore, when they had testified and spoken the word of the Lord, returned to _____ and preached the gospel to many _____ _____ of the Samaritans."
5. "But an _____ of the Lord spake unto Philip, saying, Arise, and go toward the south unto the way that goeth down from Jerusalem unto Gaza; the same is _____."
6. And he arose and went; and behold, a man of Ethiopia, a _____ _____ of great authority under Candace, queen of the Ethiopians, who was over all her treasure, who had come to Jerusalem to _____.
7. And Philip ran to him, and _____ him reading Isaiah the prophet . . .
8. He was led as a sheep to the slaughter; and as a lamb before his shearer is dumb, so he openth not his mouth; in his _____ his judgment was taken away.
9. And Philip opened his mouth, and beginning from this scripture, _____ unto him _____.

Find FIVE (5) mistakes in this paragraph.
8:36-40

Philip preached Jesus from Jeremiah the prophet to this negro. Near to where they were was a body of water. The eunuch seeing the water said: "Behold here is water; what doth hinder me to be baptized?" The horses were called to a halt and the eunuch went down alone into the water and was baptized. From this text, apart from the Greek, it would be impossible to determine the mode of baptism. The Azotus mentioned is the city of Gaza on the Philistine plain. Philip was at this time a single man who could make this trip even as Paul did on his missionary journeys.

UNDERLINE the words that are out of place.
(ONE word for each question)

1. Acts 9:1-2. 1) Saul. 2) Slaughter. 3) Synagogues. 4) Share.

166

2. Acts 9:1-2. 1) Letters. 2) Leniency. 3) Lord.
3. Acts 9:3-8a. 1) Damascus. 2) Drew nigh. 3) Dream.
4. Acts 9:3-8a. 1) Light. 2) Letters. 3) Liberty. 4) Lord.
5. Acts 9:3-8a. 1) Goad. 2) Go. 3) Grown.
6. Acts 9:3-8a. 1) Boast. 2) Blind. 3) Broken. 4) Best.
7. Acts 9:3-8a. 1) Conviction. 2) Conversion. 3) Confession. 4) Constitution.
8. Acts 9:8b-22. 1) Ananias. 2) Arise. 3) Amazed. 4) Azotus.
9. Acts 9:8b-22. 1) Saints. 2) Suffer. 3) Share. 4) Seen.
10. Acts 9:8b-22. 1) Brother. 2) Bear. 3) Bring.

Affirm or Deny But Tell the Reason Why

1. I say that Simon the sorcerer was never really converted.
   Affirm _____ Deny _____ Tell why.
2. I say the "despised Samaritans" were the first Gentile converts.
   Affirm _____ Deny _____ Tell why.
3. I say that Acts 8:14 ("Now when the apostles that were at Jerusalem heard that Samaria had received the word of God, they sent unto them Peter and John") offers proof that Peter was not the first Pope.
   Affirm _____ Deny _____ Tell why.
4. I say that Peter and John were sent to Samaria to investigate the faith of these Samaritans and see if they were on the right track.
   Affirm _____ Deny _____ Tell why.
5. I say that **nowhere** did **anyone** ever connect prayer with receiving the Holy Spirit.
   Affirm _____ Deny _____ Tell why.
6. I say that the Samaritans did not have the Holy Spirit until the apostles arrived and gave it to them.
   Affirm _____ Deny _____ Tell why.
7. I say the Holy Spirit "fell on them" in answer to prayer; therefore we should pray the same prayer today.
   Affirm _____ Deny _____ Tell why.
8. I say that Luke does not tell us all of the circumstances of Simon's sin and that it must have been a real temptation to Peter and John.
   Affirm _____ Deny _____ Tell why.
9. I say that Simon must have thought about it a long while before he made the offer to Peter and John.
   Affirm _____ Deny _____ Tell why.
10. I say that Simon would have had to wait until the Lord's day to be forgiven of his sin.
    Affirm _____ Deny _____ Tell why.

True or False

_____ 1. The main thought of Luke in the whole work of Peter was the conversion of Cornelius.

_____ 2. The eunuch was the first Gentile convert to Christianity.

_____ 3. Cornelius could have been saved if he had continued in his devoutness.

_____ 4. Cornelius could have been saved in his pious life if he had had no opportunity to hear of Christ.

_____ 5. Cornelius was an officer of the Roman army maintained in Caesarea to keep law and order.

_____ 6. Cornelius probably obtained his faith through association with the Jews.

_____ 7. No worship to Jehovah in sincerity goes unrewarded.

_____ 8. Cornelius observed the Jewish hours of prayer.

_____ 9. The angel appeared at noon. (To Cornelius).

_____ 10. The angel had on garments that literally shown with their brightness.

_____ 11. Cornelius did not connect the angel with God.

_____ 12. The angel told Cornelius to go himself to Joppa and fetch Simon Peter.

_____ 13. The angel did not want Cornelius to mix Simon the apostle with Simon the tanner, so he told him of his surname.

_____ 14. Cornelius sent only his two household servants as messengers to fetch Peter.

_____ 15. It was at the sixth hour when the men arrived in Joppa.

_____ 16. The vision of Peter and Cornelius were exactly similar.

_____ 17. To have eaten what was in the sheet would have been to sin, so thought Peter.

_____ 18. The sheet descended from heaven three times.

_____ 19. The men from Cornelius stood outside of the house at the outer gate and called in to inquire of the whereabouts of Simon Peter.

_____ 20. The messengers of Cornelius made the mission of Peter as attractive to the Jewish mind as possible.

Multiple Choice

1. Who heard the news of Peter's work in Caesarea? 1) The apostles and disciples. 2) The apostles and brethren. 3) The apostles and brethren of Judea.

2. Who contended with Peter at Jerusalem? 1) The apostles. 2) The disciples. 3) They of the circumcision.

3. Their charge was: 1) He should not have preached to them. 2) Eaten with them. 3) Baptized them.
4. To convince these of Jerusalem, Peter: 1) Preached the gospel to them. 2) Only told them of the baptism of the Holy Spirit. 3) Told them how the Lord had convinced him.
5. Peter concluded his defense by saying: The Holy Spirit had: 1) Overcome them. 2) Fallen on them as on us in the beginning. 3) filled them.
6. Peter's closing words were that: 1) God had accepted the Gentiles in that He had given them the Holy Spirit. 2) The Gentiles had been baptized in the Holy Spirit, therefore were saved and accepted. 3) God had plainly told him to accept these unclean persons.
7. "Now when they heard these things they": 1) Praised the Lord. 2) Contended with Peter. 3) Held their peace and glorified the Lord.

The Labors of the Early Disciples
11:19-21

Here is a list of TEN words. Pick out the ones that DO NOT relate to this section. The correct ones are all QUOTED from the text.
1. Scattered. 2. Scarcely. 3. Tribulation. 4. Tremble. 5. Traveled. 6. Cyprus. 7. Syria. 8. Phoenicia. 9. Antioch. 10. Hebrews.

Who's Who in 11:22—12:25.

Who said the following?
1. "There will be a famine over all the world."
2. "Rise up quickly."
3. "Now I know of a truth, that the Lord hath sent forth his angel. . ."
4. "Peter is standing before the gate."
5. "It is his angel."
6. "Tell these things unto James and the brethren."
7. "Put them to death."
8. "The voice of a god, and not of a man."

Who did the following?
1. Went to seek for Saul in Tarsus.
2. Became the ones who were first called "Christians."
3. Killed James the brother of John with a sword.
4. Slept at the door of the prison.
5. Had a prayer meeting in her house.
6. Went down to Caesarea.
7. Made "Blastus" their friend.
8. Arrayed himself in royal apparel, and sat on the throne.
9. Smote Herod.
10. Went back to Antioch with Paul and Barnabas.

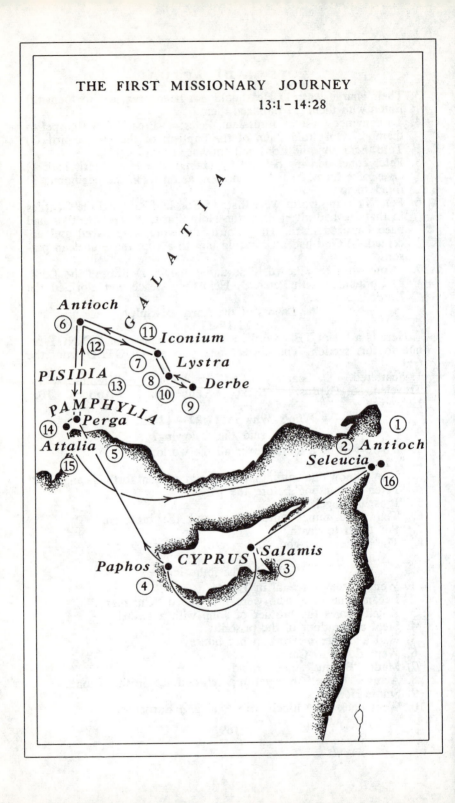

THE FIRST MISSIONARY JOURNEY
13:1 – 14:28

THE CHURCH IN THE UTTERMOST PART OF THE WORLD
13:1—28:31

THE FIRST MISSIONARY JOURNEY
1. AT ANTIOCH. 13:1-3.

1 Now there were at Antioch, in the church that was there, prophets and teachers, Barnabas, and Symeon that was called Niger, and Lucius of Cyrene, and Manaen the foster-brother of Herod the tetrarch, and Saul.

2 And as they ministered to the Lord, and fasted, the Holy Spirit said, Separate me Barnabas and Saul for the work whereunto I have called them.

3 Then, when they had fasted and prayed and laid their hands on them, they sent them away.

1 Luke begins this portion of his treatise as if it were the beginning of a separate narrative. Although it is a part of the whole, yet one could start reading at Acts 13:1 and find a complete story as he read through the rest of the book.

The spread of the gospel into the uttermost part of the earth begins from the metropolis of Antioch in Syria, and with two of the leaders of this church.

It will be of interest to note that Barnabas and Saul along with the others are called "prophets and teachers" of this church. The other servants of the church were: (1) Symeon that was called "Niger," i.e. Symeon who was called "black." There is no need to immediately conclude that Symeon was a Negro. There are many men who because of their dark hair or complexion are called "black." (2) "Lucius of Cyrene" must have been one of the first to come to Antioch as we read in 11:20 that men from this city of northern Africa were the first to preach Christ in Antioch. (3) "Manaen the foster brother of Herod the Tetrarch;" this was Herod Antipas, the Tetrarch of Galilee; and since we learn from Josephus that this Herod and his brother Archelaus were children of the same mother, and afterward educated together at Rome, it is probable that this Christian prophet or teacher had spent his childhood with these two princes, who were now both banished from Palestine to the banks of the Rhine.

Saul is placed last on the list of the five; this is probably in the order of importance. Who were prophets, and who were teachers?

399. Who were the prophets and teachers of the Antioch church? Name them from memory.
400. Do you believe "Symeon" was a Negro?
401. Who was "Lucius of Cyrene?"
402. What interesting word does Josephus give us of one of the leaders?

171

This we are not told. The word "prophet" is suggestive of far more than only foretelling the future; it carries with it the thought of exhortation and divine utterance. Read the notes on "The gifts of the Holy Spirit," as to how the gift of prophecy was given.

2 The leaders of the Antioch church were busy about the work of God. "They ministered to the Lord, and fasted." Of just what this ministration to the Lord consisted we are not told, but from other examples of the work of the church we know that they were caring for both the physical and the spiritual needs of the saints. Why were they fasting? It could have been the usual habit of consecration then prevailing in the early church. We are disposed to this view. While they were thus engaged, the Holy Spirit spoke to Symeon, Lucius and Manaen, concerning Barnabas and Saul.

"Separate me Barnabas and Saul for the work whereunto I have called them."

That God had previously called Saul we are certain. But when the Lord spoke to Barnabas concerning this task we do not know, but that He did we are here assured.

3 The setting aside described in verse three is what is commonly referred to as an ordination service. There was a setting aside. It could be overlooked that this is an example for all those who would do similar work today. Consider the facts of this case as an example:

(1) There must be men qualified, men who are already busy in the Lord's work.
(2) They must feel and realize that God has called them to this task. (Not of course in the same way that these two were called.)
(3) The local congregation directed by the elders sets them aside.
(4) Fasting and prayer are to precede the setting aside.
(5) The hands of the elders, in this case called "teachers," are laid upon their heads. (Since it was not the hands of the apostles we know nothing miraculous was imparted.)
(6) They are sent away to a definite work.

2. AT SELEUCIA. 13:4.

4 So they, being sent forth by the Holy Spirit, went down to Seleucia; and from thence they sailed to Cyprus.

4 The Holy Spirit directed in this whole procedure, so it could be

403. How did these men become prophets? Prove your answer.
404. What did you conclude the word "ministered to the Lord" means?
405. Why were they fasting? How often?
406. Who did the Lord speak to regarding Barnabas and Saul?
407. When had God called Barnabas?
408. What example for us is given in the church at Antioch?
409. Give from memory the six steps in setting aside men for the work of God.

truly said that "they were sent forth by the Holy Spirit." They were to leave the country of Syria, hence their first stop was the seaport of Antioch called Seleucia. This port was about fifteen or sixteen miles from Antioch. The mountains of Cyprus could be viewed from the coast of Syria. It should be said here that John Mark was taken with Barnabas and Saul as their minister.

On one of the ships in the port of Seleucia the three found passage and sailed to the isle of Cyprus.

3. IN SALAMIS. 13:5.

5 And when they were at Salamis, they proclaimed the word of God in the synagogues of the Jews: and they had also John as their attendant.

5 Salamis was on the coast of Cyprus. The town was populated with a substantial number of Jews, their synagogues were to be found throughout the city. The town was an important place in this time; from Salamis the eastern portion of the island was governed. What response was given by the Jews to the preaching of the Word of God? No definite word is given but it does seem that had there been any tangible results it would have been mentioned. The stay must have occupied several days. The first mention of the presence of John Mark is here made; although as it has been said, he accompanied Barnabas and Saul from Jerusalem (12:25) and doubtless set sail with them from Seleucia.

4. AT PAPHOS. 13:6-12.

6 And when they had gone through the whole island unto Paphos, they found a certain sorcerer, a false prophet, a Jew, whose name was Bar-Jesus;
7 who was with the proconsul, Sergius Paulus, a man of understanding. The same called unto him Barnabas and Saul, and sought to hear the word of God.
8 But Elymas the sorcerer (for so is his name by interpretation) withstood them, seeking to turn aside the proconsul from the faith.
9 But Saul, who is also called Paul, filled with the Holy Spirit, fastened his eyes on him,
10 and said, O full of all guile and all villany, thou son of the devil, thou enemy of all righteousness, wilt thou not cease to pervert the right ways of the Lord?
11 And now, behold, the hand of the Lord is upon thee, and thou shalt be blind, not seeing the sun for a season. And immediately there fell on him a mist and a dark-

410. How far is Seleucia from Antioch?
411. How many in the missionary party? Who were they?
412. Why could it be said that Salamis was an important city.
413. What work for the Lord was done in Salamis?

ness; and he went about seeking some to lead him by the hand.

12 Then the proconsul, when he saw what was done, believed, being astonished at the teaching of the Lord.

6 The next move of the evangelists took them on a journey of one hundred miles. They traversed the whole isle of Cyprus before Luke saw fit to record the next incident. The words used in the text: "had gone through the whole island" have the thought of a leisurely journey that would offer opportunity to stop off in several places on the way. It might be suggestive of visiting the previous work of those on this island. (11:19).

Like the work of Philip among the Samaritans the first fact made known to us is a note of opposition to the gospel. In Samaria it was Simon the sorcerer; in Paphos it is Bar-Jesus the sorcerer.

The city of Paphos was of considerable size, being the capitol of the island. The proconsul or ruler under the Roman Senate, was Sergius Paulus. Bar-Jesus was closely associated with the proconsul. This ruler was a man of understanding and was searching for the truth of God. Bar-Jesus being a Jew was evidently combining what knowledge he had of the Jewish religion with sorcery to give him the position he held.

7-8 It must have been in the providence of God that this sorcerer was a Jew, for when Sergius Paulus heard that two Jews came preaching a message purporting to be the truth or Word of God, he would quite naturally think of what he had heard from Elymas of the Jewish religion and be anxious to hear more on this subject. He called in Barnabas and Saul that they might speak to him. But when Elymas (a Grecianized form of the Arabic word for "wise") realized the mission of these two he knew that unless he could defeat their counsel his influence and position were lost. The opposition put forth by Elymas was to "withstand" Barnabas and Saul. Just what method he used in doing this, we are not informed; we are told, however, of occasions with the Jews which were very similar to this one. The method used by the Jews was to rail and contradict

414. How far from Salamis to Paphos?
415. What thought is contained in the words "had gone through the whole island?" Of what is it suggestive?
416. What is the first fact given concerning the work in Paphos?
417. What special position did the city of Paphos have on the island?
418. Under whom did the proconsul rule the island?
419. If the proconsul was "a man of understanding" why have a sorcerer in his court?
420. What method of sorcery do you imagine Bar-Jesus employed?
421. Why is it said that the providence of God enters the fact that Bar-Jesus was a Jew?
422. What does the name Elymas mean?

Paul while he was speaking. When no valid objection is known this is the only recourse. The whole effort of the sorcerer was to turn the proconsul from the acceptance of "the faith."

9-12 On this occasion we have the movement of Saul to the fore-front. Previous to this both men had been speaking (7b). Now Saul is prompted by the Holy Spirit to execute the will of God in the form of a miracle. Through the inspiration of the Spirit of God, Saul lays bare the true character of this perverted Jew. He says:

(1) This one is full of "all guile" or cunning deceit. This presents something of his hypocrisy in the use of his knowledge of God. (2) He is also full of all "villany." This bespeaks the evil ends to which he directed his efforts. (3) His name is "Bar-Jesus," i.e. "son of Jesus" or "son of Salvation," but here Paul shows that the exact antithesis is true, he is "the son of the devil." (4) He is an enemy of all right-eousness. Since he was not sincere in his profession he was truly an enemy of all righteousness. (5) All of these wicked attributes were directed toward the perversion of "the right ways of the Lord."

This sorcerer sought to place a false construction upon the things spoken by Saul and Barnabas, thus perverting the truth. The efforts of Elymas were only bringing confusion to the mind of the proconsul. This must be stopped; a rebuke is given by Saul. The reason for such a severe rebuke can be observed in the fact that the person re-buked was altogether worthy of such since he was sinning against his own conscience. The purpose was to save Sergius Paulus from the condemnation of error. The punishment was given to lend mean-ing and power to the rebuke. It is described in such great detail that we are prone to think that it is the statement of an eye witness. The result sought was secured. "Then the proconsul, when he saw what was done, believed, being astonished at the teaching of the Lord."

We should not leave our comment of this work in Paphos with-out a word about the change of Saul's name. There seem to be two general positions on this matter: (1) First, that "Saul" was the Hebrew name used up to this time; now since the apostle is to pass into the districts of the Gentiles the use of his Roman name "Paul" becomes prominent. This is only a theory which is based up-on cases of Jews who did something similar to this. It cannot be denied that "Saul" is Hebrew and "Paul" is Roman. But it must also be

423. How did Elymas oppose the work of Barnabas and Saul?
424. What change of leadership took place in Paphos? Why do you imagine this was so?
425. Give the four attributes of Bar-Jesus given by Paul in his rebuke.
426. What is meant by "perverting the right ways of the Lord?"
427. What twofold reason do we have for the severity of the rebuke?
428. Why was the rebuke accompanied by punishment?
429. Give the two ideas proposed for the change of Saul's name.

said that it cannot be demonstrated that Saul had borne the name of "Paul" prior to this incident. (2) The other thought is that the occurance of the preaching before Sergius Paulus, attended as it was with its good results, gave to Saul the name of the proconsul Sergius Paulus. The change of his name is associated with this event and it is entirely possible that such did take place since many men have been similarly nicknamed by some incident of their lives. This, however, is purely conjectural.

5. IN PERGA. 13:13.

13 Now Paul and his company set sail from Paphos, and came to Perga in Pamphylia: and John departed from them and returned to Jerusalem.

13 Paul now steps into the lead in the cause of Christ. When Paphos was entered Luke stated: "and when **they** had gone through the whole island unto Paphos" . . . now upon leaving the city the historian says "Now **Paul and his company** set sail from Paphos . . ." A great change had taken place. God had been leading Paul to this very moment. He had waited and worked patiently until God prompted him to take this position.

The town of Perga is located some few miles up from the coast of Asia Minor in the province of Pamphylia. From this place we find John Mark leaving. He sailed from here back to his home in Jerusalem. This incident displeased Paul intensely and formed the basis for a disagreement between him and Barnabas at a later time. (15:37-40). Why John Mark left is a subject of quite some discussion. The ideas vary from homesickness to divine unction. It does seem that since Paul says: "He would not go with us to **the work**" that the reason lay in some objection to the work to be done. Whether it was a faint heart in consideration of the trials ahead we have no way of knowing, but we are disposed to this view. We must not leave the work of Mark here for he was later accepted back into the favor of Paul as a man to be received and heeded. (Col. 4:10; II Tim. 4:11). He also labored in the gospel with Barnabas (15:40) and wrote our second gospel which bears his name.

6. AT ANTIOCH OF PISIDIA. 13:14-52.

a. In the synagogue, the first sermon of Paul. 1.

14 But they, passing through from Perga, came to Antioch of Pisidia; and they went into the synagogue on the sabbath day, and sat down.

430. What great change is noted in the description of Luke relative to the approach and leaving of Paphos?
431. Tell three facts concerning the departure of John Mark from Perga.
432. Why do you think he left?

15 And after the reading of the law and the prophets
the rulers of the synagogue sent unto them, saying,
Brethren, if ye have any word of exhortation for the
people, say on.

16 And Paul stood up, and beckoning with the hand said,
Men of Israel, and ye that fear God, hearken:

17 The God of this people Israel chose our fathers, and
exalted the people when they sojourned in the land of
Egypt, and with a high arm led he them forth out of
it.

18 And for about the time of forty years as a nursing-father
bare he them in the wilderness.

19 And when he had destroyed seven nations in the land
of Canaan, he gave them their land for an inheritance,
for about four hundred and fifty years:

20 and after these things he gave them judges until Samuel the prophet.

21 And afterward they asked for a king: and God gave
unto them Saul the son of Kish, a man of the tribe of
Benjamin, for the space of forty years.

22 And when he had removed him, he raised up David
to be their king; to whom also he bare witness and said,
I have found David the son of Jesse, a man after my
heart, who shall do all my will.

23 Of this man's seed hath God according to promise
brought unto Israel a Saviour, Jesus;

24 when John had first preached before his coming the
baptism of repentance to all the people of Israel.

25 And as John was fulfilling his course, he said, What
suppose ye that I am? I am not he. But behold, there
cometh one after me the shoes of whose feet I am
not worthy to unloose.

26 Brethren, children of the stock of Abraham, and those
among you that fear God, to us is the word of this salvation sent forth.

27 For they that dwell in Jerusalem, and their rulers, because they knew him not, nor the voices of the prophets
which are read every sabbath, fulfilled them by con-
demning him.

28 And though they found no cause of death in him, yet
asked they of Pilate that he should be slain.

29 And when they had fulfilled all things that were written of him, they took him down from the tree, and
laid him in a tomb.

30 But God raised him from the dead:

31 and he was seen for many days of them that came up

with him from Galilee to Jerusalem, who are now his
witnesses unto the people.

32 And we bring you good tidings of the promise made unto the fathers,

33 that God hath fulfilled the same unto our children,
in that he raised up Jesus; as also it is written in the
second psalm, Thou art my Son, this day have I begotten thee.

34 And as concerning that he raised him up from the
dead, now no more to return to corruption, he hath
spoken on this wise, I will give you the holy and sure
blessings of David.

35 Because he saith also in another psalm, Thou wilt
not give thy Holy One to see corruption.

36 For David, after he had in his own generation served
the counsel of God, fell asleep, and was laid unto his
fathers, and saw corruption:

37 but he whom God raised up saw no corruption.

38 Be it known unto you therefore, brethren, that through
this man is proclaimed unto you remission of sins:

39 and by him every one that believeth is justified from
all things, from which ye could not be justified by the
law of Moses.

40 Beware therefore, lest that come upon you which is
spoken in the prophets:

41 Behold, ye despisers, and wonder, and perish;
For I work a work in your days,
A work which ye shall in no wise believe, if one de-
clare it unto you.

One could hardly imagine a more brief statement of fact than that
given to describe the long arduous journey from Perga to Antioch
of Pisidia. (A carefully detailed description of this rough terrain is
given by Conybeare and Howson in their book on the "Life and
Epistles of the Apostle Paul.") The distance traveled was about 120
miles.

The synagogues of various cities offered the starting place for
the preaching of the gospel. The Word of God was to be taken to "the
Jew first" and this was the place where devout Jews could be found;
such persons would give careful consideration to the things spoken.
It is then natural to find here recorded that on the Sabbath day
Paul and Barnabas found seats in the synagogue of Antioch.

433. Tell in a brief way of the country traversed from Perga to Antioch of
Pisidia (read Conybeare and Howson).

434. How far is it from Perga to Antioch?

435. Why was the gospel to be taken "to the Jew first?" Why would the
synagogue be an especially good place to carry out this commission?

The order of the synagogue service is given in informal detail in verse 15a. It was customary for the law and the prophets or the psalms to be read; following this the application of the verses was to be given. It appears upon this occasion that previous arrangements had been made for Paul and Barnabas to give "the word of exhortation." The rulers of the synagogue sent word to Barnabas and Paul that if they had any word of exhortation, now was the time to speak.

It was customary to ask visiting Jews to address the people, since they would not only give instruction but would possibly have some news of the conditions of Israel in general. This would have been especially true in this circumstance since Paul and Barnabas had but recently returned from the Holy City. But most of all, these two servants of Christ were anxious to declare the message of salvation. Paul immediately responded to the situation and arose to speak. The apostle had a gesture which he often used to attract the attention of those to whom he spoke; he employed this gesture here as he arose to address the synagogue. Paul preached to those of Antioch in Pisidia about:

Jesus of Nazareth as the Christ of God.

Paul used the same method in demonstrating this fact as did Stephen, Peter, Philip; proof from the Old Testament Scriptures. His introduction was very similar to the one used by Stephen.

Introduction: 16-22.

1. Paul calls for the attention of both the Jews, "Men of Israel," and the proselytes, "ye that fear God." 16b.
2. The power of Israel's God as shown in the deliverance from Egyptian bondage. 17.
3. God's love for Israel in the wilderness. 18.
4. The God of Israel fights for His people. Compare Deut. 7:1 for a list of the seven nations conquered from the departure out of Egypt to the reign of David, the whole time in which God was giving them full possession of the land. 19.
5. Judges given until Samuel the prophet. 20.
6. The request for a king granted in Saul, son of Kish, who ruled for forty years. 21.
7. Saul removed to make room for David, the man after the heart

436. What is the order of the synagogue service?
437. What arrangements were made between Paul and Barnabas and the rulers of the synagogue?
438. Why would the Jews of Antioch be especially anxious to hear from Paul and Barnabas?
439. What was the theme of Paul's Message? How did he develop it?
440. To whose introduction is the one used by Paul similar?
441. What two classes of people were spoken to by Paul?

of God. 22. The statement made concerning David is a combination of I Sam. 13:14 and Psa. 89:20.

This introduction was given to attract attention and interest as well as to create a favorable atmosphere for the theme to follow. Those of Antioch now knew that Paul was well acquainted with the history of Israel; to this history they had listened with great pride and interest; they intently followed the narrative.

Proposition: Some reasons why we can know that Jesus of Nazareth is the Christ or Israel's Saviour.

The thought of the proposition is presented in verse twenty-three. A beautiful transition is made from David to Christ. Paul knew when he started his message that when he arrived in his message to king David he would then tell of "David's seed." This would bring him to the theme of his discourse.

I. The testimony of John the Baptist and the prophets. 24-29.
    1. John's testimony. 24-26.
       a. No doubt John was well known among these Jews and hence the witness of John would carry real weight with those that heard. 24, 25.
       b. A word of exhortation is given to receive the evident fulfillment of the promise to Abraham. 26.
    2. Testimony of the prophets. 27-29.
       The trial, death and burial of Jesus were all in fulfillment of that which had been written.
II. The testimony of the resurrection. 30-37.
    1. God raised Him from the dead and allowed Him to be seen for many days by His disciples. 30, 31.
    2. This was all done in fulfillment of prophecy respecting the blessings promised to David. 32-37.

The conclusion. 38-41.
    1. Through this One is found remission of sins. 38.
    2. Thus it could be said that there was found in Christ that which never could be found in the law, i.e. "justification." 39.
    3. The warning. 40, 41.
       Evidently the reception of the message was such that Paul saw they were in danger of stubbornly resisting the truth—

442. What two men form the extremities of Paul's introduction?
443. What is the proposition of Paul's message?
444. Show how the transition is made from the history of Israel to Jesus as the Christ.
445. What two reasons are presented in verses 24-29 for accepting Jesus as the Messiah?
446. Why would the testimony of John the Baptist be of any value?
447. How does verse 26 fit into the outline?

he quotes an appropriate prophetic word on this point. He evidently did not deem it wise to call for a decision under such a circumstance.

b. The desire to hear more the next sabbath. 42.

42 And as they went out, they besought that these words might be spoken to them the next sabbath.

42 There were some who refused the message of eternal life but there were more who were interested. They did not fully understand but there was something in the word spoken that caused them to want to hear more. It would be seven days until the next gathering of the people. Requests were heard on every side that this same message might be repeated the next Sabbath.

c. The interest of the Jews and devout proselytes. 43.

43 Now when the synagogue broke up, many of the Jews and of the devout proselytes followed Paul and Barnabas; who, speaking to them, urged them to continue in the grace of God.

43 Luke tells us in specific description of the actions of those in Antioch. As Paul and Barnabas came out of the synagogue a crowd of interested Jews and devout Gentiles followed them; these persons were doubtlessly asking questions and listening attentively to the words of Paul and Barnabas. An unusual word is given concerning those who thus manifested their concern over the message of the truth. They were said to be "in the grace of God" (43b). It is not to be concluded that they were possessors of salvation for the context plainly suggests otherwise. They were, however, in the generic sense under or in the grace of God; Jehovah was well pleased with their interest and at the same time they were the recipients of the message of redemption. If they would continue in their interest, prompted as it was by the gracious message of the gospel, they would most certainly become children of God.

d. Great gathering the next sabbath. Contradiction of the Jews. 44, 45.

44 And the next sabbath almost the whole city was gathered together to hear the word of God.

45 But when the Jews saw the multitudes, they were filled with jealousy, and contradicted the things which were spoken by Paul, and blasphemed.

44 What were the two servants of the Lord doing in the days from one sabbath to the next? While Paul was in Ephesus he spoke to

448. Of what did the prophets testify concerning the Christ?
449. What reasoning is given in verses 30-37?
450. What was the real objection of the ruling Jews?

the brethren "night and day with tears." This was done not only publicly but "from house to house." (20:18-21). We are persuaded that his conduct was no different here in Antioch.

When the next sabbath came, such an interest had been stirred up concerning this new message that almost the whole city gathered in and around the synagogue to listen to these two strangers who were so possessed by their message.

45 It was all right with the ruling Jews for these men to bring a new doctrine into their town just so long as it did not hinder their influence or hold on the people. But as these Jews saw more and more people crowding into the synagogue, and then, when they saw them begin to fill the street around the synagogue, fear and jealousy entered their hearts. By the time Paul and Barnabas were ready to speak, these Jews were "filled with jealousy." There was only one way to oppose the efforts of these men. The rulers were respected by the people; hence, if they contradicted the things spoken, even if the contradictions would not stand inspection, they would be heeded. The message was too new. It could not be accepted without some degree of skepticism. And after all, had not these Jews always been their teachers? The contradictions were backed up with equally baseless railings. This procedure was carried out by the rulers of the Jews and not without some measure of success.

e. Turn to the Gentiles with good results. 46-48.

46 And Paul and Barnabas spake out boldly, and said, It was necessary that the word of God should first be spoken to you. Seeing ye thrust it from you, and judge yourselves unworthy of eternal life, lo, we turn to the Gentiles.

47 For so hath the Lord commanded us, saying,
I have set thee for a light of the Gentiles,
That thou shouldest be for salvation unto the uttermost
most part of the earth.

48 And as the Gentiles heard this, they were glad, and glorified the word of God: and as many as were ordained to eternal life believed.

46 "Where sin abounded, grace did abound more exceedingly." God's grace is always sufficient for every accusation of the great "accuser of our brethren." On this occasion the answer was a bold statement by both of the messengers of the results forthcoming from such actions. The Jews had been addressed throughout the message. Now they are told in no uncertain words that it was a privilege that they were abusing. God had decreed that the Jews were to be the first to hear the glad tidings but now if they were going to thus

451. Why would the contradictions of these men be heeded above the words of Paul and Barnabas?

treat it they would be in reality thrusting from themselves the Word of God and judging themselves unworthy of eternal life. There was only one alternative if the Jews thus refused the message. It yet must be heard, "lo, we turn to the Gentiles."

47 Paul and Barnabas could say now that the true meaning of Isaiah's words were known to them and were here being fulfilled by the refusal of the gospel by the Jews:

"I have set thee for a light of the Gentiles, that thou shouldest be for salvation unto the uttermost part of the earth."

The mere words were known but their full impact and application was unknown until it now became apparent that they were going to be fulfilled by the very force of the circumstances.

The quotation from the prophet was received with great joy by the Gentiles. From the hearts of these Gentiles there arose praise and adoration to God for the hope thus given in His word.

48 The latter portion of verse forty-eight has been the source of many a controversy: "As many as were ordained to eternal life believed." What is its meaning? We quote from D. D. Wheden on pages 164-165 of his **Commentary On Acts** as a clear concise statement of the thought here involved:

"Ordained to eternal life—Should be rendered, disposed to eternal life. It plainly refers to the eager predisposition just above mentioned in the heart of many of these Gentiles on learning that old prophecy proclaims a Messiah for them. As many as were so inclined to the eternal life now offered committed themselves by faith to the blessed Jesus.

Rarely has a text been so violently wrenched from its connections with the context, and strained beyond its meaning for a purpose, than has been this clause in support of the doctrine of predestination. There is not the least plausibility in the notion that Luke in this simple history is referring to any eternal decree predestinating these men to eternal life. The word here rendered ordained usually signifies placed, positioned, disposed. It may refer to the material or to the mental position. It is a verb in the passive form, a form which frequently possesses a reciprocal active meaning; that is, it frequently signifies an action performed by one's self upon one's self. Thus, in Romans 9:22, the vessels of wrath fitted to destruction are carefully affirmed, even by predestinarians, to be fitted by themselves. Indeed, the very Greek word here rendered ordained is frequently used, compounded with a preposition, in the New Testament itself, in the passive form with a reciprocal meaning. Thus, Rom. 13:1, Be

452. How did these men judge themselves unworthy of eternal life?
453. What were the words of the prophet that were fulfilled on this occasion?
454. What contrast is found here?
455. What is a better word than "ordained" in verse 48?
456. Why the straining and wrenching of this text?

subject unto the higher powers, is literally, place yourselves under the higher powers. So, also Rom. 13:7; I Cor. 16:16; James 4:7, and many other texts. The meaning we give is required by the antithesis between the Jews in verse forty-six and these Gentiles. The former were indisposed to eternal life and so believed not; these were predisposed to eternal life, and so believed. The permanent faith of the soul was consequently upon the predisposition of the heart and the predetermination of the will."

f. The spread of the word. 49.

49 And the word of the Lord was spread abroad through- out all the region.

49 The apostle Paul was never content to preach the word only in the city visited but the whole region or province in which the city was situated was to hear the word also, and so it was here in Pisidia, as it will be in Asia and other places "the word of the Lord spread abroad throughout the region."

g. The persecution and leaving the city. 50, 51.

50 But the Jews urged on the devout women of honorable estate, and the chief men of the city, and stirred up a persecution against Paul and Barnabas, and cast them out of their borders.

51 But they shook off the dust of their feet against them, and came unto Iconium.

50 The rulers of the synagogue were men of real authority in all matters religious; however false or baseless their objections might be it seems they were heeded. The persons approached by the Jews of Antioch were the "honorable women" of the synagogue. Whether these women were Jews or only devout proselytes we are not told. They were probably the wives of the chief men of the city and thus influenced their husbands to promote a general persecution that would lead to the casting out of Paul and Barnabas.

51 The shaking of the dust from their feet was not an impetuous act of anger but rather in fulfillment of Jesus' words (Matt. 10:14) as a judgment of God against these persons. The eternal life offered through the gospel had been refused. Here now was the climax of their refusal.

457. Upon what is the permanent faith of the soul dependent?
458. How could it be said that "the word of the Lord spread abroad through- out the region?"
459. Who were the "honorable women?" Why approach them in this man- ner?
460. Show the significance of the shaking the dust off their feet.

h. The joy of the disciples amid tribulation. 52.
52 And the disciples were filled with joy and with the
Holy Spirit.

52 How unlike the Christians of today were these new converts of
Pisidia. When the preacher leaves a field today a general "let down"
passes throughout the congregation; and especially would this be so
if there were no prospect of securing another man to take the place
vacated. How different in the church at Antioch. In spite of all
the hard conditions "the disciples were filled with joy and with the
Holy Spirit." There is only one answer to this remarkable situation—
the preaching and teaching of Paul accompanied by the willingness
on the part of those that heard produced these results.

7. AT ICONIUM. 14:1—6a.

1 And it came to pass in Iconium that they entered together into the synagogue of the Jews, and so spake that
a great multitude both of Jews and of Greeks believed.
2 But the Jews that were disobedient stirred up the souls
of the Gentiles, and made them evil affected against the
brethren.
3 Long time therefore they tarried there speaking boldly
in the Lord, who bare witness unto the word of his
grace,
granting signs and wonders to be done by their hands.
4 But the multitude of the city was divided; and part
held with the Jews, and part with the apostles.
5 And when there was made an onset both of the Gentiles
and of the Jews with their rulers, to treat them shamefully and to stone them,
6 they became aware of it, and fled unto the cities of

1-3 Together Paul and Barnabas journeyed to the town of Iconium
and entered the synagogue. The attendance at such services was
for but one purpose, i.e. to preach Jesus as the Christ. There is an
enlightening comment given regarding the preaching of these men
here in Iconium. We all know that some preaching is not the kind
that reaches the hearts of men. Luke states that Paul and Barnabas
"so spake" that a great multitude of both Jews and Greeks believed.
We would do well to follow closely the method and message of the
apostles that we, too, might "so speak" as to reach the hearts of
those to whom we preach.

While some among the Jews opened their minds and obeyed the

461. In what way were the converts of Antioch unlike the Christians of today? What reason can be given?
462. What is meant by being "filled with the Holy Spirit?"
463. What significant word is given regarding the preaching of Paul and
Barnabas in Iconium?

truth, there were others who refused the message, being disobedient not only to the truth but to their own conscience as well.

The Gentiles were only the guests of the Jews as they attended the synagogue services. The Gentiles in this place as in many others saw something in the religion of the Jews that attracted their interest. But since they were ignorant of this new religion the words of the members of this belief would quite naturally be accepted as authoritative. Hence, when the rulers of the synagogue began to speak out against the doctrines of these two strangers their words were heeded by a good share of the uncircumcised. Some of the Gentiles were actually antagonistic toward the apostles as well as being opposed to those among their own group who had embraced this new belief.

Unless there was some real threat of bodily harm in the persecution, Paul could see no reason for leaving a place of labor. So, in spite of the active opposition of the jealous Jews there rang forth from the synagogue (and doubtless from house to house) the news that this Jesus of Nazareth was the Christ.

The Lord honored and confirmed their message with signs and wonders. It is of real interest to note that each time miracles are mentioned they are associated with the hands of either the apostles or those upon whom the apostles had laid their hands. Never do we hear the Christians of these towns working miracles "through their great faith."

4-6a The whole city of Iconium was shaken by the message of grace. Unfortunately however, it was divided about equally for and against the apostles. This fact would only encourage the apostles to draw the more closely to their source of power; but when knowledge of a plot to stone them reached their ears, and when they perceived that not only the envious Jews but also the Gentiles and rulers of the city were involved, they were forced to make a hasty retreat. The province of Lycaonia is the next to be entered in the preaching of the Word.

8. IN LYSTRA. 14:6b-20.
    a. General statement. 6b, 7.
        6b unto the cities of Lycaonia, Lystra and Derbe, and the region round about:
        7 and there they preached the gospel.

6b-7 In verses 6b-7 we have a general statement of the preaching of the gospel in the towns of Lycaonia, Lystra and Derbe. The suggestion is also made in 6b that the persons living near these cities heard the word from these faithful evangelists.

464. How could the Jews stir up the Gentiles so readily?
465. Why the signs and wonders? How performed?
466. Why leave Iconium?
467. What suggestion of extension is made in 6b?

b. The healing of the lame man. 8-10.

> 8 And at Lystra there sat a certain man, impotent in his feet, a cripple from his mother's womb, who never had walked.
> 9 The same heard Paul speaking: who, fastening his eyes upon him, and seeing that he had faith to be made whole,
> 10 said with a loud voice, Stand upright on thy feet. And he leaped up and walked.

8-10 In the Greco-Roman town of Lystra there apparently was no synagogue, for the account of the preaching suggests that Paul proclaimed the Word in the streets of the town. To be more exact as to the location of the preaching, we might say that the healing of the cripple seems to have occurred close to the city gates (cf. verse 13) so that possibly the city gates afforded a place for the gathering of the populace.

It so happened that on one occasion of preaching a cripple was found in the audience who was destined to be the object of God's power. As he listened he came to have a great faith in what was being said. We might well ask, "What was being said?" We could reply from Paul's words to the man that he must have been listening to a message that created hope and faith in the possibility of his being "made whole." So Paul, in his preaching of Jesus must have referred to some of the miracles that God had performed by the apostles' hands on other similar occasions. Then it would seem, to make such a recital tangible, he looked over the crowd for a suitable candidate to further confirm his word. Upon seeing this impotent man sitting in rapt attention, he fastened his eyes upon him and noticing that he had faith to be made whole, said with a loud voice, "Stand upright on thy feet." Now this would be no small task for the man had never walked from the day of his birth. Behold the power of God: "He leaped up and walked." How like the record in the third chapter of this book.

c. The multitudes worship them as gods. 11-13.

> 11 And when the multitude saw what Paul had done, they lifted up their voice, saying in the speech of Lycaonia, The gods are come down to us in the likeness of men.
> 12 And they called Barnabas, Jupiter; and Paul, Mercury, because he was the chief speaker.
> 13 And the priest of Jupiter whose temple was before the

468. What difference is found in the preaching at Lystra and any other town?
469. What caused the crippled man to have any hope of being made "whole?"
470. Show the wonderful power of God in the healing of the lame man.

city, brought oxen and garlands unto the gates, and would have done sacrifice with the multitudes.

11-13 But how different was the response received than what was expected. Paul doubtless hoped that this multitude would react like the one at the Gate Beautiful; that this miracle performed would cause them to stand in awe and silence and give him a chance to bring a message concerning the God who wrought this act. But these were not "devout Jews," but superstitious Gentiles. The persons of this province had been taught the Greek language. This was probably the language used by Paul in speaking to them. But these Gentiles were likewise earnest devotees of the Greek gods. As the lame man leaped to his feet there swept across the multitudes, like a wave on the surface of a lake, a low murmuring of astonishment, but the wave returned toward the speaker in a swelling babel of voices. None of this could be understood by Paul for they spoke in their native tongue—"the speech of Lycaonia." These simple, rude folk must have an immediate explanation for this phenomenon. What is it? It could not be of man and yet these appeared to be men before them. The conclusion was that it was from the gods, but which gods? The only gods they knew were those of the Greeks, hence they began to fancy that they could see in the countenances of these two strangers a resemblance to two of these deities. "Barnabas, as more dignified and reposeful in mien, suggested Zeus, the king of the gods; while Paul, as the 'chief speaker' was Hermes, the messenger of the gods."

The word of this strange conclusion was taken to the priest of the temple of Zeus or Jupiter, (or possibly he was among those who listened). The priest saw but one thing to do and that was to make preparations for a sacrifice to these deities in the guise of men. This servant of Jupiter soon had garlands and oxen ready. The oxen were led toward the city gates where Paul and Barnabas were doubtless the center of attraction. Since the expressions of worship to Paul and Barnabas were made in the native tongue of the Lycaonians, the apostles could not know in its entirety just what was transpiring.

d. The objection of Paul and Barnabas. 14-18.

14 But when the apostles, Barnabas and Paul, heard of it, they rent their garments, and sprang forth among the multitude, crying out

15 and saying, Sirs, why do ye these things? We also are men of like passions with you, and bring you good tidings, that ye should turn from these vain things unto

471. What was unexpected about the response of these people? Why?
472. Explain in your own words the reaction of these folks to the miracle?
473. Why call them Jupiter and Mercury?
474. Why didn't Paul and Barnabas know immediately what was happening?

a living God, who made the heaven and the earth and the
sea, and all that in them is:

16 who in the generations gone by suffered all the nations
to walk in their own ways.

17 And yet he left not himself without witness, in that he
did good and gave you from heaven rains and fruitful
seasons, filling your hearts with food and gladness.

18 And with these sayings scarce restrained they the multitudes from doing sacrifice unto them.

14-18 But when they finally did understand they immediately tore
their garments in their deep concern over the matter, and even as
they thus rent their garments they sprang forth or rushed into the
midst of the multitude until they could approach the priest and his
attendants and cry out: "Sirs, why do ye these things?" Paul then
took advantage of the situation not only to dispel their false conception but also to deliver a message from the true God.

The first words of Paul's message were given to draw attention
away from him and Barnabas that it might be directed toward the
true object of worship. To tell these misguided folk that the ones
whom they worshiped as deities were only men would have been useless unless it came from the men themselves.

The apostle spoke to these men of the true purpose for being
among them. It was not to be worshiped, but to bring "good tidings."
The first thought of these "good tidings" was that men should turn
from the worship of such vain speculations as these mythical Greek
gods. In turning they were not asked to refuse these gods only because they were false, but that they might turn to the worship of
the true God, the one and "living God," who made the heaven and
the earth and the sea, and all that in them is. This attribute of
Jehovah would show Him superior to any and all other gods, for
none of them claimed this distinction. The words of verse sixteen
are especially applicable to those present for Paul is saying in
essence: "In times past, i.e. before Christ came, Jehovah permitted
all the nations to continue in their course of life, but now since
Christ has come (whom Paul had just preached) you are to heed
Him." Paul was saying: "Previous to this time you might have
acted in the fashion you are now acting and God would have suffered you, but it is now inexcusable." Paul pointed out that although
the Lord permitted their course of life, it was not because He did not
leave a witness of His "everlasting power and divinity" (cf. Rom.
1:20). Paul calls attention to the fields of the Lycaonian peasants
that had brought forth for many years a plentiful harvest. Paul is

475. How did Paul utilize the situation to an advantage?
476. What was the purpose of Paul's first words?
477. What was the twofold purpose in turning from the Greek gods?
478. Explain verse 16.

saying that they should have been caused to stop and consider this witness to the one who controlled such activity. When they rejoiced at the good crop, or when they profited thereby, they should have looked beyond these mere physical evidences back to the one great origin of such things.

Even with these plain words of repudiation and explanation the hands of the priests and the hearts of the mob were scarce restrained from carrying out their intention.

e. Paul stoned. He is raised up. 19, 20a.

19 But there came Jews thither from Antioch and Iconium: and having persuaded the multitudes, they stoned Paul, and dragged him out of the city, supposing that he was dead.

20a But as the disciples stood round about him, he rose up, and entered into the city:

19-20a How fickle is public opinion! The same mob that was ready to worship Paul and Barnabas as gods one day was ready the next day, or a few days later, to cast stones at them as the representatives of the evil one.

The Jews from Antioch and Iconium stirred up the multitude; they doubtless persuaded these simple folk that Paul and Barnabas were in league with Satan. The mob had been somewhat embarrassed with the thwarting of the original plan and now they had a reasonable excuse to give vent to their feelings on these who would not accept their worship. The stoning that took place was probably led by the men of Lystra for had the Jews led the assault they would have been more deadly in their effort. Paul was knocked down and stunned. He was so broken and bruised of body that they took him to be dead. Someone roughly took hold of the crumpled form of the apostle and dragged him outside the city gates, there to lie in full view of the temple in which he could have been heralded as a god.

Timothy, Eunice, his mother, and Lois, his grandmother, were probably among those disciples who stood weeping as they looked sadly upon the bruised and broken body of the one who had brought them the Word of life. To the amazement of all Paul arose from this ordeal (it would seem with the assistance of God.) He slow-

479. What was the witness Jehovah had in Lystra?

480. What thought do you suppose the Jews used in stirring up these people?

481. In what way was the stoning an act of vengeance on the part of those of Lycaonia?

482. Who led them in the stoning? How do you know?

483. Show in the stoning the wonderful testimony of the apostle's sincerity.

484. Who were probably among the weeping disciples—where did they stay overnight?

ly rose to his feet and with the aid of those around him returned to
the city, possibly into the home of Timothy.

9. AT DERBE. 14:20b, 21a.

20b and on the morrow he went forth with Barnabas to
    Derbe.

21a And when they had preached the gospel to that city,
    and had made many disciples,

20b-21a The next day, or "on the morrow," we are told, he was
able to set out with Barnabas for the town of Derbe, between thirty
and forty miles away. It lay on the southeast among the foothills
of Tarsus. But the memory of this scene was ineffaceable. It was
one of the many "perils from his own countrymen and from the
heathen," one of his being "in death oft," which sank deepest into his mind. "Once," says he, "I was stoned." Henceforth, in
remembrance of his sufferings, he regarded himself as "always bearing about in the body the putting to death of Jesus" and could
tell the Galatians, in whose province he had thus suffered, "Let
no man trouble me for I bear in my body the marks of the Lord
Jesus," the marks of the stones showered on him at Lystra, and
the scourgings with great whips or thick rods, lacerating the flesh to
the bone, which He had endured no fewer than eight times. (II Cor.
11:23-28; 4:10; Gal. 6:17.)

"A long bare slope, with bushes and loose stones scattered over it,
and a few ruined buildings of comparatively modern date, lead up
to a broad low mound which crowns it, and under this, in all prob-
ability, lie, the remains of the Derbe of Paul. It was the frontier city
of the Roman province, towards, the southeast, and, as such, was
honored by a connection with the name of Claudius, as Claudio-
Derbe. 'Many disciples' had joined the new faith in Derbe and thus
another church of former heathen had been formed." (Geikie **Hours
With The Bible,** Vol. II, pages 286-289).

10. LYSTRA, 11. ICONIUM, 12. ANTIOCH. 14:21b-23.

21b they returned to Lystra, and to Iconium, and to An-
    tioch,

22 confirming the souls of the disciples, exhorting them to
    continue in the faith, and that through many tribula-
    tions we must enter into the kingdom of God.

23 And when they had appointed for them elders in every
    church, and had prayed with fasting, they commended
    them to the Lord, on whom they had believed.

21b-23 It is just as important to confirm the saints as it is to convert the sinners. It must have been with this thought in mind that

485. Where does Paul mention the stoning in his epistles?
486. Describe the site of Derbe—what response to the gospel?

Paul and Barnabas retraced their steps to revisit these brethren.

By consulting the map you can notice that when Paul and Barnabas arrived in Derbe they were not a great distance from Paul's home town of Tarsus. What a temptation it must have been to tarry here in Derbe where no persecution hindered until such a time as the weather permitted travel through the mountain passes and then to journey homeward through Tarsus of Cilicia. But there was a higher call than that of self-preservation and security. It was the call of the need of the children they had begotten in the gospel. To these persons Paul and Barnabas had not imparted the word only but their very selves. How readily is the truth received when its application is seen in the lives of those who speak it. So it was that when Paul and Barnabas urged these brethren to remain faithful and to remember that "through many tribulations we must enter into the kingdom of Heaven," those to whom the words were spoken could see their literal fulfillment in the lives of those who spoke.

The thought of **appointing** for them elders in every city carries the idea of being chosen by vote. Lest we obtain from this thought the impression that there was here carried out a "church election" note this quotation from Cunningham Geikie:

"Yet it would be a great mistake to imagine that because the election of officers rested with the congregations, their nominations for election was unrestrictedly left to them. Such an arrangement would at any time invite rivalries, disputes, and divisions while, in such assemblies as the earliest 'churches' there would, at least in the case of those gathered from the 'Gentiles,' be very little security for the right persons being selected. Where the voters were of such a class that Paul could decribe them, to themselves, as 'foolish,' 'weak,' 'base,' 'despised,' 'beneath notice,' or, in other words, the very humblest . . . . and that not only in circumstances or position, but even in morals and necessarily in corresponding ignorance—it would have been contrary to every dictate of prudence to leave them without guidance. The fitting persons for office would, therefore, we may assume, be indicated by the apostles or by the rulers whom they had accepted and set apart." (Pages 291-292.)

13. **THROUGH THE PROVINCES OF PISIDIA AND PAM-PHYLIA.** 14:24.

24 And they passed through Pisidia, and came to Pamphylia.

487. What is meant by points 10-11-12?

488. What temptation must have presented itself to Paul when he arrived in Derbe?

489. Why was the truth so readily received and followed by the disciples of these cities?

490. What is the "kingdom of heaven" spoken of here?

491. Explain the procedure of the appointing elders in these cities?

24 Following the confirming of the saints in Antioch of Pisidia and appointing elders for the churches, they passed again over the 120 to 140 miles of rough terrain that lay between Antioch and Perga.

14. **AT PERGA.** 14:25a.

25 And when they had spoken the word in Perga,

25a The mountain passes would not be open until the middle of May, so it must have been about this time that Paul and Barnabas "bade their last farewells to the brethren at the Pisidian Antioch and made their way down to Perga where they seemed to have stayed some time preaching the Word as they had been unable to do so when there before. It has been suggested that upon the first visit to Perga the missionaries arrived in the middle of the summer and that it was the habit of the people of the town to leave the now sultry plains of Perga for the cooler climate of the mountains back of the city. Hence there was not opportunity to preach on the first visit.

15. **AT ATTALIA.** 14:25b.

25b they went down to Attalia;

25b "Then, perhaps in July, they went to Attalia and sailed out of its small harbour, round which the streets now rise, one above the other, like the seats of a theatre, with a fringe of square towers surmounting the flat top of the hills—and then coasted along the land eastward, often in full view of the vast mountains, beyond which they had gathered to Christ, the first fruits of the Gentiles of Asia Minor, won with so much sufferings; and yet worth it all, as the earnest of the conversion of the great heathen world to the faith of the Cross" (ibid, page 293).

16. **IN ANTIOCH.** 14:26-28.

26 and thence they sailed to Antioch, from whence they had been committed to the grace of God for the work which they had fulfilled.

27 And when they were come, and had gathered the church together, they rehearsed all things that God had done with them, and that he had opened a door of faith unto the Gentiles.

28 And they tarried no little time with the disciples.

492. How far from Antioch to Perga?
493. What time of the year was it when the Apostles left Antioch?
493. Why not preach in Perga on the first visit?
495. What was the physical appearance of Attalia?
496. Explain the touching situation that must have faced the missionaries as they sailed homeward.

26-28 How many times had the minds of those in Antioch turned to the labors of those two whom they had sent forth to the work of preaching? How had they fared? Where had they labored? What success had the glorious glad tidings had in the far away places? All these questions and many more were answered as the church in Antioch assembled to hear the report of Paul and Barnabas. The news that God had opened a door for the preaching of the gospel among the Gentiles was received without question in this church since from the earliest history of the assembly the gospel had been "preached unto the Greeks also." Thus concludes the first missionary journey.

EXAMINATION OVER THE FIRST MISSIONARY JOURNEY
13:1—14:28

True or False

1. There were five leaders in the Jerusalem church.
2. The half brother of Herod the tetrarch was one of the leaders in the Antioch church.
3. The church in Antioch had a period of fasting before they fasted for the separating of Barnabas and Saul.
4. It was in the form of a surprise to Saul that God would call him to such a work.
5. The basis for our present day ordination is not found in the scripture.
6. The gospel was preached in the synagogue in Seleucia.
7. John Mark acted as an assistant to Saul and Barnabas.
8. There was a large synagogue in Salamis in which they preached the Word. This was the only place in which they preached.
9. It was fifty miles from Salamis to Paphos.
10. Bar-Jesus was a Jew.
11. Saul told Elymas that he would be blind for the rest of his life.
12. The Word of God was preached at Perga upon the first visit.
13. John Mark's home town was Antioch.
14. Both Paul and Barnabas spoke in Antioch of Pisidia.
15. Paul's message in Antioch was very similar to that of Stephen's in Jerusalem.

Identify These Thoughts

(Give just a sentence of explanation for each thought.)

1. ". . . and with a high arm led he them forth out of it."

497. Explain in your own words verses 26-28.

2. ". . . gave them their land for an inheritance, for about four hundred and fifty years."
3. "Thou art my Son. This day have I begotten thee."
4. ". . . everyone that believeth is justified from all things, from which ye could not be justified by the law of Moses."
5. "Beware therefore, lest that come upon you which is spoken in the prophets. Behold, ye despisers, and wonder, and perish."
6. ". . . urged them to continue in the grace of God."
7. "But when the Jews saw the multitudes, they were filled with jealousy."
8. "It was necessary that the word of God should first be spoken to you."
9. ". . . as many as were ordained to eternal life believed."
10. "But they shook off the dust of their feet against them."

Fill in the Blanks

1. "And it came to pass in Iconium that they entered together into the synagogue of the Jews, and _____ spake that a great multitude both of _____ and of _____ believed."
2. But the multitude of the city was divided; and part held with the _____ and part with the _____.
3. The gods are come down to us in the likeness of men. And they called Barnabas, _____ and Paul, _____ because he was the chief speaker.
4. But when the apostles, Barnabas and Paul, heard of it, they _____ their _____ and sprang forth among the multitude, crying out and saying, Sirs, why do ye these things? We also are men of like _____ with you. . . .
5. But there came Jews thither from _____ and _____; and having persuaded, the multitudes, they _____ Paul, and dragged him out of the city, supposing that he was dead.
6. . . . and on the morrow he went forth with Barnabas to Derbe. And when they had preached the gospel to that city and had made _____, they returned to Lystra.

Multiple Choice

1. Upon the return visit to the churches, Paul and Barnabas: 1) Preached and gave the Lord's Supper. 2) Preached and appointed elders. 3) Exhorted the brethren.
2. Pisidia and Pamphylia were: 1) Cities. 2) Villages. 3) Provinces.
3. Upon the second visit to Perga they 1) Passed through. 2) Preached and appointed elders. 3) Just preached.
4. Attalia was: 1) A seaport. 2) A town in the journey at which they preached. 3) A province.
5. When back in Antioch Paul and Barnabas had something to

say about the Gentiles; they said: 1) God gave them a great opportunity. 2) God had baptized them in the Holy Spirit also. 3) God had opened a door of faith unto them.

THE TROUBLES OVER CIRCUMCISION AND THE JERUSALEM COUNCIL
15:1-35

1. FALSE TEACHERS TROUBLE THE BELIEVERS. 1

1　And certain men came down from Judaea and taught the brethren, saying, Except ye be circumcised after the custom of Moses, ye cannot be saved.

1 It is very difficult for us to truly understand the vast importance of the law to the Jew. What would it mean to give up their allegiance to that divine injunction they had revered for so long? Only by thinking what it would mean to give up the most treasured of earthly law or government could we approximate the position of the Jew. In reading upon this subject I ran upon this very splendid statement by Cunningham Geikie:

"The religions of antiquity were, in all cases, intensely ritualistic. A sacrifice or a private function must, alike, be carried out in exact accordance with prescribed rules if it were to have a claim on the gods, but when everthing had been done as required, they were put under an obligation to answer favorably which they were bound to honor. Yet, in the sphere of ordinary life, nearly all races of men were free. They could eat and drink as they pleased, mix with their fellowmen, perform the common offices of daily existence, or of social intercourse, without interference from the priest. Among the Jews, however, as among their ancient fellow-countrymen in Mesopotamia—the Accadians, or as among the ancient Egyptians, with whom they had lived for centuries before the Exodus, not only every detail of religion, but every minute particular of ordinary life, was the subject of religious prescriptions, believed to be divine, and therefore to be obeyed, on peril of offending and even insulting the Higher Powers.

The Jew must bear on his person the mark of a holy observance, must perform endless cleansings of a more or less formal nature, must repeat, at prescribed times, each day, so many prescribed prayers, must eat and drink only prescribed supports and refreshments, prepared in prescribed modes, must submit from his cradle to his grave

498. How could we approximate the position of the Jew in his giving up the law of Moses?
499. How was the religion of the Jews like all religions of antiquity and yet different?

ANTIOCH OF SYRIA

Situated 300 miles northwest of Jerusalem, on the Orontes sixteen miles from its mouth, Antioch was founded by Seleucus Nicator about 300 B.C. It was the capital of Syria under the Seleucidae and also of the Roman province of Syria. In population and importance it was the third city in the Roman Empire, ranking next to Rome and Alexandria. Its principal street was lined from end to end with Colonnades. The city was called "Antioch the Beautiful" and "The Crown of the East". Its great trade drew to it many Jewish colonists, who enjoyed all the privileges of citizens. The city was notoriously immoral, and yet it is famous as the birthplace of Gentile Christianity. The people of Antioch are said to be noted for their low wit. (**Historical Geography of Bible Lands.** p. 82.)

to 'customs' and 'traditions' sacredly binding authority at every step of his daily life, this authority faced him. He must perform prescribed pilgrimages from any adopted country, however distant, to the national shrine at Jerusalem to satisfy what he conceived the demands of Jehovah.

Among the Western races, Paul had to discuss questions of doctrine, such as the resurrection and immortality, or the grounds of a soul's justification before God, and had to denounce gross sins and novel and equivocal innovations, of which he had to say, 'We have no such customs, neither the churches of God.' In Palestine and among the Jews everywhere, the burning question of the age, was the position of the uncircumcised converts to Christianity, toward circumcision. Could they be saved without becoming, at least to this length, Jews, or even without further observing the whole Jewish Ceremonial Law? Or would they be accepted by God though they lived without recognition of either?" (**Hours With The Bible,** pp. 317-318).

There were those in the church in Jerusalem who were not only persuaded that no Christian could be saved without being circumcised and keeping the Law of Moses but they felt it their divine responsibility to so teach others. Word had evidently come to these in Jerusalem of the results of the first missionary journey. Even as word of the conversion of the Gentiles in Antioch had come to them some years before. (cf. 11:22).

This time the ones who left Jerusalem to visit Antioch were not sent out by the apostles but took it upon themselves to represent them none the less. Upon entering Antioch they immediately began to throw the minds of the Christians there into utter confusion: teaching that "except ye be circumcised after the custom of Moses ye cannot be saved." Note that the mere teaching of circumcision as a religious rite was not the point of difficulty, but rather that it was being layed upon them as a test of fellowship. Paul practiced circumcision as a matter of expediency (cf. 16:1, 2) but when it came to binding it as a matter of salvation he would not allow it— "no, not for one hour."

Into the peaceful and happy atmosphere of the congregation in Antioch there was brought by these that came from Jerusalem the stench of strife and dissension. It would be natural that Paul and

500. Who were the Accadians? (Look it up in a Bible dictionary).
501. What was the difference in the questions and problems of those in the West and those in Palestine? What was the "Burning Issue" in Palestine?
502. What caused the Judaizers to leave Jerusalem and to come to Antioch to teach their doctrine?
503. If it were "not the mere teaching of circumcision as a religious rite" that constituted the difficulty what did?
504. Why could not Paul the apostle settle this difficulty in Antioch without going to Jerusalem?

Barnabas led in defending their position, but no definite conclusion could be reached. When there is not authority present that is recognized by both parties of a dispute then it becomes impossible to reach a satisfactory decision. This seemed to be the situation in Antioch.

2. PAUL AND BARNABAS SENT TO JERUSALEM. 2, 3.

2 And when Paul and Barnabas had no small dissension and questioning with them, the brethren appointed that Paul and Barnabas, and certain other of them, should go up to Jerusalem unto the apostles and elders about this question.

3 They therefore, being brought on their way by the church, passed through both Phoenicia and Samaria, declaring the conversion of the Gentiles: and they caused great joy unto all the brethren.

2, 3 Paul's mind was greatly troubled over this difficulty and well it might be for it was even as he said, a matter upon which rested the decision as whether he was "running or had run in vain." Either he was right in accepting the Gentiles in the way he had or these of the circumcision were right; there was no middle ground. There was only one thing to do and that was to go to the source of the trouble . . . this thought was strengthened, or possibly formed, by a vision which Paul had respecting such a visit (Gal. 2:1, 2).

It was decided that certain others should go along. Titus is the only one named. The Antioch church furnished the means whereby the journey could be made. The hearts of the travelers were made glad by the warm hospitality of the churches in Phoenicia and Samaria as well as the way in which they rejoiced over the conversion of the Gentiles.

3. THEIR RECEPTION IN JERUSALEM. 4, 5.

4 And when they were come to Jerusalem, they were received of the church and the apostles and the elders, and they rehearsed all things that God had done with them.

5 But there rose up certain of the sect of the Pharisees who believed, saying, It is needful to circumcise them, and to charge them to keep the law of Moses.

4, 5 Notice carefully the actions of the party upon their arrival in Jerusalem. First, the entire church assembled with the apostles and elders—the matter was laid before them all; doubtless Paul

505. Did Paul originate the idea of going to Jerusalem? If not, who did?
506. Why was this an extremely important visit? Who went with Paul? Who paid the transportation expenses?
507. What encouragement did they receive on the way?

and Barnabas rehearsed to the congregation what they had told the church in Antioch upon their return from the journeys. But it was not received in the same attitude. The fact that a good work had been done was admitted by all but the one cloud on the horizon that blotted out everything else to one group present was that all these Christians were admitted to the fellowship without circumcision. Those who were of the sect of the Pharisees arose and said as much. In the statement here the dissenters went to the full extent of their position and said not only to circumcise such but to command them to keep the Law of Moses. The case had been fully stated and both sides had been heard; the assembly was dismissed and the matter was then taken up by those who had the authority to decide.

4. THE ELDERS AND APOSTLES MEET TO SETTLE THE DISPUTE. 6-29

a. Peter's speech. 6-11.

6 And the apostles and the elders were gathered together to consider of this matter.

7 And when there had been much questioning, Peter rose up, and said unto them, Brethren, ye know that a good while ago God made choice among you, that by my mouth the Gentiles should hear the word of the gospel, and believe.

8 And God, who knoweth the heart, bare them witness, giving them the Holy Spirit, even as he did unto us;

9 and he made no distinction between us and them, cleansing their hearts by faith.

10 Now therefore why make ye trial of God, that ye should put a yoke upon the neck of the disciples which neither our fathers nor we were able to bear?

11 But we believe that we shall be saved through the grace of the Lord Jesus, in like manner as they.

6 The apostles and elders came together to consider this matter. In this private meeting there was yet a further discussion of the matter and no little disputing between those present (possibly between the elders and Paul and Barnabas). It is best sometimes to allow for an expression of all present before any logical conclusion can be drawn. Until all the evidence is in there can be no real comprehensive decision. It would seem that such was the procedure here

508. What was the first act of Paul and Barnabas upon arriving in Jerusalem?
509. What was admitted by all? What was lacking according to some?
510. Who alone had the power to decide on the issue?
511. Why do we say that the dispute in the private meeting was between the elders and Paul and Barnabas?

in Jerusalem. At whatever circumstance, following the words of disputes: Peter arose to state his position.

7-11 The apostle to the circumcision spoke here on this subject as he had spoken some years before on the same subject to the same listeners. He had not forgotten the lesson Jehovah had given him in Joppa and Caesarea. He further stated here that God Himself had selected him of all the apostles that by his mouth should the Gentiles receive the gospel. A simple statement of reiteration was all that was necessary to call to their mind the reception of the Holy Spirit by the household of Cornelius. Yea, and likewise to call to mind that his was the work and choice of God. Here, now is the point of Peter's speech—he says in essence: "If you now demand that the Gentiles be circumcised and keep the Law of Moses, you are acknowledging that either you did not believe God the first time or that you are unwilling to accept His decision." Peter calls such action and thought "tempting God" and further than this he says, "Why try to bind on the Gentiles the yoke of the law? Do you like it? Do you obey it? Yea, did even our fathers keep it? Nay, it became a galling burden to be borne. Why then bring the Gentiles under such a yoke?" As a final word of proof Peter reminds the Jews that in the light of their failure to keep the law of customs and commandments they would necessarily have to be saved by "the grace of the Lord Jesus." If that is true, and surely any sincere Jew could see that it was, then why complain when God cleansed the hearts of the Gentiles through faith and saved them on the same basis of grace?

This silenced the assembly. There was not much that could be said in light of the irresistable logic of Peter's words; and most especially since previous to this time they had glorified God at the conversion of the uncircumcised household of Cornelius. (cf. 11:18).

b. Paul and Barnabas tell of their work. 12.

    12 And all the multitude kept silence; and they hearkened unto Barnabas and Paul rehearsing what signs and wonders God had wrought among the Gentiles through them.

12 In the midst of the silence Paul and Barnabas again rehearsed in detail the miracles and wonders God granted to them in confirming His word among the heathen. The emphasis here put upon the miracles and wonders wrought by God was based upon the same

512. Why all these speeches?
513. Had Peter ever addressed this same group on this same subject before? When? Where?
514. What was the point of Peter's speech?
515. Show the common sense of Peter's closing remarks. (Verse 11).
516. Give the point of the speeches of Paul and Barnabas.

promise as that of Peter, i.e. if God so worked with the apostles as they carried the gospel to the heathen, surely He was not displeased with the work of these men but was rather putting His stamp of approval upon it.

c. The speech of James. 13-21.

13 And after they had held their peace, James answered, saying, Brethren, hearken unto me:

14 Symeon hath rehearsed how first God visited the Gentiles, to take out of them a people for his name.

15 And to this agree the words of the prophets; as it is written,

16 After these things I will return, And I will build again the tabernacle of David, which is fallen; And I will build again the ruins thereof, And I will set it up:

17 That the residue of men may seek after the Lord, And all the Gentiles, upon whom my name is called,

18 Saith the Lord, who maketh these things known from of old.

19 Wherefore my judgment is, that we trouble not them that from among the Gentiles turn to God;

20 but that we write unto them, that they abstain from the pollutions of idols, and from fornication, and from what is strangled, and from blood.

21 For Moses from generations of old hath in every city them that preach him, being read in the synagogues every sabbath.

13-18 Now for the final word upon the subject. This was given by James the Lord's brother. There is much traditional material written concerning the piety and standing of James among the Jews in Jerusalem. Be that as it may, it at least appears that he was a leader in the church at Jerusalem.

While all were silent in giving attention to the words about to be spoken, James said in essence: "Here is my judgment. You have just heard from Peter how God visited the Gentiles and took out of them some who would be His . . . Yea, this is even as the prophet Amos said . . . do you recall the prophecy? Possibly you do but you missed its application. Hear again the prophet and see afresh the fulfillment of his words. 'After these things'—Yea, the very things that have come to pass in our history, i.e. the fall of the Jewish nation and the general dissolution of this proud people . . . After these things something is going to happen. What will it be? Jehovah will

517. Who was this man James?

518. What did he add that had not already been said?

519. Tell me about the "building again of the tabernacle of David"—what is it and how is it said to be built again in the time of James?

.return to build again the tabernacle or house of David, which is fallen. . ."

How is this to be understood? Surely not in the literal building again of the house of David, for such was far from being so when James spoke . . . and yet James states that this prophecy is having its fulfillment. The only possible explanation is a spiritual one, that the house of David to be built again was a spiritual house. Yea, the ruins to be set up were to be from those Jews who had suffered under the penalty of their own rebellion and had yet found favor with God through Jesus Christ. They together were being builded into "a habitation of God in the Spirit . . . That the residue of men seek after the Lord" (Eph 2:22; Acts 15:17.) This refers to the small remnant among the Jews who would find Christ and thus have part in this wonderful promise of the prophet. And then comes the word that bears directly upon the issue at hand. James says that in the building of David's house through Christ not only would there be those few Jews who would find a part in this house but "all the Gentiles, upon whom my name is called." This settles the issue. From times of old God had determined that these things would be so.

19-21 What a splendid act and decision it was on the part of James to make such a statement. Well could he be called "James the Just." The judgment of James was not only the expression of his own heart, but that of all who had honestly listened to the evidence: that, any from among the Gentiles who turned to God through Christ were not to be troubled with the Jewish law and traditions.

That this decision might be known to all and that no further trouble come up over it, it was decided to put it in written form. In this letter it would be well, James suggests, that some provision be made for the social intercourse of the Jews and Gentiles; and therefore certain restrictions about eating should be included so they might dine together; also to abstain from those obvious sins connected with idol worship and from fornication. The reason for the apparent compromise in these restrictions of eating is found not in the spirit of compromise but in that of wisdom; "for Moses from generations of old hath in every city them that preach him, being read in the synagogues every sabbath" and to thus give no forbearance in light of this was not the part of wisdom. This seemed to settle the issue in the private meeting.

d. The letter on circumcision. 22-29.

22 Then it seemed good to the apostles and the elders, with the whole church, to choose men out of their company,

520. What word given by James relates directly to the issue at hand?
521. Why agree so readily with James?
522. Why the restrictions in the letter?

and send them to Antioch with Paul and Barnabas;
namely Judas called Barsabbas, and Silas, chief men
among the brethren:

23 and they wrote thus by them, The apostles and the
elders, brethren, unto the brethren who are of the Gentiles in Antioch and Syria and Cilicia, greeting:

24 Forasmuch as we have heard that certain who went out
from us have troubled you with words, subverting your
souls; to whom we gave no commandment;

25 it seemed good unto us, having come to one accord, to
choose out men and send them unto you with our beloved Barnabas and Paul,

26 men that have hazarded their lives for the name of
our Lord Jesus Christ.

27 We have sent therefore Judas and Silas, who themselves
also shall tell you the same things by word of mouth.

28 For it seemed good to the Holy Spirit, and to us, to lay
upon you no greater burden than these necessary things:

29 that ye abstain from things sacrificed to idols, and from
blood, and from things strangled, and from fornication;
from which if ye keep yourselves, it shall be well with
you.   Fare ye well.

22-29 The whole church was called together by the apostles and
elders and with the suggestion of their leaders they chose two of
their chief men; Judas, called Barsabbas and Silas and sent them
with Paul and Barnabas to bear the letter. Here is the letter, the
first written document of the apostolic church, written under the
inspiration of the Holy Spirit . . . written with the purpose and
theme of unity . . . Oh, how the same message is needed today! (Refer to verses 23-29).

5. THE WORK IN ANTIOCH. 15:30-35.

30 So they, when they were dismissed, came down to
Antioch; and having gathered the multitude together,
they delivered the epistle.

31 And when they had read it, they rejoiced for the consolation.

32 And Judas and Silas, being themselves also prophets,
exhorted the brethren with many words, and confirmed
them.

33 And after they had spent some time there, they were
dismissed in peace from the brethren unto those that
had sent them forth.

34 But it seemed good unto Silas to abide there.

35 But Paul and Barnabas tarried in Antioch, teaching
and preaching the word of the Lord, with many others
also.

30-35 The multitude of the Syrian disciples were no doubt eagerly awaiting the return of their leaders from this all important meeting. What was the decision? Could it indeed be settled? When the four did enter the city gates of Antioch there was an immediate gathering of the Christians and they all listened as the epistle was read. With one accord they accepted it and rejoiced greatly that they were indeed "free from the law." A double benefit was to be found in their return, for Judas and Silas who brought the letter were gifted with the ability to prophesy. So, for the space of no few days a revival was conducted in this place. As we read so often in the words of the preachers of that day the brethren were "exhorted" by these men of God and thus were confirmed. The same results would follow today if we had something of the same type of preaching. It would seem that some arrangement had been made with the church at Antioch for this time of preaching for the text states that following this effort "they were dismissed in peace from the brethren" . . . We realize from what follows that Silas stayed in Antioch or returned to Antioch shortly after his trip to Jerusalem. Some ancient authorities insert the phrase . . . "But it seemed good unto Silas to abide there."

It is always with a deep sense of joy that we constantly read throughout this book of Acts that "Paul tarried to teach and preach the word of the Lord" . . . This was his one task that he was continually performing. Not only Paul but Barnabas and "many others also." What a challenging example for the churches today.

6. PETER'S VISIT TO ANTIOCH. Galatians 2:11-21.

11-21 Although this visit is entirely omitted in Acts it has been concluded that according to the chronology of events it did occur at this time.

This is a most interesting incident. This is the first disagreement between two apostles. Notice that it was not a disagreement over a matter of faith (although Peter made it such) it was all the more unusual in light of the epistle that had just been sent from James and the apostles in Jerusalem. Why did Peter withdraw himself from the Gentiles? Because "certain came from James." Of what was he afraid? The answer can be found in the phrase "eat with them." He was fearful lest these from James find him in a Gentile house eat-

523. What double benefit was received in Antioch when the foursome arrived from Jerusalem?
524. What good element was found in the preaching at Antioch? What do you think of it?
525. What do you know of the activities of Silas at this time?
526. How do we know that Peter visited Antioch at this time?
527. What is one of the first important things to notice about this disagreement?

ing at their table. Why? Had not the decree made provisions for that very thing? Yes indeed it had, but a little closer look at the provisions of the decree will serve to show that no specifications were made for the purification of the meat, no word was given about clean and unclean meats, etc. These were the points of the law that troubled Peter. Troubled him not before God, but before men. He could not make such distinctions before God even as he himself had admitted, and as God revealed to him in Joppa and Caesarea. But he feared the censure of man more than he did God, hence his changeableness.

Did not these from James understand that such legal requirements were abolished? No, they only understood the letter of the decree given, and anything beyond that, whether done in the spirit of the epistle or not, was to be condemned. Peter knew this and withdrew himself, and forthwith set up a defense for his actions (even as many of us are wont to do today.) In this dissimulation he won quite a number to his viewpoint, including the good man Barnabas. In all this Peter stood self-condemned. He stood condemned before God. But in this the Lord knew that Peter was the kind of a man that would break down and admit his guilt once he was faced with it.

Paul acted as God's spokesman in this situation. It must have occurred in some public gathering that the rebuke was given for Paul says that he rebuked him "before them all." From what is said in Galatians it would seem to us that the rebuke must have taken place in the midst of one of Peter's public efforts to obtain adherents to his views. Right in the heat of Peter's efforts Paul "withstood him to the face." The merciless logic of Paul's words cut Peter to the heart and cut out from under him the very foundation of his position.

It would be well for us to note that Paul included himself in the statements about the Jews and bound upon Peter nothing that he himself was not also obligated to keep.

The concluding remarks of Conybeare and Howson express well our feelings on the conclusion of this matter: "Though the sternest indignation is expressed in this rebuke, we have no reason to suppose that any actual quarrel took place between the two apostles. It is not improbable that St. Peter was immediately convinced of

528. What makes this disagreement rather unusual?
529. Why didn't Peter refer to the "decree" or letter as his source of authority for eating with the Gentiles?
530. How did the natural character of Peter help the situation?
531. Of what was Peter afraid? Why was he self-condemned? What influence did he have?
532. Where was Peter when Paul rebuked him? What did he say in essence?

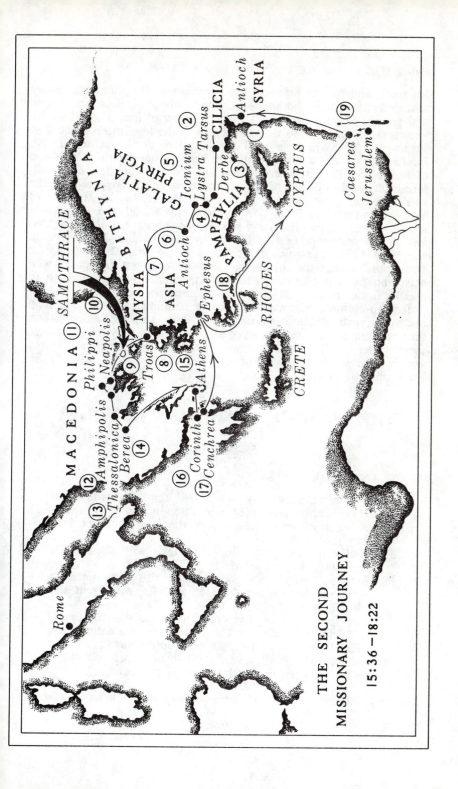

THE SECOND
MISSIONARY JOURNEY

15:36 – 18:22

his fault, and melted at once into repentance. His mind was easily susceptible to quick and sudden changes; his disposition was loving and generous; and we should expect his contrition, as well as his weakness, at Antioch, to be what it was in the high priest's house at Jerusalem. Yet, when we read the narrative of this rebuke in St. Paul's epistle, it is a relief to turn to that passage at the conclusion of one of St. Peter's letters, where, in speaking of the 'long suffering of our Lord' and of the prospect of sinless happiness in the world to come, he alludes, in touching words, to the Epistles of **'our beloved brother Paul.'** We see how entirely all past differences are forgotten,—how all earthly misunderstandings are absorbed and lost in the contemplation of Christ and eternal life. Not only did the Holy Spirit overrule all contrarieties so that the writings of both apostles teach the church the same doctrine, but the apostle who was rebuked is not ashamed to call the attention of the church to epistles in one page of which his own censure is recorded.

It is an eminent triumph of Christian humility and love. We shall not again have occasion to mention St. Peter and St. Paul together, until we come to the last scene of all, but though they might seldom meet whilst laboring in their Master's cause, their lives were united 'and in their deaths they were not divided'." **(Life And Epistles Of St. Paul.** pp. 201-202).

THE SECOND MISSIONARY JOURNEY
15:36—18:22
52-54 A.D.

1. IN ANTIOCH. 15:36-40.

36 And after some days Paul said unto Barnabas, Let us return now and visit the brethren in every city wherein we proclaimed the word of the Lord, and see how they fare.

37 And Barnabas was minded to take with them John also, who was called Mark.

38 But Paul thought not good to take with them him who withdrew from them from Pamphylia, and went not with them to the work.

39 And there arose a sharp contention, so that they parted asunder one from the other, and Barnabas took Mark with him, and sailed away unto Cyprus;

40 but Paul chose Silas, and went forth, being commended by the brethren to the grace of the Lord.

533. Why is II Peter 3:15, 16 of great encouragement in this connection?

36 When Jesus spoke to the prostrate Pharisee as he lay in the dust of the Damascus road he commissioned him to carry the glad tidings "far off among the Gentiles." To the heavenly vision the apostle was never disobedient. And so it came to pass after a few weeks spent in the town of Antioch, that, although his labors were fruitful, and the work pressed on in a happy harmonious fashion, he once again heard the call of the man from across the sea. The faces of those whom he had brought into the "kingdom of God's dear Son" haunted him and he longed once again to be with them that he might be assured that the tempter had not tempted them and thus he would have labored in vain.

37-40 These thoughts prompted his suggestion to his co-laborer Barnabas: "Let us go again and visit our brethren in every city where we have preached the word of the Lord and see how they do." This plan, however, of a combined visitation of the churches was marred by an outbreak of human infirmity. The two apostolic friends were separated from each other by a quarrel, which proved that they were indeed, as they had lately told those of Lystra, "men of like passions with you." When two individuals agree perfectly and manage in a harmonious fashion between themselves it at the same time becomes difficult to agree over the company of a third person. This was the situation with Paul and Barnabas. Although they could work in perfect accord with each other, each respecting the other's viewpoint, when a third person entered the union, his feelings and opinions had to be considered and in this, the two good friends disagreed violently. Paul felt that John Mark was very definitely unqualified to enter the work that they were contemplating. Indeed, had he not already turned back upon the same route?

As we said in the previous notes it appears that the decision of John Mark to return to Jerusalem had something to do with the "work" in which the apostles were engaged. Maybe Barnabas knew John Mark a little more intimately than did Paul. At any rate, we know they were related (cf. Col. 4:10.) John Mark indeed did prove himself to be a profitable servant of Christ Jesus. Paul the apostle acknowledged this (Cf. Philemon 24; II Tim. 4:11; Col. 4:11). The overruling hand of God's providence is seen in all the circumstances, for not only was the original plan of the apostles fulfilled, i.e. of revisting all the churches established in the first missionary journey;

534. What purpose prompted the second missionary journey?
535. Why did Paul and Barnabas agree for so long and now suddenly disagree?
536. What objection did Paul have to John Mark?
537. Why was Barnabas attracted to Mark?
538. Did Mark ever redeem himself in the eyes of Paul? (reference).
539. Show the over-ruling hand of God in the whole matter.

the churches in Asia Minor by Paul, and those on the isle of Cyprus by Barnabas, but along with it much more was done.

It appears that Barnabas and Mark left first and then Paul and Silas "went forth, being commended by the brethren to the grace of the Lord."

2. THROUGH THE PROVINCES OF SYRIA AND CILICIA. 15:41.

41 And he went through Syria and Cilicia, confirming the churches.

41 Here is another of those brief descriptions of Luke concerning the work and travels of the apostle. What churches were to be found in the parts of Syria and Cilicia? The answer can be found in the early labors of Paul and Barnabas and certain others of the early disciples (cf. 14:19-21). Doubtless through the preaching of Paul churches were established in Cilicia during his stay in his home town (cf. 9:26-30).

3. AT DERBE. 16:1a.

1a And he came also to Derbe,

4. IN LYSTRA. 16:1b-3.

1b and to Lystra: and behold, a certain disciple was there, named Timothy, the son of a Jewess that believed; but his father was a Greek.

2 The same was well reported of by the brethren that were at Lystra and Iconium.

3 Him would Paul have to go forth with him; and he took and circumcised him because of the Jews that were in those parts: for they all knew that his father was a Greek.

1 It is here that Luke records a personal word of God's servant, Timothy. Timothy is the one worker of the many with whom Paul associated whom he personally complimented and commended. (Cf. Phil. 2:19-22). Perhaps we should say that only in the case of Timothy did the Holy Spirit see fit to record Paul's commendation. As we look at the life and high standards that were set for this evangelist, we can say with Paul, there is none like him.

2-3 What a lesson can here be learned. Since Paul has been in Lystra and Derbe, ever since Timothy had gone under the waters

540. What churches were visited in the journey through Syria and Cilicia?
541. Lystra was the home town of which Christian worker?
542. What is different in the words of Paul regarding Timothy, than in those regarding other workers?
543. What lesson can we learn from Timothy in Lystra?

of baptism he had been laboring in the kingdom of God. Timothy was not looking to becoming a companion and co-laborer with the apostle; he was only interested in serving God where he found opportunity. But when Paul saw him thus laboring and heard from the brethren how he served the Lord, "him would Paul have to go forth with him."

Before we say anything further on these verses in Chapter sixteen, please remember that Paul had just a few brief days before finished a heated discussion with Peter over the matter of circumcision, and but a few days before this he had returned from a council on the subject in Jerusalem.

Lo, the hand of the apostle is found in the act of circumcision. The apostle Paul circumcised Timothy. How can it be? Had he not withstood Peter to the face on the division of the Jews and the Gentiles? Was not this rite he was now performing the expression of such division? How can it be that Paul would do such a thing? Such exclamations might be expected from some; but not from those who read the text carefully, nor from those who have perused the epistles of Paul:

"To the Jews I became as a Jew, that I might gain Jews; to them that are under the law, as under the law, not being myself under the law, that I might gain them that are under the law" (I Cor. 9:20, 21).

Here indeed we have an application of the principle set forth. And so it is with our Heavenly Father. Only when we feel and know that He has identified Himself with our sufferings, sorrows, temptation can we love Him as we do. When we realize that He understands because He in the person of His Son "was tempted in all points like as we are," was "a man of sorrows and acquainted with grief" can we go to Him and feel that our souls are in competent hands. So with you and with me, dear friend, we must become as a Jew, enter into the burden of the soul, into the sorrow of that heart, and so fulfill the law of Christ. Then we will know what Paul meant when he said: "It is more blessed to give than to receive."

5. THROUGH THE CITIES OF ICONIUM AND ANTIOCH. 16:4, 5.

    4 And as they went on their way through the cities, they delivered them the decrees to keep which had been ordained of the apostles and elders that were at Jerusalem.

    5 So the churches were strengthened in the faith, and increased in number daily.

544. Why wasn't it inconsistent for Paul to circumcise Timothy? What lesson can we gain?

4-5 The writer does not mention which cities were included in these visits, but doubtless Antioch and Iconium were among them. At any rate when the letter was read and expounded upon (you can read it by turning to 15:20-23) the brethren were encouraged in their Christian walk and as a consequence increased in number daily.

6. THROUGH THE REGION OF PHRYGIA AND GALATIA.
16:6a. Cf. Gal. 4:13-15; I Cor. 16:1, 2.

6a And they went through the region of Phrygia and Galatia,

6a Although it is not mentioned in the book of Acts we could conclude from the account given in Galatians that during the time that Paul was in the region of Galatia he contracted some type of illness that made it necessary for him to remain here for some time. During the period of his convalescence he was enabled to do a wonderful work for Christ among the inhabitants of Galatia, much to his surprise, we are led to believe. The words of Canon Farrar are very much to the point. We reproduce them for their fine expression:

"The providential cause which led to St. Paul's stay in the country was, as he himself tells us, a severe attack of illness, and the manner in which he alludes to it gives us reason to infer that it was a fresh access of agony from that "stake in the flesh" which I believe to have been acute ophtalmia (inflamation of the eye or eyeball), accompanied, as it often is, by violent cerebral disturbance (pertaining to the brain). In his letter to his Galatian converts he makes a touching appeal which in modern phraseology might run as follows:

'Become as I am, brethren, I beseech you' (i.e. free from the yoke of external and useless ordinances), 'for I, too, made myself as you are. Jew that I was, I placed myself on the level of you Gentiles, and now I want you to stand with me on that same level, instead of trying to make yourselves Jews. I do not wish to speak by way of complaint about you. You never did **me** any personal wrong. Nay, you know that when I preached the gospel among you on my first visit, it was in consequence of an attack of sickness which detained me in the midst of a journey; you could not, therefore, feel any gratitude to me as though I had come with the express purpose of preaching to you; and besides, at that time weak, agonized with pain, liable to fits of delirium, with my eyes red and ulcerated by that disease by which it pleases God to let Satan

545. What did Paul and Silas do when they arrived in Antioch and Iconium? What was the result?
546. What happened in the regions of Galatia and Phrygia?
547. Was Galatia a town, city, country, province or what?

buffet me, you might well have been tempted to regard me a deplorable object. My whole appearance must have been a trial to you—a temptation to you to reject me. But you did not. You were very kind to me. You might have treated me with contemptuous indifference; you might have regarded me with positive loathing; but instead of this you honored, you loved me, you received me as though I were an angel—nay, even as though I were the Lord of angels, as though I were even He whom I preached unto you. How glad were you to see me. How eagerly you congratulated yourselves and me on the blessed accident—nay, rather, on the blessed providence of God, which had detained me amongst you. So generous, so affectionate were you towards me that I bear you witness that to aid me as I sat in misery in the darkened rooms, unable to bear even a ray of light without excruciating pain, you would, if that could have helped me, have plucked out your eyes and given them to me. (Gal. 4:12-15)." **Life Of Paul,** p. 264-266).

It might be well to turn to the book of Galatians and read its six short chapters to learn of the concern of Paul for these Christians in the section where he bestowed so much effort.

It appears from the text that this tour and stay in Galatia only occurred as a result of the prevention of the Holy Spirit from speaking the Word in Asia. Get a good look at the map so you will know the location of Asia and of Galatia. This whole trip was a long and difficult one; for a detailed account of the terrain read the comments upon it by Conybeare and Howson (**Life And Epistles Of The Apostle Paul,** pp. 233-238).

7. **WHILE IN THE ABOVE STATED REGIONS THEY WERE FORBIDDEN BY THE HOLY SPIRIT TO SPEAK THE WORD IN ASIA. THEY PASSED THROUGH THE PROVINCE OF MYSIA AND ASSAYED TO GO INTO THE PROVINCE OF BITHYNIA BUT THEY WERE AGAIN FORBIDDEN. 16:6b-8a.**

6b having been forbidden of the Holy Spirit to speak the word in Asia;

7 and when they were come over against Mysia, they assayed to go into Bithynia; and the Spirit of Jesus suffered them not;

8a and passing by Mysia,

548. Of what nationality were the Galatians?

549. Did Paul establish one church, many churches, or no churches there?

550. When, why and where did he write to those in Galatia?

551. Was it the original intent of the apostle to go into Galatia? If not, what was his original plan?

552. Give two reason why the province of Asia would seem to be the most obvious place to go for preaching.

213

6b "The province of Asia would surely be the most obvious of development in the gospel," so thought the apostle Paul. There were more cities in this province, hence more people to whom to bring the glad tidings. There were more favorable natural conditions; i.e., the terrain was not so rough as in the neighboring provinces and to this province he had tried to go once before.

7-8a But the leader of these men looked not upon the "outward appearances" but upon the will of God. Knowing the mind of God, the Holy Spirit made it known to the apostles in some way that would let them know that God did not want the Word preached by them in Asia at this time; nor even in the more northerly province of Bithynia. Every door was shut in their faces and their path was hedged in with refusals. There was no way to go but straight ahead.

Once again we need a little clarification as to the location and meaning of the statements made in these verses. A reference to the map will give some idea as to their location. Note please the circumstances in 16:7 "over against Mysia" which means right at the border of the province, then second, from the position at the border of Mysia they planned or began to travel toward the northern province of Bithynia. There were several large towns here in which the gospel could have been preached. Once again we read the rather strange words "but the Spirit of Jesus suffered them not." Just how the Holy Spirit communicated this information we have no way of knowing. Whether subjectively or objectively it would be impossible to say. Then note: "Passing by Mysia," this can also be translated "passing through Mysia." A look at the map will clear this up. Thus were they driven straight across the country to the seaport of Troas.

8. **AT TROAS.** 16:8b-10.

    8b   they came down to Troas.

    9   And a vision appeared to Paul in the night: There was a man of Macedonia standing, beseeching him, saying, Come over into Macedonia, and help us.

    10 And when he had seen the vision, straightway we sought to go forth into Macedonia, concluding that God had called us to preach the gospel unto them.

8b, 9 The location and history of these towns is very important to a thorough understanding and appreciation of the story. Look it up and read it.

When Paul, Silas and Timothy arrived in Troas they very shortly knew why God had forced them along in the way He had. It happened that on a certain night a visitor appeared unto the apostle. A

553. To what does the term Bithynia refer?
554. What is the meaning of the phrase "over against Mysia?"
555. The meaning of "Passing by Mysia?"

man from across the Aegean Sea. His visit in this visionary form was to earnestly request that Paul cross the waters and come into Macedonia "and help us."

10 Here it is that the pronoun of the author of Acts changes from "they" to "we" and "us". Note the change in verses eight through eleven. The conclusion, of course, is that here in Troas the physician, Luke, joined the evangelistic party. Whether this was his home or not we cannot say, but we personally like to believe that it was. Paul must have spoken to Luke, Silas and Timothy about the vision. They all concluded that the circumstances pointed in just one direction and that was over into Europe. God himself had commissioned them to bear the glad tidings to Macedonia.

9. AT SAMOTHRACE. 16:11a.
11a Setting sail therefore from Troas, we made a straight course to Samothrace,

11a In passing it does seem from what happens in Troas upon the return trip (20:6-12) that some work for God must have been done here, by Luke perchance, even before Paul and company arrived. Or maybe the foursome had a meeting that is not recorded by Luke.

Here is a brief description of that charming little isle of Samothrace at which they anchored the first night out from Troas . . . "On the first day they sailed past Tenedos and Imbros straight for Samothrace and anchored for the night to leeward of it. Did Paul as he gazed by starlight, or at early dawn on the towering peak which overshadows that ancient island, think at all of its immemorial mysteries or talk to his companions about the Cabiri, or question any of the Greek or Roman sailors about the strange names of Axiocheros, Axiochersos, and Axiochersa? We would gladly know, but we have no data to help us, and it is strongly probable that to all such secondary incidents he was habitually indifferent." (**The Life Of Paul,** Farrar, p. 273).

10. AT NEAPOLIS. 16:11b.
11b and the day following to Neapolis;

11b Cunningham Geikie says concerning Neapolis: "We can infer the appearance of the port, in some measure, from that of Levantine coast-towns now. There would be the same mixture of East and West, the same privision for harbourage, and the same style

556. How can we say that to go into Macedonia was to enter Europe?
557. What is significant in the change of pronouns in Verses 8-11?
558. What does 20:6-12 have to do with the Lord's work in Troas?
559. What is Samothrace?
560. Why no description of the country through which the missionaries were passing?

of houses; but also, I fear, a little of the neglect which seems to mark all places in the East or near it.

Philippi, to which the travelers were going, lay about ten miles inland, but was easily reached from Neapolis, as that town was the coast-ending of the great Egnatian Road which crossed Macedonia and Thrace, on the one hand, and stretched away, on the other, to Thessalonica on the west. Climbing a defile through the hills which lie close behind Neapolis, by the massive squarely paved causeway of that military highway, between precipices almost over-hanging the sea, the missionaries would have a glorious view be-hind them on gaining the crest, if they chose to interest themselves in anything but their errand . . . Looking down them toward Philippi, a plain, level as the sea, lay at their feet, framed, in the nearer and further distance, in a background of mountains, of which some, within a sweep of thirty miles rose to a height of from four to eight thousand feet." (Geikie, op. cit. pp. 377-378).

Neapolis was a city of considerable size. With such a city was it not passing strange that the word was not preached here? Strange unless we understand the purposes of the preachers. "To the Jew first, and also to the Greek" was the order. Finding no opening here they went on to the next city.

11. **AT PHILIPPI.** 16:12-40
a. A description of Philippi. 12.

12 and from thence to Philippi, which is a city of Macedonia, the first of the district, a Roman colony: and we
were in this city tarrying certain days.

12 As to the statement that Philippi was "a city of Macedonia, the first of the district, a Roman colony," we quote from authors who have done research on this matter that we might understand the expression.

"The city of Philippi was a monumental record of two vast em-pires. It had been once an obscure place called Krenides from its streams and springs; but Philip, the father of Alexander, had made it a frontier town to protect Macedonia from the Thracians and had helped to establish his power by the extremely profitable work-ing of its neighboring gold mines. Augustus, proud of the victory over Brutus and Cassius, won at the foot of the hill on which it stands, and on the summit of which Cassius had committed suicide, —elevated it to the rank of a colony which made it, as Luke calls

561. How far was Philippi from Neapolis?
562. What is the Egnatian Road?
563. Describe briefly the site of Philippi.
564. Why no preaching in Neapolis?
565. What is the meaning of the phrase, "a city of Macedonia, the first of the district, a Roman colony?"

it, if not the first yet certainly 'a first city of that district of Macedonia.' And this, probably, was why Paul went directly to it.

"When Perseus, the last successor of Alexander, had been routed at Pydna (June 22, B.C. 168), Macedonia had been reduced to a Roman province in four divisions. These, in accordance with the astute and Machiavellian policy of Rome, were kept distinct from each other by differences of privilege and isolation of interests which tended to foster mutual jealousies. Beginning eastward at the river Nestus, Macedonia Prima reached to the Strymon; Macedonia Secunda, to the Axius; Macedonia Tertia to the Peneus; and the Macedonia Quarta, to Illyricum and Equirus. The capitals of these divisions respectively were Amphipolis, Thessalonica,—at which the proconsul of the entire province fixed his residence, Pella, and Pelagonia. It is a very reasonable conjecture that Paul, in answer to the appeal of the vision, had originally intended to visit—as, perhaps, he ultimately did visit,—all four capitals. But Amphipolis, in spite of its historic celebrity, had sunk into comparative insignificance, and the proud colonial privileges of Philippi made it in reality the more important town." (**The Life Of Paul,** Farrar pp. 280-81).

b. The prayer meeting and the conversion. 13:15.

13 And on the sabbath day we went forth without the gate by a river side, where we supposed there was a place of prayer; and we sat down, and spake unto the women that were come together.

14 And a certain woman named Lydia, a seller of purple, of the city of Thyatira, one that worshipped God, heard us: whose heart the Lord opened to give heed unto the things which were spoken by Paul.

15 And when she was baptized, and her household, she besought us, saying, If ye have judged me to be faithful to the Lord, come into my house, and abide there. And she constrained us.

13-15 It would seem that the party arrived in the middle of the week—for after waiting certain days the sabbath day is mentioned. There was no synagogue in Philippi; the only Jews who were faithful at all in their expression of worship were a few women who met on the banks of a river that flowed by the city.

How did Paul and the others know there was such a meeting?

566. How many divisions to Macedonia? What were their capitals? What bearing do they have in Paul's work?

567. What is "the panoply of the Roman soldier?" What does it have to do with Philippi and the writings of Paul?

568. At what time of the week did they arrive in Philippi? How do you know?

THYATIRA.

A city in Asia Minor, the seat of one of the seven churches mentioned in Rev. 1:11; 2:18, the waters of Thyatira are said to be so well adapted for dyeing that in no place can the scarlet cloth out of which fezes are made, be so brilliantly or so permanently dyed as here. The principle god of this town was Apollo, worshipped as the sun-god under the surname Tyrimnas. (**Unger's Bible Dictionary** p. 1093)

But Apollo was not the god of the woman that we know from this town. Lydia was a worshiper of Jehovah in the midst of idolatry; and this she did wherever she went. How often it is that we leave our religion when we move. Such religion is none at all. It is no wonder that the Lord opened the heart of Lydia. We would find the Lord opening our hearts to His truth more and more if we had the same devotion and determination.

Only by inquiry and that diligently. In Athens they called Paul "a babbler" and I can well imagine that he did plenty of talking here for Jesus the Messiah.

Sitting down, perhaps in a circle or semicircle there gathered this group of earnest believers. Paul, Silas, Timothy and Luke were seated with them. These men came for just one purpose and that was to preach the Word and this they immediately proceeded to do. There was in this gathering a business woman from a small province across the Aegean Sea, "Lydia, a seller of purple (i.e. dyes), of the city of Thyatira." A rather strange word is given concerning this woman. Luke says, "Whose heart the Lord opened to give heed unto the things which were spoken by Paul." Did not the Lord open the hearts of the rest of the women there that day? If so, in what way? Let us not conjecture, the text is before us, look at it carefully. It is said of Lydia that she "heard us." There follows then the consequence, her heart was opened by the Lord. It becomes perfectly obvious then that through the hearing of the truth she obtained the basis for her belief. The previous background of this woman fitted her with the disposition to want to accept the message. This fact is emphasized in the thought that although she was a business woman she thought enough of the Lord to lay this aside for the Sabbath, and not only so, but to make some provision for worship wherever she might be. This, we say, gives some indication of her heart attitude. But is it not said that the Lord opened her heart? Yes, indeed He did, by using this opportunity to His glory. This seems to be the action of the Lord in so many instances. When the background is right, God brings the preacher and the prospect together and the result is an "opened heart."

The New Testament conversions all end with the baptism of the convert. Not with their prayer experience, but their baptism. Not with their testimony, but with their baptism. Hence we find it so in the case of Lydia. Not only this business woman, but "her household" was baptized. So we must find at the riverside along with Lydia certain of her household servants. The disposition or desire to believe is the one greatest subjective step one can take toward salvation. For example, witness these household servants. It is more than probable that they had no feelings either pro or con on the subject of salvation in Jesus of Nazareth, but when they beheld the interest and acceptance of this teaching by their mistress they were aroused to thought, and because of their respect

569. Where did they preach in Philippi? How did they discover such a place?
570. Give three facts about Lydia.
571. Explain how the Lord opened the heart of Lydia.
572. What is the final step in all New Testament conversions?

of her judgments they were already disposed to acceptance. (It is not that they accepted the message without a personal knowledge and decision, but the example of Lydia did help.) How true this is of our times. There are many who stand at the fringe of the religious circle, whose minds and hearts have never been aroused in such a way as to make them disposed to believe.

We cannot imagine from what has been said before, that any of Lydia's household were infants; this is an entirely unwarranted conclusion in light of the context.

The conversion of Lydia carried in it for her a sense of appreciation and responsibility. She felt that to these messengers she owed her salvation, and not only so, but also her hospitality. This was not a passing thought but a deep persuasion of her soul; hence, she earnestly entreated, and that with persistence, that these new found friends make her house their home. And so it came to pass that the house of a well-to-do business woman became the meeting place of the first church in Philippi. In what strange and wonderful ways does the Almighty work!

c. The incident of the maid with the evil spirit. 16-18.

16 And it came to pass, as we were going to the place of prayer, that a certain maid having a spirit of divination met us, who brought her masters much gain by soothsaying.

17 The same following after Paul and us cried out, saying, These men are servants of the Most High God, who proclaim unto you the way of salvation.

18 And this she did for many days. But Paul, being sore troubled, turned and said to the spirit, I charge thee in the name of Jesus Christ to come out of her. And it came out that very hour.

16-18 A great deal of time was not spent in this town but some very interesting events took place in those brief days. "The work" of Paul was to tell to every creature the glad tidings of his Lord. "This one thing" he did everywhere and all the time. A church had been established in this place composed of those who, like Lydia and her household, had been "called out" by Paul's preaching. Services were held at least once a week and probably more often. The

573. What is the one greatest subjective step one can take toward salvation? What example is here given? Explain.

574. Why would you say that no infants were baptized in the household of Lydia?

575. What is the first effect of Lydia's conversion as shown in her conduct?

576. Where was the first meeting place of the church at Philippi?

place of meeting continued to be the banks of the river that flowed by the city.

It came to pass that one day, as they were making their way
through the city to the river, someone noticed a rather strange looking young woman who had begun to follow them. This continued
for a few days and then one day she began to cry out in a loud
voice so all could hear: "These men are servants of the Most High
God, who proclaim unto you the way of salvation." When Paul first
met this woman he could see nothing objectionable in her company, even if she were a soothsayer, for, had not the Master come
to help not those who were well but those who were sick?

But when this maid began thus to cry out and that for many days,
Paul's spirit was sore troubled. It was not that the words were
not true, for they did carry the very truth of God, but they came
from the wrong source. Paul knew as many of us need to know that
the message cannot be separated from the messenger. It was not
the maid that Paul disliked, but the spirit within her. It appears
this was a particular kind of spirit called "a python." Among the
many comments on this passage we like those of J. W. McGarvey:

"Literally translated, it was a Python spirit by which the maid was
possessed, the word Python identifying its manifestations with
those of the women who gave out the oracles at Delphi in Greece;
and who were supposed by the heathen to be inspired by the serpent
called Python, to whose wisdom these oracles were accredited.
Luke's language cannot be regarded as an endorsement of this supposed inspiration, but he distinctly recognized a real spirit in the
maid, and styles it a Python spirit for the reason given. The case was
undoubtedly one of demon possession, such as so frequently occurs
in our gospel narratives, and with which Luke's readers were pre-
sumed to have become acquainted through his former narrative."
(**ibid,** page 96).

"In the name of Jesus every knee should bow, of things in heaven
and things on earth and things under the earth . . ." These words of
Paul surely find a wonderful application in the power of Jesus over
this spirit; yea, this spirit "from beneath." When the Master calls,
we can but obey, and the body and mind of the maid were liberat-
ed from their bondage.

577. If they used the home of Lydia for a meeting place why continue to go
down to the river side? How often did they meet?
578. What did "the maid having a spirit" do before she began crying out?
579. Why was Paul troubled at her actions?
580. What lesson is there in this for us today?
581. What is meant when it is stated that the spirit was called "a python?"
582. What statement of scripture finds a wonderful application in the casting out of the demon?

d. The result of casting out the evil spirit. 19-24.

19 But when her masters saw that the hope of their gain was gone, they laid hold on Paul and Silas, and dragged them into the marketplace before the rulers,

20 and when they had brought them unto the magistrates, they said, These men, being Jews, do exceedingly trouble our city,

21 and set forth customs which it is not lawful for us to receive, or to observe, being Romans.

22 And the multitude rose up together against them: and the magistrates rent their garments off them, and commanded to beat them with rods.

23 And when they had laid many stripes upon them, they cast them into prison, charging the jailor to keep them safely:

24 who, having received such a charge, cast them into the inner prison, and made their feet fast in the stocks.

19-21 But when the spirit came out of the girl so did the source of her master's gain. It wasn't but a little while until they discovered that they had an empty vessel on their hands. When no longer people came to have their fortunes told or to be directed to some lost article, her masters were not angry with the maid but with the men who wrought this great change. It was not at all unusual for men in that day and time to seek revenge under such conditions, and this they did. These men would have no trouble locating Paul and Silas for they had the maid to direct them. And so it could very well have happened that one day as Paul and Silas and certain others were on their way to, or possibly returning from, the place of worship, they saw approaching them a group of men who by their appearance showed that they were exceedingly troubled about something. Paul and Silas soon knew that the trouble was in the form of anger, and that they were the objects of such feelings. Whether or not Paul and Silas knew why these men were angry with them we do not know; but when they had been dragged through the streets with a curious mob gathering about them, and were finally placed before the rulers of the city, they then knew that it was the "good deed done" to the possessed girl that brought them here. The writer Luke here drops the first person pronoun for he was not arrested.

Of course the real cause of the actions of those who thus dragged them into the market place would make no basis for an accusation. This rapidly grew into a mob scene and moreover the mob seemed to understand the objection even before the accused, before it

583. What came out along with the spirit? The result?
584. In what portion of the story is the first person dropped? Why?
585. How did they locate Paul and Silas?

was voiced by the lying masters. The cry goes out before the magistrates: "These men, being Jews, do exceedingly trouble our city (they should have said 'trouble our business'), and set forth customs which it is not lawful for us to receive, or to observe, being Romans." This charge carried in it the thought of treason, treason against a government of which these people were proud, having been adopted into it as a free colony. As we have suggested the mob who stood around already knew of the charge and hence upon these words they arose as one man in demanding punishment for these "Jew". No trial, no defense, no justice.

22-24 It seems from what follows in this incident that the magistrates were overpowered in their better judgment by the populace, and like Pilate "their voice prevailed" and off came the garments of Paul and Silas. Now for the first time the marks of the Roman rods were laid upon Paul's back. The instrument used was in the form comparable to our old-fashioned carpet beater. A handle, in which were fastened long iron shafts, these were bound together at the top, the shafts remained flexible between the two ends. The backs of these two messengers of glad tidings were cut with many stripes. Following this painful experience they were hurried off to jail. They were led to the jailer, who was charged with keeping them safely as dangerous characters.

The jailer no doubt thought he had under his care two desperate criminals who deserved the severest treatment. He put them not only into the prison, but into the dungeon, and to make them even more sure he had fastened their feet in stocks. The description of Geikie of the place in which they were confined is surely worthy of our consideration:

"Prisons were arranged on very much the same plan over all the empire. They were generally connected with municipal or government buildings, and consisted of two parts. Of these, the outer, was a chamber opening from the praetorium, and surrounded by cells, which enjoyed the light and what air could reach them from the external chamber. It was here that Paul was confined at Caesarea, where the prison was in 'the praetorium of Herod.' From this outer ward, however, there was a passage to the 'inner prison' called robur or lignum, from the bars of wood which formed the 'stocks' in which prisoners were secured. It had no window

586. What was the objection of the slavemasters to Paul and Silas? What did they say before the magistrates?
587. What did the mob know before the accused found it out?
588. What thought was carried in the accusation? Why especially important to these people?
589. To what other scene might this one be likened?
590. What is the meaning of "beaten with rods?"
591. What was so terrible about the "inner prison?"

or opening, except the door, which, when shut, absolutely excluded both air and light. Into this Paul and Silas were thrust, though the magistrates who thus mistreated them were only local justices, without authority to act summarily or otherwise, in criminal matters. To protect himself from their possible escape, they were, here, set by the Jailer with their feet in the stocks or lignum. The horrors of this 'inner prison' are often dwelt upon in the story of the early Christian confessors. Its awful darkness, its heat, and stench, were fearful, as may be well supposed; for prisoners were confined in it, night and day, without either exercise or renewal of air." **(Hours With The Bible, Vol. II, pp. 389, 390).**

e. Praise and prayer in jail. 25.
   25 But about midnight Paul and Silas were praying and
      singing hymns unto God, and the prisoners were lis-
      tening to them;

25 What a wonderful example of the transcendence of the spirit over the body is the singing of these men in this black hole. Their feet were in stocks, their bodies were confined but their spirits were not bound; no, not any more here than when they walked the streets of the city. The soul is confined only in the sense that it must remain for a few years in this earthly house. It makes little difference where this house of clay might be, the spirit is not bound any more in one place than in another. Possibly Paul could remember when he was not the prisoner, but the judge; not in Philippi, but in Jerusalem. Remembering the divine release of the twelve Paul and Silas could have been singing in triumphant expectancy. Be that as it may, the singing was heard by both those in the prison house and the Father in heaven.

There are two or three midnight services described in the book of Acts and each time there is something wonderful and unusual about them. The prisoners were still awake and listening to these strange men and their songs, as the sound was coming forth from the inner prison.

f. The earthquake; prisoners released. 26.
   26 and suddenly there was a great earthquake, so that the
      foundations of the prison-house were shaken: and im-
      mediately all the doors were opened; and everyone's
      bands were loosed.

26 The service was interrupted when the prison-house began to rock and shake. An earthquake! This was from God. It was of sufficient strength to push the door posts back and allow the doors to

592. What was not bound in this prison house?
593. When did Paul occupy exactly the opposite position to the one he here was in? Who heard the singing?

swing open; also to separate the stones of which the prison was made and allow the pegs to come loose that held the chains, which in their turn were fastened to the handcuffs and stocks of the prisoners.

g. The desperation of the jailer. 27.

27 And the jailor, being roused out of sleep and seeing the prison doors open, drew his sword and was about to kill himself, supposing that the prisoners had escaped.

27 This earthquake startled the prisoners to such an extent that they had no thought of escape even though their bonds were loose. It startled the jailer also, but in a different manner. Having taken care of the prisoners and having placed them under the care of his subordinates, he had fallen asleep. The earthquake brought him to consciousness with a jolt. His first thought was of his work and the first thing to meet his eyes was the open doors all around him. Seeing no one in the halls of the jail he immediately concluded that the place was empty; all had escaped. True to his position as a Roman soldier he preferred taking his own life to that of a trial and death.

h. The intervention of Paul. 28.

28 But Paul cried with a loud voice, saying, Do thyself no harm: for we are all here.

28 He had drawn his short sword and had it pressed against his breast when—a cry in the darkness—"Do thyself no harm for we are all here." Startled, he stopped. Relieved of the danger, another thought came to his mind. "If this is so, it will not be so for long unless I do something about it." Hence he called for lights.

i. The inquiry of the jailer for salvation. 29, 30.

29 And he called for lights and sprang in, and, trembling for fear, fell down before Paul and Silas,

30 and brought them out and said, Sirs, what must I do to saved?

29-30 Soon his helpers in the jail brought torches and lamps and in a matter of minutes order was restored and the prisoners were again made reasonably secure. Frightened as they were there was probably no thought of violence. Then the jailer, trembling with fear, came to kneel down before Paul and Silas, for somehow he had associated what had happened with these two unusual prisoners. His question to them, "Sirs, what must I do to be saved?" doubtless was a general one and related to his physical safety as well as

594. Describe the effect of the earthquake.
595. Why didn't the prisoners escape?
596. Did the jailer hear the singing?
597. Why kill himself?
598. Why call for lights?

his spiritual. He was without question inquiring as to the salvation of his soul but because of the circumstances present I am persuaded that it also had a bearing on his general well-being.

j. The reply and explanation. 31, 32.
>   31 And they said, Believe on the Lord Jesus, and thou shalt be saved, thou and thy house.
>   32 And they spake the word of the Lord unto him, with all that were in his house.

31, 32 Paul was never one to allow any occasion for preaching Christ as Saviour go without "buying it up," so the apostle's answer related directly and exclusively to the spiritual safety of this man. His answer was direct and all inclusive. "Believe on the Lord Jesus Christ and thou shalt be saved, thou and thy house." But, "Who was this Jesus Christ?" We have no real reason to believe that the jailer had even so much as heard the name of Christ before this occasion. As to the salvation of his house, they were in the same plight as he. Forthwith the jailer called in the members of his household, who seemed to be living either in the same building as he, or adjacent to it. Paul and Silas "spake the word of the Lord unto him." In this they, like Philip, told of this Jesus of Nazareth and of their need for His salvation.

k. The results. 33, 34.
>   33 And he took them the same hour of the night, and washed their stripes; and was baptized, he and all his, immediately.
>   34 And he brought them up into his house, and set food before them, and rejoiced greatly, with all his house, having believed in God.

33, 34 In this message there was that which caused the jailer to want to make restitution for what he had done amiss. One thing was surely the ill-treatment he and others had given these heralds of glad tidings. The jailer who had so roughly handled these men now tenderly washed the dried and clotted blood from their backs. This "word of the Lord" likewise carried information on the need of baptism. Not at some later date or as a result of salvation, but as something to be done in answer to the question "What must I

599. Why fall down before Paul and Silas?
600. In what type of safety was the jailer interested?
601. How did Paul "buy up" an opportunity?
602. Did the jailer understand what Paul meant by his first statement? If not, why not?
603. When Paul and Silas spoke unto them the "word of the Lord" what two things did it cause the jailer to do?
604. How could the jailer eat with prisoners and still carry out his job?
605. When does Luke say he rejoiced?

do to be saved?" Here then is another household to join with that of Lydia and others to form the church of Philippi. If you want to know about this church and if you want to come to know some of the other members of this congregation, find the book of Philippians and read Paul's epistle to these folk.

What a season of rejoicing for the jailer and his family, as well as for Paul and Silas, as they sat down together in the home of the jailer to eat together as brethren. This was perfectly consistent with the responsibility of the keeper which was only "to keep them safely." It might be well to point out that only after this man had manifested the fruit of repentance and was baptized does Luke say that he rejoiced that he had "believed in God."

1. The suggested release of Paul and Silas. 35-37.

35 But when it was day, the magistrates sent the serjeants, saying, Let those men go.
36 And the jailor reported the words to Paul, saying, The magistrates have sent to let you go: now therefore come forth, and go in peace.
37 But Paul said unto them, They have beaten us publicly, uncondemned, men that are Romans, and have cast us into prison; and do they now cast us out privily? nay verily; but let them come themselves and bring us out.

35 The earthquake, the preservation of the prisoners and even possibly the conversion of the jailer must have reached the ears of the rulers soon after it had occurred for we know of no other explanation for the unusual actions of these men. The day before Paul and Silas were guilty of treason and were to be treated with the highest contempt and suspicion. Now, they are to be set at liberty, to go in peace, yes, even before they have spent a full day in prison.

36, 37 From what Luke records in several places rest was not the interest of the apostles, surely not in this one at least, for they sang and prayed until midnight, then the earthquake, then the preaching, which probably took no little time, then the meal and now the soldiers are sent from the magistrates with their surprising word. If Paul said anything about his Roman citizenship before this it was not heard, but now it would be heard and with its full import. No Roman citizen could be punished without a trial and to do so was to involve the offenders in a very serious crime. Probably the two thoughts that prompted the magistrates to say

606. How account for the unusual actions of the magistrates?
607. Show the strenuousness of the work of Paul and Silas.
608. What were the two probable reasons of the magistrates for releasing them?
609. What right of Roman citizenship was here violated?

"Let these men go" were:

1. Because whoever these men were they were beaten without
a trial and trouble could arise over this.

2. They were somehow connected with this earthquake and
these rulers wanted nothing more to do with such unusual men.

The jailer came to speak to Paul of his release. Paul didn't give
his answer to his new found brother but went immediately to these
soldiers and spoke to them. He said in essence:

"What kind of action is this? A secret or private release to save
face? We were beaten before all. 'We', I say, and I mean that 'we'
are Roman citizens, beaten without a trial. Now, do you expect
us to sneak out the back door as if you were right and we were
wrong? Nay, verily, your magistrates have beaten us before all,
let all know that we are released."

   m. The report of Paul's reply to the magistrates, their action. 38,
      39.

      38 And the serjeants reported these words unto the magis-
          trates: and they feared when they heard that they
          were Romans;
      39 and they came and besought them; and when they had
          brought them out, they asked them to go away from
          the city.

38-39 I can well imagine that the soldiers were glad for once that
they were not the rulers. And when the rulers heard these words
"they feared" and well they might. The request of Paul was carried
out to the letter. Paul and Silas were besought not to carry their
case any further. By the hands of the magistrates themselves they
were released and brought out. One additional request was made by
these rulers and that was that they please leave the city. Anyone
could see what a source of embarassment to the rulers their presence would be.

   n. The final visit with the brethren at the house of Lydia. 40.

      40 And they went out of the prison, and entered into the
          house of Lydia: and when they had seen the brethren,
          they comforted them, and departed.

40 From the prison the two went immediately to Lydia's house.
There was no reason why they should hasten out of the city. When
Paul and Silas appeared what an occasion of rejoicing and thanksgiving there must have been in the house of Lydia. All the saints
of Philippi were soon called together, if they were not already there.

610. Why not accept the wrong rather than to contend for Roman rights?
611. Was Paul's request granted? What was the additional request of the
     magistrates?
612. Where did Paul go from prison? What did he do? Who stayed in
     Philippi?

To them Paul delivered further words of encouragement and exhortation. Probably his words were based upon his recent experience. He then departed. It was not without a good deal of genuine sorrow that Paul took his leave of this newly established church. But they were not left alone for both the Lord and the good physician Luke were to labor with them in Paul's absence.

12. PASSING THROUGH THE CITIES OF AMPHIPOLIS AND APOLLONIA. 17:1a.

1 Now when they had passed through Amphipolis and Apollonia,

1a For a brief description of these towns you are referred to Cunningham Geikie, pages 398-401, a part of which we quote here:

"Leaving Philippi, with its mingled memories of suffering and happiness, Paul and Silvanus and Timotheus took an easy day's journey of about three and thirty miles to the beautiful town of Amphipolis. It lies to the south of a spendid lake, under sheltering hills, three miles from the sea and on the edge of a plain of boundless fertility. The strength of its natural position, nearly encircled by a great bend of the river, the mines which were near it, and the neighboring forests, which furnished to the Athenian navy so many pines, fit 'to be the mast of some great Admiral' made it a position of high importance during the Peloponnesian wars . . . They proceeded the next day thirty miles further, through scenery of surpassing loveliness, along the Strymonic Gulf, through the wooded pass of Aulon, where St. Paul may have looked at the tomb of Euripides, and along the shores of Lake Bolbe to Apollonia. Here again they rested for a night, and the next day, pursuing their journey across the neck of the promontory of Chelcidice, and leaving Olynthus and Potidaea, with their heart-stirring memories, far to the south, they advanced nearly forty miles further to the far-famed town of Thessalonica, the capital of all Macedonia, and though a free city, the residence of the Roman Proconsul."

13. IN THESSALONICA. 17:1b-10a.

1b they came to Thessalonica, where was a synagogue of the Jews:

2 and Paul, as his custom was, went in unto them, and for three sabbath days reasoned with them from the scriptures,

3 opening and alleging that it behooved the Christ to suffer, and to rise again from the dead; and that this Jesus, whom, said he, I proclaim unto you, is the Christ.

613. How far from Philippi to Amphipolis? From Amphipolis to Apollonia? What was Amphipolis?
614. Why not stop in the two above towns?

THESSALONICA.

Situated on a bay of the Aegean Sea, called the Thermaic Gulf, the city had for its original name Therma and was called Thessalonica after the sister of Alexander the Great. It was the metropolis of Macedonia and under the name of Saloniki is a "strategic Balkan metropolis" today; present population is about 200,000. The emperor Augustus Caesar made it a free city as a reward for aid given him by it during his war with the Roman Senate. From its position on the much used Roman road, the Via Egnatia, and as a port it was an important trade center as well as a center of influence over the surrounding country. (I Thes. 1:7, 8) It was almost on a level with Corinth and Ephesus for a port of trade. There were many Jews here in Apostolic time and there is yet a large Jewish population.

4 And some of them were persuaded, and consorted with Paul and Silas; and of the devout Greeks a great multitude, and of the chief women not a few.

5 But the Jews, being moved with jealousy, took unto them certain vile fellows of the rabble, and gathering a crowd, set the city on an uproar; and assaulting the house of Jason, they sought to bring them forth to the people.

6 And when they found them not, they dragged Jason and certain brethren before the rulers of the city, crying, These that have turned the world upside down are come hither also;

7 whom Jason hath received: and these all act contrary to the decrees of Caesar, saying that there is another king, one Jesus.

8 And they troubled the multitude and the rulers of the city, when they heard these things.

9 And when they had taken security from Jason and the rest, they let them go.

10a And the brethren immediately sent away Paul and Silas by night

1b-3 As has already been observed the reason for coming to Thessalonica was that here was a synagogue of the Jews, and hence there was afforded an opening for the gospel. To Paul the presence of a synagogue was an invitation to preach Christ. Being acquainted with the service of the synagogue, and most especially with the law, he was able to utilize this opportunity to the fullest. The order of service in the synagogues allowed opportunity for free expression by any deemed worthy to speak. This chance was eagerly sought by the apostle. In the large town of Thessalonica the numerous Jews must have maintained a thriving place of worship. In this place as in all other Jewish assemblies it was necessary not only to convince the Jew that a certain man from the city of Nazareth in Galilee was the Messiah, but totally apart from that startling fact, that when the Messiah did come He was not to rule from an earthly throne but to hang from a Roman cross. Indeed, the cross to the Jews was a "stumbling block." Like the eyes of the two on the road to Emmaus "they were holden" to these things. And if, as in the case of the two, the Messiah Himself were to open the scriptures to them, and show from the law, the prophets and the Psalms that it "behooved the Christ to suffer, and to rise again from the dead," they would scarcely believe.

615. How is it Paul could speak so readily in the synagogues?

616. What two facts had to be established in the Jewish mind before they could become Christians?

617. Why was the cross a "stumbling block" to the Jew?

For three sabbaths Paul "opened and alleged" these very truths, or we might say, giving scriptural statement and proving that these things were so. For three weeks Paul made an appearance in the synagogue and without a doubt he was found on the streets going "from house to house." He further states in his epistle to the Thessalonians that while there he spent some time laboring at his trade as tentmaker. This was done by way of example and that he might not be a burden to any of the brethren. It might be well to refer to the two letters of Paul to the Thessalonians and read a first hand account of the effect of his preaching upon these folks.

Note: It would at the same time be interesting and profitable to read the many geographical and historical comments given concerning these various towns (Conybeare and Howson is one of the best), but it is not the purpose of this book to emphasize that portion of the study.

4 Upon consideration of the scriptural facts presented by Paul some among the Jews believed and embraced Christianity. They cast their lot with these two strangers. Of the many, many interested Gentiles who attended the services a vast multitude were added to the Lord. Yea, among these would-be-proselytes there were some from among the influential women of the town who became Christians. These Gentiles were the ones Paul said "turned from 'dumb idols' to serve the true and living God." Conspicuous among the Jews to accept Christ was Aristarchus who was with Paul at Ephesus, at Jerusalem, and sailed with him to home and imprisonment.

5 But there was a monster abroad in the town which would influence certain of the leaders among the Jews and having done so would use them as his ambassadors to oppose and persecute the work of God. I refer to the monster of "jealousy" or "envy".

The disbelief of these men involved more than a mere refusal to accept the promise of Paul's message; it had in it a hatred for the man himself. "Why was it," they thought, "in three weeks a new doctrine so full of apparent contradictions of the law, could secure such a following when we who have been teaching the law and traditions of God for all these years have not interested half so many? There is only one thing to do; these heretics must go, and with them their influence and teaching."

618. What is the meaning of "opened and alleged?"
619. How long did Paul preach before he was persecuted?
620. Who supported Paul while he was here? Why?
621. Who was in the majority among the converts, the Gentiles or the Jews?
622. What noted co-laborer of Paul was converted here in Thessalonica?
623. What was the monster abroad in the town? How did it effect the Jews? Paul and company?

No amount of argument from the Old Testament would suffice
to remove these men. There must be a general opposition from the
town itself, and on such a scale as to involve the power of the city
magistrates. Thessalonica being a Free City of Rome had complete control of its civic affairs and the word of the seven "Politarchs"
was final. It was also true that the conditions of the town were
particularly adaptable to the ends of these jealous Jews. In this
town and in other such Roman cities it was considered disgraceful to participate in manual work. But all did not have the money
to live the life of the noble—the result? A town full of idlers and
parasites, men who would literally "do anything for a price." These
idlers or "certain vile fellows" gathered a crowd. To this crowd
a word was sufficient, and a cry was soon raised against Paul and
Silas: Why such an opposition was raised no one really seemed to
know; something about "treason" against Caesar. "We have no king
but Caesar" was doubtless soon on the lips of everyone.

They were led by the Jews to the house of one, Jason, where it
was known that these men were staying. Somehow the Lord saw
to it that on this day Paul and Silas were not home. Jason was
home and they found certain others whom they took to be followers of the Way. Pulling and hauling these through the streets
they soon appeared before the authorities.

6-9 "In dealing with the seven Politarchs, under the very shadow
of the proconsular residence, they were dealing with judges of much
higher position and much more imbued with the Roman sense of
law than the provincial "duumviri" of Philippi. These men were not
going to be rushed into anything rash and the whole affair looked to the critical eye of these men too ludicrous for belief that
hard-working citizens like Jason and his friends could be seriously contemplating revolutionary measures."

Not only to the rulers did it thus appear but also to the ordinary
citizens of the town. A short hearing soon proved that it was only a matter of religious opinions and of no such proportions as at
first suggested. But even so, such a thought must not be left afloat
in the town. A certain bond was taken from Jason and the others
as security against a continuation of this preaching of "another
king, one Jesus." That such a bond was taken is no evidence that
Jason wanted to discourage their preaching, but when Paul and
Silas arrived home and learned of the events of the day, they forth-

624. Who were the Politarchs?
625. Who were the helpers of the Jews in their opposition to the apostles, how
     secure their help?
626. Who was Jason?
627. What difference is noticed between the judges here and those in Philippi?
628. What was the accusation?
629. Why take security from Jason?

with decided that this was indication that they were to move on to another field.

10a The extreme care of the apostle that he "might not burden any of you" (I Thess. 2:9) would seem to have an application here. After all, the hard earned money of these citizens meant something. "All things are lawful; but not all things are expedient." So it was that that same night Paul and Silas were taken out of the city and they set their course toward a country town called Berea. It could have been that Timothy was left behind here, as Luke was in Philippi, to strengthen and confirm the church.

14. AT BEREA. 17:10b-14a.

10b unto Beroea: who when they were come thither went into the synagogues of the Jews.

11 Now these were more noble than those in Thessalonica, in that they received the word with all readiness of mind, examining the scriptures daily, whether these things were so.

12 Many of them therefore believed; also of the Greek women of honorable estate, and of men, not a few.

13 But when the Jews of Thessalonica had knowledge that the word of God was proclaimed of Paul at Beroea also, they came thither likewise, stirring up and troubling the multitudes.

14 And then immediately the brethren sent forth Paul to go as far as to the sea:

10b "As usual, we notice how lightly Luke passes over the difficulties and dangers which drove Paul from place to place." The night journey of fifty or sixty miles is passed over without a word. Even though there were several rivers to cross and many other dangers on this mountain road not a sentence is given in allusion to it. The town of Berea is off the Egnatian Way in a southerly direction. It is suggested by some that Paul resorted to this out-of-the-way town in order to escape the pursuit of the Jews.

We must not conclude as we read these accounts of preaching and persecutions that Paul had no feelings on these matters, for we read in I Thessalonians that the apostle considered the Thessalonians as receiving the word "in much affliction" and in this same letter he alludes to his being "shamefully treated at Philippi."

11 But if the life of the Christian missionary has its own breaths of gloom, it also has its lights, and after all the storms which they had

630. How does the statement "all things are lawful; but not all things are expedient" apply here?
631. Who was left behind?
632. How far was the night journey to Beroea?
633. How did the apostle say they received the word in Thessalonica?

encountered they were cheered in their heaviness by a most encouraging reception.

Here in Berea they found a group of Jews who actually acted like civilized beings. Maybe it was because they were away from the city and its conceits, or because they had better leaders, or for many other supposed reasons. At any cause, instead of prejudice and bitterness Paul and Silas received interest and consideration. The interpretation placed upon the Old Testament prophecies by Paul were daily taken home to be compared with the scripture text. They read anew and with a new meaning these treasured words. There could only be one result to this type of procedure. "Many of them therefore believed."

12 The stay in Berea must have run into two or three months, as it was late fall or early winter when they arrived. This is learned by a knowledge of when travel was possible in these parts. Sir William Ramsey suggests that Paul preached in the town of Berea in some kind of public place for the hearing of the Greeks and in this way the "women of honorable estate, and of the men, not a few" came to believe. Others would place the Greeks as interested listeners in the synagogue services. Be that as it may, there were a substantial number of Greek converts, and among them some men and women of influence.

13-14a From Berea "once and again" Paul had a great desire to revisit Thessalonica and see how the Kingdom fared in that place. But for some unknown reason he was hindered from doing so. Somehow, although Paul did not reach Thessalonica, word of his preaching did. The Jews in Thessalonica were like Saul of old "yet breathing threatenings and slaughter against the disciples of the Lord," and as Saul had pursued them to foreign cities, they pursued Paul to Berea.

The method of opposition was very similar to that at Thessalonica and it was equally as successful. Almost identical words used by Luke in discussing the departure from the two towns. Timothy and Silas were to stay in Berea and carry on the work of Christ. It seems that the hatred of the Jews was centered in Paul and his preaching and not with these other two. We might also say that word was being expected daily from the brethren in Thessalonica and Paul was very anxious to hear of their state. Timothy remained in Berea to receive this word.

Why was it that others accompanied the apostle wherever he went? Some say it was because of the weakness of his body, and to

634. What encouragement did they receive in Beroea?
635. How long were they in Beroea? How do you know?
636. According to Ramsey how were the Greek converts made?
637. What great desire did Paul have while here?
638. Of what do you think the pursuit of these Jews reminded Paul?

go alone would constitute a real danger. This surely cannot be un-
questionably verified. It could have been that they were blessed by
his company. I know I would have been. At any rate, he was taken
to the seaport near Berea and there a ship was secured to Athens.
The brethren from Berea sailed with him all the way to Athens.
(Sophater could have been among them.)

15. IN ATHENS. 17:14b-34.

    a. The brethren from Berea go with Paul as far as Athens and
       take back a command for the coming of Silas and Timothy. 14b-
       15.

      14b and Silas and Timothy abode there still.
      15 But they that conducted Paul brought him as far as Ath-
         ens: and receiving a commandment unto Silas and
         Timothy that they should come to him with all speed,
         they departed.

14b, 15 When once here Paul instructed them that they should
return and charge Timothy and Silas to come as quickly as possible. The time of their arrival in Athens would be determined by
the news from Thessalonica.

    b. Paul is provoked in spirit and reasons in the synagogue. 16, 17.

      16 Now while Paul waited for them at Athens, his spirit
         was provoked within him as he beheld the city full
         of idols.
      17 So he reasoned in the synagogue with the Jews and
         the devout persons, and in the marketplace every day
         with them that met him.

16, 17 "Waiting in Athens." That seems to be the phrase descriptive of what Paul was doing in this pagan metropolis. This
would suggest the thought that he had not originally decided to
make this a point of work in his evangelistic efforts. But what
would a Christian do while thus waiting? To Paul, Christ was his
whole life; "for me to live is Christ" . . . "Christ is all."
    In the large town of Thessalonica he found the synagogue and
preached Christ; in the rural town of Berea, he did the same. And
in the immense city of Athens he also "reasoned in the synagogue

639. How could Timothy and Silas stay in the town and be free of persecu-
    tion?
640. What was being expected daily as they were in Beroea?
641. Why did Paul have someone with him wherever he went?
642. Who was Sopater?
643. When were Silas and Timothy to come to Athens?
644. What was Paul's first work for Christ in Athens?

with the Jews and the devout persons." The only difference Athens
made with Paul was that it stirred him with the deepest indignation to look upon the "city full of idols." The idols referred to were
of course, the many statues that lined the streets and filled the
squares. As one writer observed, "a statue looked out of every
cave near Athens." These "images" were of the various Greek
gods and goddesses as well as likenesses of many of the famous
warriors and statesmen. Paul was surely right in thus evaluating
them, for although these carved figures were not worshiped, they
advertised the multiplicity of gods who were.

How different is the response of men to similar circumstances.
To many, such a condition would have been so overwhelming in
magnitude as to make it seem impossible to do anything for Christ,
but not for Paul. It only caused a great desire to arise in his heart
that the truth be known in this place. This found expression not
only in the synagogue services but "everyday in the market place."
The town was full of idlers, and in such a large city there was
no trouble in securing a hearing from those on the street. In the
Agora or public market (the same place Socrates had used for
his teaching) Paul talked until they came to call him "a babbler."

c. The contact with the Epicurean and Stoic philosophers. 18-21.

18 And certain also of the Epicurean and Stoic philosophers
encountered him. And some said, What would this
babbler say? others, He seemeth to be a setter forth of
strange gods: because he preached Jesus and the resurrection.
19 And they took hold of him, and brought him unto the
Areopagus, saying, May we know what this new teaching is, which is spoken by thee?
20 For thou bringest certain strange things to our ears:
we would know therefore what these things mean.
21 (Now all the Athenians and the strangers sojourning
there spent their time in nothing else, but either to tell
or to hear some new thing.)

18-21 In such a town as Athens it was inevitable that Paul should
encounter some of the many philosophers. The Epicurean and Stoic
teaching had a great following in this place; a sizable sect of each was
meeting in the city. We will not take the space here to go into the
history and beliefs of these two philosophies. Suffice it to say that

645. What were the "idols?"
646. Where else did Paul preach besides the synagogue?
647. Which two philosophical schools did Paul encounter? What did they
teach?

the Epicureans believed that the highest good from life could only be secured in pleasure. Their founder suggested that the pleasures to be sought should be in the intellectual realm, but his followers failed to take his advice and sought the highest good in all types of pleasures, the most natural and common being in lust. The Stoics on the other hand held that the highest good could be found in a complete self-discipline amounting to the denial of the natural and necessary desires of man. One philosophy produced degenerates, the other suicides.

Well, it so happened that representatives from either side stayed one day to hear Paul. They were intrigued, their curiosity was aroused, and although totally ignorant of the very fundamentals of Christianity they none the less were interested in this Jew who so earnestly set forth this strange teaching. What was Paul teaching here? Was he dabbling with the principles of the two opposing philosophical thoughts? No, No! He was preaching "Jesus and the resurrection." He preached in plain understandable terms in this place what he had preached wherever he went. And this we also need to do today. Of course it would not be expected that they would all understand or acccept. Some called him "a babbler," others said that he was a preacher of "foreign divinities," but all heard him and all were interested. So interested, indeed, that they literally hurried Paul up to the steps of Mars' hill, up to the open air amphitheatre where these philosophers and others might gather around while Paul stood before them to tell more about this new teaching.

A description of the attitudes of these men: . . . "their greatest orator had hurled at them the reproach that, instead of flinging themselves into timely and vigorous action in defense of their endangered liberties, they were forever gadding about asking for the very latest news; and St. Luke—every incidental allusion of whose brief narrative bears the mark of truthfulness and knowledge—repeats the same characteristic under the altered circumstances of their present adversity. Even the foreign residents caught the infection, and the Agora buzzed with inquiring chatter at this late and decadent epoch no less loudly than in the days of Pericles or of Plato." (Farrar, ibid p. 302).

Surely we could say here that Paul was making application of his attributes of love. He was to say "love hopeth all things," and that "love believeth all things." These Athenians became more insolent than they were interested. Paul was surely standing as

648. What did these philosophies produce? Why?
649. What did Paul preach to these men?
650. What is the Agora? Mars Hill?
651. What was the matter with the attitude of the Athenians?

Pansainias stated on "the stone of impudence, where men had to
defend their facts while the listeners sat around."

   d. Paul's message on the unknown God. 22-31.

22 And Paul stood in the midst of the Areopagus, and said,
    Ye men of Athens, in all things I perceive that ye are
    very religious.
23 For as I passed along, and observed the objects of your
    worship, I found also an altar with this inscription, TO
    AN UNKNOWN GOD. What therefore ye worship in
    ignorance, this I set forth unto you.
24 The God that made the world and all things therein,
    he, being Lord of heaven and earth, dwelleth not in
    temples made with hands;
25 neither is he served by men's hands, as though he need-
    ed anything, seeing he himself giveth to all life, and
    breath, and all things;
26 and he made of one every nation of men to dwell on
    all the face of the earth, having determined their ap-
    pointed seasons, and the bounds of their habitation;
27 that they should seek God, if haply they might feel
    after him and find him, though he is not far from each
    one of us:
28 for in him we live, and move, and have our being;
    as certain even of your own poets have said,
    For we are also his offspring.
29 Being then the offspring of God, we ought not to
    think that the Godhead is like unto gold, or silver, or
    stone, graven by art and device of man.
30 The times of ignorance therefore God overlooked;
    but now he commandeth men that they should all every-
    where repent:
31 inasmuch as he hath appointed a day in which he will
    judge the world in righteousness by the man whom he
    hath ordained; whereof he hath given assurance unto
    all men, in that he hath raised him from the dead.

22-31 "Ye men of Athens, in all things I perceive that ye are
very religious." As G. Campbell Morgan remarks, this entire address is conciliatory. The whole speech is directed toward gaining the ear and heart of those who listened. Here is a brief outline of Paul's message to the Athenians:

652. What is the meaning of the term "conciliatory?"
653. What was "the stone of impudence?"
654. The theme of the message?

239

THE UNKNOWN GOD

Introduction: 22-b-23.
  The observance of idols.
Proposition:
  Characteristics of the Unknown God.
  I. Creator of all. 24-26.
      1. Made all things
      2. Lord of heaven and earth
      3. Dwells not in any one place
      4. Not served by men's hands
      5. The maker of nations
  II. Within reach of all. 27-29.
      1. In Him we live, move and have our being
      2. We are His offspring or creation
      3. Cast away then these idols and worship the true God
  III. Gives salvation to all. 30-31.
      1. The days of ignorance are over
      2. Men now should repent and turn to Christ
      3. This to be done in lieu of the final judgment
  Consider the following comments upon this outline:
Introduction: 22b-23a.
  He begins his message on a common ground. The thought is:
"I am to bring you a religious message and I deem it quite appropriate" for, "In all things I perceive you are very religious." To
be more specific in this general thought, and at the same time
to lead into the proposition of his address, he says: "For as I passed along, and observed the objects of your worship I found also an
altar with this inscription: To an Unknown God."
  The proposition: "What therefore ye worship in ignorance, this
I set forth unto you." It might be well to read verses 18b and 23b
together to get the full import of Paul's defense. 18b, "and some
said, what would this babbler say?" Others, "He seemeth to be a
'setter forth of strange gods'," verse 23b. "What therefore ye worship in ignorance, this **I set forth unto you.**" What a fine, pointed,
winsome approach.

I. CREATOR OF ALL. 24-26.

  This unknown God, the one whom all of you are really reaching
out to find, is the one who has made all things; the world and all
things therein. Thus, we could say of Him, that He is "Lord of
heaven and earth." This at once cuts out all gods of the various

655. From memory give the three divisions of the sermon.
656. How does Paul begin his message?
657. What is the proposition?
658. How can we say that God is "Lord of heaven and earth?"

elements and forces connected with this earth or the heavens above. Being such a great God, He would not be found in some house of human construction. How ridiculous for God to create all things and then be confined to some object of His creation! Man is totally dependent upon God for all that he has; God upon man for nothing.

II. WITHIN REACH OF ALL. 27-29.

This unknown, but knowable God, created man to begin with, and then from this one man brought forth the many nations that are now on the face of the earth. These peoples all enjoy Spring, Summer, Fall and Winter. They all live in the very part of the globe best suited to their needs. Now, in these things which this unknown but knowable God has given is the means of discovering something of His character. Paul was to say elsewhere that . . . "The things that are made declare His everlasting power and divinity" (Rom. 1:20). In thus using their senses and analyzing the things that are made in the light of whence they came they could "feel after and find him."

But lest these men conclude that God was in some far off place and was to be thought of in a completely objective manner, Paul hastens to tell them that He is nearer than the very air we breathe, for He is the source of life and the sustainer of life. It naturally follows then that we are "the offspring of God". To add force to this wonderfully new idea Paul quotes from two of their Grecian poets, Aratus and Cleanthes, who said in essence: "For we are also his offspring". This being so, and we know that it is, it must also be that all images of man whether of gold, silver, stone or wood, however wonderfully carved and artistically fashioned, could never be a representation of deity.

III. GIVES SALVATION TO ALL. 30-31.

Paul says here as Peter said in Acts 3:17, "I know that in ignorance ye did it" . . . In times past the conditions described could be attributed to "ignorance" but a new day has come, a new hour has struck. God only "overlooked" those times because He looked

659. If He is "Lord of heaven and earth" what does that fact do with the gods of the Greeks?
660. What is the relationship of man and God, God and man?
661. From whence came all the nations on the face of the earth?
662. How did Paul state that man was to "feel after" and find God?
663. God bears what relationship to life?
664. Where did Paul secure his quotation from their poets?
665. What naturally follows from the conclusion that we are God's offspring?
666. In what way did God "overlook" their ignorance?

beyond them to this day, this time. In this day, and in this message there is a remedy for all the ignorance and sin of the days past.

Now the application, now the demand upon the hearers, now the action from the message. This great God who created and sustains all things asks you and all men everywhere, in the light of your knowledge, and of the coming judgment "to repent!" Think it over. Change your mind and life. You are not right in the sight of this great God. Your beliefs, your philosphies, your life is at variance with His being and truth. It is imperative that you do this. God has set a day in His calendar when He will call all men before His bench of righteous judgment to be examined by His law. This God will not do this Himself but through His Son, the man whom He has set apart for this task. It is certain that this one will carry out this work, and all men can believe it is so, for God brought Him out of the grave for that very purpose.

That was enough. A burst of coarse derision interrupted his words. The Greeks, the philosophers themselves could listen with pleasure, even with some conviction, while he demonstrated the nullity of these gods of the Acropolis at which even their fathers four centuries earlier had not been afraid to jeer, but now that he had got to the point . . . "While Paul discussed round their altar the doctrine of an unknown God, while he enunciated philosophies, even though his enunciations contradicted their philosophies, they listened; but when he said, 'Now He commandeth men that they should all everywhere repent, inasmuch as He hath appointed a day in which He will judge the world in righteousness', they mocked. Men often find an intellectual excuse for refusing to be moral when God demands morality. Paul, discussing an altar and a theory of God, will fail unless he says, 'But now . . . **Repent'.** That is the point where men begin to mock, and postpone." (G. Campbell Morgan, pp. 424-425).

e. The results. 32-34.

32 Now when they heard of the resurrection of the dead, some mocked; but others said, We will hear thee concerning this yet again.
33 Thus Paul went out from among them.
34 But certain men clave unto him, and believed: among whom also was Dionysius the Areopagite, and a woman named Damaris, and others with them.

667. What was the demand upon the hearers? Why?
668. Why was it so imperative?
669. What connection does the resurrection have with the coming judgment?
670. What caused "some to mock?"
671. Who was converted?

32-34 But not all mocked and not all postponed. "Some believed, among them was a prominent man of the city, 'Dionysius the Areopagite.' Here was a Christian official of the very place where others mocked. There always seems to be women among the converts . . . Christianity was surely a glorious boon for them. There were no doubt others, but one who stood out above the others was "a woman named Damaris".

We find out from the Thessalonian letter that Silas and Timothy did meet Paul in Athens and that Paul was much refreshed by the news of the young evangelist. Timothy was soon sent back to Thessalonica and Silas to somewhere else, possibly Derbe. Paul left Athens as he came, alone.

Because there are some among us that say Paul made a failure in Athens, I would like to remind them of the facts of history, which say that the church in Athens was one of the strongest congregations of the empire in the second and third centuries.

16. IN CORINTH. 18:1-17.

1 After these things he departed from Athens, and came to Corinth.

2 And he found a certain Jew named Aquila, a man of Pontus by race, lately come from Italy, with his wife Priscilla, because Claudius had commanded all the Jews to depart from Rome: and he came unto them;

3 and because he was of the same trade, he abode with them, and they wrought; for by their trade they were tentmakers.

4 And he reasoned in the synagogue every sabbath, and persuaded Jews and Greeks.

5 But when Silas and Timothy came down from Macedonia, Paul was constrained by the word, testifying to the Jews that Jesus was the Christ.

6 And when they opposed themselves and blasphemed, he shook out his raiment and said unto them, Your blood be upon your own heads; I am clean: from henceforth I will go unto the Gentiles.

7 And he departed thence, and went into the house of a certain man named Titus Justus, one that worshipped God, whose house joined hard to the synagogue.

8 And Crispus, the ruler of the synagogue, believed in the Lord with all his house; and many of the Corinthians hearing believed, and were baptized.

672. What does the epistle to the Thessalonians add to our knowledge of the work in Athens?

673. What facts of history disprove the idea that Paul made a failure in Athens?

9   And the Lord said unto Paul in the night by a vision,
    Be not afraid, but speak and hold not thy peace:

10 for I am with thee, and no man shall set on thee to
    harm thee: for I have much people in this city.

11 And he dwelt there a year and six months, teaching the
    word of God among them.

12 But when Gallio was proconsul of Achaia, the Jews
    with one accord rose up against Paul and brought him
    before the judgment-seat,

13 saying, This man persuadeth men to worship God con-
    trary to the law.

14 But when Paul was about to open his mouth, Gallio
    said unto the Jews, If indeed it were a matter of wrong
    or of wicked villany, O ye Jews, reason would that I
    should bear with you:

15 but if they are questions about words and names and
    your own law, look to it yourselves; I am not mind-
    ed to be a judge of these matters.

16 And he drove them from the judgment-seat.

17 And they all laid hold on Sosthenes, the ruler of the
    synagogue, and beat him before the judgment-seat. And
    Gallio cared for none of these things.

1 As we have said, Paul left Athens as he had entered, alone.
One could go either by land or by sea from Athens to Corinth. The
distance by land was about forty miles. It was a five hour voyage
by sea. Since the sea would afford the least difficulty and since
there were a number of towns through which Paul would have
passed going by land, we believe he sailed across the brief span
of water that separated the two towns.

2,3 When Paul arrived in Corinth he was practically without funds,
nor would he take aught from the Corinthians. It was only after quite
a stay in this place that Silas and Timothy came to him with an
offering from Philippi. During the intervening time Paul worked at
his trade as tentmaker. He was fortunate enough to find lodging
with a couple of the same trade, "Aquila and Priscilla". Aquila
was born in Pontus (one of the many provinces of what has come
to be known as Asia Minor). He moved from his native home to
Rome. He had but lately been evicted from this place along with
all other Jews by a decree issued by the Emperor Claudius. It seem-

674. How far was it from Athens to Corinth by land? By sea?
675. What was the first difficulty that faced the Apostle upon arriving in
     Corinth?
676. Who helped Paul in a financial way while in Corinth?
677. Tell two facts about this man Aquila.
678. Why were the Jews forced to leave Rome?

ed that some stir had been caused in the Jewish quarter by one "Chrestus" (a corruption of the name "Christ"). Rather than investigate the uprising the Emperor, who had no particular liking for the Jews, blamed them all and sent them all from the city. This decree soon became a dead letter however, for all the Jews did not leave and many of them soon returned. Aquila and wife were among those who left. They found in Corinth a ready opportunity for their work.

Corinth is situated on a peninsula and has two seaports. The town had been populated through the efforts of Julius Caesar with a great many retired soldiers and freedom. These were placed here to protect and maintain the city in keeping with the desires of its founder. Being situated strategically as a coast town, there were people of all nations to be found on its streets and trading in its shops. Add to this the fact that the religion of Corinth had fallen into the deification of lust and you can see that it would be small wonder that Paul needed encouragement from the Lord. (Cf. 18:9.)

4 Aquila and Priscilla were evidently Christians when Paul met them. At least no word is given of their conversion and we do find them later laboring for Christ in Ephesus. (Cf 18:19). No real adequate knowledge of Paul's two years labor here can be obtained without a careful reading of his two epistles to the Corinthian church. Even though Luke is very brief in his comments on the work, his description is none the less very complete. While laboring night and day in this town Paul spoke to all "that came unto him" and of course, once a week he "reasoned in the synagogue" . . . While in Corinth he later stated he was determined "to know nothing among them but Jesus Christ, and Him crucified." As he thus preached in the Jewish assemblies he attracted a number of Gentiles and some Jews to his new message.

Lest we hurry over these verses and others which describe Paul's "labors in the word," let me pause to reflect on the real physical, moral and spiritual effort that was here put forth by this man of faith and prayer. What an example for us that we, too, might "spend and be spent" for the same gospel.

5 When one day Paul was joined by the welcome presence of Silas and Timothy from Macedonia, he was even better able to labor for the Lord. It would seem that as Paul searched the Old Testament scriptures in light of the need of the Jews and the obvious fulfillment of these scriptures he was **"constrained"** to testify to the Jews that Jesus was their "anointed one" or Christ.

679. Why would it be likely that tenmakers could find a job in Corinth?
680. Why would encouragement be needed to preach the gospel in Corinth?
681. Describe briefly the labors of Paul in Corinth. How could you obtain a complete knowledge of his work there?
682. What is meant by the little phrase "constrained by the word?" (18:5)

6 As the Jews were thus pressed to face the issue, "they opposed themselves and blasphemed". What a descriptive sentence: "They opposed themselves and blasphemed." Their objection in reality was not to Paul nor to the scripture, but a contradiction of their own true belief. Their railing and words of opposition were only a rejection of that which they really needed and wanted. "But unto this day . . . . a veil lieth upon their heart." (I Cor. 3:15)

Paul made a public declaration of his response to these Jews. It probably happened in the synagogue. He shook out his raiment and said unto them, "Your blood be upon your own heads. I am clean; from henceforth I will go unto the Gentiles." It was not that Paul was never again to preach to the Jews, for we find him later so doing, but his mission to them "first" was finished. He was now to turn his ministry unto the uncircumcised. At least this was so in Corinth.

7, 8 But note the irony of it all. Paul left the synagogue, but to go where? Next door! And what influence did this message have on the synagogue? "Crispus, the ruler of the synagogue, believed in the Lord with all his house." This man, Paul baptized personally (I Cor. 1:14). Relations must have been exceedingly delicate between the two groups—those who met so close together. The wisdom of such action would have to be determined by its fruits. (Cf. Matt. 11:19). The conversion of the Corinthians described in verse 8b was surely not without opposition from these Jews.

To be called "a Corinthian" in Paul's day would be equaled today by calling a man a drunkard or a woman a prostitute. Such was the reputation of this town. So when we read that "Many of the Corinthians hearing, believed, and were baptized" it was a real victory for the gospel. At the same time there was potentially present a great problem, yea, today's problem . . . backsliding.

9, 10 The Lord of the harvest had a real plan for this wild, wicked city. There were many potential children of God in the markets, shops, the houses of this place. If Paul's stay in Corinth was going to be like his previous efforts he would be about ready to depart now that Timothy and Silas had arrived. They could stay here with the brethren as they had in Thessalonica, Berea and Athens. But one night the Lord altered this program.

683. What is the meaning of "opposed themselves and blasphemed?"
684. Why shake out his raiment?
685. Did Paul ever preach to the Jews again? If so, why say: "from henceforth I will go unto the Gentiles?"
686. Show the irony of his decision. Was this a wise thing to do? What does Matt. 11:19 say about it?
687. Why is it such a victory for the gospel to read that "many of the Corinthians became Christian?"
688. In what sense did God have "people" in Corinth?

It would seem from what the Lord told him that Paul's decision to move on was not only because his two helpers had arrived, but because of the Jews' intense hatred for him and lest they harm him physically. The Lord said unto Paul in the night by a vision, "Be not afraid, but speak and hold not thy peace; for I am with thee, and no man shall set on thee to harm thee; for I have much people in this city.

11 For one year and six months the word of God sounded forth from the house hard against the synagogue. How we can glory in this little phrase "teaching the word of God among them." We do not know just how he did it, but that he did we are certain. In this is the salvation of the world and the church: no teaching, no salvation. It is the task of every preacher and Christian worker to be more than a mere public proclaimer. He must be a preacher **both** publicly and privately.

12-16 And how is it that Paul came finally to leave Corinth? Well, it happened this way: A new proconsul named Gallio came into office and the Jews felt that by taking advantage of his inexperience they could turn the public opinion against Paul. For some reason they never tried this plan on the proconsul who preceded Gallio, possibly because they knew they had no real cause. According to history, Gallio was a very good and wise man. He was the brother of Senca who referred to him as "sweet Gallio" and said: "No mortal man is so sweet to any single person as he is to all mankind." The Jews had not reckoned with the wisdom of this man for he no sooner heard their charges than he saw through their subtle plan. They would have no case with this man unless some law of Rome had been violated, hence the Jew's cry: "To worship God contrary to the law." This was only a half truth. The insinuation was the law of Rome, but they knew, and so did Gallio, that it was "their law" that troubled them. He told them as much, and further stated that he had no interest whatsoever in these matters. So, before the apostle could say a word, or the Jews could speak further, the governor commanded his soldiers to clear the court. Out from the presence of the judge went the chagrined and infuriated Jews.

17 Remember Crispus, "the ruler of the synagogue?" Well, here is mention made of his successor, "Sosthenes". The soldiers had no sooner cleared the court than they took hold of this one who evidently was the leader in this wicked farce and gave him the

689. What were Paul's original plans and how were they altered?
690. What is needed today for the salvation of the world and the church?
691. How did the Jews plan through Gallio to rid themselves of Paul?
692. What was the insinuation of the Jews? What was their real objection?
693. How did Gallio rid himself of the Jews?
694. Why beat Sosthenes? Why didn't Gallio stop them?

beating he so righly deserved. These Greek soldiers knew that
the whole thing was unjust; they were exasperated beyond control. Gallio looked on while the incident took place, but it made
little difference to him how his soldiers chose to amuse themselves.

17. AT CENCHREA. 18:18.

18 And Paul, having tarried after this yet many days,
took his leave of the brethren, and sailed thence for
Syria, and with him Priscilla and Aquila: having shorn
his head in Cenchreae; for he had a vow.

18 Thanks to Gallio Paul was permitted to remain in Corinth as
long as he deemed necessary. This is the only town where this took
place. It might be well to say that while here the two epistles to
the Thessalonians were written. For some reason Paul wanted to
hasten to Syria. Taking his leave of the saints in Corinth, whom he
loved so well, he made plans to sail for Syria. He took with him
Priscilla and Aquila. Upon arrival at the seaport town of Cenchrea
he cut his hair in fulfillment of a vow he had made earlier. This vow
was probably one of thanksgiving for some act of God's goodness.
It was similar to that of a Nazarite but there is no reason to assume
that it was such. There was at this time or later, a thriving little
church, of which Phoebe was a deaconess, located at Cenchrea.
(Cf. Rom. 16:1).

18. IN EPHESUS. 18:19-21.

19 And they came to Ephesus, and he left them there:
but he himself entered into the synagogue, and reasoned with the Jews.
20 And when they asked him to abide a longer time, he
consented not;
21 but taking his leave of them, and saying I will return
again unto you if God will, he set sail from Ephesus.

19-21 "A few days sail, if the weather was ordinarily propitious,
would enable his vessel to anchor in the famous haven of Panorunus
(the port of Ephesus) which was then a forest of masts at the center of the Mediterranean trade, but is now a reedy swamp in a
region of desolation." (Farrar).
Leaving Priscilla and Aquila somewhere in the town of Ephesus,
Paul immediately looked out the synagogue in the town. It must
have been the sabbath day when Paul and his friends landed in
Ephesus. Paul could see what a glorious opportunity this great city
presented for the gospel; but he must not tarry, he could leave the

695. What connection with Corinth do I and II Thess. have?
696. Why did Paul cut his hair in Cenchrea? What kind of vow was it?

two workers he had brought with him. Promising the interested Jews that he would return "if God wills," he took his leave of this great city.

19. AT CAESAREA. 18:22a.

22a And when he had landed at Caesarea, he went up and saluted the church,

22a Landing at the seaport he went up to the church in Caesarea and saluted the brethren. He probably saw Philip the evangelist and his gifted daughters, Cornelius and many others.

20. IN ANTIOCH. 18:22b.

22b and went down to Antioch.

22b Here he arrived after some three years absence and having traveled more than twenty-six hundred miles. Ah! What a report he had to give and what an experience of reunion it must have been. This concludes the **second missionary journey.**

A TEST OVER THE FIFTEENTH CHAPTER AND THE SECOND MISSIONARY JOURNEY

Answer the following questions. A sentence or two will suffice.

1. What was taught by "certain men from Judaea" that caused such a stir?
2. Why go to the apostles and elders about the trouble?
3. What encouragement did Paul and Barnabas have on their way to Jerusalem?
4. Who especially objected to uncircumcised Christians? What sect?
5. Who said that God had chosen him that by his mouth "the Gentiles should hear the word of the gospel and believe?"
6. What was the "yoke" which neither the fathers nor the Jews of Peter's day could bear?
7. What was the point of argument in the speeches of Paul and Barnabas?
8. What did James add that had not been said before?
9. Why ask the Gentiles to abstain from: "What is strangled, and from blood?"
10. What did Paul tell Peter when he withstood him to the face?
11. What purpose did Paul have in making a second journey?
12. Why disagree over John Mark?
13. Why circumcise Timothy?
14. What were the "decrees" that were delivered to the churches?

697. Who was Phoebe? Why not stay in Ephesus? Whom did Paul see in Caesarea? What amount of time involved in the second journey? How many miles?

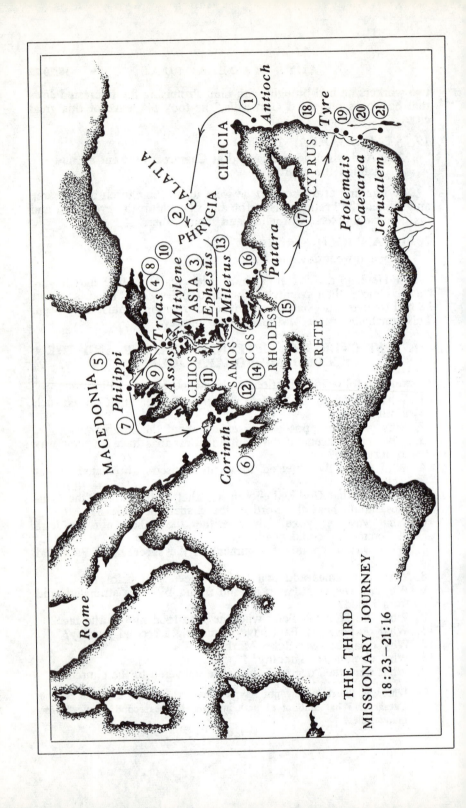

THE THIRD
MISSIONARY JOURNEY
18:23—21:16

15. What did Paul do in Phrygia and Galatia?
16. Why would a "man from Macedonia" be any different than any other man?
17. What is a "Roman colony?"
18. What was the occupation and home town of Lydia?
19. How did the Lord open the heart of Lydia?
20. Why did Paul rebuke the spirit in the maid at Philippi?
21. What was an accusation of the slavemasters before the magistrates in Philippi?
22. Was the jailor listening to the singing and praying of Paul?
23. Why ask the magistrates to deliver them personally?
24. Why did the magistrates "fear" Paul and Silas?
25. For how many sabbaths did Paul reason from the scriptures in the synagogue at Thessalonica? What was his message?
26. Who did Paul stay with in Thessalonica? How did this man get into trouble?
27. Where was Luke left to labor? Timothy? Silas and Timothy?
28. Why did Paul leave Berea?
29. What provoked Paul's spirit in Athens?
30. What is an Epicurean? A Stoic?
31. What is the "Areopagus"?
32. How did Paul develop his sermon on the "unknown God"?
33. When did some on Mars hill mock at Paul? At what point in his sermon?
34. Why live with Priscilla and Aquila in Corinth?
35. Who was Titus Justus? Who was Crispus?
36. Who was Gallio? Who was Sosthenes?
37. Where did Paul cut his hair? Why?
38. Why not stay at Ephesus?

THE THIRD MISSIONARY JOURNEY
18:23—21:16

1. IN ANTIOCH OF SYRIA. 18:23a.

23a And having spent some time there,

23a Of Antioch Luke says: . . . "Having spent some time there" . . . How long is "some time?" Let us think for a moment on this. According to a careful chronology it was one year or slightly more from the time he left Ephesus on his second journey until he returned to this metropolis on his third journey. A week or more must have been spent in traveling from Ephesus to Caesarea and then to Antioch. While here it is thought that he heard of the destructive

698. How do we arrive at the thought that it was two months or a little more that Paul stayed in Antioch?

251

work of the Judaizing teachers in the churches of Galatia. Just when he received this information we do not know, but we are sure that upon hearing of it, he was very anxious to go to the source of the trouble that he might put this heresy to rout. If we allow eight or ten months for his visit to the churches of Galatia (and it surely must have been this long if not longer), we would then understand Luke's words in 18:23a to mean about two months or slightly over.

2. THROUGH THE PROVINCES OF GALATIA AND PHYRGIA. 18:23b.

23b he departed, and went through the region of Galatia, and Phrygia, in order, establishing all the disciples.

23b For comment on what was here accomplished read the notes above.

Read also the book of Galatians, since it was written after Paul arrived in Ephesus. I would once again suggest that a knowledge of the lands through which this long trip was made would help immeasurably in your appreciation of Paul's work.

3. AT EPHESUS. 18:24 — 19:41

a. Apollos teaching the baptism of John is corrected by Priscilla and Aquila. 24-28.

24 Now a certain Jew named Apollos, an Alexandrian by race, an eloquent man, came to Ephesus; and he was mighty in the scriptures.

25 This man had been instructed in the way of the Lord; and being fervent in spirit, he spake and taught accurately the things concerning Jesus, knowing only the baptism of John:

26 and he began to speak boldly in the synagogue. But when Priscilla and Aquila heard him, they took him unto them, and expounded unto him the way of God more accurately.

27 And when he was minded to pass over into Achaia, the brethren encouraged him, and wrote to the disciples to receive him: and when he was come, he helped them much that had believed through grace;

28 for he powerfully confuted the Jews, and that publicly, showing by the scriptures that Jesus was the Christ.

24, 25 As the work of the Lord was begun in Corinth by Paul and continued by Apollos, so in Ephesus the work was begun by Apollos and continued by Paul. "What Paul did for Apollos in Corinth, Apollos did for Paul in Ephesus." What a wonderful lesson can be gained from a study of the life and work of this Apollos.

699. How long did Paul stay in the region of Galatia and Phrygia? Why?
700. How was the work in Ephesus like the work in Corinth?

1. A Jew. 2. An Alexandrian. 3. An eloquent man. 4. Mighty
in the scriptures. 5. Instructed "in the way of the Lord." 6. Fervent
in the spirit. 7. Spoke and taught accurately the things concerning
Jesus, knowing only the baptism of John.

We can say with G. Campbell Morgan that like Paul, Apollos
combined the powers of the Hebrew religion with the learning of
his Greek background. Paul was a "Hebrew of the Hebrews," but
he was also reared in the Greek city of Tarsus. How the Lord does
place His hand upon the very one He can use best in every given circumstance. How well fitted was Paul to be an apostle to the Gentiles. He had all the background of his Hebrew training to enable
him to speak to the Jews, all the personal experience of living under Grecian culture to assist in his approach and message to the
Gentiles. This also was the combination with this man Apollos.

Alexandria was the center of learning in Paul's day, a large uni-
versity being located there. This might account for the eloquence of
this one. He was not only an orator, but one who touched the emotions of his listeners and used the word of God as the basis of
his discussion. What an example for New Testament preachers of
today.

The statement that "He was mighty in the scriptures" does not simply mean that he quoted one passage after another, but rather like
Nehemiah of old "gave the sense thereof." He had a grasp of the
interrelationship of the scriptures, something to which Paul was
alluding when he said "rightly dividing the word of truth."

It might be interesting to read Matthew 3:3 in connection with the
statement that Apollos was instructed in the "way of the Lord." Here
in Matthew we have a prophecy carried over from Isaiah 40:3 concerning John the Baptist. "A way, a highway" was to be prepared
by John the Baptist for Jesus. This way was prepared by John's
preaching and his promise. John told of the soon coming of the
Messiah and His kingdom. In this doctrine Apollos had been carefully taught, either by John himself or by some one of his disciples.
We might ask: "Didn't Apollos even so much as know that the
Messiah had already come?" Oh, yes, I'm sure he did for we find
later that he taught and spoke with a fiery spirit the "things concerning Jesus." But his teaching and preaching on this subject were
limited to that which was known and taught by John the Baptist.
John knew that the Messiah had come. He knew also that He was

701. Give from memory four of the seven characteristics of Apollos.
702. Show how Paul was especially fitted for his work.
703. How was Apollos prepared by God for his work?
704. What might have accounted for the education of Apollos?
705. Show how Apollos was more than just an orator.
706. What is meant by being "mighty in the scriptures?"
707. How does Matthew 3:3 relate to the preaching of Apollos?

to have a kingdom and that very soon He would set it up. He knew of his miracles and power. Something probably of His life and teaching reached John's ears. Apollos must also have heard of the death of this Jesus and possibly something of His being raised. But Apollos knew nothing of the message of the cross, or resurrection. He was probably looking for this Nazarene to appear again and set up His Messianic kingdom.

26 This man was found in the synagogue of the Jews speaking out boldly on these matters. There were two attendants of that synagogue who also knew of the Way of God and the things concerning Jesus, but their knowledge was complete and their message unto the salvation of the soul. Be it said to the everlasting honor of this good man Apollos that although he had much in which he could take pride he was not bigoted. We can observe this in the response that was given to Priscilla and Aquila when they took him aside and instructed him more accurately in the Way of the Lord. Apollos was glad to admit his past mistake and from henceforth include in his message this new found truth.

27 It would seem that the acceptance of this new position prompted his decision to leave the town of Ephesus. It would be, to say the least, a disadvantage to boldly proclaim one thought for a space of time and then rather suddenly make almost an about-face on the same subject. When he decided that he could work in a more effective way for Christ in Achaia than in Asia, he left. Priscilla and Aquila probably told him of the work in Corinth. The brethren encouraged him in the thought and wrote letters of recommendation to the brethren in Achaia. The fact that there were Christians in Ephesus before Paul arrived is fine testimony of the good work of Priscilla and Aquila.

28 The disciples (or believers) in Corinth did receive Apollos. Indeed, he became such a favorite of some that they formed a sect around him. (Cf. I Cor. 1:12). Luke say that the greatest contribution of this evangelist was his ability to "help them much that had believed through grace." The Jews that opposed Paul's preaching of Christ in Corinth were due for a real setback and that "publicly" when this man Apollos put in his appearance.

708. What was missing from the message of Apollos?
709. What very honorable thing can we say about Apollos?
710. How did Priscilla and Aquila go about correcting Apollos? Any example for us today?
711. Why did Apollos leave Ephesus?
712. Do we find an example in these verses of a so-called "church letter?"
713. How is it that there were Christians in Ephesus before Paul arrived?
714. How did Apollos get along in Corinth? What did he do?

b. Paul corrects some on the baptism of John, baptizes them, lays hands on them; they receive the spiritual gifts. 19:1-7.

1 And it came to pass, that, while Apollos was at Corinth, Paul having passed through the upper country came to Ephesus, and found certain disciples:
2 and he said unto them, Did ye receive the Holy Spirit when ye believed? And they said unto him, Nay, we did not so much as hear whether the Holy Spirit was given.
3 And he said, Into what then were ye baptized? And they said, Into John's baptism.
4 And Paul said, John baptized with the baptism of repentance, saying unto the people that they should believe on him that should come after him, that is, on Jesus.
5 And when they heard this, they were baptized into the name of the Lord Jesus.
6 And when Paul had laid his hands upon them, the Holy Spirit came on them; and they spake with tongues, and prophesied.
7 And they were in all about twelve men.

1, 2 God did will, and Paul **did** come back to the city of Ephesus. It would seem that he was in a hurry to arrive for Luke says that he came through "the upper country" instead of coming along the longer, but more convenient highway route.

What an interesting passage is before us. Why is it that Paul met these twelve men rather than any others in this place? Well, it is not to be concluded from this text that these twelve were all the disciples in Ephesus, but rather that he encountered in these men something of interest for our learning and example.

"Did ye receive the Holy Spirit when ye believed?" . . . Note: Not **"since"** ye believed as the King James version has it. To say **"since"** ye believed would suggest a "second blessing." But the American Revised Version is accurate when it suggests that the reception of the Holy Spirit was co-existent with saving faith.

Why did Paul ask this question of these persons? This question cannot be answered with certainty but it would seem that Paul saw something in the lives of these persons that made him wonder. Possibly some lack of evidence of the fruit of the Spirit (Cf. Gal. 5:22).

715. What is meant by the statement that "God did will" and Paul did come back to Ephesus?
716. What shows that Paul was in a hurry to get to Ephesus?
717. Why mention Paul's meeting with the twelve disciples?
718. Why not use the word "since" in the question of Paul?

Be that as it may, the inquiry was made and now notice their response. "We did not so much as hear whether the Holy Spirit was" . . . (the word "given" has been supplied by the translators). Of course this does not mean that these men were ignorant of whether there was or was not such a being as the Holy Spirit, but rather they were unacquainted with the fact that the Holy Spirit had made His advent.

3-5 When Paul realized this he immediately inquired into the one action that brings the Holy Spirit into the life and body of man— water baptism. If this is not true, why bring the subject of baptism into the answer of their question? Some are inclined to the opinion that Paul was asking these persons whether they had received the spiritual gifts "since" they believed, but this is not so for it does not read "since" but "when ye believed."

When they said that they were baptized into John's baptism, then Paul knew that they were like Apollos, i.e. in need of instruction. The fourth verse must be but the briefest outline of Paul's instruction to them. They needed to know all that Apollos did (possibly they were his converts). John's baptism was a baptism of testimony, testimony to the repentance of sins and a testimony of belief in Jesus of Nazareth as the Messiah. Paul must have spoken to them of the meaning of the cross and the necessity of the baptism of the Lord Jesus (Cf. Mark 16:15-16). But forget not that the first purpose of their baptism was the reception of the Holy Spirit. When they were thus taught they were baptized by immersion for the remission of sins (cf. 2:38) and they received from God the gift of the Holy Spirit.

6, 7 Immediately following their baptism (or so it would seem) Paul granted to these men the spiritual gifts of prophecy and tongues (and doubtless others, but these are all that are evident on this occasion). This was done by the laying on of Paul's hands and for the purpose of granting inspired leadership for the infant church until the New Covenant could be placed in permanent written form.

c. Paul preaches in the synagogues and the school of Tyrannus. 19:8-12.

719. What does this text tell us as to the time when we receive the Holy Spirit?
720. Why do *YOU* think Paul asked this question of the twelve?
721. What did the twelve mean by their answer to Paul's question?
722. Why inquire into their baptism?
723. What about the thought of spiritual gifts in connection with this incident?
724. What did these twelve men need to know? What verse describes their instruction?
725. What baptism is the baptism "in the name of the Lord Jesus?"
726. What special spiritual gifts were given to these men? How?

8 And he entered into the synagogue, and spake boldly for the space of three months, reasoning and persuading as to the things concerning the kingdom of God.

9 But when some were hardened and disobedient, speaking evil of the Way before the multitude, he departed from them, and separated the disciples, reasoning daily in the school of Tyrannus.

10 And this continued for the space of two years; so that all they that dwelt in Asia heard the word of the Lord, both Jews and Greeks.

11 And God wrought special miracles by the hands of Paul:

12 insomuch that unto the sick were carried away from his body handkerchiefs or aprons, and the disease departed from them, and the evil spirits went out.

8-10 The appearance of the apostle in the synagogue was welcomed upon his first visit to Ephesus (cf. 18:19, 20) and now they manifest their open mindedness by giving heed to his bold preaching for the space of three months. Now here is a question: "If Paul established a church in Ephesus by 'reasoning and persuading' concerning **'the kingdom of God'** what must then be the relationship of the kingdom of God and the church?" There is only one conclusion and that is that the kingdom of God and the church are one and the same institution. (Cf. Col. 1:13; Rev. 1:7).

I like the two words of description as to Paul's preaching: "reasoning and persuading." Let's have more of it.

But a determined minority so quenched the voice of their conscience that they became "hardened" toward the truth. This caused them to enter into disobedience and to express this disobedience in words of ridicule and contradiction. When such evil speaking was done before the general assembly of the church there was only one thing to do and that was to leave the synagogue. It would seem that when Paul withdrew the disciples, he took with him the largest proportion of the synagogue congregation.

The town of Ephesus was about 600,000 in population. In this large city Paul and the Ephesian Christians must find a place to meet. The school room of one Tyrannus was secured. This evidently was

727. Did the Jews mean what they said upon Paul's first visit to Ephesus? (Cp. 18:19-20)

728. What is the relationship of "the kingdom of God" and the church? What two descriptive words are given concerning Paul's preaching?

729. How long did Paul continue preaching before opposition arose?

730. What real sin did the disobedient ones commit?

731. What determined the separation?

732. What was the population of Ephesus when Paul was there?

a large lecture room in which lessons on rhetoric were given. Ramsey suggests that the hours for work were from early in the morning until 10 o'clock and then a period of five hours intervened in which the noon meal was eaten and time was taken for rest and relaxation. He suggests that in this way Paul could work at his trade and at the same time speak during these hours to those who could and would hear. Whatever the circumstance, from this schoolroom there was heralded forth the word of life for the space of two years. Paul was not content simply to arouse those of the city, but also the many living in the great province of Asia. And so we read: "so that all they that dwelt in Asia heard the word of the Lord, both Jews and Greeks."

The seven churches of Asia referred to in Rev. 1:4 as well as the church at Colossae (Col. 1:2) were doubtless established at this time.

11, 12 In this great town full of superstition and sin God granted special acts of power through the hands of the apostle. Such acts would even stop the Ephesian in his onward rush to destruction. Just what these miracles were that were performed personally by Paul Luke does not say, but another unusual circumstance that came as a result of the apostle's effort is described. The power of God was so in evidence among them that nothing appeared impossible. If the hands of the apostle could heal, why not some of his personal effects? Paul, as we have said, was working at his occupation of tent making. In this work he would naturally wear an apron to protect his person and garments. Such aprons or coverings were eagerly sought by some to be carried to the sick that Paul had not time to visit. Strange to say, diseases **were** cured, and not only so, but by the use of such even evil spirits were cast out. We cannot imagine that this was done with the approval of the apostle.

   d. Exorcists overcome by evil spirits. The name of the Lord magnified. 19:13-20.

     13 But certain also of the strolling Jews, exorcists, took upon them to name over them that had the evil spirits the name of the Lord Jesus, saying, I adjure you by Jesus whom Paul preacheth.

     14 And there were seven sons of one Sceva, a Jew, a chief priest, who did this.

733. What was the "school of Tyrannus?"

734. What suggestion of Ramsey seems to help in our understanding?

735. How could "all Asia hear the word" with only one preacher?

736. What does Rev. 1:4 and Col. 1:2 have to do with Paul's work?

737. What were the special miracles wrought by Paul? Why?

738. How is it that the Ephesians used the aprons or handkerchiefs?

739. Did these items really effect the cures? How?

740. Show how the use of the aprons and handkerchiefs was not wise.

15 And the evil spirit answered and said unto them, Jesus
    I know, and Paul I know; but who are ye?

16 And the man in whom the evil spirit was leaped on
    them, and mastered both of them, and prevailed a-
    gainst them, so that they fled out of that house naked
    and wounded.

17 And this became known to all, both Jews and Greeks,
    that dwelt at Ephesus; and fear fell upon them all,
    and the name of the Lord Jesus was magnified.

18 Many also of them that had believed came, confessing,
    and declaring their deeds.

19 And not a few of them that practised magical arts
    brought their books together and burned them in the
    sight of all; and they counted the price of them, and
    found it fifty thousand pieces of silver.

20 So mightily grew the word of the Lord and prevailed.

13-16 That such efforts of healing were not, to say the least, "wise"
can be seen from the effect that they had upon unbelievers. When
word got around that the sick were being healed by proxy, it seemed to some that there must not be any limitations on the power of
the name of this one whom Paul preached. Certain ideas came into
the hearts of "strolling" Jews whose time and interest were taken
up with nothing better than dabbling in the black arts. The par-
ticipants in the particular incident described here were seven de-
generate sons of one Sceva, who was, at one time at least, a high
priest. Others had been using the name in a supernatural way saying, "I adjure you by Jesus whom Paul preacheth." So two of the
boys of Sceva (perhaps more but two are mentioned) hit upon a
plan of casting out a demon which was quite unique. Their plan
was to get the poor possessed man into a room and once there they
could then rebuke the spirit and cast it out by their new power. But
they were entirely unprepared for the results of their efforts. They had
no sooner pronounced the magical formula than the evil spirit had
a word to say in answer to them: "Jesus I know, and Paul I know,
but who are ye?" Imagine the surprised look on the faces of the two
young lads when they heard these words. And then their surprise
turned to fright as the possessed man leaped upon them. Fight as
they did he "mastered them both." In the scuffle their clothes were
torn and their bodies injured. There was only one thing to do and

741. Who were these "strolling Jews?" Who was Sceva?
742. Why did these sons want to cast out a demon?
743. What was the plan of these two sons in casting out a demon?
744. When did surprise turn to fright?
745. How was it that this incident with the two sons turned out to good?
746. How was the death of Ananias and Sapphira a parallel for this case?

that was to get out of this room and escape from this madman. What a sight it must have presented to those who saw them fleeing from the house "naked and wounded."

17 But the result was good. The news of the incident spread far and wide to both "Jews and Greeks." When they heard of it "fear fell upon them." The respect here given was evidently due to the fact that although Paul was very successful in casting out demons, yea, even the "aprons and handkerchiefs" of the apostle could do the same, yet when this power was at all mishandled, the power of its misuse was as great as its use. Hence the name of Jesus was "magnified" rather than degraded.

18-20 When Ananias and Sapphira were carried out to their graves for lying, "fear came upon every soul." Of the rest of the church Luke says that "they durst not join themselves to them," i.e. if there were some who were at all hypocritical like the two described, they made no effort at all to "join themselves to them," fearing lest a similar fate befall them. The good accomplished here in Ephesus went far beyond that in Jerusalem. The positive good accomplished was that it brought the hypocrites out of hiding to come in a confession of their sins (See Jas. 5:16). The fear of the consequences of pretending truly took hold of the hearts of these people. Oh, that it might be so today. To be specific, Luke tells us of $75,000 worth of books that were burned. What were these "magical books?" Perhaps that would best be held for a question of discussion. It would suffice to say that they were in direct opposition to The Way and were thus aligned in some fashion with the evil one.

e. Paul's far reaching plans. 19:21, 22.

21 Now after these things were ended, Paul purposed in the spirit, when he had passed through Macedonia and Achaia, to go to Jerusalem, saying, After I have been there, I must also see Rome.

22 And having sent into Macedonia two of them that ministered unto him, Timothy and Erastus, he himself stayed in Asia for a while.

21, 22 Before we discuss Paul's future plans, it might be well to place before our minds the important thoughts that relate to this time in the chronology of events. First let us say that Paul was laying plans for a collection for the poor saints in Judea. With this in mind he had written a letter to the Corinthians instructing them concerning it. He mentions in his letter to the Corinthians that the

747. How did the good accomplished in Ephesus supercede that of Jerusalem?
748. How is it that $75,000 went up in smoke?
749. How does the collection for the poor saints of Judea fit into this narrative?

THEATER AT EPHESUS.

Ephesus, the capital of the province, was in a fertile district and stood partly on lowland and partly on the hills near the mouth of the Cayster. It had a fine harbor so that at the beginning of the Christian era it was the emporium of that part of the peninsula north of the Taurus. During the ages, however, its harbor became filled up with earth brought down by the river, and its great trade passed over to Smyrna. Besides the two great roads that led easterly there were coast roads, one leading northerly to Smyrna, the other southerly to Miletus. Ephesus was the center of the worship of Diana, a goddess similar to the Greek Artemis, who was worshiped under different names throughout Asia Minor. The manufacture of shrines of silver, marble, and terra cotta, used in the worship of this deity, was a lucrative business in Ephesus. (Acts 19:24-27.) Its temple of Diana was a grand specimen of Ionic architecture and was one of the "seven wonders of the world." The length of the building was 425 feet, the breadth 220 feet, and its columns, of which there were 137, were sixty feet high, and six feet in diameter. The temple and its precincts were held most sacred and furnished safe asylum even to criminals. It was also used as a bank for the safekeeping of treasures. This great structure, like other portions of Ephesus, is now a mass of ruins. Paul made Ephesus one of his chief centers of missionary enterprise. Paul himself did not probably visit all the cities of the surrounding country where churches were established, but directed the work carried on by his various associates. The apostle John is said to have spent the closing years of his life in Ephesus.

Historical Geography of Bible Lands, pages 105-106.

Galatians and those of Macedonia were also to have a part in this collection. Some writers assume that the letter to the Galatians was written from Antioch before he left on the third journey.

Now as to Paul's plans. He had purposed "in the spirit" that he was to pass from Ephesus into Macedonia and Achaia taking up the collection, as we before stated. He planned also to winter in Corinth. And from thence to Jerusalem to take the offering to those in need. Then Paul says, "I must also see Rome."

In writing to the Corinthians Paul stated that "a great door is opened unto me and there are many adversaries" (I Cor. 16:9). Because of the very promising work in Ephesus Paul decided to stay until Pentecost. Therefore he sent on ahead Timothy and Erastus. Erastus was the treasurer of the city of Corinth and Timothy was given the highest recommendation in the letter the apostle had already written to Corinth (I Cor. 16:7-11) also (Rom. 16:23).

f. The riot of the silversmiths. 19:23-41.

23 And about that time there arose no small stir concerning the Way.

24 For a certain man named Demetrius, a silversmith, who made silver shrines of Diana, brought no little business unto the craftsmen;

25 whom he gathered together, with the workmen of like occupation, and said, Sirs, ye know that by this business we have our wealth.

26 And ye see and hear, that not alone at Ephesus, but almost throughout all Asia, this Paul hath persuaded and turned away much people, saying that they are no gods, that are made with hands:

27 and not only is there danger that this our trade come into disrepute; but also that the temple of the great gooddess Diana be made of no account, and that she should even be deposed from her magnificence whom all Asia and the world worshippeth.

28 And when they heard this they were filled with wrath, and cried out, saying, Great is Diana of the Ephesians.

29 And the city was filled with the confusion: and they rushed with one accord into the theatre, having seized Gaius and Aristarchus, men of Macedonia, Paul's companions in travel.

30 And when Paul was minded to enter in unto the people, the disciples suffered him not.

750. When and from where was the book of Galatians written?
751. What were the three places Paul purposed to visit upon leaving Ephesus?
752. Give one fact of interest about Timothy and Erastus.
753. What was meant by the "effectual door?"

31 And certain also of the Asiarchs, being his friends, sent unto him and besought him not to adventure himself into the theatre.

32 Some therefore cried one thing, and some another: for the assembly was in confusion; and the more part knew not wherefore they were come together.

33 And they brought Alexander out of the multitude, the Jews putting him forward. And Alexander beckoned with the hand, and would have made a defence unto the people.

34 But when they perceived that he was a Jew, all with one voice about the space of two hours cried out, Great is Diana of the Ephesians.

35 And when the townclerk had quieted the multitude, he saith, Ye men of Ephesus, what man is there who knoweth not that the city of the Ephesians is temple-keeper of the great Diana, and of the image which fell down from Jupiter?

36 Seeing then that these things cannot be gainsaid, ye ought to be quiet, and to do nothing rash.

37 For ye have brought hither these men, who are neither robbers of temples nor blasphemers of our goddess.

38 If therefore Demetrius, and the craftsmen that are with him, have a matter against any man, the courts are open, and there are proconsuls: let them accuse one another.

39 But if ye seek anything about other matters, it shall be settled in the regular assembly.

40 For indeed we are in danger to be accused concerning this day's riot, there being no cause for it: and as touching it we shall not be able to give account of this concourse.

41 And when he had thus spoken, he dismissed the assembly.

23-27 When Paul said there was an open door for the Word, he probably had reference to the good results from the Sceva incident. Further words concerning the many adversaries can be gained from reading I Cor. 4:9-13.

An unexpected adversary arose to close the door of opportunity. It was not the Jews this time, but the vested interests of the town leaders. A certain rich man in the city found out what was causing his business to "fall off" so sharply. This man's name was Demetrius and his work was that of a silversmith. The main outlet for his work

754. What was different about the adversary here in Ephesus?
755. What angered Demetrius?

was in the little silver shrine and image that he made by the hundreds to be sold to the devotees of Diana, goddess of the Ephesians. Her great temple was located in the city. The reason these shrines were not selling like they once did was all centered in a certain wandering preacher named Paul. He was a preacher of faith in a God "not made with hands." So successful were his efforts that "all Asia" was being influenced. This man Demetrius was a very candid speaker. Upon calling the silversmiths together, and "those of like occupation," he made no apology for the statement that he was interested in "their wealth" first and the promotion of worship of Diana second. When you strike a man in his pocket-book you have struck a vital and sensitive spot.

1. "We are losing money."
2. "Paul's preaching is the cause of it."
3. "Therefore Paul's preaching must be stopped."

This was the reasoning of this craftsman. "And besides that," he told the ever increasing crowd, "it could be that even this temple of Diana (perhaps gesturing in the direction of it) could be made of no account." And then appealing to the popular mind, he laid the trap into which so many fall. He said in thought, "Ten thousand Ephesians can't be wrong." The general popularity of the goddess is here given as a measure of correctness and truth.

28-34 The gathering called together by Demetrius occurred either in the street or in some place of public meeting. It wasn't long until they had the interest of most of the people of the city. In no time at all a great uncontrollable mob gathered. The word was thrown about that Paul and his preaching was the center of the objection. Two of Paul's companions were seized upon by some of the mob. Now the whole vast howling throng rushed into the immense amphitheatre. (It still stands to this day.) By this time Paul heard of the trouble and had ascertained the cause. He was about to enter in among the crowd and reveal himself to them and to speak to this gathering. He had spoken to mobs before. But the Christians in Ephesus who were with Paul saw the utter futility of such effort and hence strongly entreated the apostle that he not attempt it. Then a rather unusual word is given concerning this critical decision:

"And certain also of the Asiarchs, being his friends, sent unto him and besought him not to adventure himself into the theatre."

756. How wide was the influence of Paul's preaching?
757. What were the first and second interests of Demetrius?
758. What was the trap laid by Demetrius?
759. Where was the place of meeting for the gathering of Demetrius?
760. Why seize Gaius and Aristarchus?
761. Why did Paul want to enter into the crowd? Why prevented?

Who were these men? What influence would they have over Paul? In answer to this we quote again from Cuningham Geikie, Hours with the Bible, Vol. III, pages 98-99:

"The provinces of Asia Minor had officials of high rank, named after their province. Bythyniarchs, Galatarchs, Lyciarchs, or in 'Asia', Asiarchs, who were presidents of the sacred rites, and of the public games and theatrical amusements, exhibited yearly in honour of the gods and of the emperors, providing for the vast outlay solely at their private expense. One was chosen each year, but those of past years were still associated, through courtesy, with him, or at least retained the great liberality implied in their office. So wide had the influence of Paul become by this time that some of these high dignitaries were friendly to him, and sent, beseeching him not to venture into the theatre; knowing, perhaps, his fearlessness and valuing his safety."

This theatre held no less than 5,000 and by the time it was reasonably full of people, all shouting their devotion to Diana, the place indeed "was in confusion." As new persons came into this place and inquired as to why such a meeting was being held, "some cried one thing and some another, . . . and the more part knew not wherefore they were come together."

Some in this multitude felt that a defense must be made for the Jews, the thought being that just because this man Paul was a Jew there was no reason to blame the Jews as a race. The one the Jews selected to make this defense was one of their number called Alexander. He was evidently recognized as a speaker of some ability. He was hurried through the crowd to a place where all could see him. When lifted up before the multitude, Alexander waved his hands for quietness and they seemed to give heed to him, at least for the moment—but then someone cried out, "He's a Jew. Down with him! Great is Diana of the Ephesians." The multitude caught up the word and so by the space of two hours there was an incessant cry from this vast crowd, "Great is Diana of the Ephesians." Thus was this effort on the part of the Jews frustrated.

35-41 When the mob had about exhausted itself emotionally and physically, (cf. p. 164) "a dignitary who commanded respect appeared on the scene; the town clerk—an official who had charge of the municipal archives, official documents, and had the duty of reading them out to the town assemblies." This man was accustomed to addressing crowds, and besides this he had authority behind what

762. Who were the "Asiarchs" and what influence would they have over the apostle? Why not ask the Holy Spirit?
763. Why was the assembly "in confusion?"
764. Why the attempted speech of Alexander?
765. How did the town clerk select an expedient time to speak?

he said. To give this man trouble would be to bring the "rough Imperial law down on their heads." So it was that when he stood in a place to be seen and heard the great crowd was hushed and they gave heed to what he was about to say.

What a wonderfully clever speech is this of the town clerk. He surely understood the crowd and the need. Notice his procedure.

1. There was a **need** to satisfy their religious pride.

So the town clerk says: "Why are you acting as you are? Who is there that doesn't know of the position of Ephesus and Diana? The fame of Diana is spread throughout the whole world. Why, everyone has heard of the image which has fallen down from Jupiter—'Seeing then that these things cannot be gainsaid, ye ought to be quiet and do nothing rash'."

2. There was a **need** for many to understand the charges being made against Gaius and Aristarchus—were they guilty or not guilty?

So the town clerk mentions two things concerning Diana of which these men are not guilty.

a. They never robbed our temples.

b. They never blasphemed our goddess.

The town clerk was careful not to speak of what they had done, or to meet the issue as to what Paul had done.

3. There was a **need** for a solution to the grievance of Demetrius and the craftsmen.

So the town clerk reminded all, and Demetrius in particular, that the regular courts were open and there were proconsuls to act as judges in the case. This procedure was for a local offense—to be handled by the courts of Ephesus. The clerk goes further to explain that if they had a matter that entered into the realm of Imperial jurisdiction, it would be settled in the regular gathering of that court which met three times a month.

4. Above everything else there was a **need** that the mob be quieted down and dispersed.

To this end all the previous remarks were directed. And they had their effect. Now the town clerk could press upon them the conclusion that he had hinted at previously.

Since (notice the pronoun) "we" have no good reason for this wild gathering, if "we" were called into account for it before the Roman authorities, we would have no defense to make. Should the

766. Why give heed to the town clerk?
767. How was the need for the satisfaction of religious pride met?
768. How did the town clerk side-step the guilt of Paul and his companions?
769. How was the grievance of Demetrius going to be settled? What were the two courts?
770. How was the mob to be dismissed? Why the change of pronouns?

authorities accuse us of riot, we would be in a serious position. His words were so well received by all that when he dismissed the assembly they all dispersed and went home.

4. AT TROAS. II Corinthians 2:12, 13.

12-13 Although not mentioned in the book of Acts, the visit to Troas mentioned here in II Corinthians must have occurred right after he left Ephesus. Here are the reasons I say this: Because of the writting of the epistle of I Corinthians. He evidently wrote the first epistle to the Corinthians from Ephesus while he was yet laboring there. He had received the sad news in Ephesus of the problems that existed in the church at Corinth. To solve these problems he wrote this first epistle to the Corinthians. He sent it by the hand of Titus. Paul fully expected the return of Titus to Ephesus before he left but he did not come. When at last it became imperative that Paul leave Ephesus, he went out from the city looking for Titus on the way. Oh, how the apostle longed to meet Titus that he might know how his strong corrective epistle was received. With these thoughts in mind you can understand clearly the words of II Cor. 2:12, 13. Paul thought that surely he would meet Titus in Troas. But when Paul arrived he found not Titus. What a disappointment. No "relief of spirit". Although there was an open door in Troas to preach the word he could not enter it because of this weight upon his heart. This need seemed to demand immediate action and solution. So bidding the brethren in Troas a fond farewell he pressed on into Macedonia looking anxiously for "Titus my brother."

5. IN MACEDONIA. 20:1, 2.

1 And after the uproar ceased, Paul having sent for the disciples and exhorted them, took leave of them, and departed to go into Macedonia.

2 And when he had gone through those parts, and had given them much exhortation, he came into Greece.

1-2 From the first verse of this 20th chapter it would seem that Paul decided that the riot would be the formal cause of his leaving the city of Ephesus. How long he stayed in the city after the riot we do not know but I am personally disposed to believe that he left very soon afterward. At any rate, after coming to Troas in such a depressed condition he continued on into Macedonia, hoping all the while that he would meet Titus on the way. And he did. You know from previous study that the cities of Macedonia were Philippi, Thessalonica and Berea.

771. Why say that the meeting of Titus in Troas must have occurred at this time?

772. Was it wrong for Paul not to enter the open door for the Word here at Troas?

773. What prompted Paul to leave Ephesus?

As near as we can read chronologically from Paul's epistles he met Titus at Philippi. Titus brought the wonderful news that the church in Corinth had received the epistle of Paul with a humble spirit and that most all who were in sin had repented. So it was that Paul wrote the second letter to Corinth from Philippi, and possibly sent it on head of himself by the hand of Titus. In this epistle he expresses his thoughts upon meeting Titus (II Cor. 7:5-10). To each of these churches he gave "much exhortation". This was encouragement and instruction and must have taken several months. After a progressive visit from Philippi to Berea he left Macedonia and came into Greece, most specifically into the province of Achaia in Greece and the city of Corinth in Achaia.

6. AT CORINTH IN GREECE. 20:3-5.

3 And when he had spent three months there, and a plot was laid against him by the Jews as he was about to set sail for Syria, he determined to return through Macedonia.
4 And there accompanied him as far as Asia, Sopater of Beroea, the son of Pyrrhus; and of the Thessalonians, Aristarchus and Secundus; and Gaius of Derbe, and Timothy; and of Asia, Tychicus and Trophimus.
5 But these had gone before, and were waiting for us at Troas.

3-5 Paul stayed here only three months but what momentous events occurred during these three months. Here is an outline of what I believe took place at this time:
1. His labors with the Corinthian church (of which we have no details).
2. He wrote the epistle of Romans. This is borne out in the epistle itself. (Cf. Romans 15:23, 24; 16:23)
3. So we would conclude that the letter to the Galatians was written from here also.
4. Learning of the plot for his life he changed his plans.
5. A collection was taken from here by Paul according to previous instructions (Cf. I Cor. 16:1-2).

774. Which were the cities that Paul visited in Macedonia?
775. Did Paul meet Titus?
776. Why was Paul depressed?
777. Where did Paul meet Titus? What news did he bring?
778. From where was the book of II Corinthians written? What is its message?
779. To what churches did Paul give "much exhortation?"
780. In what country is Corinth?
781. Did the seven men accompany Paul on his trip through Macedonia?

Just another word concerning the plot laid for his life. It would seem that he learned of this plot just as he was preparing to go down to the seaport of Cenchreae.

Those who would attack the apostle probably were not only interested in "his life" but also his money which he had collected in quite a sum from the churches of Galatia and Macedonia. But Paul had thought of this long before this occasion and hence had not the money on his person but had suggested that seven brethren accompany him on the journey to carry this bounty with him to Jerusalem. (Cf. I Cor. 16:3) These seven men had been picked up (at least some of them) as Paul passed through Macedonia.

It would seem that upon learning of the plot for his life Paul did not venture down the road to Cenchreae but rather turned to take again the land route to Macedonia. The seven brethren, however, did sail away from Corinth and were waiting for Paul in Troas when he arrived. Some writers would have the seven men accompany Paul as far as Thessalonica and sail from there to Troas.

7. **AT PHILIPPI.** 20:6a.

6a And we sailed away from Philippi after the days of unleavened bread,

6a To arrive here Paul had to make a day's journey off the main road. But the church and the leaders in this place were especially near to the heart of Paul. And then we conjecture that he went to secure Luke as his traveling companion and fellow worker. At any rate, Luke joined Paul here (Luke had been here since his mention in the second journey and they sailed away from the seaport of Neapolis "after the days of unleavened bread."

These "days of unleavened bread" mark the time element in a very good way. Notice two things about it.

1. Almost a whole year had elapsed since he left Ephesus. (Cf. I Cor. 16:8) Note that he had left Ephesus before Pentecost the previous year. You must know that the "days of unleavened bread" follow after the eating of the passover, and that the Passover and Pentecost are just fifty days apart. So now it is less than fifty days to Pentecost when Paul sails for Troas.
2. He only has some forty days to reach Jerusalem with his bounty by Pentecost. This he was determined to do.

782. When did Paul learn of the plot for his life?

783. How did the Apostle protect himself from the robbers?

784. Without referring to the text give three events that occurred in Corinth.

785. Why go a day's journey out of the way if Paul was in a hurry to arrive in Jerusalem?

There must have been unfavorable winds in the sailing, for it only took one day on a previous voyage; now the same trip took five days.

8. IN TROAS. 20:6b-13.

6b   and came unto them to Troas in five days; where we tarried seven days.

7   And upon the first day of the week, when we were gathered together to break bread, Paul discoursed with them, intending to depart on the morrow; and prolonged his speech until midnight.

8   And there were many lights in the upper chamber where we were gathered together.

9   And there sat in the window a certain young man named Eutychus, borne down with deep sleep; and as Paul discoursed yet longer, being borne down by his sleep he fell down from the third story, and was taken up dead.

10   And Paul went down, and fell on him, and embracing him said, Make ye no ado; for his life is in him.

11   And when he was gone up, and had broken the bread, and eaten, and had talked with them a long while, even till break of day, so he departed.

12   And they brought the lad alive, and were not a little comforted.

13   But we, going before to the ship, set sail for Assos, there intending to take in Paul: for so had he appointed, intending himself to go by land.

6b Paul was in Troas for seven days. Why spend such a length of time here when they were in a hurry to arrive in Jerusalem? No real authoritative answer can be given but it does seem that since they left immediately they waited there until the day came when they could worship with the saints. It could have been that they landed in Troas on Sunday.

b. The worship on the first day of the week. 7.

7 Be that as it may, when the Lord's Day came they gathered together as a church and "broke bread" or had the Lord's Supper. It would seem from the circumstances that the Jewish reckoning of time was used here and that after sundown on the Sabbath was the beginning of the first day of the week. It could have been that here at Troas as in Corinth a meal was eaten before or in conjunction with the Lord's Supper—as some call it the "love feast". It

786. What is meant by "the days of unleavened bread?" What import here?
787. Tell of the sailing conditions from Philippi to Troas?
788. Why spend so much time in Troas?
789. How do you know a meal was eaten in conjunction with the Lord's Supper?

was evidently customary to have a discourse at these gatherings and this time they had the priceless privilege of hearing the apostle Paul.

8-13 The meeting was being held in a third story room and many torches had been set in the sockets around the walls of the room. The windows were naturally open for ventilation and seated on the window sill of one of the openings was a young man named Eutychus.

Someone suggested that this young man had worked all day and that the fatigue of his body overcame his interest in the message of the apostle and that when fully asleep he relaxed and toppled out of the open casement. Whatever was the cause of his sleep he did fall to his death on the street or ground outside the house.

It would seem that Paul was the first to leave the house and hurry around to where the young man lay. Paul treated Eutychus like Elijah treated the widow's son. He compassionately fell on his prostrate form and drew him close to him in his arms. There must have been a prayer ascending from Paul's heart as he did this. Paul looked up to the anxious ones standing around him and said: "Trouble not yourselves, for his life is in him." (K. J. V.) Now mark it carefully that Eutychus was "taken up" before Paul arrived and those that handled him and tenderly laid him out on the ground or whatever, took him to be dead; and without a doubt he was.

Upon returning to the third story room the "breaking of bread" took place for which they had originally gathered. We might remark that the Lord's Supper here called the "breaking of bread" was partaken of on Sunday regardless of what time of reckoning for time is used. If you count the time from sundown to sundown (Jewish) it was on Sunday. If from midnight to midnight (Roman) it was on Sunday. Then following "the breaking of bread" a meal was also taken—it usually was so done in the early church.

Paul took up his message following the meal where he had been interrupted and continued speaking even unto the break of day. Even Eutychus managed to participate in the last of Paul's visit. The saints here were greatly strengthened by the preaching and their faith was increased by the restoration of this young man.

Luke was present to hear this lengthy sermon but he only makes mention of the incident with Eutychus and then says that Paul plainly instructed him and the other seven brothers (brethren) to go ahead

790. Why have the windows open? Why sit in the window?
791. Why do you think Eutychus fell asleep?
792. What Old Testament comparison can be made in the raising of Eutychus from the dead?
793. What do you think about the idea that Paul was first to reach the young man?
794. Was Eutychus really dead?
795. How can you prove that the Lord's Supper was on Sunday regardless of the time reckoning?

down to the ship and sail along the coast and pick him up at the town of Assos. Paul wanted to walk from Troas to Assos. Why walk? It was twenty miles or more and Paul had been up all night. He must have been fatigued in body and mind, but as some of you must know, solitude with God is the most restful experience one can find; if not for the body, at least for the spirit. As he walked these twenty miles, over none too easy a road, he had many things to settle alone with God.

9. AT ASSOS. 20:14a.

14a And when he met us at Assos, we took him in,

14a The ship in which the voyage was made must have been a local merchant vessel that had a regular route of pick-up and delivery to these various parts. Assos was one of them, as Paul had no doubt previously learned, and when the ship arrived here he was already at the dock to board the ship and sail the rest of the way.

10. AT MITYLENE. 20:14b.

14b and came to Mitylene.

14b This was the chief town on the island of Lesbos. It was on the east side of the island about ten miles from Asia Minor. "Mitylene was originally built on a small island, and perhaps joined to Lesbos by a causeway which offered two excellent harbors, one on the North and the other on the South." (Ibid.) Here they anchored overnight as was customary.

11. OVER AGAINST CHIOS. 20:15a.

15a And sailing from thence, we came the following day over against Chios;

15a This is a large island and is separated from the mainland by a channel of varying width—at the narrowest place it is only five miles wide and is blocked by a series of small islands. Through this channel Paul's ship sailed and anchored here in this protected channel "over against Chios."

12. AT SAMOS. 20:15b.

15b and the next day we touched at Samos; and the day after we came to Miletus.

15b This is yet another large island with a narrow strait between it and the mainland—another overnight stop.

796. Why walk instead of going by ship?
797. What type of vessel was it in which Paul sailed?
798. What was Mitylene?
799. What is meant by the statement "over against Chios?"

13. **IN MILETUS.** 20:16-38.

a. Past Ephesus to Miletus. 16, 17.

16 For Paul had determined to sail past Ephesus, that he
   might not have to spend time in Asia; for he was hasten-
   ing, if it were possible for him, to be at Jerusalem the
   day of Pentecost.
17 And from Miletus he sent to Ephesus, and called to
   him the elders of the church.

16-17 Before arriving in Miletus there are two points to be considered.

1. King James version states that they "tarried at Trogyllium"
   but the American Revised leaves this place out—why so? The
   answer is found in the fact that the most ancient manuscripts
   omit this phrase; it exists in tradition of Asia Minor.
2. Paul sailed right past the port of Ephesus as he wished not to
   stop there. He knew that if he did he would be detained by his
   many friends and he did not wish to be so. He wanted to arrive
   in Jerusalem by Pentecost to allow a ready distribution of the
   bounty he had collected.

Upon arriving at Miletus and finding that there would be time to
speak to the Ephesian elders while here, he forthwith sent a letter to
them that they would hasten over the thirty miles that separated them
and meet him here at Miletus.

b. Paul's past ministry, as exemplified at Ephesus. 18-21; 26.

18 And when they were come to him, he said unto them,
   Ye yourselves know, from the first day that I set foot
   in Asia, after what manner I was with you all the time,
19 serving the Lord with all lowliness of mind, and with
   tears, and with trials which befell me by the plots of the
   Jews;
20 how I shrank not from declaring unto you anything that
   was profitable, and teaching you publicly, and from
   house to house,
21 testifying both to Jews and to Greeks repentance toward God, and faith toward our Lord Jesus Christ.

Here is a brief outline of his address:
(The New Century Bible by J. Vernon Bartlet.)
1. Paul's past ministry, as exemplified at Ephesus. 18-21 and 26.
2. His attitude to his own future. 22-24.
3. And also ultimate as touching his hearers. 25.

800. Why does King James Version state that they tarried at Trogyllium?
801. Why not stop at Ephesus?
802. How far from Miletus to Ephesus?

4. Conditions at Ephesus in the near future. 23-30.
5. The self-sacrificing spirit of this example. 31-35.

Under (1) of this outline we give the fine paraphrase of these verses by Cunningham Geikie. (N.T. series, Vol. III, p. 367-369)

1. Paul's past ministry, as exemplified at Ephesus. 18-21 and 26.

18. "You personally know, from the first day I set foot in Asia, the life I lived among you always, through over three years, 19. serving the Lord with all lowliness of mind, and with tears over backsliders, and with trials which befell me by the plots of the Jews: 20. you know how I did not shrink from telling you anything that was for your good, and how I taught you both publicly, in your assembly, and privately, from house to house, 21. testifying to Jews and Greeks alike, their need of repentance towards God, and faith towards our Lord Jesus Christ . . . 26. Therefore, since my farewell demands my reckoning with myself as to the past, I boldly witness to you this day, that I am pure from the blood of all men."

22 And now, behold, I go bound in the spirit unto Jerusalem, not knowing the things that shall befall me there:
23 save that the Holy Spirit testifieth unto me in every city, saying that bonds and afflictions abide me.
24 But I hold not my life of any account as dear unto myself, so that I may accomplish my course, and the ministry which I received from the Lord Jesus, to testify the gospel of the grace of God.

2. His attitude to his own future. 22-24.

22. "And now, behold, I go (by an inner impulse I cannot resist) to Jerusalem, not knowing what specially will befall me there: 23. beyond the fact that the Holy Ghost testifies to me in every city I visit, that bonds and afflictions await me in it. 24. But I do not hold my life of any account, as dear to myself, so that I may finish the course assigned me by God; no clinging to life hindering me: and, with my course, the ministry which I received from the Lord Jesus, to testify the good news of the grace of God to man."

25 And now, behold, I know that ye all, among whom I went about preaching the kingdom, shall see my face no more.
26 Wherefore I testify unto you this day, that I am pure from the blood of all men.

803. From memory give three of the points in Paul's address to the Ephesian elders.
804. What was the attitude of the apostle while laboring in Ephesus?
805. What was the theme that Paul preached to both Jews and Greeks in Ephesus?
806. How was Paul made free from the blood of all men?
807. Why was Paul so determined to Jerusalem?

3. And also ultimate as touching his hearers. 25.

25. "And now, behold, I know that ye all, among whom I went about preaching the kingdom, shall see my face no more."

> 27 For I shrank not from declaring unto you the whole counsel of God.
> 28 Take heed unto yourselves, and to all the flock, in which the Holy Spirit hath made you bishops, to feed the church of the Lord which he purchased with his own blood.
> 29 I know that after my departing grievous wolves shall enter in among you, not sparing the flock;
> 30 and from among your own selves shall men arise, speaking perverse things, to draw away the disciples after them.

4. Conditions at Ephesus in the near future. 28-30.

28. "As, therefore, I am thus guiltless in this matter, it is for you, who have taken my place, to take heed to yourselves, and to all the flock, in which the Holy Ghost has made you bishops, or overseers, to feed the church of God, which He purchased for His own, with His own blood. 29. For I know that after my departing, last year, wolves—pitiless evil-working teachers—now that I am no longer there to keep them off, will come in among you from without, not sparing the flock; 30. and that, from among yourselves, men will rise, speaking perverted words, to draw away the disciples from the truth, to follow themselves."

> 31 Wherefore watch ye, remembering that by the space of three years I ceased not to admonish every one night and day with tears.
> 32 And now I commend you to God, and to the word of his grace, which is able to build you up, and to give you the inheritance among all them that are sanctified.
> 33 I coveted no man's silver, or gold, or apparel.
> 34 Ye yourselves know that these hands ministered unto my necessities, and to them that were with me.
> 35 In all things I gave you an example, that so laboring ye ought to help the weak, and to remember the words of the Lord Jesus, that he himself said, It is more blessed to give than to receive.

5. The self-sacrificing spirit of his example. 31-35.

31. "Therefore be watchful, remembering that for three whole years, I never ceased to admonish everyone, night and day with tears,

808. What was the relationship of these men to the church of the Lord? Their work?
809. What characterized the admonishment of the apostle?
810. What was to be the source of their inheritance and the guide of their whole life?

to keep the faith. 32. And now I commend you to God, and to the word of His grace—the truth I taught you, which must be the guide of your whole life, and is able to build you up, and to give you an inheritance you crave, in the kingdom of the Messiah, among all them who are sanctified. 33. I coveted no man's silver, or gold, or apparel. 34. Indeed, ye yourselves know that these hands ministered to my necessities, and to those of them that were with me. 35. In all things I have shown you by my example, that (laboring as I did, you ought to help the weak, and to remember the words of the Lord Jesus, how He Himself said, it is more blessed to give than to receive."

c. The tender farewell. 36-38.

36 And when he had thus spoken, he kneeled down and prayed with them all.

37 And they all wept sore, and fell on Paul's neck and kissed him,

38 sorrowing most of all for the word which he had spoken, that they should behold his face no more. And they brought him on his way unto the ship.

36-38 The feeling in the message just delivered led naturally to a prayer meeting. Paul had done all he could do for these brethren. He now commits them to God for His leading and working. The posture here assumed by Paul was to kneel. What does it mean? Simply that it is a good posture in prayer—nothing more.

There was a real love between Paul and the elders of Ephesus; there were tears and for many of them, genuine grief at the parting: most of all because of the foreboding words of Paul that they would see his face no more. He had told them of the promised bonds that awaited him in Jerusalem and then to say that he would never return broke their hearts.

But the work of Christ must go on in spite of broken hearts, separation, grief or any other of the changing experiences of life. And so it was that the elders followed the apostle and the others right down to the water's edge and bade them a very tender farewell.

14. **AT COS.** 21:1a.

1 And when it came to pass that we were parted from them and had set sail, we came with a straight course unto Cos,

1a It would seem that a favorable wind was blowing and that the trip to Cos was made rather rapidly—it was a distance of some forty

811. How do we know that Paul made tents in Ephesus?

812. What saying of Jesus is given here by Paul that is not recorded in the gospels?

813. Why kneel in prayer?

814. What caused the greatest grief to the Ephesian elders?

815. What were the sailing conditions to Cos? How do you know?

nautical miles; the direction is due south. An island of twenty-three miles in length separated from the mainland by a narrow channel. Here the ship cast anchor probably near the large city of Hippocrates. In the morning they were ready to sail down the channel of Cos.

15. AT RHODES. 21:1b.

1b and the next day unto Rhodes,

1b This was another celebrated island in Paul's day, an overnight stop for Paul's ship.

16. AT PATARA. 21:1c, 2.

1c and from thence unto Patara:

2 and having found a ship crossing over unto Phoenicia, we went aboard, and set sail.

1c, 2 The vessel boarded at Philippi now had either completed its voyage or was proceeding further up the coast of Asia Minor. But how was Paul now to arrive in Jerusalem by Pentecost? Providence intervenes and the words of Luke seem to suggest that they were pleasantly surprised to find a ship here at Patara sailing for Phoenicia. (Maybe even on the same day they found it). They immediately put out into the open sea and proceeded on the last leg of their trip.

17. IN THE SIGHT OF CYPRUS ON THE LEFT. 21:3a.

3a And when we had come in sight of Cyprus, leaving it on the left hand,

3a The writer has found words of Conybeare and Howson so expressive on this point that we reproduce them here:

"The distance between these two points is three hundred and forty geographical miles; (between Patara and Tyre) and if we bear in mind that the northwesterly winds in April often blow like monsoons in the Levant, and that the rig of ancient sailing vessels was peculiarly favorable to a quick run before the wind, we come at once to the conclusion that the voyage might easily be accomplished in forty-eight hours. Everything in Luke's account gives a strong impression that the weather was in the highest degree favorable; and there is one picturesque phrase employed by the narrator which sets vividly before us some of the phenomena of a rapid voyage. That which is said in the English version concerning the "discovering" of Cyprus and "leaving it on the left hand" is the original for a nautical expression implying that the land appeared to rise quickly as they sailed past it to the southward. It would be in the course of the second day (probably in the evening that "the high blue eastern land appeared." The highest mountain of Cyprus is a rounded summit, and there would be snow upon it at that season of the year. After the second night the first land in sight would be the high range of Lebanon in Syria (21:3), and they would easily arrive at Tyre before the evening." (Life and Epistles of the Apostle Paul, pages 532-533).

816. How did providence intervene at Patara?

18. AT TYRE. 21:3b-6.

3b we sailed unto Syria, and landed at Tyre; for there the
ship was to unlade her burden.

4 And having found the disciples, we tarried there seven
days: and these said to Paul through the Spirit, that
he should not set foot in Jerusalem.

5 And when it came to pass that we had accomplished
the days, we departed and went on our journey; and
they all, with wives and children, brought us on our
way till we were out of the city: and kneeling down
on the beach, we prayed, and bade each other farewell;

6 and we went on board the ship, but they returned home
again.

3b-4 While the ship was tarrying here, unloading her cargo Paul
found the followers of the Way in the town and met with them for
seven days; this must have included a Lord's Day. He probably
carried on a one week revival here as he had in the same length of
time at Troas.

There were prophets among the saints in Tyre, and these through
the revelation of the Holy Spirit besought Paul not to go to Jerusalem.
No word is given by Luke of Paul's response to this divine suggestion, but Paul's actions speak louder than his unrecorded words. When
the days of the ship's stop were fulfilled they pressed on, even as
Someone Else, "steadfastly toward Jerusalem".

5, 6 But not without the tenderest of partings, the disciples of Tyre
followed the servants of God out of the city, down to the beach. It
would seem that following the final gathering with Paul and the
brethren that the whole congregation, women, children, and men all
walked with the preachers down to see them off.

What a touching scene of farewell ensued. What words of trust
and love were exchanged. And then I can read into the closing words
of Luke a certain loneliness that he must have felt . . . "but they returned **home** again."

19. IN PTOLEMAIS. 21:7.

7 And when we had finished the voyage from Tyre, we
arrived at Ptolemais; and we saluted the brethren,
and abode with them one day.

817. How could the 340 miles between Patara and Tyre be covered in only 48 hours?

818. What picturesque phrase sets forth the nautical note in this trip from
Patara to Tyre?

819. How long a stop at Tyre and what did Paul do?

820. What warning was given at Tyre? Paul's response?

821. How can we see a touch of loneliness in the words "but they returned
home again?"

7 Although there is much that could be written concerning the history of this town we will not here write of it. There was an opportunity at this place to speak to the brethren but the purpose of arriving in Jerusalem for the feast hurried them on through this town. They paused only to greet the saints in a one day gathering.

20. CAESAREA. 21:8-14.

8 And on the morrow we departed, and came unto Caesarea: and entering into the house of Philip the evangelist, who was one of the seven, we abode with him.

9 Now this man had four virgin daughters, who prophesied.

10 And as we tarried there some days, there came down from Judaea a certain prophet, named Agabus.

11 And coming to us, and taking Paul's girdle, he bound his own feet and hands, and said, Thus saith the Holy Spirit, So shall the Jews at Jerusalem bind the man that owneth this girdle, and shall deliver him into the hands of the Gentiles.

12 And when we heard these things, both we and they of that place besought him not to go up to Jerusalem.

13 Then Paul answered, What do ye, weeping and breaking my heart? for I am ready not to be bound only, but also to die at Jerusalem for the name of the Lord Jesus.

14 And when he would not be persuaded, we ceased, saying, The will of the Lord be done.

8, 9 It was some thirty or forty miles from Ptolemais to Caesarea. One day's journey would see them within the city gates.

Here we meet an old friend, "Philip the evangelist, who was one of the seven." How long it has been and what a multitude of experiences have taken place since we were with him on "that road that goeth down from Jerusalem to Gaza." But we did read that Philip was "found at Azotus" and passing through he preached the gospel to all the cities **till he came to Caesarea.** (Acts 8:40)

And here he is in this same city, still the evangelist of Christ. It must have been eight or ten or even more years since he made his home here. The reason for his stay could possibly be found in the family of "four virgin daughters who prophesied." These young ladies must have been but small girls when he first came to this wicked town.

Philip must have had quite a house to accommodate this whole evangelistic party. However much Paul and his company were anxious to go to Jerusalem, they could not leave Philip without visiting and even helping out in the work of the Lord in this place.

10-14 Speaking of "old friends" in the narrative of the book of

822. What old friend do we meet in Caesarea? How long had he been there?
823. How did Philip's daughters become prophetesses?

Acts, who is this one who comes as a prophet from Jerusalem? Can this be the same man that came once before from the Holy City? Remember the visit of one "Agabus" to Antioch of Syria? He there reported that a famine was coming over the "whole world". The circumstances seem to be somewhat similar for the disciples in Judea are again in want. Whether this is right or wrong we do know that Agabus has a dramatic method of delivering his divine message.

Picking up a girdle that is lying nearby he binds it around his feet, then taking it off he attempts to tie up his own hands. Upon so doing he makes his divine prediction in these words:

"Thus saith the Holy Spirit: So shall the Jews at Jerusalem bind the man that owneth this girdle, and shall deliver him unto the hands of the Gentiles."

His actions remind us of the prophets of the Old Testament days.

Upon this announcement a great concern took hold of the hearts of Luke and Aristarchus as well as the other brethren. They had all learned to love Paul very dearly and to hear of his being bound pained them greatly. The only recourse was to stop Paul from going to Jerusalem. This was a divine warning to deter him from this purpose, so thought the brethren in Philip's house. They besought him with the strongest words and emphasized them with the tears that streamed down their faces.

These words were not without effect on the apostle, but he did not so interpret them. Paul felt and knew that God wanted him in Jerusalem and to Jerusalem he would go. This word of Agabus and the other warnings were but to better prepare him for the experience.

And so it was that the apostle expressed in emphatic words his determination. The love and sympathy of his friends touched him, but he had a higher call that he must answer.

"What do ye, weeping and breaking my heart? For I am ready not to be bound only, but also to die at Jerusalem for the name of the Lord Jesus."

To these words there was only one right response: "The will of the Lord be done."

21. IN JERUSALEM. 21:15, 16.

15 And after these days we took up our baggage and went up to Jerusalem.

824. Tell where and when you heard of Agabus before.
825. Who foretold that Paul was going to be bound in Jerusalem?
826. What was the interpretation placed upon the words of Agabus by Luke and Aristarchus?
827. How did the brethren attempt to hinder Paul from going to Jerusalem? Did it affect Paul? In what way?

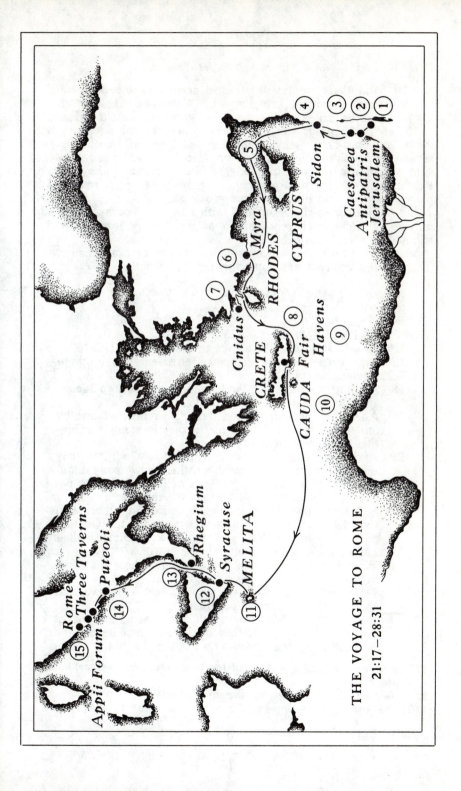

THE VOYAGE TO ROME
21:17 – 28:31

16 And there went with us also certain of the disciples
from Caesarea, bringing with them one Mnason of
Cyprus, an early disciple, with whom we should lodge.

15, 16 The baggage was again packed and the short journey was
made to the busy city. Some of the saints of Caesarea went along and
secured permission from one, Mnason, who had a house in Jerusalem,
with whom the party could lodge while celebrating the feast of
Pentecost. The city was particularly crowded at this time and a
place to stay would be a welcome provision.

Let us not forget that Paul had with him the "bounty" taken up
among the Gentile churches and that this money was to be distributed as soon as possible.

So ends the third and last missionary journey or evangelistic tour.
The distance traveled was approximately 3,400 miles.

THE VOYAGE TO ROME
21:17 — 28:31

1. AT JERUSALEM. 21:17—23:30
  a. Paul's salutation and the advice of the elders. 21:17-26.
      17 And when we were come to Jerusalem, the brethren
received us gladly.
      18 And the day following Paul went in with us unto James;
and all the elders were present.
      19 And when he had saluted them, he rehearsed one by
one the things which God had wrought among the Gentiles through his ministry.
      20 And they, when they heard it, glorified God; and they
said unto him, Thou seest, brother, how many thousands there are among the Jews of them that have believed; and they are all zealous for the law:
      21 and they have been informed concerning thee, that
thou teachest all the Jews who are among the Gentiles
to forsake Moses, telling them not to circumcise their
children, neither to walk after the customs.
      22 What is it therefore? they will certainly hear that thou
art come.
      23 Do therefore this that we say to thee: We have four
men that have a vow on them;
      24 these take, and purify thyself with them, and be at
charges for them, that they may shave their heads: and
all shall know that there is no truth in the things where-

828. How was the housing problem of Jerusalem solved for Paul and his company?
829. How far did Paul travel on the third journey?
830. This visit to Jerusalem was like what other visit? In what way?

of they have been informed concerning thee; but that thou thyself also walkest orderly, keeping the law.

25 But as touching the Gentiles that have believed, we wrote, giving judgment that they should keep themselves from things sacrificed to idols, and from blood, and from what is strangled, and from fornication.

26 Then Paul took the men, and the next day purifying himself with them went into the temple, declaring the fulfilment of the days of purification, until the offering was offered for every one of them.

17-19 Paul was received this time somewhat in the same way that he and Barnabas had been when, years before, they had brought the problem of the circumcision of Gentiles to the apostles in Jerusalem. On the day of their arrival they were given a warm welcome. The preparations for staying in the home of Mnason were made and the night was spent in rest. On the day following an important matter must needs be taken care of. Luke was present at this meeting and hence we have the pronoun "we" and "us" used in discussing the incident.

There was a real interest in the things that God had wrought through the ministry of the apostle Paul. It must have taken no little time to tell "one by one" the victories for the gospel in the many places where Paul had preached. But James and the elders listened attentively to these words, and when he had finished they gave praise and glory to the proper one—they "glorified God".

20, 21 But even before Paul had told of the first gospel triumph these men had something that was clamoring within them for utterance. The coming of Paul to Jerusalem was a matter of no small import. He had a reputation; his actions and words were followed carefully by thousands of Jews. The criticism of this one was ever present and entered the city of Jerusalem long before he did. Indeed, the Jews who hated his gospel of freedom had been constantly at the job of dinning it into the heads of all who would listen to them that this Paul was the worst of heretics. To this evident fact the elders and James now make mention. Word that Paul was in Jerusalem would soon be common knowledge and the hatred of these Jews would make it impossible for him to do anything for Christ, unless something could be done and that right away.

22, 23 It would do no good to say before all that Paul **did not** forsake Moses, for it was well known that he **did** preach among the Gentiles that they need not circumcise their children and that the customs

831. What was the response of James and the brethren over the victories of the gospel told by Paul?

832. How did the coming of Paul to Jerusalem pose a problem for the leaders of the church?

had no claim on them. What then could be done? It was not for the sake of the Gentiles that the advice of the elders was given, for they had a letter written as to their standing before God—it was for the Jews.

What is this that is asked of Paul—"Four men that have a vow?" "Be at charges for them?" This surely was the keeping of the "customs of the law". These four men were probably Christian Jews who were fulfilling the ceremonies that were connected with the law of the Nazarite. J. W. McGarvey seems to feel that these men had contaminated themselves through contact with a dead body before their vow was fulfilled and that they were now purifying themselves in the temple.

24-26 "To be at charges for them" had to do with purchasing the animals that they must sacrifice and of entering the temple to tell the priest that the days of their purification were fulfilled. This they could not do for they were unclean. Paul could further identify himself with these men by his cleansing himself of uncleanness. He was counted unclean on the general basis of the law as given in Leviticus 15:1-3. He could be purified in one day.

Now I ask you, was this an act of compromise on the part of Paul? The writer especially likes the words of J. W. McGarvey on this point. He says: "I think it must be admitted that subsequent to the writing of the epistle to the Ephesians, and more especially that to the Hebrews, he could not consistently have done this; for in those epistles it is clearly taught, that in the death of Christ God has broken down and abolished 'the law of commandments contained in ordinances' which he styles 'the middle wall of partition' (Eph. 2:13-15); that the Aaronic priesthood had been abolished (Heb. 7, 8); and that the sacrifice of Christ had completely superseded that of dumb animals (Heb. 9, 19). But in Paul's earlier epistles, though some things had been written which, carried to their logical consequences, involved all this, these points had not yet been clearly revealed to his mind, and much less to the minds of the other disciples; for it pleased God to make Paul the chief instrument for the revelation of this part of His will. His mind, and those of all the brethren, were as yet in much the same condition on this question that those of the early disciples had been in before the conversion of Cornelius in reference to the salvation of the Gentiles. If Peter, by the revelation made to him in connection with Cornelius, was made to understand better his own words uttered on Pentecost (2:39), it should cause no surprise that Paul in his early writings

833. Why not solve the problem by simply stating that Paul DID NOT forsake Moses?
834. Were Christian Jews concerned in this matter, or non-Christian?
835. Why were these four men purifying themselves?
836. What is meant by the phrase "be at charges for them?"

JOPPA BY THE SEA.

We have already discussed Joppa in an earlier picture. Let us pause here to look carefully at this drawing. Here is a port to which Jonah went when he took the ship to Tarshish. We have all come to the port of birth and boarded the ship of life to sail out into the sea of time toward the port of eternity or the judgment. The ship in which Jonah found himself was a place of escape from God—a place to hide from God. To many people the ship of life has become a place to hide from God—a means of escaping God. But there is a storm ahead and we are going to need our God in a very real manner.

On the shore of Joppa's port is a fishing boat. This might suggest to us that all of life is a fishing trip. Jesus made this comparison. In the sea of life we will indeed catch something, but what will it be? Will it not depend on the type of net you use? and upon the diligence you exercise in the task and upon the providence of God? Tell me, my soul, what is thy purpose as you sail upon the sea of life?

uttered sentiments the full import of which he did not comprehend until later revelations made them plain. That it was so is but another illustration of the fact that the Holy Spirit guided the apostles into all the truth, not at one bound, but step by step. In the wisdom of God the epistle to the Hebrews, the special value of which lies in its clear revelations on the distinction between the sacrifices and priesthood under Moses and those under Christ, was written but a few years previous to the destruction of the Jewish temple, and the compulsory abrogation of all the sacrifices of the law; and that thus any Jewish Christian, whose natural reverence for ancestral and divinely appointed customs may have prevented him from seeing the truth on this subject, might have his eyes opened in spite of himself." (**ibid.** pp. 208, 209).

Paul probably thought that surely all would now be well, for in a day or two the seven days for the purification of these men would be accomplished and he would have the testimony of his help to give to all who were concerned in this affair. But the Holy Spirit had testified to him in every city that "bonds and afflictions" awaited him at Jerusalem, and he was very shortly to experience the fulfillment of the Spirit's words.

b. Jews from Asia cause Paul's arrest. 21:27-40.

27 And when the seven days were almost completed, the Jews from Asia, when they saw him in the temple, stirred up all the multitude and laid hands on him,

28 crying out, Men of Israel, help: This is the man that teacheth all men everywhere against the people, and the law, and this place; and moreover he brought Greeks also into the temple, and hath defiled this holy place.

29 For they had before seen with him in the city Trophimus the Ephesian, whom they supposed that Paul had brought into the temple.

30 And all the city was moved, and the people ran together; and they laid hold on Paul, and dragged him out of the temple: and straightway the doors were shut.

31 And as they were seeking to kill him, tidings came up to the chief captain of the band, that all Jerusalem was in confusion.

32 And forthwith he took soldiers and centurions, and ran down upon them: and they, when they saw the chief captain and the soldiers, left off beating Paul.

33 Then the chief captain came near, and laid hold on

837. How explain that Paul was not compromising in what he did?
838. How would the purification in the temple help Paul's position with the Jews?

him, and commanded him to be bound with two chains;
and inquired who he was, and what he had done.

34 And some shouted one thing, some another, among
the crowd: and when he could not know the certainty
for the uproar, he commanded him to be brought into the castle.

35 And when he came upon the stairs, so it was that he
was borne of the soldiers for the violence of the crowd;

36 for the multitude of the people followed after, crying out, Away with him.

37 And as Paul was about to be brought into the castle,
he saith unto the chief captain, May I say something
unto thee? And he said, Dost thou know Greek?

38 Art thou not then the Egyptian, who before these days
stirred up to sedition and led out into the wilderness
the four thousand men of the Assassins?

39 But Paul said, I am a Jew, of Tarsus in Cilicia, a citizen
of no mean city: and I beseech thee, give me leave to
speak unto the people.

40 And when he had given him leave, Paul, standing on
the stairs, beckoned with the hand unto the people; and
when there was made a great silence, he spake unto
them in the Hebrew language, saying,

27, 28 Imagine the surprise that must have appeared in the eyes of
certain Jews from Asia when they saw in the streets of Jerusalem the
familiar, but despised figure of Saul of Tarsus. These were some of
the very Jews who had opposed him in Ephesus. When they first saw
him he was walking with a certain Greek named "Trophimus". This
fact only served to heighten their hatred of him and his liberal
ways.

Then, one day, while these same Jews were worshiping in the temple, whom did they there behold but this despised heretic. In a moment they were crying out in hatred against him. And what were
the words of their cry? "Men of Israel help. This is the man that
teacheth all men everywhere against the people (the Jews) and
the law and this place."

And then to give a real charge that could result in his death they
cried out what they **knew** was not so: "And moreover he brought
Greeks also into the temple, and hath defiled this holy place."

29-32 This was a trumped-up charge based wholly on hatred. They
had only seen him with **one** Greek and that not in the temple, but in
the streets, and they **supposed** he had brought him into the temple.

839. Why were the Jews from Asia filled with even more hatred than usual
when they saw Saul in Jerusalem?
840. What was the lie told by the Jews?

But they were not content with words only. Even as they cried they took hold of the apostle, while yet he was in the very act of worship. He was pulled and hauled across the temple floor toward the door of the Holy Enclosure; out into the Gentile quarter; and straightway the temple guards shut the doors to shut out this heretic. The spirit of the mob had taken hold of these Jews and they forthwith proceeded to beat Paul to death. This was done just outside the Gate Beautiful.

The Roman authorities who ever kept a watchful eye out for the ever increasing Jewish tumults soon spied the crowd and heard the cries. Word went up to the tribune in the tower of Antonia as to what was taking place; indeed, he was told that: "All Jerusalem was in confusion." When these unarmed Jews saw the Roman soldiers bearing down upon them they had good reason to "leave off beating Paul." But a short time before five to ten thousand of them had been trampled to death close to this very spot; so says Josephus.

The tribune soon had officially laid hands on Paul and bound him to two of his soldiers with handcuffs. Paul was now the prisoner of the Roman government. The "bonds and afflictions" had indeed come.

33-40 Turning to those close by, Claudius Lysias asked "Who is he?" Some shouted one thing and some shouted another and all of them shouted something. Amid this uproar no sense could be had so in disgust at these noisy, unreasonable Jews, Claudius Lysias commanded: "Take him to the castle." But Paul was not to be led away alone for the crowd followed him shouting what they shouted at another prisoner of Rome: "Away with Him." Coming to the steps of the castle, the crowd pressed so closely upon Paul that he had no room to proceed, but proceed he must, so the soldiers hoisted Paul upon their shoulders and in this manner he was carried up the stairs to the tower. But the apostle paid not the slightest heed to all this tumult for his mind and heart were filled with another matter. Even as he was set down on his feet again he burst out with this question to the chief captain: "May I say something to thee?"

It wasn't what Paul said but the language that he used that gave the tribune a start. Lysias thought he knew the one he had arrested, but when he heard the Greek tongue he realized he was wrong. The man he thought Paul to be was an Egyptian, and no common prisoner either, but rather that notorious outlaw who drew away

841. Where was Paul as he was being beaten by the Jews?
842. What was told to the tribune that brought such immediate action?
843. What was the first act of Lysias upon rescuing Paul?
844. What was in the mind of Paul as he was being carried on the shoulders of the soldiers?
845. Why was the tribune surprised when he heard Paul speak Greek?

four thousand men of the assassins after him. These (p. 192) "assassins" seemed to be an underground organization bent on the overthrow of the Roman government; so it was especially desirous that such be captured. Who then is this man about whom such a tumult is made? The tribune asked if Paul was not the one he thought him to be. Paul gave answer to this in the pointed concise words:

"I am a Jew, of Tarsus in Cilicia, a citizen of no mean city."

The emphasis placed upon the city was to impress the tribune with his position in the Roman world. To his citizenship not only of Tarsus but of the Roman empire he was soon to allude.

Perhaps to answer better the question of just who Paul was he was given permission to speak to the mob. But the purpose was thwarted, for if Paul used Greek to attract the attention of the Roman army officer, he was to use Hebrews to draw the attention of those of his own race.

Stepping forward, as best he could with the bonds upon him, he made the familiar gesture to his audience for attention. He secured it and a great stillness fell over the mob gathered before him. The great consuming love of the apostle for his kindred according to the flesh is here manifested. He loved them that they might be saved.

c. Paul addresses the Jewish mob. 22:1-21.

1 Brethren and fathers, hear ye the defence which I now make unto you.
2 And when they heard that he spake unto them in the Hebrew language, they were the more quiet: and he saith,
3 I am a Jew, born in Tarsus of Cilicia, but brought up in this city, at the feet of Gamaliel, instructed according to the strict manner of the law of our fathers, being zealous for God, even as ye all are this day:
4 and I persecuted this Way unto the death, binding and delivering into prisons both men and women.
5 As also the high priest doth bear me witness, and all the estate of the elders: from whom also I received letters unto the brethren, and journeyed to Damascus to bring them also that were there unto Jerusalem in bonds to be punished.
6 And it came to pass, that, as I made my journey, and

846. Who were the Assassins?
847. Why mention the city from which Paul was?
848. How was the purpose of the captain thwarted by Paul?
849. To what purpose did Paul love his kinsman?

drew nigh unto Damascus, about noon, suddenly there shone from heaven a great light round about me.

7 And I fell unto the ground, and heard a voice saying unto me, Saul, Saul, why persecutest thou me?

8 And I answered, Who are thou, Lord? And he said unto me, I am Jesus of Nazareth, whom thou persecutest.

9 And they that were with me beheld indeed the light, but they heard not the voice of him that spake to me.

10 And I said, What shall I do, Lord? And the Lord said unto me, Arise, and go into Damascus; and there it shall be told thee of all things which are appointed for thee to do.

11 And when I could not see for the glory of that light, being led by the hand of them that were with me I came into Damascus.

12 And one Ananias, a devout man according to the law, well reported of by all the Jews that dwelt there,

13 came unto me, and standing by me said unto me, Brother Saul, receive thy sight. And in that very hour I looked up on him.

14 And he said, The God of our fathers hath appointed thee to know his will, and to see the Righteous One, and to hear a voice from his mouth.

15 For thou shalt be a witness for him unto all men of what thou hast seen and heard.

16 And now why tarriest thou? arise, and be baptized, and wash away thy sins calling on his name.

17 And it came to pass, that, when I had returned to Jerusalem, and while I prayed in the temple; I fell into a trance,

18 and saw him saying unto me, Make haste, and get thee quickly out of Jerusalem; because they will not receive of thee testimony concerning me.

19 And I said, Lord, they themselves know that I imprisoned and beat in every synagogue them that believed on thee:

20 and when the blood of Stephen thy witness was shed, I also was standing by, and consenting, and keeping the garments of them that slew him.

21 And he said unto me, Depart: for I will send thee forth far hence unto the Gentiles.

I like very much the outline of this speech as given by Wm. Dallmann in his book "Paul" page 219. In introducing the speech Dallmann has written:

"Chrysostom says: 'What nobler spectacle than that of Paul at this moment. There he stands, bound with two chains, ready to make his defense to the people. The Roman commander sits by to enforce order by his presence. An enraged populace looks up to him from below. Yet in the midst of so many dangers, how self-possessed is he, how tranquil!'

1. Paul spoke of his birth and training as a strict Pharisee, with rare courtesy adding 'as ye all are this day'.
2. Paul spoke of his persecuting those of 'this Way', the Christians, as they well remembered.
3. Paul told of his conversion while engaged in persecution.
4. Paul told of his commission from God Himself to preach the Gospel to the Gentiles.

Gentiles. That stung them to the quick. They gave him audience unto this word and then lifted up their voices and shouted: 'Away with such a fellow from the earth, for it is not fit that he should live!' " Here are a few points in this speech that I deem worthy of special note:

1. The general knowledge of the teaching of Christ revealed in the manner in which Paul refers to it. He gives no introduction to the subject but simply refers to it as "this Way".
2. The use of the term "brethren" in the fifth verse. Here as in the earlier part of his speech he appears to be anxious to gain a favorable impression with these Jews if at all possible.
3. I refer you to the harmony of the account of Paul's conversion that is given previously in 9:13.
4. The connection of baptism to the remission of sins in verse 16. This same connection is found in 2:38; 8:38, 39; 8:12; 16:33, 34, etc. Paul was "converted" on the road to Damascus, but was saved" or forgiven when he obeyed the gospel. (II Thess. 1:7-9)
5. The vision in the temple in Jerusalem, which vision or trance is not spoken of anywhere else. (17-21)

"That fatal word—Gentiles—.Up to this moment they were charmed by his use of the Hebrew language; and perchance they thought to hear some new promise of the coming Messiah, the one that would break this Roman power. Strange indeed was the record of this man's life. Paul hoped withal to free himself of the charge of a heretic. He

850. How did Paul show rare courtesy on this occasion?
851. Why so object to one word?
852. How do we know of the general knowledge of the teachings of Christ?
853. How is the term "brethren" applied in verse one?
854. How is baptism obedience to the gospel?

evidently felt that what convinced him in his stubborness would persuade these Jews.

d. The response of the mob. Paul imprisoned. 22:22-30.

22 And they gave him audience unto this word; and they lifted up their voice, and said, Away with such a fellow from the earth: for it is not fit that he should live.

23 And as they cried out, and threw off their garments, and cast dust into the air,

24 the chief captain commanded him to be brought into the castle, bidding that he should be examined by scourging, that he might know for what cause they so shouted against him.

25 And when they had tied him up with the thongs, Paul said unto the centurion that stood by, Is it lawful for you to scourge a man that is a Roman, and uncondemned?

26 And when the centurion heard it, he went to the chief captain and told him, saying, What art thou about to do? for this man is a Roman.

27 And the chief captain came and said unto him, Tell me, art thou a Roman? And he said, Yea.

28 And the chief captain answered, With a great sum obtained I this citizenship. And Paul said, But I am a Roman born.

29 They then that were about to examine him straightway departed from him: and the chief captain also was afraid when he knew that he was a Roman, and because he had bound him.

30 But on the morrow desiring to know the certainty wherefore he was accused of the Jews, he loosed him, and commanded the chief priests and all the council to come together, and brought Paul down and set him before them.

22, 23 But their prejudice was so deep-seated that nothing either logical or divine would free them from it. "Then began one of the most odious and despicable spectacles which the world can witness, the spectacle of an Oriental mob, hideous with impotent rage, howling, yelling, cursing, gnashing their teeth, flinging about their arms, waving and tossing their blue and red robes, casting dust into the air by handfuls, with all the furious gesticulations of an uncontrolled fanaticism" (Farrar, page 535).

"Away with such a **fellow** (a word of the deepest contempt) from the earth. He contaminates the earth with his presence."

The chief captain simply repeated his former command, probably in disgust at a waste of time. "Take him into the castle and when you have him there examine him with 'flagellum'. Maybe that will make him 'take sense'."

24-28 The tribune must know why these many men shouted against this one so.

"The soldiers at once tied his hands together, stripped his back bare, and bent him forward into the position for that horrid and often fatal examination by torture which, not far from that very spot, his Lord had undergone.

Thrice before, on that scarred back had Paul felt the fasces of Roman lictors; five times the nine-and-thirty strokes of Jewish thongs; here was a new form of agony, the whip—the horrible flagellum—which the Romans employed to force by torture the confession of truth." (ibid.)

But even as they tightened the ropes on his hands, Paul turned to the captain who stood by watching the proceedings and asked in a quiet voice, "Is it lawful for you to scourge a man that is a Roman and uncondemned or untried?"

This question had more than one thought in it for it was not only strictly against the Roman law to beat a Roman citizen before a trial but it was also strictly forbidden to put bonds on such a one.

This question stopped the action of the soldiers immediately and the captain hurried to the tribune with the blunt question: "What art thou about to do?—For this man is a Roman."

Claudius Lysias probably began to wonder just **who** this stranger was. He thought him to be an Egyptian and he spoke Greek—when he gave him permission to speak he spoke Hebrew—when he wanted him examined he turned out to be a Roman. With these thoughts in his mind, the chief captain approached Paul and asked this question, "Tell me, art **thou** a Roman?" Perhaps looking up and down the ordinary looking figure and clothes of Paul he could see that this man was a Jew and a poor one at that. How could he be a Roman citizen?

In a day when the honor of being a citizen was an expensive one this army captain had a right to wonder.

855. How did Paul imagine he would convince these Jews?
856. What does Farrar say about the mob?
857. How did the tribune propose to find out what this one had done?
858. Describe the "examination" Paul was about to receive.
859. What three types of beatings were given Paul?
860. What two Roman laws were violated here?
861. Show the real perplexity of Claudius Lysias.
862. Why emphasize the "*thou*" in the question of the tribune to Paul?

"**I** know how much it cost **me** to get this citizenship," he remarked, in a dubious tone of voice. "But I have been a citizen from my birth," was the calm answer to his unexpressed suspicion. (ibid 537).

29, 30 Paul's claim was accepted and the whips were dropped and the soldiers who were to lay on the lash left him.

But this only served to heighten the trouble of the chief captain— he had captured this man, indeed he had saved him from death, he had bound him, he could not go back on his decision, but who was he and what had he done? The law of Rome had been violated and he had a prisoner on his hands of whom he knew nothing. Something must be done. It was the Jews that called for his death, let them explain the charges against him.

So sending word to the Sanhedrin to gather, he loosed Paul and brought him on the morrow to stand before the highest court of Jewish law.

    e. Paul addresses the council. 23:1-10.

     1 And Paul, looking stedfastly on the council, said, Brethren, I have lived before God in all good conscience until this day.

     2 And the high priest Ananias commanded them that stood by him to smite him on the mouth.

     3 Then said Paul unto him, God shall smite thee, thou whited wall: and sittest thou to judge me according to the law, and commandest me to be smitten contrary to the law?

     4 And they that stood by said, Revilest thou God's high priest?

     5 And Paul said, I knew not, brethren, that he was high priest: for it is written, Thou shalt not speak evil of a ruler of thy people.

     6 But when Paul perceived that the one part were Sadducees and the other Pharisees, he cried out in the council, Brethren, I am a Pharisee, a son of Pharisees: touching the hope and resurrection of the dead I am called in question.

     7 And when he had so said, there arose a dissension between the Pharisees and Sadducees; and the assembly was divided.

     8 For the Sadducees say that there is no resurrection, neither angel, nor spirit; but the Pharisees confess both.

     9 And there arose a great clamor: and some of the scribes

863. How did the tribune become a Roman citizen?
864. What problem did Lysias hope to solve by bringing Paul before the Sanhedrin?

of the Pharisees' part stood up, and strove, saying, We find no evil in this man: and what if a spirit hath spoken to him, or an angel?

10 And when there arose a great dissension, the chief captain, fearing lest Paul should be torn in pieces by them, commanded the soldiers to go down and take him by force from among them, and bring him into the castle.

Fredrick Farrar remarks as to the place of the assembly of the council (Page 504).

1 "The Sanhedrin met in full numbers. They no longer sat in the Lishcath Haggazzith, the famous hall, with its tessellated pavement which stood at the south side of the Court of the Priests. Had they still been accustomed to meet there, Lysias and his soldiers would never have been suffered to obtrude their profane feet into a chamber which lay within the middle wall of partition—beyond which even a procurator dare not even have set a step on pain of death. But at this period the Sanhedrin had probably begun their meetings in the Chanujoth, or 'booths', the very existence of which was a proof of the power and prosperity of 'the Serpent House of Hanan'. To this place Lysias led his prisoner and placed him before them."

Paul was determined to secure a fair hearing of his cause and case before the proper authorities. It must have been with this thought in heart that he looked stedfastly on the council.

He did not refer to them as Peter and John had (4:8) "Rulers of the people and elders."

Paul here simply called them "Brethren" possibly because he himself had been a member of this body of men. First he wanted it known that he was "not guilty".

"Brethren, I have lived before God in all good conscience until this day."

2, 3 Maybe it was the familiarity with which Paul addressed the council or the bold statement of innocence or perchance the guilty conscience of the high priest that irritated him. In a moment of hot rage he cried out to those near Paul, "Smite him on the mouth." Instantly the heavy hand of some soldier struck Paul full in the face. Smarting from the blow, the apostle flashed out with the words: "God shall smite thee, thou whited wall!" What! "Sittest thou to judge me according to the law, and commandest me to be smitten contrary to the law?"

865. What does Farrar say about the place of the meeting of the Sanhedrin? How proven?
866. Why call the council "brethren?"
867. Why have Paul struck on the mouth?

4, 5 Those observing this incident (members of the Sanhedrin) had so schooled themselves in self-deception that the truth or falsity of Paul's statement made no appeal to them. The only thing apparent to them was that the high priest had been reviled. They were shocked! "Revilest thou God's High Priest?"

Why had Paul so spoken? Did he not know who occupied the chair of this office? It is perfectly possible that he didn't for the Sadducees "passed the chair" with disgraceful frequency. Since Paul had been away from Jerusalem he had not informed himself on just who was or who wasn't the high priest.

Then also Frederick Farrar suggests that the apostle's poor eyesight played a part in the reason for his words. He says:

"Owing to his weakened sight, all that he saw before him was a blurred white figure issuing a brutal order, and to this person, who in his external whiteness and inward worthlessness thus reminded him of the plastered wall of a sepulchre, he had addressed him in indigant denunciation." (ibid 541).

Immediately upon learning the "identity of the delinquent", Paul retracted his previous statement for he well knew it was a direct violation of the scriptures. (Ex. 22:28).

6-9 Paul, like Peter, John, the twelve, and Stephen, knew that there was to be no justice or mercy administered by **this** court.

The council hadn't changed since Paul was associated with it. It was divided "into two parties—the Sadducean priest and the Pharisaic elders and scribes."

As the apostle surveyed the council, he decided that an act of strategy was the best way out.

"Brethren, I'm a Pharisee, a son of Pharisees and for the hope of the resurrection I am called into question."

This bold statement lined him up with one side of the Sanhedrin and at once touched the sore spot between the two parties. The statement of the apostle was indirectly true for the preaching of the resurrection of Christ was several times opposed. The scribes of the Pharisees could not let this opportunity pass. Here was a chance to contend for "the truth". Up one of them jumped. "We find no evil in this man. And what if a spirit hath spoken to him, or an angel?"

This touched off the powder keg of emotion and ill feeling. It was only a matter of minutes until everyone was arguing and har-

868. Why call the high priest a "whited wall" if he did not know him?
869. How is the "self-deception" of the Sanhedrin seen?
870. How is it that Paul did not know who was high priest?
871. How does Paul's poor eyesight fit into this picture?
872. What scripture was violated by Paul's words?
873. Why use the act of strategy he did?
874. Was the statement of the apostle true?

anguing his neighbor. In the midst of this wild disorder stood the apostle.

Some of them had hold of him, those of the Pharisees in defense and those of the Sadducees in hatred. He was pulled and hauled between them until he was threatened by the force of the pulling to be torn limb from limb.

10 Now Claudius Lysias **must** have been confused and disgusted. What kind of people were these Jews? He could make no sense out of their words or actions.

He gave the command to those soldiers near him to interfere in this insane melee and rescue their prisoner. This they did and probably none too gently.

If ever it was that the apostle needed encouragement, it was now. He had come to Jerusalem with a free will love offering for his Jewish brethren. He came with a sincere prayer that they would receive him. He was glad to try for reconciliation in the temple purification. He was falsely accused, and tried to get a hearing on the steps of the castle while he stood in Roman chains. He only escaped a cruel beating by an appeal to his Roman citizenship. He found nothing but hatred and insolence from the highest court of his people. Here he was bound in a Roman prison.

   f. The Lord encourages Paul. 23:11.
      11 And the night following the Lord stood by him, and said, Be of good cheer: for as thou hast testified concerning me at Jerusalem, so must thou bear witness also at Rome.

11 But in this dark hour the Lord stood by him to speak to him in the most wonderful and cheering words. "Be of good cheer for as thou hast testified concerning me at Jerusalem, so must thou bear witness also at Rome."

It was no promise of release from bonds nor a fore-note of victory, but simply that he would live and testify for the Messiah. This was enough.

   g. The plot for Paul's life and his escape. 23:12-30.
      12 And when it was day, the Jews banded together, and bound themselves under a curse, saying that they would neither eat nor drink till they had killed Paul.

875. How was Paul's life endangered?
876. What were the probable feelings of Claudius Lysias at the result of the trial?
877. Give three facts that point to an evident need for encouragement on the part of Paul.
878. What was the thought of the Lord's encouragement?

13 And they were more than forty that made this conspiracy.

14 And they came to the chief priests and the elders, and said, We have bound ourselves under a great curse, to taste nothing until we have killed Paul.

15 Now therefore do ye with the council signify to the chief captain that he bring him down unto you, as though ye would judge of his case more exactly: and we, before he comes near, are ready to slay him.

16 But Paul's sister's son heard of their lying in wait, and he came and entered into the castle and told Paul.

17 And Paul called unto him one of the centurions, and said, Bring this young man unto the chief captain; for he hath something to tell him.

18 So he took him, and brought him to the chief captain, and saith, Paul the prisoner called me unto him, and asked me to bring this young man unto thee, who hath something to say to thee.

19 And the chief captain took him by the hand, and going aside asked him privately, What is it that thou hast to tell me?

20 And he said, The Jews have agreed to ask thee to bring down Paul tomorrow unto the council, as though thou wouldest inquire somewhat more exactly concerning him.

21 Do not thou therefore yield unto them: for there lie in wait for him of them more than forty men, who have bound themselves under a curse, neither to eat nor to drink till they have slain him: and now are they ready, looking for the promise from thee.

22 So the chief captain let the young man go, charging him, Tell no man that thou hast signified these things to me.

23 And he called unto him two of the centurions, and said, Make ready two hundred soldiers to go as far as Caesarea, and horsemen threescore and ten, and spearmen two hundred, at the third hour of the night:

24 and he bade them provide beasts, that they might set Paul thereon, and bring him safe unto Felix the governor.

25 And he wrote a letter after this form:

26 Claudius Lysias unto the most excellent governor Felix, greeting.

27 This man was seized by the Jews, and was about to be slain of them, when I came upon them with the soldiers and rescued him, having learned that he was a Roman.

28 And desiring to know the cause wherefore they ac-
    cused him, I brought him down unto their council:
29 whom I found to be accused about questions of their
    law, but to have nothing laid to his charge worthy of
    death or of bonds.
30 And when it was shown to me that there would be
    a plot against the man, I sent him to thee forthwith,
    charging his accusers also to speak against him before
    thee.

12-15 Paul's escape from the council only stirred up a greater hatred. It was the very morning following his experience with the Sanhedrin that more than forty men agreed together neither to eat nor
drink until they had slain Paul. These forty thought even as Paul
thought so long ago that they were doing a service to God in this
murderous act. When they came to the high priest and elders to secure
their cooperation in this nefarious scheme they expressed no shame.
Indeed, they seemed to expect approval and congratulations.

16-18 This was not the first or the last time murder was employed
as a means of quelling apostasy. The place was worked out in the
secrecy of the forty men but soon others heard and at a certain place
the name of "Paul" struck a responsive chord of interest in the mind
of a young lad who heard it. He stopped to listen more fully to the
gossip that involved the name of one so dear to him. What he heard
made his heart leap within him. These men were assassins and this
was a plot of murder of his own uncle. That afternoon Paul had a
visitor. How surprised and glad he must have been to see his nephew.
But in a moment Paul's face took on a serious expression as he
heard his nephew tell him—

"Uncle, they are plotting to kill you. I heard men saying that to-
morrow morning the priests are going to ask Claudius Lysias to
bring you down before the council as if they would inquire more
accurately concerning your case, but men will be lying in wait on
the way and they will rush upon you and kill you."

Immediately upon hearing of this Paul acted in the wise way he
was wont to. He called one of the ten centurions or captains near
by and asked him to take his nephew to the chief captain for he
had something to say to him.

19-22 See how kindly and gently the chief captain treats this young
lad. As nervous and shy as the boy would be he took him by the hand
and led him aside to hear what he had to say. When Lysias heard of

879. How was the plot to kill Paul like Paul's previous persecution of the
     church?
880. How was the intenseness of the hatred of the 40 men expressed?
881. Who averted the disaster?
882. Who escorted Paul's nephew to Lysias?
883. How did the chief captain show his kindness to the lad?

this plan he saw in it a great danger, not only to justice but to his own office. So great was the danger that 470 soldiers must be called to help.

23-30 As once before, there was only one recourse to save his life and that was to leave Jerusalem. This time Paul was to ride out on horseback.

There was to be a letter to accompany this impressive appearing group. The centurian in charge was to take it to the governor Felix to explain the case history of the prisoner.

If you will read carefully the letter in verses 26-30 you will notice a subtle lie or two told by Lysias to cover up his hasty actions. He says (in verse 27) that he rescued Paul from the Jews "having learned he was a Roman." Now you know it wasn't until after he had taken him into the castle that he learned he was a Roman.

The tribune makes no mention of the attempted scourging. So has man attempted through any and all means to "appear righteous" before his fellow-man.

2. **AT ANTIPATRIS.** 23:31, 32.

    31 So the soldiers, as it was commanded them, took Paul
        and brought him by night to Antipatris.
    32 But on the morrow they left the horsemen to go with
        him, and returned to the castle:

31, 32 "A long march down the hills to the sea plain brought them, next day, to Antipatris, a town built by Herod the Great and named after his father, Antipater, now know as Ras-el-Ain, on the Roman road to Caesarea, about forty miles from Jerusalem and about twenty from the seat of the Procurator. A large mound covered with heaps of stone, old foundations, broken columns, and chiselled blocks, half buried among thorns, is now all that remains of the town, but a copious spring bursting from the mound—a chief source of the permanent stream Aujeh—shows that one great element of health and local beauty had been among the attractions that fixed its site." **(Geikie, pp. 390-391).**

Paul now only needed seventy horsemen to guard him. The 400 infantry men after some rest returned to Jerusalem.

3. **IN CAESAREA.** 23:33—27:1.

    a. Paul is brought before Felix the governor. 23:33-35.
      33 and they, when they came to Caesarea and delivered
          the letter to the governor, presented Paul also before
          him.

884. What real danger did the tribune see in the plot on Paul's life?
885. Name the two falsehoods that Lysias put in his letter.
886. How far was Antipatris from Jerusalem? From Ceasarea?

34 And when he had read it, he asked of what province he was; and when he understood that he was of Cilicia,

35 I will hear thee fully, said he, when thine accusers also are come: and he commanded him to be kept in Herod's palace.

33-35 Coming into the beautiful city of Caesarea, the party went immediately to the governor's house. Audience was soon obtained and they stood still while Felix read the letter. There was only one point of import missing in the letter.

"Of what province art thou?" asked the governor.

"Tarsus in Cilicia" was evidently the reply of Paul. Why ask this question? Well, it was customary to judge a man either at the place of his birth or where the crime was committed. Felix knew where the supposed crime had occurred. He evidently asked this question to complete the picture in his mind or to secure an opportunity for relieving himself of the responsibility of judgment if he could not decide the case.

"I will hear you when your accusers are also come." Directing his remarks to the soldiers standing near by, Felix said: "Keep him in the Praetorium."

This was no ordinary prison but was one built by Herod in the palace. It was to house those of royal position and here acted as a place of detention.

b. Paul's trial before Felix the governor. 24:1-22.

1 And after five days the high priest Ananias came down with certain elders, and with an orator, one Tertullus; and they informed the governor against Paul.

2 And when he was called, Tertullus began to accuse him, saying,
Seeing that by thee we enjoy much peace, and that by thy providence evils are corrected for this nation,

3 we accept it in all ways and in all places, most excellent Felix, with all thankfulness.

4 But, that I be not further tedious unto thee, I entreat thee to hear us of thy clemency a few words.

5 For we have found this man a pestilent fellow, and a mover of insurrections among all the Jews throughout the world, and a ringleader of the sect of the Nazarenes:

6 who moreover assayed to profane the temple: on whom also we laid hold:

8 from whom thou wilt be able, by examining him thyself, to take knowledge of all these things whereof we accuse him.

887. Why inquire as to the province of Paul?
888. In what type of prison was Paul placed?

9 And the Jews also joined in the charge, affirming that these things were so.

10 And when the governor had beckoned unto him to speak, Paul answered,
Forasmuch as I know that thou hast been of many years a judge unto this nation, I cheerfuly make my defence:

11 seeing that thou canst take knowledge that it is not more than twelve days since I went up to worship at Jerusalem:

12 and neither in the temple did they find me disputing with any man or stirring up a crowd, nor in the synagogues, nor in the city.

13 Neither can they prove to thee the things whereof they now accuse me.

14 But this I confess unto thee, that after the Way which they call a sect, so serve I the God of our fathers, believing all things which are according to the law, and which are written in the prophets;

15 having hope toward God, which these also themselves look for, that there shall be a resurrection both of the just and unjust.

16 Herein I also exercise myself to have a conscience void of offence toward God and men always.

17 Now after some years I came to bring alms to my nation, and offerings:

18 amidst which they found me purified in the temple, with no crowd, nor yet with tumult: but there were certain Jews from Asia—

19 who ought to have been here before thee, and to make accusation, if they had aught against me.

20 Or else let these men themselves say what wrong-doing they found when I stood before the council,

21 except it be for this one voice, that I cried standing among them, Touching the resurrection of the dead I am called in question before you this day.

22 But Felix, having more exact knowledge concerning the Way, deferred them, saying, When Lysias the chief captain shall come down, I will determine your matter.

1 The forty men in Jerusalem were going to have a long fast if they were going to eat nothing until they killed Paul. But when word got to them that Paul had left the city, they probably gave up their vow. But not the high priest Ananias. He was not one to be thwarted. When the Christians fled Jerusalem, Saul "pursued them to foreign cities." Saul went to the high priest for permission to do

so. This time the high priest was himself in pursuit. (Not of Christians, but of the very one who was once the pursuer.)

It is probable that Lysias sent word to the high priest that since Paul was a Roman citizen his case had been referred to the governor.

Paul had been in Caesarea five days when "his accusers" came. Here is an interesting chronology of the "12 days" that had elapsed since Paul came to Jerusalem.

1—May 8th Paul arrived at Jerusalem.
2—May 9th Pentecost and council held.
3—May 10th Paul goes to Temple with the four Nazarites.
4—May 11th Second day of Nazarite week.
5—May 12th Third day.
6—May 13th Fourth Day.
7—May 14th Fifth day and Paul is apprehended in the temple.
8—May 15th Before the Sanhedrin.
9—May 16th The conspiracy against Paul; at nine o'clock at night Paul is dispatched to Caesarea.
10—May 17th Reaches Caesarea.
11—May 18th)
    19th)
    20th) At Caesarea.
    21st)
12—May 22nd Trial before Felix.

(This chronology is taken from Lewin, as quoted by Dallmann).

2-9 Ananias was prepared to make the most of this appearance. With this in mind he had brought along a Roman orator who understood better the procedure of Roman law. Of course this lawyer or orator was paid, but he was determined to "do his mercenary best."

Paul was called out of the prison and all were summoned before the governor and the trial began.

Tertullus was the first to speak and his first effort was to secure the good will of Felix. This Roman orator said everything he could in favor of Felix. It wasn't what he did say that mattered, it was rather what he did not say that suggested flattery.
Indeed:

(1) By the effort of Felix the country **did** enjoy a measure of peace. He even called himself "The Pacifier of the Providence" yet there was much discord and Felix was the cause of a good deal of it.

(2) And it was true that "evils were corrected". Yes, and how many

889. Show the great difference in the relation of Paul to the high priest here from that of previous times.
890. How did Ananias hear that Paul had left Jerusalem and was now in Caesarea?
891. When Paul was tried before Felix how many days elapsed since he first arrived in Jerusalem?

other "evils" were promoted by this one? And some of the correct-ed evils resulted in the slaughter of numerous Jews.

Felix like other kings felt he had "divine right" in his rule, hence the use of the world "providence" in verse 2.

Tertullus says that it was not only here before the governor that the nation made mention of these things, but at all times and in all ways with thankfulness. (What a liar.) This smooth speaker says in essence that: "I could go on like this for hours but I do not wish to bother you with it."

What is the meaning of "clemency?" It refers to compassion or re-mission—just another word of flattery. Now to the charges against Paul.

   1. "We (the Jews, since he was speaking for them) have found this
.   man a 'pestilent fellow'."
This was but a general charge as much as to say that "this man is a monster" or "this one is a desperate character", a "dangerous criminal". This was only given to throw a dark aura around the apostle.

   2. He is a mover (originator) of insurrections. Not confined to
      one location, but "among the Jews throughout the world".
When the Jews were pressed for a charge against Jesus they resort-ed to that of insurrection. This would be a very pointed appeal to a Roman ruler.

   3. A ringleader of the sect of the Nazarenes.
This was a military term applied to those who were in the front rank of the army, a foremost man—of the sect. The term Nazarenes was a term of contempt referring to Jesus of Nazareth. This sect was mentioned by Tertullus as if it were a low class of people. Thus Paul then was a ringleader of this rabble.

   4. A profaner of the temple. Literally "attempted"—"endeavor-
      ed"—to profane the temple.
Why would a Roman governor be interested in this thought? Be-cause it was a capital offense in both Roman and Jewish law. The accusation they had against Paul had to do with bringing a Gen-tile into the Jewish quarter. This was strictly forbidden on penalty of death. This the Roman ruler knew.

892. Why bring Tertullus along?
893. In what way was Tertullus deceptive in what he said to Felix?
894. Mention two of the sins of "The Pacifier of the Providence."
895. What is the meaning of the word "providence" in verse 2?
896. What obvious lie did Tertullus tell?
897. Why call Paul "a pestilent fellow?"
898. What is the meaning of the term "insurrection?"
899. Why call the Christians "Nazarenes?"
900. Why mention profaning the temple?

To put the Jews in the best light, Tertullus insinuates that left alone the Jews would have tried the case and settled it in justice and law, but Lysias interfered and made it ultimately necessary to appear here in Caesarea.

10-21 Of course a greater falsehood could hardly be imagined, for far from being about to judge Paul, they were about to murder him when Lysias interfered.

The orator adds in conclusion that a simple examination on the part of the governor will substantiate all that has been said. The Jews led by Ananias, although they knew how the facts had been perverted were so full of hatred they "joined in assailing him".

Notice how carefully and completely Paul answers the false charges and note also his adroit introduction. When the governor gave Paul the nod of assent to speak he spoke after this fashion:

"Since you have been for many years a judge of this nation (from 6 to 10 years, a long time when the average term was 2 years or less) I am glad to make my defense before you for I can be more confident of a fair judgment."

Then follows the reasons why the things whereof he was accused were **not** so.

(1) "A pestilent fellow"—This general charge was passed over by Paul as not even worthy of notice. Anyone who actively objected to the belief of another would be considered by the one opposed as "a pestilent fellow"—"a monster of wickedness"— This proved nothing.

(2) "A mover of insurrection". Hear Paul on this charge: "Take knowledge, O Felix, it has been but 12 days since I came to Jerusalem. A mover of an insurrection against Rome? Where? Did they find me in the temple? Did they? Can they prove that I stirred up a crowd in the synagogues? Prove it. Or in the streets of the city? I have been here in Caesarea five days. Stir up an insurrection in seven days? Ridiculous! For proof of what they have said, they have nothing."

(3) "A ringleader of the sect of the Nazarenes."
"Guilty! But I am only serving the God of our fathers by this means. Far from introducing a new god, I am following the law and the prophets who hath told of these days. I have the same hope as these, my accusers, the hope of the resurrection of

901. In what way did Tertellus attempt to put the Jews in a favorable light? How false?
902. Show the advantage of the introduction given by Paul?
903. Why not answer the first charge?
904. How did the mention of the twelve days answer the charge of insurrection.
905. How did Paul show that being a Nazarene was no offense against God?

both the just and the unjust. Far from being some kind of a heretic I do so thoroughly believe these things that I constantly **exercise** myself (a term alluding to athletic exercises at the Grecian games) so as to have a conscience void of offense before God and man."

(4) "A profaner of the temple."
This was a charge of sacrilege. As to being sacrilegious Paul had this to say of his relationship to the temple at Jerusalem: "I was in the temple to worship. I had no thought of profaning the temple or insulting my people. Indeed, I brought alms and offerings to them from foreign places. There was no tumult or crowd. This was how they found me in the temple. Certain Jews from Asia also found me in the performance of these rites. They should be here today to accuse me now as they accused me then. But since they are not here let the ones that are here say what wrong I have done. I **was** examined before the Sanhedrin and they found nothing against me. On only one point could I be called in question and that has to do with a point of doctrine and not of law. I cried before the council: "Touching the resurrection of the dead I am called in question before you this day."

22 If either Paul or Ananias thought a decision was to be made at this time they were to be disappointed. Felix knew very well of the relationship of Christianity and Judaism. Felix was not thinking primarily of justice, but like a certain other, Pilate, about his job. He was afraid to incur the disfavor of the Sanhedrin and yet he could not condemn this innocent man. A pretext was used to relieve the pressure.
"When Lysias the chief captain shall come down I will determine your matter."
He was a long time in coming for Paul stayed two years in Caesarea.

c. Paul's two years imprisonment in Caesarea. 24:23-27.

23 And he gave order to the centurion that he should be kept in charge, and should have indulgence; and not to forbid any of his friends to minister unto him.
24 But after certain days, Felix came with Drusilla, his wife, who was a Jewess, and sent for Paul, and heard him concerning the faith in Christ Jesus.

906. Who should have been present at the trial to substantiate the charges?
907. Why make the point that the charge was not one of law but rather of doctrine?
908. How account for the indecision of Felix?
909. Why did Felix make the statement that he did?

25 And as he reasoned of righteousness, and self-control, and the judgment to come, Felix was terrified, and answered, Go thy way for this time; and when I have a convenient season, I will call thee unto me.

26 He hoped withal that money would be given him of Paul: wherefore also he sent for him the oftener, and communed with him.

27 But when two years were fulfilled, Felix was succeeded by Porcius Festus; and desiring to gain favor with the Jews, Felix left Paul in bonds.

23 "He seems to have been in what was termed 'military custody' in which the prisoner was bound by a long, light chain to his arm, the other end of which was fastened to the officer." (Jacobus, page 375)

There was a thriving work for the Lord here in Caesarea, headed up by Philip, the evangelist. And so it was that Philip must have been among those who came to see Paul while he was held here. This could have been a renewing of the friendship that was established when the house of Philip was opened to Paul and his companions on the return of their missionary journey. (Cf. 21:7, 8)

Others from Jerusalem also could have visited the apostle. It could have been that during this time he wrote the epistles of Colossians, Ephesians and Philemon—some authorities so believe. I am no authority and can only say that the evidence seems to point to a later date than this for these three books.

24 It will be well to tell just now a little case history of the prospects for the gospel that Paul had in Felix and Drusilla.

First, who was this man Felix? What was his background? The story starts with two slave brothers. Paullus and Felix. For some reason not known to your writer, Paullus obtained a fortune. Through this he was able to engineer the placement of Claudius as emperor. Naturally upon the ascension of Claudius to the throne, Paullus prevailed on him on behalf of his brother, Felix. Thus was Felix, the slave, made governor of Judea, with residence in the marble house of Herod in Caesarea. "He indulged in all kinds of cruelty and lust, exercising regal power with the disposition of a slave."

Felix was the husband of three queens or "royal ladies". His first and last wife were both named Drusilla. The one mentioned in the text was the daughter of Herod Agrippa I—(the one that beheaded James and put Peter in prison (12:1, 2). She was the youngest of

910. What is meant by "military custody?"
911. Who would be logical to expect as a visitor while Paul was in prison?
912. What about the writing of three book from Caesarea?
913. Tell in your own words of the rise of Felix from a slave to a governor.

the three daughters of Herod Agrippa and also the most beautiful. When but a child she was betrothed to Epiphanes, son of Antiochus who refused to undergo the necessary rite to become a Jew. She was then married to Azizus, king of Eunesa (a small kingdom in Syria). From this marriage a son was born whom she named Agrippa.

Felix met Drusilla when he first became governor and fell in love with her. (The wife of Felix at the time was the granddaughter of Anthony and Cleopatra).

With the aid of a magician in the court of Azizus, Felix persuaded this 18 or 19 year old girl to become his wife, for as he said, "If you do not refuse me I will make you a happy woman."

She accepted his offer and was prevailed on to transgress the laws of her forefathers and marry this profligate.

Felix plainly was a sensualist and Drusilla a hypocrite of the deepest dye. Before such persons was Paul called to speak. Felix asked Paul to outline the Christian faith. This Paul did but he also fitted the material to the one listening.

Paul spoke of "righteousness" of which Felix had none. The ancient historian, Tacitus, stated that Felix felt he could commit all crimes with impunity.

25 The apostle spoke of "self-control". Drusilla, while seated beside Felix, was evidence of his lack of it.

The third thought was that of "judgment" which Felix faced unprepared.

How Paul developed these thoughts we do not know but this manner of development was so real and personal that terror took hold of the heart of the governor and lest he should give in to the truth that was pressing upon him he cried out: "Go thy way for this time; and when I have a convenient season, I will call thee unto me."

The "convenient season" was upon him. Although Felix **did** call for Paul many times, the subject of salvation and "the faith" never came to light as it did here. No word is given how the message affected Drusilla.

Tradition has it that she and her son perished in Pompeii upon the eruption of Vesuvius in 79 A.D. What a tragic death for an unrepentant sinner.

26 Strange that a wealthy man like the governor of Judea and Samaria should hope to receive a bride from a poor Jewish prisoner. But was Paul so poor? I have of late read some discussion suggesting that at this period Paul had come into some little money.

It cost money to appeal to Caesar as Paul did. It cost money to

914. What of a Biblical interest is given here of Drusilla?
915. To whom was Drusilla married when Felix asked her to marry him?
916. Show the appropriateness of the message of the Apostle to those who heard.

have two slaves or attendants (Luke and Aristarchus). This is but the reasoning of man, but it is an interesting thought.

However it happened, Felix hoped that some day it would be "convenient" for him to obtain a bribe from the apostle for his release. But Paul saw to it that it was not so. What were the subjects discussed by the apostle and Felix? I cannot imagine that Paul changed his method or message here, but that he did all he could to obtain the conversion of this notorious sinner.

28 When two years had passed, Felix in his public and political life had gone from bad to worse and was called to Rome to give an account. He was dismissed from his office and Porcius Festus took his place. The last act of Felix as governor was to gain favor with the Jews (who were the ones who were bringing the charges against him at Rome) by leaving Paul in bonds.

d. Festus visits Jerusalem. 25:1-6a.

1 Festus therefore, having come into the province, after three days went up to Jerusalem from Caesarea.

2 And the chief priests and the principal men of the Jews informed him against Paul; and they besought him,

3 asking a favor against him, that he would send for him to Jerusalem; laying a plot to kill him on the way.

4 Howbeit Festus answered, that Paul was kept in charge at Caesarea, and that he himself was about to depart thither shortly.

5 Let them therefore, saith he, that are of power among you go down with me, and if there is anything amiss in the man, let them accuse him.

6a And when he had tarried among them not more than eight or ten days,

1, 2 Festus was a "mild-mannered man, honest and just in his dealings" (whenever it did not interfere with his political advantages), withal a crafty politician. His first gesture upon coming to his new position was to pay a visit to Jerusalem and see how "the land lay" in the capital of the Jews.

The Jews were glad for his visit for it afforded them further opportunity to press their charges against Paul. These opposers of the

917. What was the response of Felix to Paul's message?
918. Did Felix ever call Paul to speak to him again?
919. What was the final fate of Drusilla?
920. What motive was there in asking Paul for money? Did Paul have it?
921. How is it that Paul was not approached on the subject of a bride?
922. How did Felix lose his job?
923. What was the first act of the new governor Festus?

gospel did not give up easily. By this time it had gotten out of the
realm of a doctrinal issue and was more of a personal grudge a-
gainst Paul.

3-6 Ananias probably smarted a long time under the rebuke,
"Thou whited wall". He influenced the elders of the Sanhedrin to feel
the same way about the apostle. However, Ananias was no longer the
high priest when Festus came to Jerusalem. Ananias was retired
but held great power in a personal and political manner over the
Jews of Jerusalem.

One by the name of Ismael, son of Fabi who had been put forward by Agrippa, was now high priest.

When Festus arrived in Jerusalem the same cry reached him that
was heard two years previous. "Saul of Tarsus must be punished,
and that right away."

Luke makes it obvious in his record that the request for Paul's
punishment was unlawful. The Jews were not going to use the
Assassins to carry out their plan, their motive was far more obvious.
Murder was a small matter to them in comparison to the defilement
of the temple.

Festus did not rebuke them for their unjust suggestion, nor did he
yield to it. His answer to them was altogether fair as well as typically Roman: "Paul is right where he should be. I am about to return to Caesarea and if you want to see him or to oppose him in
any way, come with me. Let your chief men return with me and
stand in Roman court in lawful procedure. If there is anything amiss
in the man it will be brought to light in this way."

e. Paul's trial, defence and appeal to Caesar. 25:6b-12.

6b he went down unto Caesarea; and on the morrow he sat
    on the judgment-seat, and commanded Paul to be
    brought.

7   And when he was come, the Jews that had come down
    from Jerusalem stood round about him, bringing against
    him many and grievous charges which they could not
    prove;

8   while Paul said in his defence, Neither against the law
    of the Jews, nor against the temple, nor against Caesar,
    have I sinned at all.

9   But Festus, desiring to gain favor with the Jews, an-
    swered Paul and said, Wilt thou go up to Jerusalem,
    and there be judged of these things before me?

924. How was Festus received by the Jews in Jerusalem? Why?
925. Since it was unlawful for the Jews to ask for the punishment of Paul
     how did they imagine Festus would grant their request?
926. What is "typically Roman" about the answer of Festus to the Jews?

10 But Paul said, I am standing before Caesar's judgment-seat, where I ought to be judged: to the Jews have I done no wrong, as thou also very well knowest.

11 If then I am a wrong-doer, and have committed anything worthy of death, I refuse not to die; but if none of those things is true whereof these accuse me, no man can give me up unto them. I appeal unto Caesar.

12 Then Festus, when he had conferred with the council, answered, Thou hast appealed unto Caesar: unto Caesar shalt thou go.

6b Festus was as good as his word. It was not more than eight or ten days until he went to Caesarea. On the very next day after his arrival he heard the case of Paul.

Once again the apostle was called from his prison room to make his defense. Note: He had appeared in the last two years before the following:

(1) The mob on the steps of the Tower of Antonia.
(2) The Sanhedrin in Jerusalem.
(3) Before Felix.
(4) Before Felix again in an unofficial manner.
(5) Now before Festus.
(6) He is yet to appear before king Agrippa.

This all afforded a wonderful opportunity to preach the word, which opportunity Paul used, but it was also a bit wearying and it must have been not a little exasperating as to result.

7-11 There was no Roman orator this time. All the Jews gathered round Paul and after the Jewish manner began to accuse him of many grievous charges. Luke evidently was an eye-witness of this event and he adds that proof for the charges was entirely lacking. What were the charges brought? This can be answered from the thoughts of the reply Paul gave. These charges had to do with:

(1) Sin against the law (being a Nazarene)
(2) Sin against the Jews (a pestilent fellow)
(3) Sin against the temple (attempting to profane it)
(4) Sin against Caesar (stirring up an insurrection)

The same charges of two years ago. They had not forgotten one of them. But they had no more proof this time than they had before. Festus could see that there was no real purpose in holding this man longer, but if he could be used to an advantage for his political prestige, then he would do so. The question Festus asked was ask-

927. Name three of the six persons or groups before whom Paul had been tried in the last two years.
928. What is different about this trial from the first one that Paul had here?
929. What is alike in the two trials?

311

ed only that he might obtain the favor of the Jews present. "Wilt
thou go up to Jerusalem and there be judged of these things before me?"

It is even doubtful that Festus would have taken Paul to Jerusalem
for judgment, but then to please the Jews he said this and possibly
to hear the reaction of the apostle. He was hardly prepared for
what he heard. Paul was not going to be sacrificed for the desires
of a selfish local official, especially when there was a way of securing at least a measure of justice. Paul said in thought: "No, I will
not go to Jerusalem. I am to be judged and I am standing right
where this should be carried out. Why go to Jerusalem? I could only stand before Jews there. I have done them no harm, as you very
well know. Now if I were a criminal or even a **murderer,** I would refuse not to die; but if all the charges are lies I utterly refuse to be used
as a means to further your evil ends. You will not deliver me into the
bloody hands of the Jews. I **appeal to Caesar!"**

These words did not at all please Festus. This was a poor beginning for his governorship. He was taken aback. This was the first
such case he had dealt with. "What shall I do?" He turned to his
counselors for an answer. There was only one thing to do. It was
the right of every Roman citizen to make such an appeal. Although
it was going over his head as a judge, Festus could only say: "Thou
hast appealed unto Caesar. Unto Caesar shalt thou go."

f. Paul's defense before King Agrippa. 25:1b—26:32.

13 Now when certain days were passed, Agrippa the king
    and Bernice arrived at Caesarea, and saluted Festus.
14 And as they tarried there many days, Festus laid Paul's
    case before the king, saying, There is a certain man
    left a prisoner by Felix;
15 about whom, when I was at Jerusalem, the chief
    priests and the elders of the Jews informed me, asking
    for sentence against him.
16 To whom I answered, that it is not the custom of the
    Romans to give up any man, before that the accused
    have met the accusers face to face, and have had oppor-
    tunity to make his defence concerning the matter laid
    against him.
17 When therefore they were come together here, I made
    no delay, but on the next day sat on the judgment-seat,
    and commanded the man to be brought.

930. Why did Festus ask the question about trial in Jerusalem?
931. Do you believe Paul was justified in appealing to Caesar?
932. Why did this appeal displease Festus?

18 Concerning whom, when the accusers stood up, they brought no charge of such evil things as I supposed;

19 but had certain questions against him of their own religion, and of one Jesus, who was dead, whom Paul affirmed to be alive.

20 And I, being perplexed how to inquire concerning these things, asked whether he would go to Jerusalem and there be judged of these matters.

21 But when Paul had appealed to be kept for the decision of the emperor, I commanded him to be kept till I should send him to Caesar.

22 And Agrippa said unto Festus, I also could wish to hear the man myself. To-morrow, saith he, thou shalt hear him.

23 So on the morrow, when Agrippa was come, and Bernice, with great pomp, and they were entered into the place of hearing with the chief captains and the principal men of the city, at the command of Festus Paul was brought in.

24 And Festus saith, King Agrippa, and all men who are here present with us, ye behold this man, about whom all the multitude of the Jews made suit to me, both at Jerusalem and here, crying that he ought not to live any longer.

25 But I found that he had committed nothing worthy of death: and as he himself appealed to the emperor I determined to send him.

26 Of whom I have no certain thing to write unto my lord. Wherefore I have brought him forth before you, and specially before thee, king Agrippa, that, after examination, I may have somewhat to write.

27 For it seemeth to me unreasonable, in sending a prisoner, not withal to signify the charges against him.

1 And Agrippa said unto Paul, Thou art permitted to speak for thyself. Then Paul stretched forth his hand, and made his defence:

2 I think myself happy, king Agrippa, that I am to make my defence before thee this day touching all the things whereof I am accused by the Jews:

3 especially because thou art expert in all customs and questions which are among the Jews: wherefore I beseech thee to hear me patiently.

4 My manner of life then from my youth up, which was from the beginning among mine own nation and at Jerusalem, know all the Jews;

5 having knowledge of me from the first, if they be willing to testify, that after the straitest sect of our religion I lived a Pharisee.

6 And now I stand here to be judged for the hope of the promise made of God unto our fathers;

7 unto which promise our twelve tribes, earnestly serving God night and day, hope to attain. And concerning this hope I am accused by the Jews, O king!

8 Why is it judged incredible with you, if God doth raise the dead?

9 I verily thought with myself that I ought to do many things contrary to the name of Jesus of Nazareth.

10 And this I also did in Jerusalem: and I both shut up many of the saints in prisons, having received authority from the chief priests, and when they were put to death I gave my vote against them.

11 And punishing them oftentimes in all the synagogues, I strove to make them blaspheme; and being exceedingly mad against them, I persecuted them even unto foreign cities.

12 Whereupon as I journeyed to Damascus with the authority and commission of the chief priests,

13 at midday, O king, I saw on the way a light from heaven, above the brightness of the sun, shining round about me and them that journeyed with me.

14 And when we were all fallen to the earth, I heard a voice saying unto me in the Hebrew language, Saul, Saul, why persecutest thou me? it is hard for thee to kick against the goad.

15 And I said, Who art thou, Lord? And the Lord said, I am Jesus whom thou persecutest.

16 But arise, and stand upon thy feet: for to this end have I appeared unto thee, to appoint thee a minister and a witness both of the things wherein thou hast seen me, and of the things wherein I will appear unto thee;

17 delivering thee from the people, and from the Gentiles, unto whom I send thee,

18 to open their eyes, that they may turn from darkness to light and from the power of Satan unto God, that they may receive remission of sins and an inheritance among them that are sanctified by faith in me.

19 Wherefore, O king Agrippa, I was not disobedient unto the heavenly vision:

20 but declared both to them of Damascus first, and at Jerusalem, and throughout all the country of Judaea,

and also to the Gentiles, that they should repent and turn to God, doing works worthy of repentance.

21 For this cause the Jews seized me in the temple and assayed to kill me.

22 Having therefore obtained the help that is from God, I stand unto this day testifying both to small and great, saying nothing but what the prophets and Moses did say should come;

23 how that the Christ must suffer, and how that he first by the resurrection of the dead should proclaim light both to the people and to the Gentiles.

24 And as he thus made his defence, Festus saith with a loud voice, Paul, thou art mad; thy much learning is turning thee mad.

25 But Paul saith, I am not mad, most excellent Festus; but speak forth words of truth and soberness.

26 For the king knoweth of these things, unto whom also I speak freely:for I am persuaded that none of those things is hidden from him; for this hath not been done in a corner.

27 King Agrippa, believest thou the prophets? I know that thou believest.

28 And Agrippa said unto Paul, With but little persuasion thou wouldst fain make me a Christian.

29 And Paul said, I would to God, that whether with little or with much, not thou only, but also all that hear me this day, might become such as I am, except these bonds.

30 And the king rose up, and the governor, and Bernice, and they that sat with them:

31 and when they had withdrawn, they spake one to another, saying, This man doeth nothing worthy of death or of bonds.

32 And Agrippa said unto Festus, This man might have been set at liberty, if he had not appealed unto Caesar.

13 Festus had not been in office long until he had a visit from royalty.

We might say that it was a visit of relatives, for the sister of the king was a sister to his wife. "Agrippa, the king and Bernice." These came to bring greetings (and congratulations) but also to stay "for many days". Among the many things of interest in the new post it was natural that Festus should mention the rather unique case of Paul. Luke had such a valuable source for his information that he could put the words of Festus to Agrippa in the first person. Luke causes Festus to say(paraphrasing his words):

933. What relation was King Agrippa to Festus?

14-19 "There is a carry-over case from the rule of Felix. He was left a prisoner. When I arrived in Jerusalem, I heard more about him. It seems the chief priests expected me to turn him over to them as 'a token of my esteem'. I, of course, answered that this was no custom prevailing among us Romans. (It evidently is among the Jews.) I said that our law was to face one another in the court and let the accused have equal opportunity with the accusers. They took me up on my offer and I heard their case the very next day.

Well, when the man was brought and the trial was under way I found there were no such charges as I at first imagined. I thought the man must have done some great evil to the Jews. But the only thing I could make out was an argument between them over one called 'Jesus' whom the Jews said was dead but whom Paul strongly maintained to be alive.

20-22 "Now I am not acquainted with such superstitious religious beliefs, so I asked Paul if he would go up to Jerusalem about this matter and be judged there before me. (Here Festus places an entirely different construction on his actions than truly happened). But what did the man do? He appealed to Caesar. So I have charged him to be kept for this trial before Augustus."

It could have been from the note found in verse 22 that Agrippa had heard of Paul's imprisonment even before Festus gave him the details. The verse does seem to suggest that the king was rather anxiously awaiting a chance to hear from this strange prisoner.

"I also was wishing that I could hear the man myself," said Agrippa.

23-27 "Tomorrow you shall," answered Festus.

So according to the prearranged plan there was on the morrow a gathering not soon to be forgotten. To the king it was but another opportunity to amuse himself amid royal surroundings. This was to be done in full formal dress. The army generals were there! all the chief men of social position and rulers of the city were sent invitations. Bernice and Agrippa had on their royal robes. In the midst of all this splendor Paul appeared from the prison.

Did Paul hear the gossip of the jailor the night before the gathering? Did he know just what occasioned this appearance? Did he have knowledge that he was to speak before a king? To all these questions we will have no answer but it is interesting to speculate.

Festus had called the meeting so he now makes a formal speech of introduction. Paul stands between two soldiers with the light chain

934. What seemed to be the greatest concern of Festus in the case of Paul?
935. What false construction did Festus put upon his actions?
936. Did Agrippa know of Paul before Festus told of him?
937. Describe briefly the assembly before whom Paul was to speak.
938. What did Festus say was the purpose of the trial?

dangling from his left wrist. Festus stands before Agrippa and gestures toward Paul and says:

"King Agrippa, and all others here present, behold the man. This is the one that has caused all the Jews to cry out that he should be killed. I heard this cry both here and in Jerusalem. I have tried him and found nothing at all worthy of death, but here is our problem. He has appealed to Augustus, and I will send him. But I have nothing to write of him to the emperor. I know not the details of this case. But you can help me, and especially you, King Agrippa, since you know much more about the Jewish religion than I. You can appreciate my position, that it does seem altogether unreasonable to send a prisoner with no charges."

So spoke the governor in words of flattery and not without a note of real need.

1 Everyone else had been speaking about and for the apostle. Agrippa gestures from his elevated seat to Paul and says:

"Paul, thou art permitted to speak for thyself."

PAUL'S DEFENSE BEFORE AGRIPPA
26:2-29

Introduction. 2, 3.

Proposition: "To demonstrate that Jesus is the Christ and that he, Paul, was innocent."

   I—Paul's early life. 4-8.
      1. Was among the Jews and well known by them. 4, 5a.
      2. Was a strict Pharisee. 5b.
      3. Now judged for the things he and all the Jews believed. 6, 7.
      4. Application to the king. 8.
  II—His persecution of the Christians. 9-11.
      1. He opposed Jesus of Nazareth and His teaching. 9.
      2. Intense persecution at Jerusalem. 10.
      3. Details of his madness, even to foreign cities. 11.
 III—His conversion. 12-19.
      1. On the road Damascus at noon and attended with an intense light. 12, 13.
      2. The voice, the message of Jesus to Saul. 14-18.
      3. Paul's ready and complete response to the vision and voice. 19.
 IV—Paul's labors following his conversion. 20.
  V—The application of what has just been said to the present situation. 21-23.

939. Who was in the place of highest authority in this trial?
940. Would it be a good plan for us to tell the details of our conversion even as Paul did here?

    1. The reason for his being taken in the temple was because he was carrying out the commission of Christ. 21.
    2. What he says now and has preached before is nothing but what the prophets have said should come. 22,23.
VI—The interruption of Festus and Paul's answer. 24, 25.
VII—The application of Paul's answer to the king. 26-29.
    1. The knowledge of king Agrippa of the life and death of Jesus of Nazareth. 26.
    2. Appeal to Agrippa and his knowledge of the prophets. 27.
    3. Agrippa's conviction and "almost persuasion". 28.
    4. Paul's reply. 29.

Now we shall proceed to carefully examine the details of this outline.

Introduction. 2-3.

Paul counted this occasion a real privilege, which indeed it was. But "more especially" because of "whom" he had as an audience. Not just a king, but "King Agrippa". The apostle states that he was very glad to speak to this one, but why? Well, a bit of background is in order here to appreciate what is to follow.

Here is a little chart of the Herod family to show you the relationship of this Herod to the rest of them.

TABLE OF THE HERODIAN FAMILY.

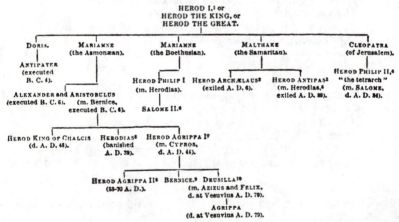

1 "Herod the King," Matt. 2; Luke 1:5. 2 Herod "Archælaus," Luke 19:12-27; Matt. 2:22. 3 "Herod" Antipas "the tetrarch," Matt. 14:1; Luke 3:1, 19; Mark 6:14. 4 Herod "Philip" "the tetrarch," Matt. 14:1, 6; Luke 3:1, 19; 9:7; Mark 6:14. 5 "Herodias," Matt. 14:3, 6; Mark 6:17. 6 Salome, Matt. 14:6; Mark 6:22, 28; Luke 3:19. 7 "Herod" Agrippa [I] "the king," Acts 12:1, 2. 8 Herod "Agrippa" II, Acts 25:13-27; 26. 9 "Bernice," Acts 25:13, 23; 26:30. 10 "Drusilla," Acts 24:24.

                                                People's Bible Encyclopedia

You can see **that this man** was the last one of the Herods to appear in history.

When Paul said that this man "knew of these things", i.e. the events of the life of Christ and of Saul's own conversion, it was surely true that he did! His grandfather attempted to kill Jesus when He was an infant. His father had attempted to kill the apostle Peter. All his life he must have heard of this one Jesus of Nazareth. It could have been that he also knew the writings of the prophets. His father being quite a student of the Jewish religion had taught him these things. At least his association with the Jews had taught him many points of their history and prophets. Herod Agrippa was himself part Jew, his mother was a Jewess.

Paul seems to have a high estimate of the knowledge of this one on such matters. The apostle says: . . . "Thou art expert in all customs and questions which are among the Jews."

This was a fine introduction designed to secure the favorable attention and interest of the king and the rest of the audience. And what an audience!

Paul now proceeds to demonstrate through the telling of the history of his own life that he is innocent of all the charges laid against him and that Jesus of Nazareth is indeed the Messiah.

I. Paul's early life. 4-8.

1. Was among the Jews and well known. 4-5.

Paul was going to take his time in explaining enough of the background to prove both his complete innocence and the validity of his conversion and commission. He says first then that he was not an intruding stranger with an unusual heresy and strange teaching. He said in thought: "King Agrippa, these persons who accuse me have known me and of me since my childhood. My whole life has been in closest association with my people, the Jews. A good share of my life has been spent in Jerusalem.

2. Was a strict Pharisee. 5b.

Then to show in the future of his discussion the validity of his change he mentions his zeal for the law. To say that he was a Pharisee was to say that he stood for the law of Moses in the strongest, strictest manner. Indeed, Paul was to later describe himself during this period as "a Pharisee of the Pharisees". The implications of this statement were well understood by Agrippa, if not by the others.

941. Why did Paul consider it a special privilege to speak before King Agrippa?
942. Show how it would surely be true that Agrippa knew of the things of the life of Christ and Paul.
943. What two things did Paul hope to prove by a background explanation of his life?
944. Why mention the fact that he was a Pharisee?

3. Now to be judged for what he and all other Jews believed. 6, 7

"And now"—This is surely suggestive of a great contrast; what he was then and what he was as he stood before the king. What a change! It must also contain a note of irony for the apostle is saying that his charges are based only on what he did believe, does now believe, and what the Jews have always believed.

". . . The hope of the promise made of God unto **our** fathers; unto which promise **our** twelve tribes, earnestly serving God night and day, hope to attain."

"The hope" referred to was the coming of the Messiah. This hope was based on a promise, a promise given by God to Abraham, Isaac, Jacob, Joseph and others. And so it was the mainspring of the Jews' hope. In this promise they saw deliverance and exaltation. How sad it was that when He came to His own . . . they received Him not. . .

Paul is saying to the king that his charges are not those of some "wicked villany" but concern the coming of the "king of the Jews".

Ah! What a descriptive phrase is given as to the great desire of the Jews for the Messiah. Mark it:

". . . earnestly serving God night and day, hope to attain."

This can point out to us how earnest, and zealous, and self-sacrificing we can be and still be wrong.

4. Application to the king. 8.

If you will recall the words of Festus to Agrippa you will remember that the governor told the king of the discussion over the resurrection (cf. 25:19). Paul evidently spoke of the resurrection of Jesus of Nazareth as a proof of the Messiahship. Indeed, the resurrection would prove that this Jesus was the Messiah, or Christ. This thought was new and startling to the king, but none the less convincing. With these thoughts in mind we can appreciate the words of Paul to Agrippa: "Why is it judged incredible with you if God doth raise the dead?"

II. His persecution of the Christians. 9-11.

1. He opposed Jesus of Nazareth and His teaching. 9.

Paul is saying: "Oh, king, if you feel in opposition to this One and this new teaching, I can say that I appreciate your feeling, having felt the very same myself. Indeed, to me it was a holy responsibility. 'I verily thought . . . **I ought** to' . . .

945. How did Paul use the word *"our"* to an advantage, as in verse 6?

946. What is "the hope" referred to in verse 6?

947. What can we learn for ourselves in the earnest desire of the Jews for the Messiah?

948. How would King Agrippa know of the resurrection? Why would he think it incredible?

"This name and its authority to me were very odious and anything I could do contrary to it, that I did."

   2. Intense persecution at Jerusalem. 10.

"And this I did in Jerusalem. (I say it with shame). I not only shut up Christians in jail, but when they were tried in the Sanhedrin for blasphemy, I gave my black pebble against them, and for their death. You ask how I could carry out the work of an officer of the law? I received permission from the chief priests to do so."

   3. Details of his madness; even to foreign cities. 11.

"Many times did the Jews find me in the synagogue. For what reason? to worship God? No. I was heretic hunting and when I found a suspect I grilled him with questions of this false Messiah until I made him blaspheme (as I thought), and then I could throw him in jail and vote for his death at the council. When there were no more to be found in Jerusalem I was so mad that I did not hestitate to pursue them even to foreign cities."

III. His conversion. 12-19.

(You are referred to the harmony of the three accounts of the conversion of Saul on pages 120-121. There is little we could add here that is not already written there.)

IV. Paul's labors following his conversion. 20.

In this one descriptive verse is compacted all the efforts of the apostle to preach the gospel in the first, second and third journeys, as well as his efforts to preach immediately following his conversion. So much time and so many events could hardly be described in so short a space.

V. The application of what has just been said to the present situation. 21-23.

   1. The reason he was taken in the temple was because he was carrying out the commission of Christ. 21.

If Paul was arrested for fulfilling divine summons, those who arrested him were in the wrong. The content of his preaching was but a fulfillment of the promise of the prophets. In this manner Paul showed that "**the** cause" for which the Jews "seized" him in the temple was indeed baseless.

   2. What I say now, I have preached before, and this is nothing but what Moses and the prophets have said would come. 22-23.

949. How would a statement of Paul's persecution of the Christians help in getting the message to King Agrippa?
950. In what manner did Paul "give his vote" against them?
951. How did Paul "strive to make them blaspheme?"
952. How did the fact that Paul was carrying out the commission of the Messiah reflect on those who arrested him?
953. How does Paul use Moses and the prophets in his message?

Paul now plainly states, for the benefit of those listening, that God was with him and approved the things he did and the contrary was true of those who opposed him. "It was only through God's intervention that I stand here before you this day. But as I do, I want to bear this news that all inspired spokesmen from Moses through all the prophets have borne: 'The Messiah was forordained to **suffer** and die'."

Further that: "He was to be raised from the dead and by this means (His death and resurrection) He would be able to give the light of hope to all people.

"Although arrested on a false charge, tried in mockery and treated shamefully, by my own people, the Lord stood by me and delivered me out of it all. I stand here before you today, O king, to testify of the same message for which I have been so treated. That message contains nothing but what Moses and the prophets said would come to pass. I want to tell to the small and the great that the Messiah was to suffer and to die and rise again from the dead. Yea, by this means He was able after His resurrection to proclaim the light of hope to all people."

VI. The interruption of Festus and Paul's answer. 24, 25.

Festus had hoped by this hearing to learn certain things that could help in his letter to the emperor. But he was totally unprepared to hear this strange tale. Will you try to imagine how this record must have sounded to a complete outsider? Festus listened in open-mouthed amazement at Paul's account of:

(1) The intense hatred of one religion against another (and both believing in the same God).
(2) The leader of one side overcome and changed to the opposite side by a bright light on a road in Syria.
(3) The wholehearted zeal of the new convert and apostle.
(4) The persecution by those with whom he once worked.
(5) And now he says the message he has to bring tells of the raising of a man from the dead.

Festus could not help but perceive that this one who spoke, spoke with intelligence on the subject of the Jewish religion. "This one is indeed a learned man, but his speculations into these matters have turned his brain. This is not helping my purpose at all—he is giving me nothing that I could write to the emperor." Festus burst forth in this loud impetuous ejaculation:

"Paul, thou art mad; thy much learning is turning thee to madness."

954. Why was Festus so amazed at Paul's mesage?
955. How could Fetus speak of Paul's learning?

Paul answers as only one led by the Holy Spirit could answer. Without a moments hesitation he replies to Festus: "I am not mad, most excellent Festus (politely using the official title for the governor), but speak forth words of truth and soberness."

Paul is saying to Festus that what he has to say is neither fanciful nor nonsensical, but rather the opposite—"truth and soberness". And then for the benefit of both Festus and Agrippa, Paul makes the next remark:

"The king knows that the thoughts I am presenting so freely are all the events of the life of Jesus and those things that have happened to me are doubtless already known by the king. None of these things happened in secret."

Now to obtain again the attention of the king that had been diverted by the interruption of Festus, Paul says: "King Agrippa, believest thou the prophets? Ah, I know of thy background and religious profession. I know thou believest."

And, Paul might also have concluded that the king believed from the expression on his face. It is my conviction that king Agrippa was deeply stirred by what Paul preached. I also believe that Paul could see this and for that reason asked the above question. It was for this same reason that Agrippa replied as he did to Paul's pointed question.

"With but little persuasion thou wouldst fain make me a Christian."

There are those who feel that the king was saying this as a jest or as a slighting remark, the thought being (according to them) that Agrippa said to Paul: "Ah, you are trying to make a Christian of me with just a **little** persuasion."

But I cannot see that such a remark fits into the tenor of the meeting. It is my conviction that King Agrippa was stirred in the same manner that Sergius Paulus was in Salamis. (13:7)

What a wonderful answer does Paul give to the statement of Agrippa. He turns the rejection of the king into a definite advantage. He says in thought: "I would that it were God's will that whether with little persuasion or with much persuasion both those of no standing (in this world) and those of great standing, would become as I am—lifting his right manacled hand—except these bonds."

VII. The break-up of the meeting. 26:30-32.

The signal that the trial and defense were over was given by the

956. How did Paul show courtesy in answering Festus?
957. How did Paul prove that what he was saying was truth and soberness?
958. Why was Paul so sure that the king believed?
959. Do you believe Agrippa was serious in his reply to Paul?
960. Show how Paul turned rejection into advantage.

rising of the king from his chair. All others also rose and began moving out of the room. Paul was again led to his place of confinement. What were the thoughts of the apostle as he returned from this meeting? He could at least feel that he was "free from the blood of all men"—including that of a king. When Bernice, Festus and Agrippa had withdrawn to themselves, Festus said: "Why, this man should not even be in prison. He has done nothing worthy of imprisonment."

To this thought both Bernice and Agrippa agree. Agrippa comments further on the subject by saying:

"This man might have been set at liberty had he not appealed unto Caesar."

Of course whether Agrippa would have agreed to his release and to the acceptance of the censure of the Jews is questionable, but this was a concession at least.

g. Preparations for leaving. 27:1, 2.

1 And when it was determined that we should sail for Italy, they delivered Paul and certain other prisoners to a centurion named Julius, of the Augustan band.

2 And embarking in a ship of Adramyttium, which was about to sail unto the places on the coast of Asia, we put to sea, Aristarchus, a Macedonian of Thessalonica, being with us.

1. Once again the pronoun "we" comes to the forefront. Luke has evidently been with Paul during the two years imprisonment in Caesarea. Some suggest that it was at this time that Luke wrote his "former treatise". It could very well have been so.

Luke was not the only one to accompany the apostle on the trip . . . "certain other prisoners" were to go to Rome. Among them was "Aristarchus", Paul's fellow-prisoner. The man into whose hands these persons were placed was named Julius. It is of interest to note that he was of that group who served as special "cohort" of the emperor. What more appropriate person to take Paul to the imperial city?

2. The ship in which they were to sail was from the little coastal town of Adramyttium. This town was located on the coast of Mysia. Evidently the boat on which they were to embark was one of the

961. What do you suppose were the thoughts of the apostle as he returned to jail?

962. Do you believe Agrippa would have freed Paul if there had been no appeal to Caesar?

963. What does the use of the pronoun "we" suggest?

964. How does the "former treatise" enter the thought here?

965. What do you know of Julius?

smaller local merchant vessels, and this was its return trip on its commercial run. The hope of Julius was that they would find another ship somewhere on the coast of Asia that was going to Rome. At any rate, baggage was packed and put on board and farewells were said at the dock. Maybe Philip, the evangelist, was in the group that waved farewell to the apostle and his companions.

If Rome were to be reached action must be taken. The time for sailing on the open sea was fast drawing to a close. According to the closest calculations it was late in the month of August when they put out from the harbor of Caesarea. Perchance the lateness of the season accounted for the willingness of Julius to sail on a vessel that was only going part of the way to their destination.

4. AT SIDON. 27:3.

3 And the next day we touched at Sidon: and Julius treated Paul kindly, and gave him leave to go unto his friends and refresh himself.

3. Sixty-five miles was the extent of the first days sailing. Maybe because Julius was one of those who listened to Paul before Agrippa, or because he learned from Luke and Aristarchus of Paul's character, he gave him special permission to visit the saints in Sidon (cf. 11:19). If we are right in thinking that most of the sailing of that time was done at night (because of the guidance of the stars) then we could say that Paul had a whole day to "refresh himself". It would seem that although Paul was somewhat of a seasoned seaman, on this occasion seasickness was hinted at in the words "refreshed himself" or "received attention".

5. UNDER THE LEE OF CYPRUS. 27:4.

4 And putting to sea from thence, we sailed under the lee of Cyprus, because the winds were contrary.

4. ". . . they put to sea again, running briskly north till above the upper coast of Cyprus, but having constantly to tack as soon as they steered west, the wind now being against them.

"Having at last, however, reached that island, they ran as close as they could under its lee; their headway still slow; their poor daily advance being, as hitherto, won only by assiduous tacking. They would, thus, often run close in towards Asia Minor, in full

966. Why take a ship that was not going all the way to Rome?
967. Who might have been at the dock to say goodbye? Prove your answer.
968. Why the haste at this time?
969. How far did they sail the first day?
970. How is it that in spite of their hurry Paul had a whole day to "refresh himself?"
971. Was Paul seasick?
972. What is meant by the expression "tacking"?

sight of the glorious range of the Taurus mountains beyond whose
snow peaks the thoughts of the apostle must often have wandered
to the churches of the central tableland which he loved so dearly as
his children in Christ and which he knew he would never see again.
How were they faring? Had grievous wolves, entering in, troubled
them? Would they quit them like men and, after all, be his crown
of rejoicing in the day of the Lord Jesus?

6. AT MYRA. 27:5, 6.

> 5 And when we had sailed across the sea which is off
> Cilicia and Pamphylia, we came to Myra, a city of
> Lycia.
> 6 And there the centurion found a ship of Alexandria
> sailing for Italy; and he put us therein.

5. "The southwest wind which, at the start, had been favorable for
sailing now made the voyage painfully tedious since they turned west-
ward after running north for a time from Sidon, but at last they
reached Myra, their next port of call." (**Cunningham Geikie,** Vol.
III, pages 475-476).

Here is a fine quotation concerning the town of Myra (Cf. 476,
Geikie): "One of the chief towns of Lycia, it lay where the coast
forms a slight bay just before it turns north as the west face of Asia
Minor, bordering the Aegean or, as we say, the Grecian Archipelago.
An open-air theatre, 355 feet in diameter, many fine public buildings, and numerous stately tombs, enriched with statues and elaborate
carving, then attracted the eye on entering its port—Andriaca, two
and a half miles from the town itself, which lay on the slope of a
hill, setting off its every detail. The old name is still known, though
the Turks call it Dembre; but its present squalor contrasts painfully with the splendour of the ruins which speak of what it was under the Romans.

6. "But what was a ship from Alexandria Egypt doing here? And
this ship was sailing for Italy. Was it not away off its course? Indeed,
it was. The same wind that troubled the ship from Adramyttium
had blown this great vessel off its course."

As to what the ship looked like, I refer you again to Geikie:

"Ships, in Paul's day, were as various in their size, within certain
limits, as they are now, that in which on this voyage, he was wreck-
ed at Malta carrying two hundred and seventy-six persons and a cargo of wheat; a dangerous one even now; I, myself, having narrow-
ly escaped shipwreck between the Dardanelles and Malta, by its

973. What do you suppose was in the mind of the apostle as they came in
sight of the Taurus mountains?
974. Give two facts about Myra.
975. How would it be possible to find a ship from Egypt at this place?

shifting. Josephus tells us that the vessel in which he was sailing to Italy carried 600 persons and it, like that of Paul, was lost, going down in the Adriatic so suddenly that Josephus and the rest 'swam for their lives all that night' just as Paul had once done. Lucian further helps us to realize the marine of those days by the account he gives of a corn-ship of Alexandria, which had come to the Piraeus—'a large, indeed an immense ship'. The ship carpenter told him, he says, that it was 120 cubits—that is, say, 180 feet long; its breadth over 30 cubits, or over 45 feet, and its depth 29 cubits or, say, 43 feet. Its lofty mast, for he mentions only one—was wonderful and so was its yard. The ropes from it to the hull were a sight to see and so was the curved stern rising high, like a bird's neck, at the one end and the prow, of similar shape to balance it at the other end. Its name—'The Goddess Isis'—shone out on both sides of the bow with such artistic ornamentation, while the top he said was of flame color and on the deck the eye was attracted, in the fore part of the ship, by the anchors, the windlasses and such like, and on the poop by the cabins and offices. The great merchantmen of the Phoenicians known as Tarshish ships had been famous in the day of Exekiel and it is not probable that shipbuilding had lost its skill in the advance of 600 years, and hence we may safely conclude that the docks and harbors of that first century saw vessels which, for costliness and splendor, though not in outline or scientific structure, would even now have been the pride of their owners and of their crews." (pp. 469-70, III)

This ship from Alexandria was to complete its voyage and it was the very one Julius wanted for their destination. So Paul and his companions were put aboard. All together there were 276 persons on board this wheat ship.

7. AT CNIDUS. 27:7a.

7 And when we had sailed slowly many days, and were come with difficulty over against Cnidus, the wind not further suffering us,

7a I see no point in using my words to describe this voyage from a second-hand viewpoint when there are those who have been there and have described it as they saw it. Note this word from Farrar:

"The distance between the two spots is only one hundred and thirty miles and under favorable circumstances they might have got to their destination in twenty-four hours. But the baffling Etesians Periodical Mediterrean winds still continued with un-

976. Give three facts concerning the ship on which Paul was to sail.
977. What disappointment was evidenced at Cnidus?
978. What determined the route of the voyage as far as Crete?
979. Why sail under the lee of Crete?

seasonable steadiness and to reach even to Cnidus occupied many weary and uncomfortable days, and when they got off at the beautiful and commodious harbor they were destined to a fresh and bitter disappointment for they could not enter it. Had they been able to do so the season was by this time so far advanced and the wind was so steadily adverse that we hardly doubt that, unless they continued their journey by land, they would either have waited there for a more favorable breeze or decided to winter in a port where there was every pleasant requisite at hand for the convenience of so large a vessel and its numerous crew. Since, however, the wind would neither suffer them to put in at Cnidus nor to continue their direct voyage, which would have passed north of Crete, the only alternative left them was to make for Cape Salmone at the eastern end of the island and there sail under its lee." (p. 564)

8. UNDER THE LEE OF CRETE. 27:7b.

7b we sailed under the lee of Crete, over against Salmone;

7b "To get to Salmone was comparatively easy, but when they had rounded it they had the utmost difficulty in creeping along the weather shore until they came to a place called Fair Haven, a little to the east of Cape Matala, and not far from an obscure town of the name of Lasea." (ibid)

9. AT FAIR HAVENS. 27:8-15.

8   and with difficulty coasting along it we came unto a certain place called Fair Havens; nigh whereunto was the city of Lasea.

9   And when much time was spent, and the voyage was now dangerous, because the Fast was now already gone by, Paul admonished them,

10 and said unto them, Sirs, I perceive that the voyage will be with injury and much loss, not only of the lading and the ship, but also of our lives.

11 But the centurion gave more heed to the master and to the owner of the ship, than to those things which were spoken by Paul.

12 And because the haven was not commodious to winter in, the more part advised to put to sea from thence, if by any means they could reach Phoenix, and winter there; which is a haven of Crete, looking north-east and south-east.

13 And when the south wind blew softly, supposing that they had obtained their purpose, they weighed anchor and sailed along Crete, close in shore.

14 But after no long time there beat down from it a tempestuous wind, which is called Euraquilo:

15 and when the ship was caught, and could not face the wind, we gave way to it, and were driven.

8-10 Why was "much time" spent at Fair Haven? Was it not in waiting for winds to change? But they did not change. The feast of the Jewish day of atonement (September 15 or 24) came and went and yet they remained in the habor. Soon it was October when the time for sailing was almost past. Something must be done for a winter's stay. Paul came forward with his advice. It was to stay where they were as it was too late for sailing and it would only result in a possible loss to the ship and injury to those on board. When Paul said "I perceive" he was speaking from experience and not necessarily from inspiration. This advice was offered to Julius, since he was the imperial representative and the one who seemed to determine the action of the voyage. The pilot as well as the owner had other ideas. And there was much to be said in their favor. Their argument was:

(1) Fair Haven is not a "commodious" place to winter—exposed as it is from almost every point of the compass. Besides that, it is a long way from any town and it will be indeed dreary and lonesome for the sailors.

(2) Phoenix is only a short 32 miles up the coast (of course it is around the Cape of Crete but we can make it). This harbor will be perfect for our wintering. A south wind will soon spring up and we will be there before day dawns.

11-15 The centurion listened to both sides and cast his vote for the owner and the captain. Sure enough a south wind did come up and they weighed anchor and pushed along the coast of Crete. The little boat that trailed behind was soon to be used as a means of landing when they reached their destination in the harbor of Phoenix. But "after no little while" the sailors must have looked up in alarm as the wind began to change and a great thunderhead gathered in the northeast. It proved to be the very tempest that they feared—"The Eurquilo" or "Noreaster".

10. **CAUDA.** 27:16, 17.

16 And running under the lee of a small island called Cauda, we were able, with difficulty, to secure the boat:

17 and when they had hoisted it up, they used helps, undergirding the ship; and, fearing lest they should be cast upon the Syrtis, they lowered the gear, and so were driven.

16-7 "When they reached the cape there came from 7,000 foot high Mt. Ida a sudden typhonic squall. . . "The winds come down from those mountains fit to blow the ship out of the water," said a skipper to Sir William Ramsey. (ibid. Given by Wm. Dallman in

980. What time of the year was it when they arrived at Fair Haven?
981. What two arguments were used as to sailing for Phoenix?
982. What encouraged the sailors to think they had obtained their goal?
983. What was the name of the wind that came upon them? It's meaning?

"Paul", p. 244). When the ship was seized in this cyclone and whirled around and could not look the wind in the face, we let her drive and ran under a small island named Cauda . . . 23 miles away."

Here the water was a little less rough. Their first effort was to take up the little boat that was in tow at the back of the ship. This had to be done if they were going to have a means of going ashore later and therefore it would act as a life boat in an emergency. It was only with the greatest difficulty that the small boat was lifted out of the water and made secure on board ship. Then there began the process known as "frapping the ship". It consisted of passing cables under the boat in such a way as to bind the timbers together and thus make it less susceptible to leaking. Whether the cables were passed around the ship vertically or horizontally has occasioned some discussion, as it seems that both methods were employed. Just how this was done amid such a storm is not known but that they did it we are sure. Following these precautions, the rudders were set and the ship was given over to the winds to be driven.

The third and final effort to prepare to meet the storm was in "lowering the gear". This consisted of taking in all the sail that was up and securing the ropes as tightly as possible. The rudder of the boat was set in such a way as to keep the course away from the Syrtis, the terrible quicksand of Northern Africa.

DRIVEN FOR FOURTEEN DAYS BY THE WIND. 18-27.

18 And as we labored exceedingly with the storm, the next day they began to throw the freight overboard;

19 and the third day they cast out with their own hands the tackling of the ship.

20 And when neither sun nor stars shone upon us for many days, and no small tempest lay on us, all hope that we should be saved was now taken away.

21 And when they had been long without food, then Paul stood forth in the midst of them, and said, Sirs, ye should have hearkened unto me, and not have set sail from Crete, and have gotten this injury and loss.

22 And now I exhort you to be of good cheer; for there shall be no loss of life among you, but only of the ship.

23 For there stood by me this night an angel of the God whose I am, whom also I serve,

24 saying, Fear not, Paul; thou must stand before Caesar: and lo, God hath granted thee all them that sail with thee.

984. Why pause at Cauda?
985. Why was the small boat trailing behind? Why take it in?
986. What is meant by "frapping" the ship?
987. Why set the rudder?

25 Wherefore, sirs, be of good cheer: for I believe God, that it shall be even so as it hath been spoken unto me.

26 But we must be cast upon a certain island.

27 But when the fourteenth night was come, as we were to and fro in the sea of Adria, about midnight the sailors surmised that they were drawing near to some country:

18-25 Following these precautions the ship was driven. For 13 days they drifted on an average of 36 miles in 24 hours—making a total of 468 miles.

The day following the frapping of the ship they began to throw overboard the wheat so as to lighten the ship, for in spite of the frapping they had evidently sprung a leak. On the third day as much of the extra gear as could be spared was thrown in the sea. In spite of this effort they contrived to "labor exceedingly" with the storm. The sun could not be seen in the day nor the stars at night. All hope that they would ever be saved from a watery grave was now gone. It might have been on the fifth day or the sixth or seventh or even later, but sometime in the midst of this dreary, frightening experience Paul gathered some of the sailors about him to give the message recorded in Acts 27:21-26. First of all he was to say, "I told you so. If you had harkened unto me in Fair Haven you would not now be where you are." But his main thought was one of encouragement. He said, "Be of good cheer for I have a message from God concerning our safety. Not one of you shall perish. There shall be loss 'tis true but only of the ship. I know this for last night an angel of God stood by me and said as much. I am a servant of God and belong to Him. The words which he spoke to me were:

'Fear not, Paul. You must stand before Caesar, your prayers have been heard on behalf of those on board and God hath granted them all to you.'

And so Paul concluded his remarks by saying, "Cheer up, for I believe that it shall be, indeed, even as He hath said." And then Paul reveals a bit more insight into the future by adding: "But we must be cast upon a certain island."

26-27 All this time no one had taken food, much of the provisions being gone and the tossing of the ship making it practically impossible. Let's not forget that Luke was aboard this vessel and is giving an eye-witness account of these events.

988. How far and how fast did they drift?
989. Why throw overboard the wheat and gear?
990. What two thoughts did Paul give in his message to the sailors?
991. What word of the future was given by the Apostle?
992. How did they know they were near land?

LANDING ON MELITA. 28-44.

28 and they sounded, and found twenty fathoms; and after a little space, they sounded again, and found fifteen fathoms.

29 And fearing lest haply we should be cast ashore on. rocky ground, they let go four anchors from the stern, and wished for the day.

30 And as the sailors were seeking to flee out of the ship, and had lowered the boat into the sea, under color as though they would lay out anchors from the foreship,

31 Paul said to the centurion and to the soldiers, Except these abide in the ship, ye cannot be saved.

32 Then the soldiers cut away the ropes of the boat, and let her fall off.

33 And while the day was coming on, Paul besought them all to take some food, saying, This day is the fourteenth day that ye wait and continue fasting, having taken nothing.

34 Wherefore I beseech you to take some food: for this is for your safety: for there shall not a hair perish from the head of any of you.

35 And when he had said this, and had taken bread, he gave thanks to God in the presence of all; and he brake it, and began to eat.

36 Then were they all of good cheer, and themselves also took food.

37 And we were in all in the ship two hundred threescore and sixteen souls.

38 And when they had eaten enough, they lightened the ship, throwing out the wheat into the sea.

39 And when it was day, they knew not the land: but they perceived a certain bay with a beach, and they took counsel whether they could drive the ship upon it.

40 And casting off the anchors, they left them in the sea, at the same time loosing the bands of the rudders; and hoisting up the foresail to the wind, they made for the beach.

41 But lighting upon a place where two seas met, they ran the vessel aground; and the foreship struck and remained unmoveable, but the stern began to break up by the violence of the waves.

42 And the soldiers' counsel was to kill the prisoners, lest any of them should out, and escape.

43 But the centurion, desiring to save Paul, stayed them from their purpose; and commanded that they who

could swim should cast themselves overboard, and get
first to the land;

44 and the rest, some on planks, and some on other things
from the ship. And so it came to pass, that they all
escaped safe to the land.

28-29 It was on the fourteenth night that a different sound was
heard above the wind and rain. The sailors immediately recognized it
as the roar of the breakers on the beach. Sounding was taken in a
short time and the depth found to be twenty fathoms (120 feet).
Another sounding was taken and it was measured as fifteen fathoms
(90 feet). The land was approaching rapidly. Lest they be thrown
on the rocks they let go four anchors from the stern of the boat.
They did not know where they were or what would become of them
and the attitude of the heart is well expressed in the little phrase that
follows the account of the lowering of the anchors:

"And they wished (or prayed) for day."

30-32 Paul was on deck before daybreak and watched with a sharp
and experienced eye the activities of all hands. The sailors can
hardly be blamed for their actions considering their background and
the circumstances. It was a matter of "every man for himself", with
them. And they would have indeed escaped and left the ship un-
manned had it not been for the vigilance of the apostle. The sham
of appearing to set out anchors from the bow of the ship was
transparent to Paul—he who had been "a night and a day in the
deep". Turning to the centurion and the soldiers who also stood by
watching the proceedings, gesturing to the sailors as they lowered
the boat he cried:

"Except these abide in the ship ye cannot be saved."

All hands were going to be needed to care for the coming
emergency and if the sailors left the others would suffer.

And so we can also learn the lesson from this circumstance—
that although Paul knew the Lord had promised the safety of all,
he was expected to do his part in the carrying out of God's plan.

The soldiers immediately sprang to thwart the purpose of the
sailors. The small boat had already been lowered and was even then
bobbing in the sea. A soldier drew his short sword and leaning
over the side of the ship severed the rope and let the small boat ad-
rift.

33-36 And then the cold grey light of dawn began to streak the sky
and when it was light enough to be seen Paul for the second time

993. Why throw out the anchors?
994. How could the words of Paul be true regarding the loss of all unless
the sailor stayed aboard?
995. What lesson can we learn from this circumstance respecting the Lord's
will?

assembled the men around him on the deck of the ship and spoke to them on this wise:

"Come now, let us take some food. It has been two weeks—fourteen days since you ate at all. Food is for your safety. You will need strength for what is ahead of us—but I assure you that not a hair of your head shall perish. Come, let us eat."

And so saying, Paul took a loaf of bread in his hands and broke it. He then did a very wonderful thing. There on the deck of the doomed ship, amid more than two hundred heathen persons, he bowed his head and raised his voice in thanksgiving to the Father above.

What a testimony this action was and how we need to let our light shine in the midst of a crooked and perverse generation. Seeing the brave, confident example of the apostle, the others took heart and began to eat.

37-41 Luke here reminds us again that he was aboard, for he counts himself among these 276 souls on board.

When they had "eaten enough" they began to do what they could for the waterlogged vessel. It was evidently now all but swamped with water. Overboard went more of the wheat.

When the day had advanced far enough to see through the storm to land they perceived a certain land they knew not what nor where, but there was also a beach. Immediately there was talk as to whether they could bring the ship up on the beach in safety. They might better their lot by trying. Surely they could not long stay where they were. The anchor chains or ropes were unfastened, the iron bands that had held the great rudder loosed; this must be used and that skillfully if any kind of safe landing were to be made. A small sail was hoisted in the fore of the ship and the great unwieldly vessel began to move. Now, what they did not see was a small island out from the shore of Malta—it would have been impossible for them to distinguish it from the mainland. But upon approaching the shore they could see the small isle of Salmonetta and the channel between it and the larger island. It was here that they encountered the "two seas" and alas a shallow channel!

According to those who have investigated the sea bed at this place, a very heavy, sticky clay is to be found here. Into this clay the bow of the ship was run with the greatest force. It stuck fast. But even as it did the heavy waves of the coast began to tear at the stern of the vessel. All could see that it would be no time until the whole ship would come to pieces. Then it was that almost all be-

996. What encouragement and testimony did Paul give at this point?
997. How many on board the ship?
998. What did they do to improve the condition of the ship?
999. Why try to sail into the land?
1000. What did they fail to see in the land before them?
1001. What caused them to go aground?

gan to think of themselves and what would happen to them under such conditions. With characteristic Roman cruelty the soldiers suggested that the prisoners be killed since such an open means of escape was before them and the soldiers would be held responsible for their lives. But then was fulfilled, indeed, the words that for Paul's sake these would be saved.

42-44 The centurion, desiring to save Paul . . . and well he might for all that he had said and done, counseled that no one be harmed but that as many as could swim go overboard immediately and make for the shore; that those that could not were to look for a spar or plank or something from the ship that would float and with that aid reach safety. This was carried out posthaste and so all 276 persons came dripping up on the beach of Malta on that cold November morning.

12. MELITA. 28:1-10.

1 And when we were escaped, then we knew that the island was called Melita.

2 And the barbarians showed us no common kindness: for they kindled a fire, and received us all, because of the present rain, and because of the cold.

3 But when Paul had gathered a bundle of sticks and laid them on the fire, a viper came out by reason of the heat, and fastened on his hand.

4 And when the barbarians saw the venomous creature hanging from his hand, they said one to another, No doubt this man is a murderer, whom, though he hath escaped from the sea, yet Justice hath not suffered to live.

5 Howbeit he shook off the creature into the fire, and took no harm.

6 But they expected that he would have swollen, or fallen down dead suddenly: but when they were long in expectation and beheld nothing amiss come to him, they changed their minds, and said that he was a god.

7 Now in the neighborhood of that place were lands belonging to the chief man of the island, named Publius; who received us, and entertained us three days courteously.

8 And it was so, that the father of Publius lay sick of fever and dysentery: unto whom Paul entered in, and prayed, and laying his hands on him healed him.

9 And when this was done, the rest also that had diseases in the island came, and were cured:

1002. Why suggest to kill the prisoners?
1003. How were all saved for Paul's sake?
1004. What month was it that this happened?

10 who also honored us with many honors; and when we
    sailed, they put on board such things as we needed.

1-6 The natives of the island were doubtless as intent upon seeing
what was in the sea before their island as those on board were in seeing what lay before them.

The first passenger had hardly come out of the water until the
natives began to gather sticks and brush for a fire. It was cold and
these strangers were wet. Thus in a short time a great bonfire was
blazing and the thankful survivors were standing around it trying to warm themselves.

Paul again shows his humility and helpful spirit. Up into the
wooded area went the apostle to gather an armful of "furzeroots" and
laid them on the fire, but even as he did so he knew that he had
gathered more than roots in that armload. Because of the heat, the
snake that had hidden there came out. Paul evidently was yet in
the position of putting the fuel on the fire when the viper slithered
out and immediately struck at him and fastened itself to his hand.
"The creature" so firmly fastened itself that it hung from Paul's hand.
All could see it. The Maltese were seen whispering among themselves.
Luke learned that they were saying of Paul —

"Surely this man was a murderer (possibly having learned that
there were prisoners among the strangers), that even though he has
escaped the sea yet justice is giving him his just deserts."

But the snake did not hang on Paul's hand long for it was shaken
off into the fire. Then were the "barbarians" the more intent upon watching this stranger, but he neither fell over dead nor did
they see him swell up at all. Then in a few moments they repeated in reverse what had happened to the apostle at Lystra. They
called him a god!

7-10 Following the episode on the beach they were taken to the
governor of the island whose name was Publius. He was a wealthy
land owner and was very kindly disposed toward these unexpected
visitors. For three days they were treated royally by Publius. The unusual escape of Paul from the bite of the serpent was probably noised
about but the islanders were to have even more proof of the power
and presence of God with this man.

They had not been any time with the governor until they were
told of the severe sickness of his father—very probably he was confined to his bed in his son's house. He was suffering from dysentery
in the aggravated form. Paul doubtless saw an opportunity to repay some of the kindness shown them and at the same time an op-

1005. What was the first act of kindness on the part of the natives?
1006. What caused the snake to come out of the roots?
1007. How were the Maltese like and unlike those of Lystra?
1008. How did Paul repay the natives for their kindness and at the same time
      open a door for the gospel?

PUTEOLI

A famous watering place of the Romans, located in a sheltered part of the Bay of Naples. Its Greek name was Dicaearchia. It was the most accessible harbor near to Rome. So Paul was brought to this port with other prisoners (Acts 28:13). Vespasian conferred great privileges upon the city. Cicero had a villa here, and Hadrian a tomb. Portions of its famous baths remain to this day, and a part of the pier at which St. Paul must have landed on his way to Rome. The present name is Pozzuoli. **(Unger's Bible Dictionary, P. 904, 905.)**

337

portunity to give testimony for his Saviour. Going into the room where the sick man lay, Paul placed his hands upon him and prayed; he was healed. This exciting and wonderful incident was soon told in every part of the island. In no time at all Paul had a business of healing on his hands. Those with all types of diseases came to be cured—and were they ?Ah, yes! Like in the days of the Saviour (and so unlike today) there were no disappointments. These persons were not without a deep sense of gratitude. Paul, Luke, Aristarchus and others were "honored with many honors". And when they sailed, the natives put on board the ship as many things in foodstuffs and other gifts as they thought they could use.

12. AT SYRACUSE. 28:11, 12.

11 And after three months we set sail in a ship of Alexandria which had wintered in the island, whose sign was The Twin Brothers.

12 And touching at Syracuse, we tarried there three days.

11 It was a ship from Alexandria, Egypt, upon which Paul started the journey and it was a ship from Alexandria upon which he was to finish the journey; but of course it was another vessel, one that had fared better than her companion during the winter period. This three month period was from the middle of November to the middle of February. According to Greek mythology, Jupiter or Zeus had two sons by one of the goddesses named Leda. These sons were supposed to have been translated into the sky and as the "shining stars" had a good influence on the ocean and hence were the patron gods of the sailors. The names of these two sons were Castor and Pollux. The ship upon which Paul and the others embarked was named after these gods.

12 It was eighty-six miles to Syracuse. This port was made up of five cities. "The walls were 22 miles in circumference and the city rivaled Carthage in wealth, according to Strabo. Cicero calls it 'glorious Syracuse, greatest of Greek cities, and fairest of all cities.' It was a colony of Corinth and for years almost mistress of the world." (Dallmann, **Paul** pp. 251-252.)

Here they stayed for three days. There is no record that Paul preached here at this time, but later a strong work was established.

13. AT RHEGIUM. 28:13a.

13 And from thence we made a circuit, and arrived at Rhegium:

1009. How are the cures of Paul and Jesus unlike those of today?
1010. What was the significance of the name of the ship upon which they sailed to Rome?
1011. What type of city was Syracuse?

14. **IN PUTEOLI.** 28:13b, 14.

13b and after one day a south wind sprang up, and on the
second day we came to Puteoli;

14 where we found brethren, and were entreated to tarry
with them seven days: and so we came to Rome.

13b, 14 "Puteoli was eight miles northwest of Naples and the greatest port of Italy, especially for wheat from Egypt, the grainary of
Rome, 140 miles away. Here stood a large pier of twenty-five arches,
of which thirteen ruined ones remain. At this pier the vessels dis-
charged their passengers and cargo. Curious crowds commonly came
to see the sight." (ibid, p. 263)

In the crowd that came to the pier were some followers of the
Way. How glad was Paul to see these brethren and how happy they
were to see him. He was prevailed upon by them to stay seven days.
During this time they doubtless had preaching and fellowship.

THE MARKET OF APPIUS AND THE THREE TAVERNS. 15.

15 And from thence the brethren, when they heard of us,
came to meet us as far as The Market of Appius and
The Three Taverns; whom when Paul saw, he thanked
God, and took courage.

15 In order to get some idea of the territory the apostle is covering at this time, we quote from Dallmann respecting the trip from
Puteoli to The Market of Appius and the Three Taverns.

"On the eighth day after landing, Paul left Puteoli for Rome, one
hundred and seventy miles away. On the Via Consularis he passed the
temple of Serapis. Going between the two mountains beyond the
city, he crosses the famous and fertile fields of Campania. After a
march of nineteen miles he spends the night at Capua, famous for
its mighty ancient amphitheatre and its statue of Venus.

He leaves on the Via Appia, built by the Censor Appius Claudius
in 312 B.C. during the Samnite War. In 280 the blind man by a great
speech had hindered a peace with Pyrrhus. He was also Rome's
first author and composed a collection of wise sayings. Eight hundred years later this 'queen of Roads', as Statius calls it, was still
in such perfect state as to astonish Procopius, secretary of General Belisarius. Procopius writes: "To traverse the Appian Way
is a five days' journey for a good walker. It leads from Rome to
Capua. Its breadth is such that two chariots may meet upon it
and pass each other without interruption, and its magnificence sur-

1012. How far to Rome from Puteoli? How long did they stay in Puteoli?
1013. When was the road of Appia built?
1014. How many days walk from Capau to Rome?
1015. Give three interesting facts about this road.

passes that of all other roads." Procopius goes on to tell us Appius had the material brought from a great distance 'so as to have all the stones hard and of the nature of millstones.' Then he had the stones smoothed and polished and cut in corresponding angles so as to bite together in jointures without the intervention of copper or any other material to bind them, and in this manner they were so firmly united that, on looking at them, we would say they had not been put together by art, but had grown so upon the spot. Milestones were all along the way. Every forty feet was a seat. About every twenty miles was a "mansion" or poststation where horses, mules, and vehicles were kept for travelers and government dispatches." (ibid, p. 264-265).

"Paul landed at Appii Forum where Appius Claudius founded a market for the country people when he built the Queen of Roads, of which the great Caesar himself had once been a curator. Suetonius says: "Claudius Drusus erected a statue of himself wearing a crown at Appii Forum. A hundred years before, Horace was here with Virgil and Maecenas . . . . to reconcile Augustus and Mark Anthony. He found the water was utterly bad. The place was full of boatmen and extortionate tavern-keepers.

"Four buildings, one a miserable inn, is all that remains of Foro Appio. The forty-third milestone is still there. Here Paul was met by Christians who had come from Rome to greet him.

Three Taverns is ten miles beyond the Market of Appius. At Antium on the sea, where Nero was born, Cicero had a villa and on his way to Mormiae he stopped at Three Taverns. While the horses were being changed he tasted the wine and wrote a letter to Atticus on the festival of Ceres, April 12, 58 B.C. Here more Christians from Rome came to greet the apostle. When Paul saw these, he thanked God and took courage." (ibid, p. 267-268)

Evidently there were groups of Christians in both places. Paul must have entered this great city with apprehension and wonder as to how he would be received among the Jewish Christians and as to how his trial would turn out. So when these persons showed their love by coming more than forty miles to greet him, he did indeed thank God and was encouraged.

15. AT ROME. 28:16-31.

16 And when we entered into Rome, Paul was suffered to abide by himself with the soldier that guarded him.

17 And it came to pass, that after three days he called together those that were the chief of the Jews: and when they were come together, he said unto them, I, brethren,

1016. What was the method of travel from Puteoli to Appii Forum?
1017. How far had the Christians traveled to see Paul?

though I had done nothing against the people, or the customs of our fathers, yet was delivered prisoner from Jerusalem into the hands of the Romans:

18 who, when they had examined me, desired to set me at liberty, because there was no cause of death in me.

19 But when the Jews spake against it, I was constrained to appeal unto Caesar; not that I had aught whereof to accuse my nation.

20 For this cause therefore did I entreat you to see and to speak with me: for because of the hope of Israel I am bound with this chain.

21 And they said unto him, We neither received letters from Judaea concerning thee, nor did any of the brethren come hither and report or speak any harm of thee.

22 But we desire to hear of thee what thou thinkest: for as concerning this sect, it is known to us that everywhere it is spoken against.

23 And when they had appointed him a day, they came to him into his lodging in great number; to whom he expounded the matter, testifying the kingdom of God, and persuading them concerning Jesus, both from the law of Moses and from the prophets, from morning till evening.

24 And some believed the things which were spoken, and some disbelieved.

25 And when they agreed not among themselves, they departed after that Paul had spoken one word, Well spake the Holy Spirit through Isaiah the prophet unto your fathers,

26 saying,
> Go thou unto this people, and say,
> By hearing ye shall hear, and shall in no wise understand;
> And seeing ye shall see, and shall in no wise perceive:

27 For this people's heart is waxed gross,
> And their ears are dull of hearing,
> And their eyes they have closed;
> Lest haply they should perceive with their eyes,
> And hear with their ears,
> And understand with their heart,
> And should turn again,
> And I should heal them.

28 Be it known therefore unto you, that this salvation of God is sent unto the Gentiles: they will also hear.

29 And when he had said these words, the Jews departed, having much disputing among themselves.

30 And he abode two whole years in his own hired dwelling, and received all that went in unto him,

31 preaching the kingdom of God, and teaching the things concerning the Lord Jesus Christ with all boldness, none forbidding him.

16 "I must also see Rome." And now Paul was to have the fulfillment of this desire but how unlike the manner in which he had anticipated viewing the capitol city. There is much that could be written respecting the scenes that greeted the apostle as he walked those forty-three miles. We could write of the tombs and statues that lined the way but others have told of those things. Let us try to hold to the text as near as possible.

Paul was given much freedom here. He had his own rented house or apartment—all that reminded him that he was a prisoner was the chain and the soldier. What a train of long wearisome events had happened since he said, "I appeal to Caesar." What a trying and tiresome journey it had been. But after only three days the tireless ambassador in bonds sent word that he wanted to meet with those who were the leaders among the Jews of Rome. Paul was especially interested in getting the true facts before these men. He wanted them to know that he was here as a prisoner, not because he had done anything against the Jewish leaders or the nation of Israel. Paul places the responsibility of his imprisonment upon the Jews. He further proves that he had done nothing against the Roman government for he states that upon examination no fault was found in him. Indeed, left up to them he would be at liberty; but the Jews intervened and made necessary an appeal to Caesar; thus did Paul account for his appearance in Rome as a prisoner. But one more final, pungent word—I sent for you that I might see you and tell you that for the "hope of Israel" (the Messiah) I am bound with this chain.

17-22 Whether or nor these elders and rulers of the synagogues in Rome were telling the truth or not I do not know, but they said that they had neither received written nor spoken word about the apostle, but that they had heard of this new sect to which Paul had just alluded and they would like very much to hear more about it first hand. These men were prejudiced to begin with for they only heard evil concerning this new "sect". But we should be glad that they were even willing to give it a hearing. So a day and time was set and they came out in great numbers to hear from this strange prisoner.

1918. How does Paul show his tireless effort in serving Christ?
1019. Whom does Paul blame for his imprisonment?
1020. What was the reason Paul assigned for his imprisonment?

23-31 Then followed a most touching scene. From morning until evening the bond-servant of Jesus Christ expounded, testified, opened, alleged, besought and proved that this Jesus was the Christ and that He did have a kingdom and subjects. Paul proved from both the law and the prophets that this was so. What was the result? "Not peace but a sword."

"The division which has resulted ever since when the truth of God has encountered, side by side, earnest conviction with worldly indifference, honest investigation with bigoted prejudice, trustful faith with the pride of scepticism."

A stormy session followed as they disagreed among themselves. Then they departed, but not before Paul gave them one final inspired warning. Paul said, "The words of Isaiah the prophet are surely fulfilled in you."

As in Antioch of Pisidia he said in conclusion "Lo we turn to the Gentiles." Here in Rome he modified the form just a bit.

"This salvation of God is sent unto the Gentiles. They will also hear."

And now for two whole years he is to abide here at Rome. Luke tells us that all were permitted to see him and that he preached concerning the kingdom of God; that he also taught concerning the Lord Jesus Christ with all boldness. We might also add that certain epistles were written at this time. How many and which ones are determined by your conception as to what happened to Paul when he appeared before Caesar. After the two years was he released? Did he indeed go to Spain and then return to Rome for a second trial? We do not know. Here is the order of the writing of the epistles as I have thought of them:

THE EPISTLES OF PAUL

The Epistle	The Date	The Journey	The Place Where Written
1. I Thess.	52 A.D.	Second	Corinth
2. II Thess.	53 A.D.	Second	Corinth
3. I Cor.	57 A.D.	Third	Ephesus
4. II Cor.	57 A.D.	Third	Macedonia at Phillippi
5. Gal.	57 A.D.	Third	Corinth
6. Romans	58 A.D.	Third	Corinth
7. Phil.	62 A.D.	Journey to Rome	Enroute to Rome

1021. Why should we suspect the Jews in Rome of not telling the truth?
1022. What was touching about the scene in Paul's lodging?
1023. Did any in Rome accept the gospel?
1024. What time and place was similar to this in Rome?
1025. What is "The Kingdom of God" of which Paul preached?
1026. What are the two theories of Paul's trial and imprisonment?

The Epistle	The Date	The Journey	The Place Where Written
8. Col.	62 A.D.	Journey to Rome	At Rome
9. Eph.	62 A.D.	Journey to Rome	Rome
10. Eph.	62 A.D.	Journey to Rome	Rome
11. I Tim.	67 A.D.	After Release	Ephesus
12. Titus	67 A.D.	After a visit to Crete	Ephesus
13. II Tim.	68 A.D.	To Tim. who was in Ephesus	Rome
14. Hebrews	68 A.D.	Some Bible scholars think that someone beside Paul wrote the epistle to the Hebrews	Rome

Thus after six years of happy effort I have finished the notes on the book of Acts. They are far from perfect. Of this I am more conscious than anyone else. But if they contribute in some way to make this marvelous book of Acts more actual to you, I shall be well repaid.

Yours in the Kingdom of God
San Jose, California
January, 1953
Don De Welt
Revised, February, 1958

ACTS TEST OVER THE THIRD MISSIONARY JOURNEY AND THE VOYAGE TO ROME
18:23—28:31

True or False

_____ 1. Paul visited numerous churches in Galatia on his third journey.

_____ 2. Among those visited in the above stated province was Berea and Thessalonica.

_____ 3. Apollos was a native of Corinth.

_____ 4. No, that is all wrong. He was from Athens.

_____ 5. Still wrong, his native home was Alexandria.

_____ 6. Apollos was "mighty in the scriptures".

_____ 7. A woman helped to teach this man the truth.

_____ 8. Apollos became a famous preacher at Corinth.

_____ 9. Paul asked twelve men in Ephesus if they had received the Holy Spirit after they had believed.

_____ 10. Acts states that the twelve men were baptized into the name of "the Father, and of the Son and of the Holy Spirit".

_____ 11. The spiritual gifts given were "tongues of knowledge".

344

_____ 12. Paul preached for six months in the synagogues of Ephesus.

_____ 13. He worked for three years in the schoolroom of Tyrannus.

_____ 14. Diseases and those possessed of demons were healed by handkerchiefs that were carried away from the body of Paul.

_____ 15. Seven sons of one Sceva really took a beating from a man possessed of a demon. (Read this carefully please)

_____ 16. The whole town of Ephesus heard about this and it caused a terrible reflection upon the standing of the church.

_____ 17. There were hypocrites even in the churches that Paul established.

_____ 18. A thousand or more dollars went up in smoke in the city of Ephesus.

_____ 19. Paul's plan from Ephesus was to go immediately from there to Jerusalem.

_____ 20. Paul wrote II Corinthians from Ephesus at this time.

MULTIPLE CHOICE

1. Paul sent who from Ephesus to Macedonia? 1) Titus and Timothy. 2) Timothy and Erastus. 3) Aristarchus and Secundus.

2. What churches were established during the stay at Ephesus? 1) The churches at Corinth and Thessalonica. 2) The seven churches of Asia. 3) The churches at Troas and Philippi.

3. The work of Christ was called: 1) The church of Christ. 2) The Gospel of Christ. 3) The Way, in the town of Ephesus.

4. Demetrius was: 1) A goldsmith. 2) A worker in brass. 3) A silversmith.

5. Demetrius was angry most of all because: 1) Diana was losing devotees. 2) He was losing money. 3) The Jews were losing followers.

6. Who was carried into the mob in the Ephesian theater? 1) Timothy and Erastus. 2) Gaius and Titus. 3) Aristarchus and Gaius.

7. Paul was kept from going into the theatre because: 1) He knew it was against the rules. 2) Friends warned him. 3) Jehovah warned him.

8. Alexander was: 1) The orator of the Jews. 2) A friend of Paul. 3) One of the Asiarchs.

9. The mob was quieted down by the: 1) City police. 2) City councilman. 3) The town clerk.

10. "The assembly" that was called out by Demetrius can be referred to in a general way as a: 1) Town meeting. 2) Church. 3) Camp meeting.

11. The town clerk gained his point by telling them that: 1) They would be only furthering the cause of Christ. 2) Called into account for their actions. 3) Dishonoring their reputation.
12. Paul departed from Ephesus: 1) At night. 2) After he had exhorted the disciples. 3) Early in the morning.
13. Paul went directly to: 1) Macedonia. 2) Greece. 3) Asia from Ephesus.
14. Paul wrote the following books from Corinth: 1) Romans and II Corinthians. 2) Galatians and Philippians. 3) Romans and Galatians.
15. II Corinthians was written from: 1) Rome. 2) Philippi. 3) Troas.

FILL IN THE BLANKS

1. Paul expected _____ to meet him at _____ with news from _____.
2. Paul was taking up a collection on the third missionary journey for the poor _____ _____ in _____.
3. There were _____ men who helped carry this money (the number of men).
4. Luke's home-town was _____.
5. Paul was in a hurry to arrive in _____ before _____.
6. The meeting in Troas occurred on the _____ day of the week.
7. The meeting was held in a three-story house and _____ fell out of the window and was taken up for dead.
8. "From _____ he sent to _____, and called to him the _____ of the church." Acts 20:17.

UNDERLINE THE MISTAKES IN THE FOLLOWING:

Paul wanted the Ephesian elders to know that after his departing grievous wolves would enter in among them, not sparing the flock.

And not only so, but that right from among themselves men would arise as partyists to draw away disciples after them.

Paul gave a statement from Jesus that was not found in the four gospels. Rhodes is the name of one of Paul's companions.

There was a change of ships at Patara. They passed Cyprus on the right. The ship from Patara unloaded at Tyre. They stayed three days at Tyre.

Some of these of Tyre were prophets. They stayed seven days at Ptolemais. Philip the evangelist was a convert of Paul. Philip was like Paul, and was an evangelizing bachelor.

There came a prophet from Jerusalem whose name was Agabus. This man took his own girdle and bound his hands and feet and said that Paul would be thus bound in Jerusalem.

Paul was to stay in the home of John Mark in Jerusalem. There were only two apostles present in Jerusalem when Paul arrived.

CAN YOU MATCH THESE THOUGHTS?
Place the matching numbers in the two lists alongside each other.

1. "All zealous for the law".
2. The Jews from Asia.
3. "He spake unto them in the Hebrew language".
4. Four men who had a vow.
5. Claudius Lysias.
6. The castle stairs.
7. ". . . scourge a man that is a Roman"?
8. The Egyptian who led 4000 Assassins.
9. ". . . far hence unto the Gentiles".
10. "No resurrection, neither angels nor spirits".
11. Neither eat nor drink till they had killed Paul.
12. The command of Ananias.
13. Paul's sister's son.
14. 200 spearmen, 200 footman, 70 horsemen.
15. The governor of Syria and Cilicia.

1. The Jews in Jerusalem.
2. The chief captain.
3. The words that set off the mob to cry: "Away with him".
4. Those over which Paul was at charge.
5. Paul addressing the Jewish mob.
6. Those who stirred up the multitudes and laid hands on Paul.
7. Where Paul stood to address the Jews.
8. "Smite him on the mouth."
9. Paul's words to the centurion.
10. The one for whom Paul was mistaken.
11. The profession of the Sadducees.
12. The forty under an oath.
13. Paul's escort.
14. Felix.
15. He who heard the plot.

WHO SAID IT?—TELL WHERE
1. ". . . We have found this man a pestilent fellow."
2. "I appeal unto Caesar."
3. "I also could wish to hear the man myself."
4. "Saul, Saul, why persecutest thou me?"
5. "Paul, thou art mad. Thy much learning is turning thee mad."
6. "With but little persuasion thou wouldest fain make me a Christian."
7. "Sirs, I perceive that the voyage will be with injury and much loss."
8. "By hearing ye shall hear, and shall in no wise understand; and seeing ye shall see, and shall in no wise perceive."
9. "We neither received letters from Judea concerning thee, nor did any of the brethren come hither and report or speak any harm of thee." 347

REVIEW EXAMINATION OVER THE BOOK OF ACTS
True or False

.... 1. Jesus promised the baptism in the Holy Spirit to 120 disciples.

.... 2. One of the qualifications for the office of the apostle was to have been with Jesus from the baptism of John until the day of ascension.

.... 3. The theme of the sermon on Pentecost was repentance from sin and faith in God.

.... 4. The lame man at the gate beautiful had been lame since his birth.

.... 5. Peter had the same type of men in his second audience as he did in the first.

.... 6. All twelve apostles were arrested and put in jail as a result of Peter's message on Solomon's porch.

.... 7. Ananais and Sapphira were carried out dead because of lying.

.... 8. An angel of God released the twelve apostles from prison.

.... 9. Gamaliel saved the apostles from a beating by a clever speech.

.... 10. Stephen was stoned for blasphemy.

True or False

.... 1. Philip and Stephen were scattered by the persecution.

.... 2. Simon the sorcerer believed but was never baptized.

.... 3. The Ethiopian eunuch was the treasurer of a queen.

.... 4. Peter and John came to Samaria for the purpose of giving spiritual gifts.

.... 5. Simon the scorcerer sinned in that he tried to impart the Holy Spirit when he had no right to do so.

.... 6. Ananais baptized Saul of Tarsus after Saul had been without food or drink for three days and nights.

.... 7. Saul did not preach immediately after his baptism, but went away into Arabia.

.... 8. Peter's first convert in Lydda was named Aeneas.

.... 9. Cornelius was baptized in the Holy Spirit before he was baptized in water.

.... 10. Herod made a speech in Jerusalem for which an angel of heaven smote him and he was eaten of worms.

True or False
THE FIRST MISSIONARY JOURNEY

.... 1. Elymas was one of the converts made in the town of Iconium.

_____ 2. There were many who heard the word and believed in Antioch of Pisidia.

_____ 3. Timothy was converted by Paul at Derbe.

_____ 4. No persecution was encoutered at Derbe.

_____ 5. Upon the return trip they did not have time for preaching.

True or False
TROUBLE OVER CIRCUMCISION

_____ 1. The trouble was caused by the Jews from Antioch.

_____ 2. Paul and Barnabas had a difficult time in being accepted as sincere by the brethren in Jerusalem.

_____ 3. Peter's speech told of the miracles God had wrought through his ministry.

_____ 4. James told how prophecy was fulfilled in the conversion of the Gentiles.

_____ 5. The letter stated that it was wrong to eat blood.

True or False
THE SECOND MISSIONARY JOURNEY

_____ 1. Paul took up a collection for the poor saints in Judea on this journey.

_____ 2. Paul established the work in Galatia on this journey.

_____ 3. The woman with a spirit of divination lived in Philippi.

_____ 4. Paul refused to leave the jail at Philippi without a proper escort.

_____ 5. Paul stayed in Thessalonica to reason three Sabbaths.

_____ 6. Jason lived in Thessalonica.

_____ 7. There was a good work done in Berea with no opposition.

_____ 8. An Epicurean is one who does not believe in showing emotion.

_____ 9. There was no one converted in Athens.

_____ 10. Silas and Timothy joined Paul in Corinth.

True or False
THE THIRD MISSIONARY JOURNEY

_____ 1. Priscilla and Aquila met Apollos in Corinth and corrected his teaching.

_____ 2. The seven sons of Sceva were interested in casting out demons.

_____ 3. Paul wrote the book of I Corinthians from Ephesus.

_____ 4. Demetrius was interested in stopping the preaching of Paul.

_____ 5. Paul took a collection from Galatia, Macedonia and Achaia for the saints in Judea.

THE HOLY SPIRIT IN THE BOOK OF ACTS

Questions you should answer *before* you study the lesson.

1. If I did learn from the book of Acts, of what value is this to present day Christians?

2. Are there some "key verses" in Acts i.e., as related to the power of the Holy Spirit in our lives today? Discuss them.

3. If we have the same experiences today as described in this book, would we also have the same results from these experiences?

4. How does *fear* both help and hinder our appreciation of the Spirit's work in our lives?

5. How many references to the Holy Spirit are found in the Acts account? Choose one: (1) twenty-one? (2) one hundred? (3) sixty? So what?

6. Since the book of Acts is so important to us, and since the subject of the Holy Spirit is so prominent in the book, why have we neglected Him so long?

7. It is very difficult for us to remember that the first book of the New Testament was not written until the second missionary journey. When the first deacons were spoken of as "being filled with the Holy Spirit" (Acts 6:3), they were thus filled before we have any scriptural record of the apostles laying their hands on them. Discuss this thought.

8. Is there any rule we can use in deciding what in Acts, concerning the Holy Spirit, relates to us and what in Acts does not relate to us? Please state it plainly.

9. Is there a rule we can learn to help us know when language is to be understood as figurative or to be understood in the literal sense? Please state it plainly.

10. Have you ever read the book of Acts with the thought of the Holy Spirit's work? If not do so now.

INTRODUCTION

We shall consider most carefully every reference to the Holy Spirit in Luke's second treatise, but we shall do so with but one thought in mind: *How can I relate this to my life and God's will for me?* We shall ask and answer four questions for each of the sixty references to the Holy Spirit in Acts. They are: (1) What does it say? i.e. Is every word clear in the translation? (2) What does it mean? i.e. What does it mean in its context? When the meaning is in question admit it and offer options. (3) What does it mean to me? (4) How—Or should I share this with someone else?

For the benefit of those who need a comprehensive view of the subject, here are all the references to the Holy Spirit in the Acts account:

1. Acts 1:2, The Lord "had given commandment through the Holy Spirit to the apostles."
2. Acts 1:4, "Wait for the promise of the Father which ye have heard from me." (cf. John 14:16).
3. Acts 1:5, "Ye shall be baptised with the Holy Spirit not many days hence."
4. Acts 1:8, "Ye shall receive power when the Holy Spirit is come upon you."
5. Acts 1:16, The Scripture, "which the Holy Spirit spake before by the mouth of David concerning Judas."
6. Acts 2:4, "They were all filled with the Holy Spirit, and began to speak with other tongues as the Spirit gave them utterance."
7. Acts 2:17, "I will pour forth of My Spirit upon all flesh."
8. Acts 2:18, "On My servants and on My handmaidens will I pour forth of My Spirit; and they shall prophesy."
9. Acts 2:33, "Having received of the Father the promise of the Holy Spirit, He hath poured forth this."

10. Acts 2:38, "Ye shall receive the gift of the Holy Spirit."
11. Acts 3:19, "Seasons of refreshing from the presence of the Lord."
12. Acts 4:8, "Peter filled with the Holy Spirit, said."
13. Acts 4:25, "Oh Lord . . . Who by the Holy Spirit, by the mouth of our father David, Thy servant, didst say."
14. Acts 4:31, "They were all filled with the Holy Spirit, and they spake the Word of God."
15. Acts 5:3, "Why hath Satan filled thy heart to lie to the Holy Spirit?"
16. Acts 5:9, "Ye have agreed together to tempt the Spirit of the Lord."
17. Acts 5:32, "We are witnesses of these things; and so is the Holy Spirit, Whom God hath given to them that obey Him."
18. Acts 6:3, "Men of good report, full of the Spirit and of wisdom."
19. Acts 6:5, "A man full of faith and of the Holy Spirit."
20. Acts 6:10, "Not able to withstand the wisdom and the Spirit by which he spake."
21. Acts 7:51, "Ye do always resist the Holy Spirit."
22. Acts 7:55, "He, being full of the Holy Spirit, looked up."
23. 24. 25. Acts 8:15, 16, "Who . . . prayed for them that they might receive the Holy Spirit; for as yet He was fallen upon none of them; only they had been baptised."
26. Acts 8:17, "They laid their hands on them, and they received the Holy Spirit."
27. Acts 8:18 "Through the laying on of the apostles' hands the Holy Spirit was given."
28. Acts 8:19, "That on whomsoever I lay my hands, he may receive the Holy Spirit."

29. Acts 8:20, "Thought to obtain the gift of God with money."
30. Acts 8:29, "The Spirit said unto Philip."
31. Acts 8:39, "The Spirit of the Lord caught away Philip."
32. Acts 9:17, "That thou mightest . . . be filled with the Holy Spirit."
33. Acts 9:31, "Walking . . . in the comfort of the Holy Spirit."
34. Acts 10:19, "The Spirit said unto him" (Peter).
35. Acts 10:20, "I have sent them."
36. Acts 10:38, "God anointed him with the Holy Spirit and with power."
37. Acts 10:44, "The Holy Spirit fell on all them which heard."
38. Acts 10:45, "On the Gentiles also was poured out the gift of the Holy Spirit."
39. Acts 10:47, "Which have received the Holy Spirit as well as we."
40. Acts 11:12, "The Spirit bade me go with them."
41. Acts 11:15, "The Holy Spirit fell on them as on us at the beginning."
42. Acts 11:16, "Ye shall be baptised with the Holy Spirit."
43. Acts 11:24, "He was a good man, and full of the Holy Spirit and of faith."
44. Acts 11:28, "Agabus . . . signified by the Spirit that there should be a great famine."
45. Acts 13:2, "The Holy Spirit said."
46. Acts 13:4 "They, being sent forth by the Holy Spirit."
47. Acts 13:9, 10, "Saul . . . filled with the Holy Spirit . . . said."
48. Acts 13:52, "The disciples were filled with joy and with the Holy Spirit."

49. Acts 15:8, "God . . . bare them witness, giving them the Holy Spirit."
50. Acts 15:28, "It seemed good to the Holy Spirit and to us."
51. Acts 16:6, "Forbidden of the Holy Spirit to speak the Word in Asia."
52. Acts 16:7, "The Spirit of Jesus suffered them not."
53. Acts 19:2, "Did ye receive the Holy Spirit when ye believed? . . . . We did not so much as hear whether the Holy Spirit was given."
54. Acts 19:6, "The Holy Spirit came on them."
55. Acts 20:22, "I go bound in the Spirit unto Jerusalem."
56. Acts 20:23, "The Holy Spirit testifieth unto me in every city."
57. Acts 20:28, "The Holy Spirit hath made you bishops."
58. Acts 21:4, "These said to Paul through the Holy Spirit."
59. Acts 21:11, "Thus saith the Holy Spirit."
60. Acts 28:25, "Well spake the Holy Spirit by Isaiah the prophet."

1. ". . . after that he had given commandment *through the Holy Spirit* unto the apostles whom he had chosen:" 1:2

   A. *What Does It Say?* In answering this important question we must understand: (1) Who is speaking? In this text, our Lord is speaking. (2) To whom is he speaking or who is being addressed? In this verse the eleven apostles are addressed. (3) For what purpose? He is addressing the apostles with the great commission—He is commanding them to go into all the world and preach the good news— this is an abbreviated form of the longer expressions in Matthew 28:18-20 and Mark 16:15, 16. Cf. Luke 24:44-49, John 20:20-23. (4) Under what conditions or circumstances does this verse appear? No geographical place is mentioned. The

thought is: Jesus was not taken up to heaven until
He first, through the Holy Spirit, gave the great
commission.

B. *What Does It Mean?* We are narrowing this question to refer *only* to the mention of the Holy
Spirit in the passage. We will answer the question
as it relates to the rest of the verse or verses *only*
if such helps our understanding of the subject of
the Holy Spirit. Acts 1:2 discusses the aid of the
Holy Spirit exercised by our Lord in His speaking—specifically in the giving of the great commission or "commandment" to the chosen apostles.
Through the help, aid, or assistance of the Holy
Spirit Jesus gave these words to Peter, James, John,
Andrew and the other eleven. In just what particular sense the Holy Spirit aided Him or accompanied Him, we do not know. Indeed, there is some
question as to which verb relates to the phrase.
Gareth Reese has well said: "exactly what we are
to understand was done by the help of the Holy
Spirit depends on with which verb this phrase is
taken. It can be taken with "chosen" (meaning:
He chose the apostles by the help of the Holy
Spirit), and is thus translated in the Syriac and
Ethiopic versions. It can be taken with "received
up" (meaning: Christ was taken up to heaven by
the power of the Holy Spirit). It can be taken
with "given commandment" (meaning: Christ
acted by the special aid of the Holy Spirit when
He gave the Great Commission). (*New Testament History*, p. 3). We prefer the last meaning.

C. *What Does It Mean To Me?* Since the Holy Spirit
aided our Lord in so many ways under so many
circumstances (see Lesson Nine), are we then to
conclude He will not also be our Helper? Of
course, the ministry of the Other Comforter is
distinct as relates to our Lord and His apostles but

many of their needs are ours and we can expect the same One to aid us.

A very basic concept appears just here: How interested is our God in the affairs of our lives? Does our God have an interest or personal concern about the "little needs" of our lives as well as the so-called "larger concerns"? We believe with our Lord that "not a sparrow falls" without our Father's knowledge. This being true, *how* does He indicate or express His interest? *How* does He answer our prayers? Angels are ministering spirits sent to fulfill His will in the lives of His children. What about the presence and purpose of the Holy Spirit in the body of each of His children? We cannot be cognizant of His immediate, subjective work but we believe He is at work. If it was "through the Holy Spirit" our Lord chose His apostles, it is also "through the Holy Spirit" that some of our choices have been made. If it was "through the Holy Spirit" Jesus gave the great commission, are we to conclude He is absent when we repeat or fulfill this commission today? Perhaps we can catch a glimpse of the depth of meaning in the little phrase "in Him we live and move and have our being"—not only by the rights of creation but by the privileges of the new creation.

D. *How Can I Share It?* If there is a greater need among His followers than the awareness of God's work in our lives through the Holy Spirit, I do not know what it is. Share this glorious truth!

2. ". . . and, being assembled together with them, he charged them not to depart from Jerusalem, but to wait for the promise of the Father, which said he, ye heard from me." 1:4

A. *What Does It Say?* The antecedent of the pronoun "them" refers to "the apostles whom he had chosen" (vs. 2). Therefore the charge concerning "the promise of the Father" is given to them. He had mentioned the same need to stay in the city of Jerusalem for the same purpose in Luke 24:49: "I send forth the promise of my Father upon you: but tarry ye in the city, until ye be clothed with power from on high." Jesus had made request to the Father concerning the other Comforter: "and I will pray (or made request) of the Father, and he shall give you another Comforter, that he may be with you forever," (John 14:16). Compare these other references to the same promise: John 15:26; 16:7; 13; Matthew 10:20; John 20:22.

B. *What Does It Mean?* God long ago promised the first Comforter—the Old Testament contains this promise in so many prophecies and types. Jesus was the first Comforter—the fulfillment of that promise. As certain as the coming of our Lord in the flesh, so certain is the coming of the Holy Spirit.

C. *What Does It Mean To Me?* This is both a specific and a general promise. Specific in the sense that He was speaking to the apostles about the coming day of Pentecost and their baptism in the Holy Spirit—general in the sense that He speaks of the time of the advent of the Holy Spirit as a gift. We must remark again that we see in the name *Comforter* far more than we usually associate with the presence of the Holy Spirit in the life of the average church member. Comfort is a personal, felt relationship—as comfort relates to a person, this presupposes some form of personal exchange and interaction on the part of the Comforter and the one being comforted. Please, please remember the Holy Spirit was promised and received twenty years before the first epistle of the New Testament was written.

D. *How Can I Share It?* There is nothing more needed in our dark, sad world than the personal, warm fellowship of God's Holy Spirit. The best way we share this truth is by a demonstration on our part. If and when we show the results of the personal indwelling Christ, we will have shared the grandest gift of God to His children.

3. ". . . for John indeed baptised with water; but ye shall be baptized in the Holy Spirit not many days hence." 1:5

A. *What Does It Say?* We have commented as to the meaning of this text in several places—we shall not write further. The words are clear: Jesus promised the apostles that as John immersed persons in water, Jesus would immerse their minds or spirits in the Holy Spirit—and this would happen soon.

B. *What Does It Mean?*
When we ask this question we confine ourselves to the *one text* under consideration. We have answered this question of Holy Spirit baptism in its larger connections in another lesson. This was a preparatory measure as related to the work of preaching the Gospel. The apostles were not ready to carry out the great commission until they were first baptized in the Holy Spirit. We do not minimize the source of strength and power granted by the Holy Spirit to the inner man (Ephesians 3:16), but we do want to say the largest meaning of this experience would seem to be to grant to the apostles the ability to recall all that Jesus taught them and to speak it with clarity and boldness as a consequence of this experience. Infallible recollection, information, and inspiration all came as a result of this experience.

C. *What Does It Mean To Me?* It would be easy to say that since we were not included in the promise we do not at all relate to this text. However, the fact of our attempt to understand it indicates a personal relationship to it. It seems to me very impressive that we have the same Comforter as the one promised to the apostles. We can be sure that as He met their needs and equipped them for their work, He will (and does) meet our needs and prepare us for our work.

D. *How Can I Share It?* If there is one large need in the heart of Mr. Church-member, it is to know something of the nearness of God. If we can teach them by word and example that God through His Spirit is in us—lives in our bodies—we will have indeed shared an important truth.

4. "But ye shall receive power, when the Holy Spirit is come upon you: and ye shall be my witnesses both in Jerusalem, and in all Judea and Samaria, and unto the uttermost part of the earth." 1:8

A. *What Does It Say?* Once again: our Lord speaks to His ambassadors, the apostles. This is a repeated promise looking to Pentecost. As a result of the power granted by the Holy Spirit, these men will be able to share the good news. Jesus plainly tells them the progressive nature of their witness.

B. *What Does It Mean?* This verse is linked with the question of the apostles concerning the restoration of the kingdom to Israel; whereas, they were *not* to know the times or the seasons for the restored kingdom, they *were* to know the time and place for an equally important (or even more important) event. The *power* promised was the baptism of the Holy Spirit. Question: "Would this experience motivate them to witness or simply bring to their remembrance all the information for their witness?" This is a crucial question as it probes the deeper meaning of the contact of the divine Spirit with the human spirit. Someone has suggested that the motivation for witness was the resurrection and the baptism in the Holy Spirit gave them the information. Judging from the Acts account, the subject of the resurrection was surely dominant. However, we can hardly imagine the experience of the Holy Spirit baptism without a personal response. The sense of awe, wonder, and amazement must have filled the hearts of the apostles as they contemplated and unavoidably felt what happened to them. These men were to bear witness of what they had seen and heard (i.e. the resurrected Christ with all authority in heaven and on earth). Essentially, the power to give this witness came from their association with Him "after His passion." The confidence to speak accurately and clearly came from the Spirit baptism.

C. *What Does It Mean To Me?* We have all the evidence to establish without question the resurrection of our Lord. The foundation for our message is firmly established. Where is our witness? We are not eye-witnesses of His majesty, but we do believe because of those things written for such a purpose. The example of these unlearned and ignorant men should move us out into our society with the same boldness to tell the same good news. We are not the eye-witnesses with infallible knowledge, nor is it likely we will be called upon to be martyrs for our words. But we do have the same motivations: a lost world—a wonderful Savior—a command to go and tell.

D. *How Can I Share It?* We have already touched on this. It has been said so many times by so many writers and speakers. If we could convince the members of our Lord's church it was their privilege to share the good news of Christ's death for our sins and that He arose from the dead, the whole world would soon be saved. We can only share what we ourselves personally possess.

5. "Brethren, it was needful that the scripture should be fulfilled *which the Holy Spirit spake* before by the mouth of David concerning Judas, who was guide to them that took Jesus." 1:16

A. *What Does It Say?* By reading this verse in its context, especially if this is done in two or three modern speech translations, it is almost impossible to misunderstand it. Here are the words of Peter to the 120 about Judas.

B. *What Does It Mean?* We are not enslaved to commentaries but we do believe they are worthy of your serious consideration. Commentaries are but the written lessons of men who have made a careful attempt to answer the question at the heading of this point (i.e. *What does it mean?*). We have listed twenty-one of what we consider the best commentaries on the book of Acts. There are four times this number available, but these are in our estimation the most helpful. (For the benefit of those who do not have this list, we include it here.)

1. *Standard Bible Commentary-Acts*, Edited by Orrin Root, Standard Publishing Co., Cincinnati, Ohio, 1966, 208 pages, $5.95.
2. *The Acts of the Apostles*, G. Campbell Morgan, Fleming H. Revell Co., 1924, 548 pages, $4.95 (?).
3. The New International Commentary, *Commentary on the Book of Acts*, F. F. Bruce, Wm. B. Eerdmans Co., 1954, 556 pages, $5.95, $6.95.
4. *New Commentary on Acts of Apostles*, J. W. McGarvey, Standard Publishing Co., 1892, 298 pages, $4.95.
5. The Evangelical Commentary, *The Acts of the Apostles*, Charles W. Carter and Ralph Earle, Zondervan Publishing Co., 436 pages, $5.95.
6. Westminister Commentaries, *The Acts of the Apostles*, R. B. Rackham, Methuen and Co., 36 Essex St., Straud, London, WC 2.
7. Restoration Reprint Library, *Studies In Acts*, W. R. Walker, 194 pages, $3.95.

8. *Commentary on the Acts of the Apostles*, J. A. Alexander, Zondervan Publishing Co., 1956, 960 pages, $12.95.
9. *Interpretation of the Acts of the Apostles*, R. C. H. Lenski, Wartburg Press, Columbus, Ohio, $5.45, 1134 pages.
10. *Pictures of the Apostolic Church—Studies in the Book of Acts*, William M. Ramsay, Baker Book House, 1959, 368 pages, $3.50.
11. *The Acts of the Apostles*, Thomas Walker, Moody Press, 568 pages, $4.95.
12. *New Testament History*, A Critical and Exegetical Commentary on the Book of Acts, Gareth L. Reese, 1966, 700 pages, $6.00.
13. *Notes on the New Testament*, By Albert Barnes, Baker Book House, 1962, $3.50.
14. *Acts Comments*, Edsil Dale, Moberly, Mo., 1960, 390 pages, $5.50.
15. *Acts of the Apostles*, A Homiletic Commentary, David Thomas, Baker Book House, 1955, 494 pages.
16. *The Acts of the Apostles*, William Barclay, The Daily Study Bible, St. Andrew Press, Edinburgh, 214 pages, $2.50.
17. Scripture Union, *Bible Study Books—Acts*, R. P. Martin, Scripture Union, 239 Fairfield Avenue, Upper Darby, Pa.; 90 pages, $1.25.
18. *The Living Word, Acts of Apostles*, Part I & II, R. B. Sweet Co., J. W. Roberts, 88 and 94 pages, $2.00.
19. *A Study of the Books of Acts*, Standing on the Promises, Charles J. Woodridge, Baker Book House, 152 pages, $2.50.
20. *The Acts of the Apostles*, William Owen Carver, Broadman Press, 280 pages, $2.95 (?).
21. *Acts Made Actual*, Don DeWelt, College Press, 418 pages, $5.95.

"Here is Peter's clear definition of Inspiration: in the Scriptures the Holy Spirit is the speaker, and (in this case) the mouth of David is the medium for his speaking. This definition is oft repeated. The Spirit—the *causa efficiens;* the human mouth (pen)—*causa instrumentalis.* The significant preposition is *dia,* 'through' a medium or an instrument. And this was done not merely 'through David' but through his 'mouth,' his very utterance. This is verbal inspiration, through which none other ever occurred according to the Scriptures themselves." (Lenski, p. 45)

C. *What Does It Mean To Me?* Since the Holy Spirit has spoken through the apostles and prophets there is nothing more important for me to do than to study and know the meaning of every word. We do not minimize the need and value of the study of other subjects, but they surely pale into insignificance as we contemplate the thought of God speaking to us. Not all men believe God has spoken

362

to us in the words of the Bible—many who do somehow miss the vast importance of such a fact. We know it. We believe it. We feel its importance. Therefore we must know it! This is heaven's incentive for Bible study.

D. *How Can I Share It?* Perhaps through you many others can understand the privilege and need for a personal word-for-word study of what God through the Holy Spirit is saying to us. You could share nothing more important than the enthusiasm you have for a knowledge of His Word.

6. "And they were all filled with the Holy Spirit, and began to speak with other tongues, as the Spirit gave them utterance." 2:4

A. *What Does It Say?* We have treated this text quite completely in other parts of our study. We refer you to them. We must say the measure of filling with the Holy Spirit was the baptism in the Holy Spirit or "being clothed with power from on high" or "receiving power after the Holy Spirit came upon them." There are five expressions all referring to the same experience: (1) Baptized in the Holy Spirit, (2) Clothed with power from on high, (3) Receive power after the Holy Spirit is come upon you, (4) Filled with the Holy Spirit—after the event, Peter refers to it as, (5) "Poured forth this which ye see and hear." The antecedent of the pronoun "they" is important. To whom does it refer? It is a source of amazement to read commentary after commentary which speak of the 120 disciples as the antecedent of this pronoun. In contrast consider: (1) Jesus used the words of John the Baptist spoken by John to the multitude (Matthew 3:1-12) and referred these words to the apostles (1:5). Indeed, the eleven were so convinced of this they wanted to supply the twelfth member to their group before the promised experience occurred. Does it seem reasonable that Jesus would baptize in the Holy Spirit those to whom He gave no promise? What purpose would be served in so doing?

B. *What Does It Mean?*

We need to realize the proper meaning of a phrase here found by an examination of every place it occurs. As an example: *"filled with the Holy Spirit."* Are we to conclude that every time we read this phrase, "filled with the Holy Spirit", we have a case of Holy Spirit baptism? There are many persons who so believe. Is this fair to the context? Here are all the uses of this expression:

1. Luke 1:35, "He shall be *filled with the Holy Spirit,* even from his mother's womb." This is in reference to John the Baptist. This would seem to indicate the filling of the Holy Spirit is not here dependent upon the conscious co-operation of the person being filled.

2. Luke 1:41, "Elizabeth was *filled with the Holy Spirit,"* We are not here told she was baptized in the Holy Spirit. It would be presumptuous to claim such an experience for Elizabeth when it is not so described.

3. Luke 1:67, "Zachariah was *filled with the Holy Spirit."* What we have said of Elizabeth we say of her husband.

4. Luke 4:1, "Jesus *full of the Holy Spirit* was led by the Spirit into the wilderness." No one would think of describing this expression of the Holy Spirit as the baptism in the Holy Spirit.

5. Acts 4:8, "Peter, *filled with the Holy Spirit,"* Does this describe a condition Peter obtained at Pentecost and sustained the rest of his life? Or is the filling with the Holy Spirit dependent or contingent upon the faith, trust or reliance of

364

the person being filled? Whatever the answer is to these questions this verse does not describe another case of Holy Spirit baptism.

6. Acts 4:31, Speaking of "their company" to which Peter and John returned after their trial before the council. Following the united prayer we read these words of "their company": "They were all *filled with the Holy Spirit*, and they spake the word of God with boldness." The first consideration would be to understand who was included in this experience. The text describes them as "their company". Are we to believe this refers to the other ten apostles? Or a larger group of disciples? At whatever juncture we would not mistake this expression for what happened on Pentecost or in the house of Cornelius. We shall discuss this passage in detail in a later section.

We could list the rest of the places in the New Testament where the expression "filled with the Holy Spirit" occurs. They are: (7) Acts 6:3, (8) 6:5, (9) 7:55, (10) 9:17, (11) 11:24, (12) 13:9, 10, (13) 13:52, (14) Ephesians 5:18. In *none* of these references do we have mention made of speaking in tongues or *any other* miraculous manifestation such as those associated with the baptism in the Holy Spirit. What is the conclusion of the whole matter? *The expression, "filled with the Holy Spirit", describes a condition and or an experience different than the baptism in the Holy Spirit. It does describe the baptism in the Holy Spirit but it does also describe another condition. All who were baptized in the Holy Spirit were filled with the Holy Spirit, but not all who were filled with the Holy Spirit were/are baptized in the Holy Spirit.*

C. *What Does It Mean To Me?* We refer you to our thoughts on pages 45 to 52 in *Volume One.* We do believe He "gave some to be apostles" for a special purpose and the baptism in the Holy Spirit equipped them for this purpose. To be the spokesmen on behalf of Christ they must have infallible expression; this they received by the baptism in the Holy Spirit. We believe it is patently plain that the "tongues" spoken were the languages of the people present.

D. *How Can I Share It?* Surely we do need to share the teaching of the importance and work of the office of the apostles. The loose application of Acts 2:4 to everyone and anyone has led to all kinds of confusion. Let's get an in-depth understanding of the total circumstance.

7. "And it shall be in the last days, saith God, I will *pour forth of my Spirit* upon all flesh: and your sons and daughters shall prophesy, and your young men shall see visions, and your old men shall dream dreams." 2:17

A. *What Does It Say?* Since we have discussed this passage in both of our books, ACTS MADE ACTUAL p. 42 and THE CHURCH IN THE BIBLE, pp. 26-32, as well as in Volume One of THE POWER OF THE HOLY SPIRIT, pp. 45-52, we refer the reader to these sources. Suffice it to say here: (1) Peter plainly states that what was happening on Pentecost was a fulfillment of Joel's prophecy. What right do we have to expect such prophecy to be fulfilled over and over again? Is there some indication in the words of Peter or Joel that we could expect a repeat fulfillment? What about the reference to "all flesh"? What about the reference to "sons and daughters and handmaids prophesying"? We answer: *a.* "All flesh" refers to the whole human race (i.e. Jews and Gentiles —the only persons present on Pentecost were Jews). In a strictly literal sense, we cannot find a fulfillment on Pentecost. "All flesh" was *not* present to receive the "pouring out" of the Holy Spirit. When did "all flesh" receive the Holy Spirit? The first Gentiles to receive the Holy Spirit were those in the house of Cornelius. We have already discussed the impossibility of using this case as a general example. We, of course, understand that Peter was enabled to speak the gospel to the house of Cornelius only because he had been baptized in the Holy Spirit on Pentecost (i.e. he had infallible guidance from the Holy Spirit as a consequence of the immersion of his spirit in the Holy Spirit). We need to remember the spirits of the apostles were immersed in the Holy Spirit on Pentecost and *stayed immersed* as long as they exercised trusting faith. *b.* Who were the *sons* and *daughters* and *handmaids* who prophesied? Please, please read the Acts account as well as all other New Testament references to the gift of prophecy. Point out an example of women praying for and receiving the gift of prophecy and we will gladly concede the point. We have no other means of impartation than the "laying on of the hands of the apostles". We have cases where the gift of prophecy was exercised, such as Philip's four virgin daughters, in which case, we have no reference as to how they obtained this gift. We *do* know they were associated with Peter and John and Paul and it is very possible the hands of the apostles were laid upon them. We *know* supernatural powers were granted through the hands of the apostles. We *do not know* any other means of obtaining these powers. We have *no* example of others obtaining such powers by prayer or through the hands of any others than the apostles. (There is no exception in the case of Annias and Paul in Acts 9:12 for this has a reference to the salvation of Paul and not to a subsequent experience). As we have said time and again, we believe every Christian should be "filled with the Holy Spirit", but in the absence of any reference to supernatural powers in the several examples of persons who *were* filled with the Holy Spirit (see Acts 4:31; 13:52; Ephesians 5:18), we see no reason to claim supernatural powers on the single fact that we are indwelled and/or filled with the Holy Spirit.

B. *What Does It Mean?* Shall we take a phrase at a time for meaning? *"It shall be in the last days, saith God"* is a reference to the period of time in which we now live. The whole study of every reference to "the last days" is too detailed here to discuss (we refer you to one of our BIBLE STUDY TEXTBOOKS for help on this subject — see MINOR PROPHETS by Paul Butler, pp. 84-90). Suffice it to say that we have been in "the last days" since Pentecost, and will be until Jesus comes again. What is here described is to happen during the period from Pentecost to the end of time. *"I shall pour forth my Spirit upon all flesh."* We know the Holy Spirit is not some type of fluid. Why then the expression "poured forth" or "pour forth"? There are several possible answers: (1) The suggestion of anointing seems to be a part of this. Oil was poured out upon those being initiated into an office, particularly, priests were "poured upon" as they entered their office. Are we to understand that at the beginning of God's acceptance of both Jews on Pentecost and the Gentiles at Caesarea that as they entered the priesthood of believers; and the Lord was anointing them for the office by granting them the Holy Spirit? It would seem reasonable inasmuch as the Holy Spirit is spoken of as the element of anointing at the beginning of our Lord's ministry (Acts 10:38). Perhaps such an expression as "poured forth" used to describe His coming or advent does indeed relate to the purpose of anointing in the beginning of our office as priests unto God as well as the beginning of His work among the believers. (2) "Poured forth" perhaps refers to the suddenness of His coming—a figure of speech in which the effect is described as the cause—as if a quantity of water or some other element were poured upon one. The sudden sensation resulting could well describe the feelings of those who were suddenly endowed with these supernatural powers. The effect could best be described with the words "poured upon". (3) Perhaps since the Holy Spirit came from heaven or from above and the sensation was first felt in the head, "poured out" would be an appropriate description.

We have discussed, we hope adequately, the expression "all Flesh"—meaning both Jew and Gentile.

8. "And your sons and your daughters shall prophecy, and your young men shall see visions and your old men shall dream dreams."

A. *What Does It Say?*

If we are to imagine all 120 disciples as being involved in the baptism in the Holy Spirit, (i.e. in the upper room), then we could also imagine some young men—some young women—even a few old men as being present among the 120. (But even if this were true, we do not believe *any* of them were Gentiles—thus *all* flesh was *not* involved.) But are we right in believing all 120 were involved

369

in the Holy Spirit immersion? To whom did Jesus promise this experience? (Acts 1:5) *To the apostles,* (cf Luke 24:49). What purpose would be served in immersing the minds of all 120 in the Holy Spirit? See our arguments for saying *only* the 12 apostles were present for the baptism of the Holy Spirit on Pentecost. (Vol. I page 50-52) If this did not happen on Pentecost when did the sons and daughters prophecy? When did the young men see visions and the old men dream dreams? We believe the power to grant these visions, prophecy, and dreams was given to the apostles by the baptism in the Holy Spirit and they in turn, or because they were thus endowed, layed their hands on certain woman, men and old men and granted these experiences to them through the Holy Spirit who was already present in them. Perhaps those in Samaria could be a case in point. When Peter and John came to Samaria to lay their hands upon certain of the believers it was for the "falling on power" of the Holy Spirit. (Acts 8:12-16) These believers were thus equipped to carry on the teaching and preaching in the approaching absence of Philip.

The young men we would equate with preachers of today and the old men as elders in the churches. Philip and Stephen were two young men with vision and the ability to preach and teach, not to mention the power to perform signs and wonders. (Acts 6:8) How were these two young men thus equipped? The hands of the apostles were laid upon them. (Acts 6:6) Certain older men were appointed in churches. (Acts 14:23) Could it not be that the figurative reference to "old men" in Acts 2:17 anticipates the supernaturally endowed elders of the apostolic church? The important point is the apostles were enabled because of the baptism in the Holy Spirit on Pentecost to thus equip these men.

B. *What Does It Mean?* If there ever was a time in the history of the Restoration Movement when we needed an understanding of the work of the Holy Spirit, it is *now!* We have sons and daughters, young men and handmaids, not to mention older men, all claiming to qualify as those who have visions and prophecy and have other supernatural gifts. What shall we say about these things? I would say there is a great deep hunger for reality and the sense of God's nearness in the hearts of some. This hunger is indeed in the heart of every humbly surrendered Christian; and *it shall be satisfied or it will dissipate and we will fall back into the world!* Form and declamation *will not* satisfy this hunger, only the power and presence of God Himself! Our people have no daily devotional life. I refer to a daily feeding of the heart upon God's Word and satisfying the longings of the heart before the throne of grace. Our people have little joy in their service, public or private. Almost no personal testimony of the delivering power of our Saviour is ever mentioned. Why? Because there is no personal meditation and no personal involvement in His Service.

C. & D. *What Does It Mean To Me? and How Can I Share It?*

No wonder we look elsewhere for His nearness and His reality! I have but little criticism for those who seek these spiritual experiences. I do not define these experiences as those who have them do. I believe they are seeking the power and presence of our dear Lord in the wrong way, (and I have given my reasons for so believing), but they are hungry. They are thirsty. They are also satisfied

371

that what they have found is His power and presence. What they claim goes beyond this. Has your daily devotion to the Lord produced a wondering, exhilarating, exciting sense of His nearness? *Isn't our God this real?* If so, why shouldn't we thus relate to Him? I would not at all define such a relationship as the gift of tongues or prophecy, etc, but rather as my human response to His overwhelming power, beauty, holiness, and nearness. Is there something wrong with tears, strong cryings and strivings as we rejoice or agonize with God in prayer? (These are not only words on paper. If they are only that, then they indeed are worse than nothing.) When we have experienced this season of prayer with Him, we do not claim some supernatural gifts, but we do come away from such a place as Moses returned from the mount.

9. ". . . Having received of the Father the promise of the Holy Spirit, he hath poured forth this, which ye see and hear." (Acts 2:33)

A. *What Does It Say?* Jesus received something from the Father. What was it? Evidently the advent of the Holy Spirit was so well known to our Lord as to be expected at a certain time. John 7:39 is a key verse in understanding this text. (Please read it.) Jesus promised "Rivers of living water" as a consequence of the Holy Spirit's presence in the believer, but one qualifying condition is mentioned: ". . . the Spirit was not yet given because Jesus was not yet glorified." When was Jesus glorified? Jesus said ". . . Father, glorify thou me with thine own self with the glory which I had with thee before the world was." (John 17:5) Jesus returned from the mount called Olivet to the "glory which He had with the Father"-and having sat down at the right hand of the majesty on high, He was glorified, and we believe, coronated or crowned king of kings and Lord of Lords. His first royal act was to send the Holy Spirit. The results of this act were the occurrences on Pentecost. We really do not know why the Son seems to be something less than the Father. (i.e., in this relationship of giving and receiving). Perhaps the word "less" is unfortunate. Could we say that here was the last act of the Son's condescension just before He returned to being equal with the Father? (Phil. 2:5-9) Please notice that it was Jesus, not God who sent, or "poured forth", the Holy Spirit. This is in fulfillment of the promise of John the Baptist. Speaking of Jesus, John said: "*He* shall baptise you in the Holy Spirit." (Matt, 3:11, 12) The apostles were anointed and thus initiated into their office by the immersion of their minds in or with the Holy Spirit. This Jesus did for them.

B. *What Does It Mean?* Among other things this text would mean that John 20:22, 23 is a promise not an experience. (i.e., at the time it was spoken.) Jesus said to the apostles: ". . . as the Father hath sent me, even so send I you, and when He had said this, he breathed on them and saith unto them, 'Receive ye the Holy Spirit. Whosoever sins ye forgive, they are forgiven; whosesoever sins ye retain, they are retained."

We conclude Jesus was speaking in John 20:22, 23 of the day of Pentecost and was here preparing the apostles for the experience. This would seem to be confirmed by what would happen upon receiving the Holy Spirit. If the apostles were endowed in the upper room by Jesus with the power to forgive and retain sins what was the purpose of Pentecost? We might also add they were sent out into the world "even as the Father had sent Him" immediately after Pentecost-but *not before.* This text means to us that we understand Jesus is receiving the fulfillment of a promise made to Him by the Father. (John 14:16; 26) The Holy Spirit is Christ's gift from the Father to the believer. He is "the other Comforter" or the One to take the place of our Lord. (i.e., in His absence) This began on Pentecost and Peter is here explaining the occurrence.

C. *How Does This Relate To Me?* A number of our comments already made have a personal application. Above all we are so glad the Comforter has come! We look to this text as a historic promise of when He came and who sent Him.

D. *How Can I Share It?* We do not wish to become redundant but it *is* so important that we teach men everywhere and as often as possible when and where and how the Holy Spirit was given. Most especially, should we teach the full meaning of Pentecost.

10. "And Peter said unto them, Repent ye, and be baptized everyone of you in the name of Jesus Christ unto the remission of your sins; and ye shall receive the gift of the Holy Spirit." (Acts 2:38)

A. *What Does It Say?* We want to give this text as full a treatment as possible for these questions are a part of it: (1) Is the gift of the Holy Spirit the Holy Spirit Himself or some gift from the Holy Spirit?

(2) Are we to understand that the Holy Spirit literally indwelt the 3,000 converts, or was this a figure of speech referring to some other form of indwelling? (3) Were there miraculous powers associated with this "gift of the Holy Spirit"? We shall first of all proceed with a word by word examination of the text to be sure we know as

closely as possible what is said, look at it: *and ye shall receive the gift of the Holy Spirit.*"

Brother Chester A. Williamson has written a splendid treatise on the subject of the indwelling Spirit. We quote extensively from him in our treatment here: "In discussing the meaning of the text from a Greek analysis Thomas B. Warren, chairman, department of Bible, Freed-Hardeman College says: ". . . either appositional genitive, thus making the statement mean 'the gift which is the Holy Spirit' or the objective genitive, thus making the statement mean 'the gift of the Holy Spirit himself'. In either case it is the Holy Spirit himself that is given to literally dwell in the heart of the believer." Brother Williamson continues: "I think it is unnecessary to paraphrase the verse in order to make an objective genitive out of the phrase. In the English language, however, 'Holy Spirit' would be classified as in the objective case because it is in apposition with the noun 'gift' which is the direct object of the verb, 'shall receive.'

"Acts 2:33 contains the same Greek construction as Acts 2:38: 'promise' (accusative case), 'of the Holy Spirit' (genitive case). Yet this promise is not 'a promise which the Holy Spirit had made'; Jesus had received it 'of the Father.'

" 'This, which ye see and hear' definitely links the promise with the prophecy mentioned in Acts 2:16,17. Note that this came from God ('saith God'), and refers to the Spirit of God ('my Spirit'), in Greek, 'from of the Spirit of Me' (making the *me* very emphatic).

"Acts 2:39 is another verse in the immediate context which must be considered. Whatever the scope of the promise referred to there, the implied promise of remission of sins for all believers who repented and were baptized and the direct promise of the gift of the Holy Spirit on the same terms must be included.

"As indicated by the quotation from Robertson and the use of the same Greek construction in Acts 2:33, the use of the genitive case in 'the gift of the Holy Spirit' does not answer the question for us as to whether the expression means, 'the gift consisting in the Holy Spirit' or 'the gift which the Holy Spirit gives.' We must look to the Scriptures for the answer.

". . . Prophecies in the Old Testament had dealt with God's 'pouring out of the Spirit' (making Him abundantly available to all believers), Proverbs 1:23; Isaiah 32:15; Joel 2:28,29; and to His imparting the Spirit, personally, to believers, Isaiah 44:3; 63:11; Ezekiel 11:19; 36:26,27.
"Jesus had spoken of the Holy Spirit as a gift, Luke 11:13; and of *receiving the Holy Spirit,* John 20:22. In John 14:16, He says, 'And I will pray the Father, and He shall *give you another Comforter,* that He may abide with you forever.'

"His death, burial, resurrection, ascension, and glorification, referred to in John 7:39, were just about to take place, and then *the Holy Spirit would be given.*

"This time, He is speaking only to His apostles, and not to the largest assembly connected with the Feast of Tabernacles. But the *forever* of verse 16, throughout which the Holy Spirit is to 'dwell with' — and *'be in'* disciples would seem to extend throughout the entire Christian Dispensation.

"In the Old Testament, when God gave commands which were to be in effect throughout the entire Mosaic dispensation and then to cease, the commands were said to be *'forever throughout your generations.'*

"But no such limiting term is used in connection with the word 'forever,' in John 14:16. According to other Scripture indications, this dispensation is not to be followed by another, and the abiding presence of the Holy Spirit is not to be withdrawn even at the end of it.

". . . But T. W. Brents leaves no room for doubt. Following are a few quotations from his great book, *The Gospel Plan of Salvation* (published 1874): 'The phrase 'the gift of the Holy Ghost' occurs Acts 2:38 and 10:45, and in both places must be understood as equivalent to 'the Holy Spirit as a gift,' yet we are persuaded that the same measure of the Spirit is not alluded to in both places.'

" . . . Regarding the promise of Jesus, recorded in John 14:16,17, Brents said: 'That this was not a figurative, but a literal in-dwelling of the Holy Spirit is plain . . . they were all filled with the Holy Spirit . . . ' Acts 2:4. It will scarcely be said that the disciples were only figuratively filled with the Holy Spirit . . . Nay, it was literally in them, as the Saviour promised them it should be.' "

11. "Repent ye therefore, and turn again, that your sins may be blotted out, that so there may come *seasons of refreshing from the presences of the Lord.*" (Acts 3:19)

    A. *What Does It Say?* Even the casual reader would not fail to see a similarity between this reference and Acts 2:38. (i.e., in the context.) Peter is preaching in both references. He is addressing many of the same people in both references. He is calling for response and making a promise in both examples. Notice an interesting parallel:

Acts 2:38—Peter said:	Acts 3:19—Peter said:
1. Repent	1. Repent
2. and be baptized	2. and turn again
3. for the remission of your sins	3. that your sins may be blotted out
4. ye shall receive the gift of the Holy Spirit.	4. there may come seasons of refreshing from the presence of the Lord.

We could equate "the seasons of refreshing from the presence of the Lord" with the gift of the

Holy Spirit" without doing violence to the text. Indeed if the other expressions are parallel, then this one is necessarily so.

B. *What Does It Mean?* If this expression has any reference to the Holy Spirit, His presence is intended to produce within the Christian a *cooling, pleasant sense of God's nearness.* Are we talking of an emotional sensation? We surely are! How could we experience "seasons of refreshing" without our emotions being involved? Please remember; if the Jews on Solomon's porch were the recipients of the blotting out of sins then they would also be of this boon of happiness which the law could never give. "The old legalism of Pharisasism knew nothing about such seasons, for all work-righteousness is like the drive, heat, and sweat of slavery." (*Lenski*)

C. *What Does It Mean To Me?* Perhaps we should say—"What it *should* or *could* mean to me." The gift of the Holy Spirit was intended to produce an exhilaration—a joy of inner-satisfaction which could be described as "seasons of refreshing"—but somehow such has never really been the experience of so many of us. Why? We do not expect it or believe it! The fruit of His presence in our lives *is* "joy" and "peace" but somehow we fail to allow this to be more than words.

D. *How Can I Share It?* We can't share what we do not personally possess. It can be much more. Pause a moment. Meditate on the thought that at this moment the wonderful living Christ abides in you! Isn't that an exciting thought; a thought? It *is* to me. I exclaim "praise God for His infinite mercy", and the corresponding sense or emotion of refreshment and satisfaction is mine! The Holy Spirit is only awaiting as a latent presence in our body. Our willingness to verbalize our belief is the key to the release of His expression of joy and peace. What a precious thought to share with others. I share it with you. Will you share it?

12. "Then Peter, *filled with the Holy Spirit* said unto them, 'Ye rulers of the people, and elders, . . .'" (Acts 4:8)

A. *What Does It Say?* We do need to read the context of this one verse. Peter and John are arrested and taken before the council for preaching the message of the resurrected Lord. This is the first expression of Peter upon being charged or questioned by the chief priest. We need to see this experience as a very literal fulfillment of Matthew 10:19, 20. (cf. Luke 21:12-17) The Holy Spirit is about to give him the words to speak.

B. *What Does It Mean?* In this connection we need to understand the phrase: *"filled with the Holy Spirit"*. Are we to understand Peter was always "filled with the Holy Spirit" and here is just a simple reference to that fact; or that upon this particular occasion he was "filled with the Holy Spirit" so as to enable him to give the answer he did? A third possibility suggests itself which seems to be even more plausible: The historian Luke, recounting the incident, reminds us that here is the fulfillment of the promise of Jesus. Cf. Matthew 10:19, 20 and in Luke's former treatise, Luke 21:12-17.

C. *What Does It Mean To Me?* We cannot imagine the Holy Spirit exercising this power without the willing co-operation of the man being used. Peter was "filled with the Holy Spirit" but only because he wanted to be, only because he was willing to be. We do not expect the same infallible guidance from the Holy Spirit as that granted to Peter but we

know unless we are willing, the Holy Spirit cannot and will not manifest His fruit in our lives.
We want to add the thought: unless we put ourselves out in the stream of humanity and face the
Pharisees and Sadducees of our day, we shall have
no occasion in which we will need the power or
the divine enablement of the Spirit.

Whatever grace and strength He can give us in
our inward man (Eph. 3:16) is promised "as we
go." Jesus' promise of "lo, I am with you always"
was conditional: "go—and lo, I am with you."

D. *How Can I Share It?* We can share this thought in
two ways: (1) With the army of the Lord—no
soldier can feel the presence and approval of his
commander who does not get out into the hand-to-
hand, person-to-person exchange. This thought we
must share with every soldier. (2) We need to
allow this truth to move us to its fulfillment in
our own lives.

13. "O Lord . . . Why *by the Holy Spirit,* by the mouth
of our Father David, thy servant, didst say." (Acts
4:25)

A. *What Does It Say?* Please read the context. Peter
and John return to "their company" from the trial
before the Sanhedrin. It is "their company" who
prays this prayer. Perhaps someone present gives
words to the thought of all. "They all lift up
their voice with one accord and say"—What is
said? Among other thoughts is the plain statement
of inspiration on the part of David. It was the
Holy Spirit who gave David the words in the second
Psalm. It is redundant to talk about the Holy
Spirit giving thoughts without words. How are
thoughts expressed without words? Are not the
words first formed in the mind before they are
written?

B. *What Does It Mean?* This prayer is an example to us in the area of faith and devotion. (See ACTS MADE ACTUAL pages 69-71) We want to emphasize here the one point of inspiration for the writings of David, indeed for the writing of all the Old Testament. (cf. II Peter 1:21) We are not at all unaware that many critics (some of them conservative) reject the phrase "by the Holy Spirit" upon which we are now commenting. Needless to say, we have been persuaded by the same evidence used by the translators of the American Standard New Testament. We commend to you a study of the book THY WORD IS TRUTH by Edward Young. We have not found a better discussion of the subject of inspiration.

C. *What Does It Mean To Me?* We need to share the same unshakable confidence in the Scriptures. This is the solid foundation upon which all of our faith rests. A clear definition of inspiration is a big need in every Christian's heart. The hazy definitions of inspiration of our day only underline this need.

D. *How Can I Share It?* You can organize a class in your church and teach the reasons why you believe the Bible to be the inspired Word of God. In the midst of this discussion, you need to clearly define what you believe about the Holy Spirit and the Bible. Here are some books to help you with this class:

1. *The Evidences of God in an Expanding Universe*, John Clover Monsma, Toronto: Longmans, 1958.
2. *The Bible and Modern Research*, A. Rendle Short, Marshall, Morgan and Scott, 1931.
3. *Therefore Stand*, Wilbur M. Smith, Boston: Wilde, 1945.
4. *Modern Science and the Christian Faith*, A Symposium, Van Kampen Press, Wheaton, Illinois, 1950.
5. *Archaeology and Bible History*, Joseph P. Free, Wheaton, Illinois: Van Kampen Press, 1950.

6. *The Monuments and the Old Testament*, Ira M. Price, Judson Press, 1925.
7. *The Five Books of Moses*, O. T. Allis, The Presbyterian and Reformed Publishing Co., 1943.
8. *The Basis Of Christian Faith*, Floyd E. Hamilton, Harper and Row Co., 1963.

13. "And when they had prayed, the place was shaken wherein they were gathered together; and they were all filled with the Holy Spirit, and they spake the Word of God with boldness." (Acts 4:31)

A. *What Does It Say?* We need to decide to whom the pronoun "they" refers. *"They* were all filled with the Holy Spirit." Who is involved here? Verse 23 of this chapter tells us Peter and John returned to "their own company" which means either the rest of the ten apostles or to a larger group—which undoubtedly included the apostles. It was this "company" who were "filled with the Holy Spirit."

B. *What Does It Mean?* Here is an example of persons filled with the Holy Spirit and with no reference made to unusual miraculous manifestations. The earthquake was external and not personal. What we mean is: no one spoke in tongues, prophesied, or indicated personal supernatural powers. All who were "filled" "spake the Word of God with boldness." Are we to understand, the urgency of the circumstance, the prayer meeting, the earthquake, all contributed to the filling of the Holy Spirit or that such persons were continually filled with the Holy Spirit and this is but a reference to that fact? We could say the ability to speak the Word of God came from the Holy Spirit, (i.e. the supernatural gift of "knowledge" was involved and such a message proceeded from the Holy Spirit); but then we remember Acts 8:4 where reference is made to all the Christians in Jerusalem, who upon being scattered by persecution, "went everywhere preaching the Word." We then would be inclined to say that "speaking the Word of God with boldness" was the personal testimony of these people. However, we have no certain conclusions to offer for there is no evidence to indicate what those conclusions should be.

C. *What Does It Mean To Me?* We need to pause and consider carefully *all* the circumstances: (1) We *do not* know just who is involved in this expression. (2) We *do not* know if the speaking or preaching of the Word of God was supernaturally induced or not. (3) Such a "filling" of the Holy Spirit would be completely apart from the New Testament for the New Testament obviously was not yet complete. (i.e. they were filled by and with the Holy Spirit Himself). (4) Such a filling seemed to react on their emotional or sensible natures. What was this reaction? It must have been: a sense of His precious nearness, His supreme power, a reaction of courage or holy boldness. We believe from what we have studied earlier that to be filled with the Holy Spirit is to be filled with our Lord; but such in this case could not have been a psychological experience produced by reading the New Testament.

D. *How Can I Share It?* Surely there is nothing more meaningful to share than the thought or truth of being filled with the Holy Spirit. Can we say we are filled with Him?; or that we are being filled with Him?; or that we shall be filled?; or were? What shall we share? Please, please, notice the lack of any dramatic supernatural manifestations. We all need and want boldness. We all have Him and want to be filled with Him. When shall it be true of us? Only when it is, can we share it. We cannot claim the persons here involved were especially or unusually prepared for this experience (or shall we call it a condition?) Perhaps we could eliminate the whole subject by convincing ourselves the apostles were the only ones here involved; but we are not so convinced and will not avoid other references in this same book that speak of persons like ourselves who were "filled with the Holy Spirit." (Acts 6:3, 13:52)

15. "But Peter said "Ananias, why hath Satan filled thy heart to lie to the Holy Spirit, and to keep back a part of the price of the land." (Acts 5:3)

A. *What Does It Say?* There are two or three actions of the Holy Spirit in this text: (1) The Holy Spirit must have enabled Peter to know the condition of the heart of Ananias. This could have either been a part of the ability granted to Peter in the Holy Spirit baptism or "the discerning of Spirits" as in I Corinthians 12:10. We much prefer the thought that Peter was able through or because of the Holy Spirit baptism to read the heart of Ananias. (2) The Holy Spirit was in the body of Ananias and his wife Sapphira as a result of their becoming Christians. (Roman 8:9) (3) The Holy Spirit is a very real person to whom a lie can be told or upon whom deception can be attempted. Ananias could have been as responsive to the Holy Spirit as he was to Satan. His heart could have been filled with the Spirit instead of the evil one.

B. *What Does It Mean?* It means we are always susceptible to two divine beings: Satan and the Holy Spirit, both of whom can fill our hearts; both who have a power to exert in our lives. The lie or scheme for deception must have been made by Satan. It is a fearful fact that the father of lies has not ceased his work since that day. We ought to learn also that the presence of the Holy Spirit is not an automatic insurance against sin. We must cooperate with Him. In the same regard, the presence of Satan is not prima facto evidence we shall sin. We must cooperate or he is powerless. We are so glad to say again; "Greater is He who is within you, than he who is within the world." (I John 4:4)

C. *What Does It Mean To Me?* We have already indicated a number of applications in this text. We might say death suffered as a result of this lie has not ceased being the penalty. Death is separation. (James 2:26) There are three deaths to die: (1) The physical death of the body, the separation of the spirit from the body. (2) The eternal death in hell, the separation of the Spirit from God. (Revelation 21:8). (3) The death "while we yet live", (I Timothy 5:6) the separation of the human spirit from the Holy Spirit by sin. When we willfully attempt to "continue in sin that grace might abound," we produce a sense of separation. A very real death takes place in our heart. May we be able to sing with real clear meaning, "nothing between my soul and the Saviour."

D. *How Can I Share It?* There is no thought any more needed by the members of our various congregations than this one. In this connection we might add here: *how* we repent of our sin in a manner to insure forsaking of it is just as important as discovering and being convinced of it. True repentance is a deep persuasion, a full involvement of mind (and emotions) resulting in a real change. We have a choice of "die daily" (I Cor 15:31) to sin's allurements, the devil's lies, or die to the blessed presence of the Holy Spirit. Separate yourself from sin or you will separate yourself from the Spirit of God.

16. "But Peter said unto her, How is it that ye have agreed together to try the Spirit of the Lord?" (Acts 5:9)

A. *What Does It Say?* We need to understand very carefully and fully the word "try" or "tempt" as it is here used. Peter exercises further power of discernment and gives us an insight into the house of Ananias and Sapphira. They had actually decided upon a test or experiment into the reality of the Holy Spirit. It is as if they said; "we will set up a circumstance in which we will find out if the Holy Spirit is all He seems to be." What a daring, unreasonable thing to do! Did they realize the danger of such a venture? The quality of God was surely of an inferior sort in their mind. In the negative sense this test was all wrong.

B. *What Does It Mean?* Have you ever wondered why God was so severe in His response to the actions of these two? Pause a moment to reflect on what is involved. It is the responsibility of man to God. Essentially we are asking: does God care what I do, either good or bad? This experiment is asking another question: "if God knows, does God care personally." All of this could be and was psychologically involved but it did not minimize or change their lie and deception.

C. *What Does It Mean To Me?* Perhaps it has occurred to you, as it has to me, that God would be just as responsive in a positive experience as He was in this negative one. Shall we put Him to the test? In what area shall it be? Let us agree together to try the Spirit of God as to: (1) a character defect such as a certain touchiness or an enlarged ego that sets off a burst of temper—This has been a problem for a very long time. Since the Holy Spirit is in the character-developing business, He could help in this. Will He? Ask Him and see! It has been my experience to find prayer for character development more immediately answered than any other BUT, since *we are to change*, God puts us in a position (in answer to our prayers) where we *can* choose and change. We have the Divine "Standby" ready to reinforce our feeble resistance of Satan. He will provide "the way of escape" (I Corinthians • 10:13) but you must ask for it and take it! Try Him and see—He is the giver of life! (2) In changing an impossible set of circumstances in human relations, every local church is either in such a circumstance, or has been, or will be. Only the moving agent in God's work of providence can handle this problem; we refer to the Holy Spirit. If we actualy, in faith, involve the Spirit of God and put Him to the test, some wonderful changes will begin to take place. We ought never to forget our changed attitude toward the same circumstances is also the Spirit's own work!

D. *How Can I Share It?* Surely this is obvious in what has already been said. In this experience the rule is: "we most truly have what we most fully give away."

17. "We are witnesses to these things: and so is the Holy Spirit, whom God hath given to them that obey Him." (Acts 5:32)

A. *What Does It Say?* Peter, speaking on behalf of all the apostles, is making a defense before the Sanhedrin. The council has charged them "not to speak at all nor to teach in the name of Jesus." They had "filled Jerusalem" with their teachings. Peter is now telling why they so taught and preached. "We *must* obey God rather than men." We have personally seen Him and heard Him after His passion. It would be criminal not to tell this good news. Peter states that there was someone else who also beheld the crucifixion, burial and resurrection of Jesus. He was the Holy Spirit! This unusual witness is given by God to all who obey God. Peter started by stating the necessity of obeying God. He concludes by this marvelous benefit or gift who comes as a consequence of this obedience. The thought is generic in the realm of obedience (i.e. the promise of the Spirit's presence and witness is consequent upon an attitude of total submission to God), but it could also be specific. Only those who accept our Lord in repentance of sin and baptism for the remission of sin can expect the Holy Spirit as a result of their obedience. (Acts 2:38) Does this text say the Holy Spirit is given to the obedient ones as a witness in them and through them? Please, please *think* before you reject this thought.

B. *What Does It Mean?* If this text means anything, it means we have the Holy Spirit Himself as a gift from God as a result of our obedience. What is a witness? Only an observer? "One who testifies for another" is a witness. The apostles were arrested and imprisoned for witnessing. They "filled Jerusalem" with their teaching. The New Testament is the report of the witness of the Holy Spirit. He has borne His witness through the inspired writers and speakers. Is that all?

C. *What Does It Mean To Me?* The whole idea of the Holy Spirit being an advocate or lawyer for the facts of the gospel is a new one to me. Are we to understand these two thoughts separately? That is: (1) We have the Holy Spirit through our obedience to the gospel, (2) He, the Holy Spirit, bore His witness through the apostles and other inspired men in the first century? Is there some way in which He becomes a witness in and through those who receive Him as a gift? We all freely admit He spoke through Peter and John, enabling them to witness. Did Peter and John intend to contrast only themselves and the Sanhedrin council? Were they saying: "We have obeyed God and have the Holy Spirit. You haven't and do not. We witness because of our obedience and the Holy Spirit"? But if they meant this then the converse would also be true. If the council obeyed God and accepted Jesus as their Messiah and Saviour, then they would receive the Holy Spirit *as a witness.*

D. *How Can I Share It?* What shall we share? The wonderful promise: if we obey God, initially in repentance and baptism, we shall receive the Holy Spirit. Shall we also share the thought that He will witness through us to the lost world of the salvation facts: "He died for our sins, was buried, and rose again"? (I Corinthians 15:1-4) Shall we tell others that when we went in obedience to the command of our Lord we found the assistance of the Holy Spirit in strengthening our inward man (Ephesians 3:16) and the sense of "lo, I am with you always" as we opened our mouth for Him? If you believe it, you will. If you do not, you will **not.**

18. "Look ye out therefore, brethren, from among you, seven men of good report, full of the Spirit and of wisdom, whom we may appoint over this business." (Acts 6:3)

A. *What Does It Say?* This text says several very surprising things: (1) There were several persons in the congregation or community of believers in Jerusalem who were "filled with the Holy Spirit." (and of wisdom and of faith) We cannot imagine such abilities of faith and wisdom were supernatural gifts such as those mentioned in I Corinthians

12:1ff. We say this because the task was serving tables and supernatural faith would hardly be required. This, of course, is only our human reasoning about the subject. If we are to say through the laying on of the hands of the apostles, these seven men were granted supernatural powers, then such laying on of hands must have preceded the ceremony of 6:6. We are always on inconclusive ground when we argue from silence and use such silence to serve our own purposes. (2) It seems more significant that such men could be identified as "full of the Holy Spirit and of wisdom." This presupposes a personal association among the believers much more personal than we usually have. A recognition of the influences of the Holy Spirit upon the human personality was also well enough known as to be identified.

B. *What Does It Mean?* It means being filled with the Holy Spirit was such a common experience (should we call it "condition" or "relationship"?) that many persons were involved. It also means the characteristics of the Holy Spirit were well enough known as to be recognized in the personality of the disciples of our Lord. Would it be possible today to select several persons who would be described as "full of the Holy Spirit"? If so, just what would be the identifying characteristics? The lives of Philip and Stephen as examples should be most carefully studied as those who qualify for this grand quality.

C. *What Does It Mean To Me?* This has always been a somewhat elusive but extremely desirable quality. It should now be much more in the realm of definition and reality. We know much more clearly than ever before what it means to have Him. Could we condense this definition by saying: we are so in love with our wonderful Lord that He dominates and overrides our every thought? Jesus has become "all" and "in all" to us. The Holy Spirit was sent not to glorify Himself but our Saviour. This He can do when we visualize Him as "Christ in us", as "the other Jesus" *living in us*. There are two constant needs just here: (1) constant association with our Lord through the gospel accounts, and (2) a constant, conscious effort to allow Him to shape our thinking. All of the, sometimes only sentimental gospel songs, will take on a depth and power of meaning we never before knew possible.

D. *How Can I Share It?* "What I have that give I thee"—these are the words of Peter to the lame man at the Gate Beautiful (Acts 3:1 ff). They are also our words to the lame in the precincts of God's temple today. If we feel many are indeed "lame" in the area of spiritual power we must remember only what we ourselves have can be shared with anyone else. Do we want others to be filled with the Holy Spirit? A good sample (example) is the beginning of help.

19. ". . . and they chose Stephen, a man full of faith and of the Holy Spirit, . . ." (Acts 6:5)

A. *What Does It Say?* This a mere statement of fact. We have discussed in the 17th reference all of the implications here involved. We can find nothing more to say of the expression "full of . . . the Holy Spirit."

B. *What Does It Mean?* Please read what we have said earlier. But we *must* add: a character study of Stephen is surely in order just here. What being "filled with the Holy Spirit" meant to Stephen is best seen in his life. Please read all of the sixth and seventh chapters of Acts once again and mark the qualities of Stephen. Here are a few qualities we observed. We might call this study "What being filled with the Holy Spirit did for Stephen": (1) He was full of "grace and power" (Acts 6:8). We could talk about the surface fact that being filled with the Holy Spirit meant he also had the hands of the apostles laid upon him (Acts 6:6) and because of this he was enabled to perform these "signs and wonders" among the people. Just why the apostles would thus supernaturally equip these men when their task was "serving tables" we do not know. Either we do not understand all the implications of the phrase "serve tables" or the laying on of the hands of the apostles was only for the purpose of setting them into the work. We prefer the former thought. In close continual human relationships, there is a great need for God's compassionate insight. There must have been many words, thoughts, needs, and burdens shared with Stephen as he came into the home, a representative of the Lord with their only means of life. Are we to understand that the qualities he possessed as a person and a Christian (i.e. *wisdom, faith, grace*) were intensified by the Holy Spirit? We do not know, but we simply cannot believe the presence of the Holy Spirit will change anyone who does not want a change or can develop any quality of character without the person's willing desire to have it so. (2) We might call Stephen "God's full man" and point out the text says of him that he was full of (a) wisdom, (b) faith, (c) grace, (d) power, and all of these because he was full of the Holy Spirit. We are tempted to enlarge upon these points but this is not a homiletical treatment.

C. *What Does It Mean To Me?* The whole study of the life of Stephen can mean much to us: He was willing to serve in the lowest areas of life. He used what he had and the Holy Spirit increased it a hundred-fold. He was unashamed and unafraid to speak to those of his own synagogue. There must have been a heated exchange of scripture references as he discussed the Old Testament prophecies fulfilled in Jesus of Nazareth. He faced stubborn, deceitful, lying, ignorant men, and it was said of him: "he had the face of an angel." Under these conditions we usually do not come out with that description. Wasn't it the Holy Spirit who made the difference? Isn't He the source, the power, of transformation today?

D. *How Can I Share It?* God has a great desire to fill more men. He is looking for those whose hearts are turned toward Him. Perhaps we can help in the search by sharing this lesson from Stephen.

19, 20, & 22. "They were not able to withstand the wisdom and the Spirit by which he spake." (Acts 6:10) "Ye do always resist the Holy Spirit." (Acts 7:51) ". . . he, being full of the Holy Spirit, looked up steadfastly into heaven, and saw the glory of God, and Jesus standing on the right hand of God." (Acts 7:55)

20. A. *What Does It Say?* We have arranged these three references together because they are all words concerning Stephen. Stephen spoke to the synagogue of the Libertines under the impulse of the Holy Spirit. We do not know that he possessed the gift of prophecy or wisdom (Cf. I Corinthians 12:1-ff) but it is quite likely and surely appropriate. As we have earlier indicated; we would assume through the laying on of the hands of the apostles (6:6) such powers were imparted, at least such powers were given by this means elsewhere (Acts 19:1-6; 8:12-15). We have no indication Stephen prayed to receive such gifts. There was some form of debate, the arguments advanced by Stephen were under the immediate guidance of the Holy

Spirit. We would imagine reference to the Old Testament prophecies concerning the Messiah were very prominent.

B. *What Does It Mean?* However well we are led by the Holy Spirit, however true our position might be, it is always possible to reject it. If some did it to Stephen, we should not expect less or different response from some people.

C. *What Does It Mean to Me?* We need to recognize that even under the immediate guidance of the Holy Spirit, it is sometimes right to speak to an unfavorable, even antagonistic audience. We need also to remember there were undoubtedly some who accepted the message.

D. *How Can I Share It?* Wisdom is the best use of knowledge. James tells us we should pray for it. This wisdom of James 1:5ff is not the supernatural gift of wisdom, but it is very much a part of God's provision for every Christian. This is no substitute for study. We must have knowledge before we ask for divine assistance in the use of it. May we move more and more men to be like Stephen.

21. A. *What Does It Say?* The subject of resisting the Holy Spirit is one that deserves careful thought. We believe the particular resistance in this text was a refusal of the application of the Spirit's word. Stephen had just presented the Divine evidence from Hebrew history. Those listening refused it. How careful we need to be in this area. These men did not know it was the Holy Spirit they resisted. Conscious of it or not, whether you believe it or not you are doing it; resisting the Holy Spirit.

B. *What Does It Mean?* We catch a real hint of help in the phrase "as your fathers did, so do ye" (Acts 7:51b). A thoughtful rereading of chapter seven of Acts will indicate the action of "the fathers." In the immediate circumstance of "resisting the Holy Spirit", there is always a way to justify or rationalize our actions. Consider the case of Joseph and his brothers or Moses and the water from the rock.

C. *What Does It Mean To Me?* Any message from the Spirit's word should be tenderly, thoughtfully considered, not to teach a lesson to someone else, not to only find out what is said, but to ask ourselves: "What wilt thou have *me* to do?" When will we become aware of the fact that God's directions for our lives can never be fulfilled when we resist?

D. *How Can I Share It?* Read a passage of the Spirit's word to some one of your friends and explain the possibilities of either resisting or receiving—of being "cut to the heart" or broken of heart.

22. A. *What Does It Say?* The thought is clear that Stephen was on the occasion "filled with the Holy Spirit", but are we to understand he was always full of the Holy Spirit and we are here only reminded of this fact?

B. *What Does It Mean?* Stephen spoke the whole message of chapter seven under the direction of the Holy Spirit, but now, just before his death, God grants him, through the Spirit, a glimpse of the glory prepared for him. Are we to understand the Holy Spirit moved within Stephen in such a manner as to fill him or to so suffuse his mind and heart that this vision was granted him? If this is the thought here, what is the thought of 6:3 where Stephen was "full of the Spirit" even prior to his selection as a servant of the Lord for the church in Jerusalem? Perhaps we should say "being filled with the Holy Spirit" as used in the scriptures is reserved for those times when man was made especially aware of the Spirit's presence. But this cannot be said of 6:3 or several other references. We must therefore conclude there is a potential or latent filling of the Spirit and an actual or conscious filling of the Holy Spirit.

C. *What Does It Mean To Me?* Surely there are none of us who do not wish the grand relationship of being filled with the Holy Spirit (please see our discussion of this in Volume One, p. 37ff. and Volume Two, p. 11ff.). The Holy Spirit will produce His blessed fruit in our character as we are willing to permit Him, so that, on occasions of stress and need, can we expect Him to enable us to speak with boldness and faith or humility and wisdom. There are indeed times when we are consciously aware we are dominated by some emotion such as anger or grief. If we are indwelt by Him and it has been our practice to permit Him, yea, to encourage Him; to submit to Him; to eagerly invite Him to express Himself through us, then in the time of stress, He will fill our hearts and mouths and actions with His wisdom, grace. We can hardly expect such a relationship if we have not practiced His presence in the ordinary affairs of life.

D. *How Can I Share It?* The best way to share this truth is by a personal example. It should be said of us as it was of Stephen: "he was full of faith and of the Holy Spirit." This knowledge is gained by the observation of the very ordinary actions and attitudes of the individual.

23, 24, 25, & 26. "Now when the apostles that were at
Jerusalem heard that Samaria had received the word
of God, they sent unto them Peter and John: who,
when they were come down, prayed for them, that
they might *receive the Holy Spirit*: for as yet *it was
fallen upon none of them: only they had been baptized into the name of the Lord Jesus.* Then laid they
their hands upon them, and they received the Holy
Spirit." (Acts 8:14-17)

A. *What Does It Say?* Actually this passage contains
three direct references and one indirect reference.
Since they are all part of one narrative, we will
consider them together. We rejoice in anticipation
of a study of these verses for they contain the
whole system of the Holy Spirit's work: (1) The
first relationship we sustain to the Holy Spirit is
obtained as we hear the gospel, believe it, and are
baptized into Christ. When this happens, we are
given the Holy Spirit as a gift. This the Samaritans
had done. The fact of their acceptance of Christ
is stated in verse 12 *and* in verse 16. Please notice
the contrast in verse sixteen: the Holy Spirit had
not "fallen upon" *any* of them but they *all* had
been baptized into the name of the Lord Jesus.
The supernatural manifestations of the Holy Spirit,
such as speaking in tongues, prophesying, etc. were
not yet manifest among the Samaritans. Peter and
John were sent to supply this need. But in contrast to these supernatural gifts, these Samaritans
did have the Holy Spirit indwelling them, as
He does all believers. This indwelling was obtained
as a direct consequence of their acceptance of
Christ. The praying of Peter and John that the
Samaritans might "receive the Holy Spirit" *must*
be understood in light of the whole teaching here
given: please, please notice the punctuation and the
use of the word "for". The meaning of the phrase:

". . . that they might receive the Holy Spirit" (15b) *must* be understood by the modifying phrase "for as yet it (he) was fallen upon none of them." Luke is saying: the Samaritans did not have the supernatural powers of the Holy Spirit. Peter and John prayed and laid on their hands that He might thus "fall upon them." The reason for granting such powers was to carry on the work in the soon-coming absence of Philip. If certain persons were not thus supernaturally gifted, there would have been no source of Divine direction. What the New Testament does for us, those with the gifts did for them. Perhaps this record is an example of what occurred many times in many places. When persons left heathenism to accept Jesus of Nazareth as the Saviour, how could they be instructed without the direct aid of the Holy Spirit through these gifted teachers? If those who were baptized into the name of the Father, Son and Holy Spirit were to be taught "all things whatsoever I have commanded you" (Matthew 28:18-20), then there *must* be some source for this teaching. Through the baptism in the Holy Spirit this information was brought to the memory of the apostles (Matthew 10:20ff), but they could not go everywhere. Indeed, they "stayed in Jerusalem" (Acts 8:3,4). Those to whom those who were scattered spoke (Acts 8:4) became Christians. They must be taught "all things." This could not be accomplished without supernatural help; we believe the apostles went from place to place for the purpose of equipping certain persons with the supernatural aid necessary for this grand work. (2) We want to emphasize the fact that the apostles were prepared for their work by the experience of Pentecost. Jesus told them how very needful it was that they wait in the city for this event (Acts 1:5, 8; Luke 24:49). We shall not argue the point as to whether the Holy Spirit baptism did indeed create incentive as well as information. We believe the resurrection of our Lord, His appearances unto them "after His passion by many infallible proofs" (Acts 1:3) was the supreme incentive for preaching and teaching. "Simon saw that through the laying on of the hands of the apostles the Holy Spirit was given" (Acts 8:17). We did also see clearly what happened through the hands of the apostles. *Some physical manifestation must have accompanied the laying on of the apostles' hands or Simon could not have identified the experience.* What was it Simon saw as the hands of the apostles were laid upon the heads of some of these Samaritans? Did they "speak in tongues and prophesy" as the twelve disciples at Ephesus? Read Acts 19:1ff. We do not know but this seems a reasonable conclusion. Perhaps tongues were not needed here to the same extent as in Ephesus. By reading the preceeding comments you will know we believe tongues were languages and were used for evangelism and teaching. (3) Please notice: There are three manifestations of the Holy Spirit here described. Such description is given in the following words: (a) The Samaritans had been baptised for the remission of their sins (Acts 2:38,39) to receive the Holy Spirit as a gift. Such a manifestation is indicated by the following words: "only they had been baptised into the name of the Lord Jesus." (b) The Holy Spirit's supernatural powers could be activated by the laying on of the apostles' hands. The two apostles, Peter and John, were sent by the ten for this purpose. The Holy Spirit was already present in the bodies of the Samaritans, but as yet, they had not been endowed with any of the supernatural powers. Such powers would soon be needed in continuing the work of evangelism and education. Peter and John came to pray and lay their hands upon some of the Samaritan converts for this purpose. Such a manifestation is described in the following words: "who when they were come down, prayed for them, that they might receive the Holy Spirit: for as yet it (he) was fallen upon none of them . . . then laid they their hands upon them, and they received the Holy Spirit." (3) The ability to grant supernatural powers of the Holy Spirit came only through the hands of the apostles. Simon the sorcerer *did not* see that through the faith and prayer of the Samaritans, these powers were given. If this had been the case, he would have prayed and believed much earlier and would have received such powers. His former work of sorcery would have created an appetite for excercising these supernatural powers. Why didn't Simon or someone else, anyone else, have these powers prior to the coming of Peter and John? We believe the answer is in the fact that the apostles were the only ones who could grant such powers and that the apostles received ability to impart these powers as a result of their baptism in the Holy Spirit.

B. *What Does It Mean?* We have in these verses of Acts an insight into the life of the apostolic church. The church was "apostolic" in much more than a mere historical sense. These were indeed the days of the apostles, but to these men we must look for all we know about our Lord and His church. We must right at this juncture say that we believe Paul was also baptized in the Holy Spirit at some time and place best known to God. We would imagine such an experience for Paul would have occurred soon after his conversion. Perhaps we catch a hint of it in the words of Annaias to Saul: ". . . Brother Saul, the Lord, even Jesus, who appeared unto thee in the way which thou camest, hath sent me, that thou mayest receive thy sight, and *be filled with the Holy Spirit.*" (Acts 9:17) There is such a strong desire on the part of some people to claim spiritual experience they will fasten on to almost any Bible reference for authority. There are indeed many things that happened to the apostles (including Paul) which contain examples for us, but these are experiences common to all Christians. We must use thought and caution with all of God's word and most especially when we attempt to understand His work through His apostles. Our Lord chose these twelve men and Paul to do a job no one else could do. They were especially trained and taught, especially equipped for the task by the baptism in the Holy Spirit. They were the voice of Jesus, God's divine information bureau, the foundation of the church (Ephesians 2:20). We must not read one passage of Scripture without a knowledge of its connection with every other passage on the same subject. Suppose we were to believe Acts 8:14-17 contained an example for our imitation. We would then be forced to the following conclusions: (1) We have received the word, believed and were baptized but do not have the Holy Spirit. What of all the references to the contrary? (i.e. that indicate we receive the Holy Spirit at the time we become Christians, such as Acts 2:38, 5:32; 19:1ff; Gal. 3:2;) (2) If the case of the Samaritans is an example for us then we could be Christians without the Holy Spirit. What of Romans 8:9? (3) If Acts 8:14-17 is today's example who acts in the place of Peter and John? Do we have some form of apostolic succession? If so, who decides upon this? Surely those who decide who succeeds the apostles are even greater than the apostles. (4) What does the little phrase: "only they had been baptized into the name of the Lord Jesus" mean? (i.e. in connec-

tion with the "falling on of the Holy Spirit?")
There is a connection—what is it? (5) Who will
decide as to who receives the Holy Spirit? Do *all*
persons receive the Holy Spirit by the laying on
of hands? If not, who and how many?

C. *How Does It Apply To Me?* We have unavoidably
developed this question in the previous two. If we
accept the thought that the apostles were Christ's
personal representatives and were trained and
equipped for this position and work, then their
action with those of Samaria is an expected expression of this relationship. We then regard the New
Testament as a product of the same Spirit through
their hands. Mark, Luke, Jude, James were all endowed with supernatural ability through the laying on of the apostles' hands and by this means
were enabled to write. The gift of "discerning of
spirits" would also be a necessary protection
against spurious documents (i.e. those who had the
gift of discerning of spirits could tell if a manu-
script was the product of the Holy Spirit or merely
the writing of the unaided human spirit). This
gives us an explanation for the production of the
New Testament which puts confidence and conviction in our hearts.

D. *How Can I Share It?* This is such an important
reference. Every Christian should have a clear
understanding of Acts 8:14-17. It should be so
clear that he can immediately explain it to someone else and answer whatever questions are posed.

27, 28, & 29. "Now when Simon saw that through the
laying on of the apostles hands *the Holy Spirit was
given,* he offered them money, saying, Give me also
this power, that on whomsoever I lay my hands, *he
may receive the Holy Spirit.* But Peter said unto him,

Thy silver perish with thee, because thou hast thought to obtain *the gift of God* with money." (Acts 8:18-20)

A. *What Does It Say?* There are three references to the Holy Spirit in these three verses. We have printed them together because they are all a part of one narrative and are best considered together. Simon saw something: (i.e. some physical manifestation he associated with the Holy Spirit). This is very important. If what the Samaritans received when they became Christians was only the Holy Spirit Himself, minus any supernatural expressions, Simon would not have been able to identify this reception of the Holy Spirit. When the three thousand were baptized on Pentecost did anyone know *when* they received the Holy Spirit as a gift? (i.e. Was there some psycho-physical manifestation?) The record simply reads: "they then that received his word were baptized, and there were added unto them in that day about three thousand souls." There is no reference here to any outward expression of the Holy Spirit. We *do* believe the three thousand in their obedience received Him (Acts 5:32) The Holy Spirit Himself is given at the "hearing of faith" (Galatians 3:2) (i.e. at the time we become Christians). The Samaritans became Christians when they heard Philip preaching good tidings concerning the kingdom of God and the name of Jesus Christ and they were baptized, both men and women. Even Simon himself became a Christian. Could we then conclude that both Simon and the Samaritans had the Holy Spirit Himself as a gift from God upon their acceptance of Christ? We have no reason to believe otherwise. It would be helpful to list the expressions used here: (1) "the Holy Spirit"; (2) "this power"; (3) "the gift of God." The first expression we must conclude is a reference to some expression of the Holy Spirit not just the immediate or even initial reception of Him. We believe the Samaritans received the Holy Spirit at the time of their baptism. He hadn't "fallen on them" in any supernatural manner. "Only they had been baptized into the name of the Lord Jesus" and had thus received Him but had not been endowed through Him with any supernatural powers. This is a common figure of speech used on several occasions in the Bible and elsewhere in which the cause is spoken of as if it were the result.

The second reference is a deeper insight into the circumstance: *Simon did not ask for the Holy Spirit.* (Was it because he already had Him as a gift, even as do all Christians?) Simon asked for *"this power,* that on whomsoever I lay my hands, he may receive the Holy Spirit." Simon's request was for the apostles' ability to grant supernatural powers through the Holy Spirit. We believe the Holy Spirit was already present and the hands of the apostles simply released or directed the supernatural abilities of the Holy Spirit within the persons upon whom they laid their hands. This was "the power" or prerogative Simon wanted. The third reference is "the gift of God." To what does Peter refer in this phrase? Surely the Holy Spirit is the "gift" or "promise" of God. From what we have already said, we could conclude it was not only the Holy Spirit Himself which Simon wanted. This he already obtained as a gift at his baptism. He wanted "the power" to grant supernatural expressions through the Holy Spirit. This is "the gift of God" he sought to obtain with money. The apostles were gifted by God in a way Simon could never be. Why? Was it because of the avarice of his heart or because such a gift could not be given to anyone but the apostles? Obviously both conditions were present. We believe the latter was more basic a reason (i.e. even if Simon's motives were pure, his request was wrong).

B. *What Does It Mean?* Once again, we have overlapped these two thoughts. It is almost impossible to attempt a careful understanding of every word without at the same time discussing their meaning. We, however, do have a few more thoughts on the meaning here involved. Why didn't Philip lay his hands on the Samaritans? Simon saw many miracles or "signs and wonders" through Philip but he failed to see from him what he saw from the apostles. Why? The obvious answer is: Peter and John gave what Philip could not give. The purpose for these gifts or abilities granted by Peter and John has not yet been mentioned. Why were these Samaritans thus endowed? Philip was soon to leave these new Christians. In the absence of their inspired leader, the Samaritans must have those who could carry on the work. In "the falling on" of the Holy Spirit, can we imagine the use of the gift of prophesy or of knowledge? Did some of the Samaritans receive from Peter and John the power through the Holy Spirit to confirm their teaching with signs and wonders? This does seem to be a reasonable explanation to the purpose of the "falling on" of the Holy Spirit. What alternate explanations are there as to purpose? Are we to believe there was some deficiency in their lives or faith? We could hardly think so. We have no reason. If the Holy Spirit was not given to the Samaritans when they became Christians, why? Where is it plainly so stated? What does the phrase mean which says "only they had been baptized into the name of the Lord Jesus"?

C. *What Does It Mean To Me?* Why are there so many men today who are willing to lay hands on persons or accept the laying on of hands of others? Is not this presumption of the worst sort? We are *not* apostles. We *do not* have the prerogatives of apostles. Neither are we those endowed by the apostles, and if we were, we could not by our hands grant supernatural powers to others (i.e. if Philip is an example). However, there is a void, a vacuum that *must* be filled. The human heart longs after, reaches out to the living God. When we read of those in the days of the apostles who were alive and glowing with the power of the Holy Spirit (in the slang of today: "who were turned on"), we say: "This is for me" or "I *must* have it; I *will* have it." Wait only a moment to ask yourself: "Was it the supernatural powers that 'turned them on' or was it their *personal encounter* with a powerful Saviour?" We have the problem today of those who never felt the joy and exhilaration of a personal surrender and commitment to a very wonderful Saviour who are now finding in what they call "the baptism of the Spirit" what they should have found in their conversion experience. If these same people would visualize or imagine their relationship with our Lord in the same manner as they do with the Holy Spirit and go after the fulfillment or realization of that imagery with the same determination we would have no problem, for they would be completed in their surrender to Him. Tersley put it this way: "We have many who do not wish to deny the validity of their conversion but who find fulfillment in what they call 'the baptism in the Holy Spirit.' " Why not admit you were never converted and begin all over?

D. *How Can I Share It?* All depends upon what you possess. As Peter said to the poor impotent beggar:

"What I have *that* give I thee" (Acts 3:6). If you have the same power Peter and John had as a result of their baptism in the Holy Spirit, then share the results of that power *in the same manner* as did Peter and John. If you have the same powers as those manifest in the work of Philip, then let us see them! If you have the joy, delight, the bubbling happiness of the living Saviour in your life, we will know it. *Just what do you have? What you give will surely indicate what you have!*

30. "And the Spirit said unto Philip, Go near, and join thyself to this chariot." (Acts 8:29)

A. *What Does It Say?* Here again is the clear indication of the person of the Holy Spirit. We do not know if Philip heard an audible voice or if the words were formed in his mind by the divine Spirit. In whatever form here is a very real divine Person exercising the power of speech or words in direct communication to man.

B. *What Does It Mean?* This verse helps us in our thinking. The Holy Spirit is a very real person, not an inanimate influence. There are no words without a mind. We are indwelt by a Person. We might observe that the Holy Spirit did not do the preaching. He gave directions to the preacher but He honored God's ordinance that, not by angels, nor by the Spirit, but by man is the message of salvation to be given.

C. *What Does It Mean To Me?* Are we to expect the Holy Spirit to give us directions today in our efforts to win the lost? There are many who feel He does. How can we determine this? The basic issue relates to *why* or *how* the Spirit spoke to Philip. Was it because Philip was supernaturally endowed through the hands of the apostles? (i.e.

the voice of the Spirit was a part of His supernatural work granted only to those upon whom the
apostles laid their hands). Let's get the facts: (1)
Philip *did* have supernatural powers. He performed
"signs and wonders" in Samaria (Acts 8:6), (2)
Philip *did* have the hands of the apostles laid upon
him (i.e. along with the six other men chosen to
take care of the tables [Acts 6:5 ff]), (3) We *do
not* know all the reasons *why* the apostles' hands
were laid on Philip. We know it was part of the
ceremony of setting him aside for the task of
waiting on tables. Was he *also* granted special
powers by this action? We do not know. We can
assume that since others were thus supernaturally
empowered on other occasions (Acts 19:1-6) that
Philip was also; but, we simply do not know. (4)
Neither do we have any indication that Philip
obtained this power through prayer, meditation,
fasting or other spiritual exercise. (5) Our problem is sharply defined when we realize there are
those who claim direct Spirit-led guidance but who
have often made obvious mistakes in such directions, or have contradicted others who claim similar
guidance. What shall we say of these things? I
believe we should leave the case of Philip alone.
We have no conclusive evidence in either direction. We can have no real faith in our actions or
attitudes. The word of God is silent and so we are
presumptuous to speak. Could we apply Romans
14:23 and say: "Whatsoever is not of faith is sin"?
We would *like* to believe the Holy Spirit will speak
to us in some manner or that He has spoken to us
in the conversion of some present-day Ethiopian-
eunuch-encounter, but we have nothing but a
personal subjective base for this claim.

D. *How Can I Share It?* We must remember God is
yet at work in this world. Simply because we can-

not claim immediate conscious direction from the
Holy Spirit does not mean God's providence has
been eliminated. We learn of God's directions in
our lives in retrospect (i.e. we look back upon the
events of our days and evaluate and many times
marvel at the direction of God). We are like
Joseph of old who said of his forced, unhappy
visit to Egypt: "God sent me to Egypt." This kind
of confidence in the intimate interest of our heavenly Father should be shared with all.

31. ". . . the Spirit of the Lord caught away Philip; and
the eunuch saw him no more," (Acts 8:39)

A. *What Does It Say?* There is a problem as to the
meaning of the words: "caught away." Does this
refer to some supernatural ride? Was Philip simply
snatched away bodily from the road to Gaza and
dropped on one of the streets in Azotus? We think
of I Kings 18:12: "And it will come to pass, as
soon as I am gone from thee, that *the Spirit of
Jehovah will carry thee whither I know not; . . .*"
or II Kings 2:16 (please read this reference).
Others feel this expression refers only to the directions of the Holy Spirit given to Philip which
eventually led him to Azotus. Whereas we prefer
the first view, we have no way of being conclusive
in our arguments. We do want to say the Spirit's
direction in Philip's life indicates God's interest and
Philip's devotion.

B. *What Does It Mean?* In a larger connection, we
can consider the whole life of Philip as under the
direction of the Holy Spirit. This is a pleasant
thought. Was Philip or Stephen an exception? Or
were there many men and women in the apostolic
age who "walked by the Spirit" and did not fulfill
the lust of the flesh? We believe Stephen and Philip
were supernaturally empowered, but "walking by

the Spirit" is a rule for the life of all Christians (Galatians 5:16ff).

C. *What Does It Mean To Me?* I believe God is more interested and concerned with what we call the "little things" of life than we are. After all, life is life (i.e. we are as much under the care and concern of God when we eat our breakfast as when we kneel in prayer). We do not expect an angel to speak to us literally about where we should go today, nor do we listen for the Spirit to say to us: "This is the one. Speak to Him." We cannot imagine a translation experience of miraculous movement. But in doing this, we have sometimes lost the sense of God's nearness and this is a tragic loss. Something must be done to make it up. Would you read again Frank Laubach's booklet on *A Game With Minutes?*

D. *How Can I Share It?* Philip and Stephen were not ordained (i.e. classified by men as among the clergy) but they were two of the grandest examples of Spirit-filled, Spirit-led men we have in the New Testament. Please remember: there were numerous persons who were "filled with the Holy Spirit" before the problem arose over the serving of tables. When a choice was to be made, it was made among several who "were filled with the Holy Spirit." We have no reason to believe the hands of the apostles were laid upon all of these believers. We should be glad to share the wonderful truth that all believers can be like Philip or Stephen, "filled with the Holy Spirit."

32. ". . . Brother Saul, the Lord, even Jesus, who appeared unto thee in the way which thou camest, hath sent me, that thou mayest receive thy sight, and be filled with the Holy Spirit." (Acts 9:17)

A. *What Does It Say?* These are the words of Ananias. It is important that we understand just what Ananias gave to Saul. He came to accomplish two things: (1) to grant physical sight to Saul, and (2) to become an instrument in filling Saul with the Holy Spirit. Further than this lone reference, we have no knowledge of Paul's personal relationship with the Holy Spirit. There are, of course, indications in several of the 98 references to the Holy Spirit in Paul's epistles.

B. *What Does It Mean?* We are on safer ground in this question. We definitely believe the sight to which Ananias has reference is physical. Verse 18 plainly indicates this: "and straightway there fell from his eyes as it were scales, and he received his sight"; (18a). The last half of verse 18 could be a hint in answering the question as to how and when Saul was "filled with the Holy Spirit": ". . . and he arose and was baptised;". Could we assume since Saul repented of his sins and was baptized "to wash away his sins" (in the blood of Jesus, not the water) that at that time and place he received the Holy Spirit not only as a gift, but as the element of his spiritual baptism? We are asking if Saul was not baptized in the Holy Spirit at the same time he was baptized in water? We do not know but we can think of no more appropriate time. We do believe the Holy Spirit was given to Saul at his baptism as He is to all others who accept our Lord; and we believe the powers of the apostles came from the Holy Spirit baptism. Saul was beginning his life not only as a Christian but as the "one sent" by Christ. Is Ananias saying in substance: "I have been sent to give you your physical sight and your credentials as a Christian and an apostle"? Perhaps this is too much to read into the little phrase "filled with the Holy Spirit", but we are attempting a consistent explanation as related to the whole work of the Holy Spirit in Paul's life.

C. *What Does It Mean To Me?* Once again we see the use of the phrase: "filled with the Holy Spirit." It must be understood in its context. "Filled with the Holy Spirit" as here used could be much like the same words as used to describe Pentecost (Acts 2:4), but we are not positive about this. We should be very careful to understand as God intended we do by reading all we know about the incident being described. As we have pointed out earlier, there are several times when the words: "filled with the Holy Spirit" describe persons and an experience not at all like those on Pentecost or the house of Cornelius. We should indeed be "filled with the Holy Spirit", but will it be as the twelve or as Paul? Surely Paul is an example for us, but hardly in this regard.

D. *How Can I Share It?* There is something here to share: the wonderful conversion experience of Saul of Tarsus and most especially, the work of the Holy Spirit in the whole wonderful transaction. Answer the following questions and share your answers with someone: (1) Did the Holy Spirit work with Saul as he prayed for three days in the house of Judas? Why was he without food or drink? Why pray? (2) Did the Holy Spirit give Saul the vision (9:12) of Ananias coming even before he came? We are asking if God acted directly or if the Holy Spirit was His agent? (3) Does John 16:7-10 relate to Saul's conversion? If so, how? If we do no more than think seriously about the relationship of the Holy Spirit in conversion, we will have accomplished our purpose.

33. "So the church throughout all Judea and Galilee and Samaria had peace, being edified; and walking in the

fear of the Lord and *in the comfort of the Holy Spirit,* was multiplied." (Acts 9:31)

A. *What Does It Say?* The word "comfort" as here used could well be translated "consolation" or "encouragement." This is a statement related to the whole body of believers and therefore has particular interest to Christians today. The verb "walking" is a key to the meaning here. Rotherham has well translated the word: "the church *'going on its way'* ". All Christians throughout the holy land were living and working in the fear of the Lord and *the comfort of the Holy Spirit.*

B. *What Does It Mean?* How did these persons obtain *comfort* from the Holy Spirit? How was this encouragement, direction, or aid communicated from the Holy Spirit to the individual? We have two possible answers: (1) a subjective experience in which the Holy Spirit made "the Lord Himself real to the consciousness of those who went, for witness, for preaching, for insistence upon the Lordship of Christ;" . . . Just how this happened is surely much better 'felt than told' ", and (2) to quote another commentator: "This presence of the Spirit is always *mediated* through the Word by means of which He speaks to us and keeps us encouraged and strong in the faith." In the first answer, the inward strength or satisfaction is attributed to the Holy Spirit. This is a Spirit-produced emotional aid. In the second, the encouragement is obtained from the teaching of the truth (whether it is taught orally as in the case of the early church or from the written word as in our case). We realize the Holy Spirit was the author of such teaching and thus we attribute our encouragement to Him. How can we decide which position is meant by the inspired writer? in no way known to the writer.

C. *What Does It Mean To Me?* This verse should cause us to be very cautious about being dogmatic in our assertions or positions. Just how is the comfort of the Comforter communicated to the individual? We can boldly assert: "by the teaching of the Spirit's word", but we are only dogmatizing. The text does not say so, and for us to say so when the text does not, is pure presumption. One fact stands out: we should find a real source of encouragement, strength, or aid from the Holy Spirit. This must be more than a pious platitude. It must be a personal testimony!

D. *How Can I Share It?* Once again, we must say: *we only share what we have.* Is the Holy Spirit a comfort to you? It is almost redundant to say: "Is the Comforter a comfort?," but this is exactly the issue. We would become concerned if we felt God was to us something less than God or our Saviour were less than a Saviour? What shall we say when the divine Comforter gives no personal comfort? The converse can be true: if He is a Comforter to you, you can share this precious relationship with others.

34, & 35. "And while Peter thought on the vision, the Spirit said unto him, *Behold, three men seek thee.* But arise, and get thee down, and go with them, nothing doubting: for *I have sent them.*" (Acts 10:19,20)

A. *What Does It Say?* There are two references in the same context: two actions of the Holy Spirit. They are speaking and sending. We shall consider them together. This text is plain enough in statement to hardly need comment. Perhaps the words of Alexander would be helpful (if you are not reading at least ten commentaries along with my comments, you are the loser): ". . . *the Spirit* (i.e. the Divine or Holy Spirit) *said to him, Behold*

414

(or *lo,* implying something unexpected and surprising), *three men are seeking thee* (asking or inquiring for "thee"). This coincidence of time between Peter's anxious meditation and the inquiries of the men from Caesarea brings the two parts of the providential scheme into conjunction and cooperation:" (p. 398) (*Commentary On The Acts Of The Apostles*—J. A. Alexander;)

B. *What Does It Mean?* We want to ask and try to answer two questions here: (1) Why did God use the Holy Spirit as a spokesman? (2) What meaning does it have for our day? In answer to the first question, we could say: God was giving Peter information he never had before and therefore must speak to him. This is not adequate since Peter could have received all the same information from the three men if he had waited a few more minutes, but God didn't wait. Why? The answer must be: Peter would not have been convinced with any other method of explanation. How does this relate to our day? Do we have circumstances in which God has a very, very difficult time getting us to do His will? To ask this question is to answer it. God isn't trying to get us to preach to those to whom He has already commissioned us, is He? Or is He? Does God have as much interest in us as He had in Peter? Does God want His will fulfilled in our life as much as He did in the life of Peter? Here is a most crucial question: *"Was the Spirit's speaking to Peter a part of the baptism of the Holy Spirit?"* (i.e. Because Peter was baptized in the Holy Spirit, did he have a nearness and a contact with the Holy Spirit not experienced by those who had not been baptized in the Holy Spirit?) This is a possibility but *how* shall we prove it? Of course, this particular example was the opening of the door of the gospel to the Gentiles; but are we to conclude that only in such cases do we have

God's immediate interest through the Holy Spirit? Aren't some of the problems of our life just as vital and as big to us as this was to Peter? Has God's immediate interest left the world?

C. *What Does It Mean To Me?* The above comments should sharpen our interest in answering this question. We need to fearlessly answer the basic question here and several others closely associated. The basic question: Why is the account of Peter's experience given to us? (i.e. Why did God through the Holy Spirit direct Luke to write this incident?) Was it to inform all men for all time of the special means and men God used in opening the doors of the kingdom to the Gentiles? I am sure we would all agree this is an obvious answer, but is it the *only* answer? (i.e. Are we to conclude God worked once for this one purpose and therefore will not work again like this?) There are two or three factors that point in the affirmative for an answer: (1) We have no examples in the rest of Acts or the epistles which indicate God's immediate involvement in the problems of other Christians (i.e. in the same way as indicated with Peter). God did not speak to anyone else personally through the Holy Spirit in answering their perplexities. This fact gives us reason to consider the incident with Peter as of the same exceptional nature as other one-time Biblical incidents. (2) There are no teachings in the New Testament to indicate the Holy Spirit will speak personally to you or me in solving our personal problems. If there is such a teaching, I have failed to read it and would appreciate hearing from any reader about it. (3) There are many who feel the Holy Spirit does speak to them personally in solving problems, however, such persons make mistakes and get conflicting or confusing answers from the

Holy Spirit; others get contrary answers to the same questions asked by their friends. All this confusion is not from the Holy Spirit.

D. *How Can I Share It?* It seems to me we should share the thought that God *is* indeed personally interested in our problems and is presently at work answering our questions, (as much as we are willing to allow Him by His providence to answer them), but we can only discover His answers in retrospect and thank Him for all the grand direction He has given us.

36. ". . . even Jesus of Nazareth, how God anointed him with the Holy Spirit and with power: who went about doing good, and healing all that were oppressed of the devil; for God was with him." (Acts 10:38)

A. *What Does It Say?* Remember who is being addressed by Peter: the Gentiles in the house of Cornelius. Whatever these persons knew about our Lord was gathered from their attendance at the Jewish synagogues or from the general gossip of the populace. Evidently enough was known to be able to draw some lessons: these persons had heard of the baptism of Jesus by John. Peter now adds this interesting and important word: Jesus was not only baptized by John the Baptist, but was anointed by God with the Holy Spirit and power. We would consider the word "power" to be descriptive of the consequence of the Spirit's presence (i.e. because He was anointed by the Spirit, He was also empowered—our Lord was full of the Holy Spirit and of power). We commented rather extensively on the anointing action of the Holy Spirit both as to Jesus and those of Acts the second chapter. We must add here that the "good" and the "healing" of our Lord was accomplished through this same Spirit and power.

The phrase: "for God was with Him" must therefore be a summary statement. To say that "God
was with Him" is the same as saying "He was full
of the Holy Spirit and power."

B. *What Does It Mean?* We are always faced with two
   areas of interest in answering this question: (1)
   What does it mean to those to whom it was written
   or in the context of the verse? and (2) What does
   it mean today? Our primary interest in this question has to do with the first area. Considering the
   audience who first heard these words, what did
   they mean to them? Did anyone in that house
   know of Isaiah 61:1ff. or of its fulfillment in the
   life of Jesus as recorded in Luke 4:16ff. It reads:
   ". . . and he entered, as his custom was, into the
   synagogue on the sabbath day, and stood up to
   read. And there was delivered unto him the book
   of the prophet Isaiah. And he opened the book,
   and found the place where it was written, The
   Spirit of the Lord is upon me, because *he anointed
   me* to preach good tidings to the poor: . . ." Perhaps not, but it does indicate the purpose of His
   anointing. We are sure many, if not all present
   knew the meaning of the words: *Messiah, Christ,*
   and *anointed.* These were used almost as synonyms.
   This expression meant primarily that Jesus was the
   long-promised Messiah, the Christ (anointed) of
   God.

C. *What Does It Mean To Me?* This verse states the
   fundamental of the Christian faith (i.e. that we
   believe Jesus of Nazareth is the Christ, or "the
   anointed", of God). The presence of the Holy
   Spirit at His baptism in the form of a dove was
   a sign to John, to those present, and to us that
   God was with Him and was sending Him out to
   begin His divine mission: (1) good tidings to the
   poor, (2) release to the captives, (3) sight to the

blind, (4) set at liberty those that are bruised, and (5) proclaim the acceptable year of the Lord. This verse ought to remind us once again, very forceably, that even Jesus did not have power or the sense of God's nearness without the Holy Spirit.

D. *How Can I Share It?* Use a little imagination. What aspect seems most applicable to others? (1) The setting of the text as related to the household of Cornelius? (2) The act at the Jordan River of the Holy Spirit coming upon (was He not already within?) Jesus? (3) The consequent power and presence of God with Jesus because of the Holy Spirit?

37, & 38. "While Peter yet spake these words, the Holy Spirit fell on all them that heard the word. And they of the circumcision that believed were amazed, as many as came with Peter, because that on the Gentiles also was poured out the gift of the Holy Spirit. For they heard them speak with tongues, and magnify God." (Acts 10:44-46)

A. *What Does It Say?* We discussed this at some length in our earlier consideration of the baptism of the Holy Spirit (see Vol. I, p. 39-55) However, we shall attempt to approach these verses just as if we had never before studied them. Let us then carefully define each phrase: (1) "While Peter yet spake these words," What words? Are we to refer this to all that Peter said from verse 34 through 43? Or to just the conclusion of his words as in verse 43? We prefer the latter explanation. Peter had just dropped his voice at the end of the sentence in verse 43 when the Holy Spirit fell. (2) "the Holy Spirit fell on them that heard the word." Of course, this phrase is defined as "the gift of the Holy Spirit" and further described as "speaking in tongues and magnifying God." We learn later in 11:16 that Peter called this experience "the baptism in the Holy Spirit." The word "fell" as here used, must refer to the suddenness and unexpectedness of the coming of the Holy Spirit. The Holy Spirit did indeed fall on them (we consider the pronoun "them" to refer to all who were listening to Peter in the house of Cornelius. "Them that heard the word" would not include the six Jewish brethren who accompanied Peter. These men, described as "they of the circumcision that believed", Cornelius had "called together his kinsmen and his near friends"). (3) "And they of the circumcision that believed were amazed, as many as were come with Peter, because that on the Gentiles also was poured out the gift of the Holy Spirit." We find out from 11:12 there were six Jewish men who accompanied Peter from Joppa to Caesarea. The term "gift of the Holy Spirit" *must* be understood in the context in which it is given or all types of confusion will result. This is very obviously the baptismal "gift of the Spirit" (i.e. the gift of the Holy Spirit in this case is the baptism in the Holy Spirit). It is not at all strange that the baptism in the Holy Spirit should be referred to as a gift. Indeed, *all* manifestations of the Holy Spirit are at one time or another referred to as "the gift of the Holy Spirit". Consider: (A) The Holy Spirit Himself as an indwelling presence is called "the gift of the Holy Spirit" (Acts 2:38), (B) The supernatural powers exercised in and through certain persons upon whom the apostles laid their hands are referred to as "gifts" of the Holy Spirit (I Corinthians 12:1), (C) The baptism of the Holy Spirit is here referred to as "the gift of the Holy Spirit. The reason behind all these expressions is that in no instance is the presence or power of the Holy Spirit earned. It is like salvation:

"It is the gift of God" (Ephesians 2:8). (4) *"For they heard them speak with tongues, and magnify God."* If this experience was a "like gift" as that given on Pentecost, then the "tongues" here used were foreign languages and the "magnifying of God" had to do with His "mighty works" (2:11). There is some question as to whether the "tongues" of Corinthians 12 & 14 are languages, but there is no question as to Pentecost since 2:6 states ". . . every man heard them speaking in his own language".

B. *What Does It Mean?* The meaning of this particular passage is best understood by Peter. Fortunately, he explains the meaning in 11:1-18, particularly in verses 15-18. (Please, please read this passage carefully so our comments will make sense). The conclusion is stated in verse 17: ". . . who was I, that I could withstand God?" It is sometimes better to reason from the conclusion back to the beginning. In this procedure, the whole structure becomes plain. In what instance was Peter attempting to withstand God? He was unwilling (like all other Jews) to take the gospel to the Gentiles. The whole action from 10:1 to 11:18 is for the purpose of overcoming this Jewish prejudice. The climax of the action is in the baptism of the Gentile household in the Holy Spirit. It began for Peter on the housetop of Simon the tanner with the vision, then the voice of the Spirit and the three men, then the explanation of Cornelius. The final and overwhelming move of persuasion was the baptism of the Holy Spirit. Peter says: "I remembered the word of the Lord as He said to us (Acts 1:5) 'John indeed baptized in water, but ye shall be baptized in the Holy Spirit'. Peter says in effect: "I had always felt this to be the greatest experience of our life and that it was given exclusively to us, that we apostles were honored above all men by being baptized in the Holy Spirit. Wonder of wonders: A housefull of Gentiles are recipients of the same experience! How can it be? But it is. It is of and from God. I am convinced. No more action is necessary. I withstand no longer. I will accept these Gentiles. They can be recognized on an equal level with us in the family of God."

C. *What Does It Mean to Me?* There are some extremely crucial questions asked and answered in this text: (1) *Do you believe a person must be baptized in water before he is saved?* If you do, then you must see that what occurred to the house of Cornelius did not relate to salvation and happened to persons who were not Christians. We are hesitant to say this, but what else could we conclude? They were believers and they were hearing the word, but they had not been baptized and were not baptized until after their baptism in the Holy Spirit. This fact simply points up the exceptional nature of this case. The baptism in the Holy Spirit was for someone else's benefit, not for those who received it. We say this because their biggest, deepest need was salvation, and yet God through Christ baptized them in the Holy Spirit. Why? From Peter's point of view, nothing would be more convincing. He must have thought: "If God grants such a tremendous experience to Gentile persons who are not even Christians, who am I to hesitate in accepting them as converts to Christ?" I believe this is what he meant when he said: "Can any man forbid water that these should be baptized who have received the Holy Spirit as well as we?" (10:47), (2) *Can a person have the Holy Spirit and yet not be a Christian?* This is the opposite side of the above question. Romans 8:9 states: "If any man hath not the Spirit of Christ, he is none of his." This is in reference to the abiding presence of the Spirit. We believe that what happened to the house of Cornelius was of a temporary nature, that when its purpose of convincing Peter and the other Jewish Christians was fulfilled, then the experience was also fulfilled and the effects of it dissipated. We would conclude then that upon being baptized in water these persons received the Holy Spirit as an abiding presence within them and not before. (3) Why is this incident so often used as an example for present-day tongue speakers? Because it seems to fit their theology. We must face into it: most all who claim the baptism in the Holy Spirit today do not believe baptism is at all related to salvation. When we accept their experience as valid, it is tantamount to accepting their concept of salvation, that is, the forgiveness of sins. The example of the house of Cornelius offers *no help* to such persons, for reasons above stated, it becomes the prime example of the opposite! Because they had not been baptized and therefore were not Christians, their experience made the deep impression it did upon the minds of the prejudiced Jewish Christians.

D. *How Can I Share It?* We need to face into the total issue here involved and at the same time be kind and full of concern. As we talk to others about the problem of present-day tongue speakers, we must admit there is a far more vital issue also in the balance. If we admit certain persons have been baptized in the Holy Spirit and do indeed speak with tongues and at the same time we know such persons were never baptized in water for the remission of sins, we are in effect denying the fundamental issue of the purpose for Christian baptism. If not, why not? This is just as serious as a problem can become. Is baptism for the remission of sins or not? Is the Holy Spirit for persons who have never been baptized? There could hardly be a more important point of sharing. What sayest thou?

39. "Surely no one can refuse the water for these to be baptized who have received the Holy Spirit just as we did, can he?" (Acts 10:47)

A. *What Does It Say?* Comment seems unnecessary here in face of all we have said previously. However we do not wish to overlook a single thought as related to Him. The reception of the Holy Spirit here as in 11:15, 16, 17 is the baptism of the Holy Spirit. Once again we see the generic: "Holy Spirit" used to describe the specific: "baptism in the Holy Spirit." We need to remember this for a clear view this generic-specific use of terms. The generic "gift of the Holy Spirit" is used earlier in Acts to describe the specifics of: gifts, baptism, and the Holy Spirit Himself; so here also.

B. *What Does It Mean?* Upon reading some commentaries, we are strongly tempted to digress from the subject and discuss the need for and purpose of water baptism, but we shall not. Someone else has done an admirable job on that subject. We need comment on the Holy Spirit. We can add nothing here not already said.

C. *What Does It Mean To Me?* See our comments on point 36.

D. *How Can I Share It?* See our comments on point 36.

40, 41, & 42. "And the Spirit told me to go with them without misgivings. And these six brethren also went with me, and we entered the man's house. And as I began to speak, the Holy Spirit fell upon them, just as He did upon us at the beginning. And I remembered the word of the Lord, how He used to say, 'John indeed baptized with water, but you shall be baptized with the Holy Spirit. If God therefore gave to them the same gift as He gave to us, also after believing in the Lord Jesus Christ, who was I that I could stand in God's way? (Acts 10:12; 15-17)

A. *What Does It Say?* It is essential to a careful under standing that you read the tenth chapter of Acts and the first eighteen verses of chapter eleven. We will never know what these verses say until they are read in their context. We make no apology for repeating points when we feel they add to the sum total of knowledge (there are times when they do not). We refer you to points 33 & 34 which discuss the words of the Holy Spirit to Peter. Let us notice the four references to the Holy Spirit in these verses: (1) ". . . the Spirit told me . . .", (2) ". . . the Holy Spirit fell . . .", (3) ". . . baptized with the Holy Spirit . . .", (4) ". . . the same gift . . ." Each of these phrases has been considered earlier in a careful discussion. We refer you to the earlier discussion for this: for (1) to references No. 33 & 34; for (2) to No. 36; for (3) & (4) to No. 36.

B, C, & D. See above comment.

43. ". . . and they sent forth Barnabas . . . for he was a good man, and full of the Holy Spirit and faith: and much people were added unto the Lord." (Acts 11:22, 24)

A. *What Does It Say?* Luke says here what he said earlier of Stephen (Cf. 6:5). There seems to be no hint of supernatural power associated with being "filled with the Holy Spirit". Perhaps the fruit of the Spirit, such as joy, peace, love, kindness were very prominent in the attitudes and actions of both Stephen and Barnabas.

B. *What Does It Mean?* There are several commentators who relate the expression "full of the Holy Spirit" to the supernatural gifts of the Spirit. Accordingly, such persons who are "filled with the Holy Spirit" have several of these gifts. This hardly seems a tenable position since "faith and "wisdom" are both one of the gifts and in this reference and in 6:5, Stephen and Barnabas are also full of wisdom and faith. If they were full of the Holy Spirit in the supernatural sense, why was is necessary to add: "and faith" and wisdom? We believe it means that the direction of Christ our Lord (who lives in us by the Holy Spirit) was so prominent in demeanor of Stephen and Barnabas, people recognized Him and said, "They are full of the Holy Spirit." We can only offer our opinion but we hope it is helpful.

C. *What Does It Mean To Me?* Would the reader please refer to Volume II, pages 11 through 44 and read them carefully? There are two basic thoughts here: (1) Being filled with the Holy Spirit is a most desirable relationship which is attainable by all Christians; (2) This relationship is a matter or subject of character development and not of service. The supernatural gifts and baptism in the Holy Spirit were for the purpose of teaching, preaching, confirming, etc. in the work of establishing His kingdom in the hearts of men. Being filled with the Holy Spirit is for the purpose of preparing the man for whatever service he performs in Christ's kingdom. The second then becomes more important than the first. If we are not prepared to serve, we cannot serve. Please remember: when the apostles wanted some men to take care of the very physical task of distributing food, the men were to be "filled with the Holy Spirit" (6:3-5).

D. *How Can I Share It?* I believe it is extremely important we see Barnabas, Stephen, Philip and doubtless many others as men who were "filled with the Holy Spirit" in such a conspicuous manner that people knew it. Being filled with the Spirit was not, in this case, something they did but something they were. This describes a personal relationship with the Holy Spirit sustained by these men. This relationship with the Holy Spirit affected their attitudes and actions to such an extent others knew it. When we have such a relationship, we will indeed have something to share. If we are filled with the Holy Spirit, we unconsciously will be able to share this glorious fact.

44. "Now at this time some prophets came down from Jerusalem to Antioch. And one of them named Agabus stood up and began to indicate by the Spirit that there would certainly be a great famine all over the world. And this took place in the reign of Claudius." (Acts 11:27, 28)

A. *What Does It Say?* The prophecy of Agabus was evidently given in the midst of some formal service or meeting. We obtain this thought from the expression "stood up" (i.e. made a public statement). The prophets in the New Testament were classified along with the apostles as being a part of the foundation of Christ's Church (Ephesians 2:20). The Holy Spirit was the source of the prophetic powers. Foretelling seems to be only a minor part of thier work: forthtelling or teaching was a much larger share.

B. *What Does It Mean?* We could discuss the meaning of the message of Agabus, but our purpose is to discover the Spirit's work. The Holy Spirit became the intelligence or power by which or through which Agabus was able to make this prediction. Just where or how did Agabus obtain this gift? Acts 19:1-6 indicates certain persons prophesied as a result of the laying on of the hands of Paul. Agabus had been in Jerusalem with the apostles. Did they lay their hands upon him to grant this power? We do not know, but it seems quite possible.

C. *What Does It Mean To Me?* We have many present-day claims to this prophetic gift. If we have inspired teachers today, then their teaching is of equal value to the New Testament. If such teachers do not add anything to the sum total of our knowledge of God's word of what value are they? Anyone with sincere faith and devotion can study and teach the New Testament. Present-day prophets contradict each other, themselves, and the word of God. The plain answer is: their claim is false! We ask again: "In what reference do we find the gift of prophecy given through prayer? Or by the laying on of the hands of someone who was not an apostle?"

D. *How Can I Share It?* We need to challenge the source and authority of present-day prophets. We do not have an answer for all the questions asked concerning this prophecy or that one. It is enough to ask: "Whence cometh this power?" If the New Testament is silent as to example or teaching concerning how the gift of prophecy was given (i.e. apart from the hands of the apostles) we are presumptuous to claim it.

45. "Now there were at Antioch, in the church that was there, prophets and teachers, Barnabas, and Symeon that was called Niger, and Lucius of Cyrene, and

Manaen the foster-brother of Herod the tetrarch, and Saul. And as they ministered to the Lord, and fasted, the Holy Spirit said, Separate me Barnabas and Saul for the work where unto I have called them." (Acts 13:1,2)

A. *What Does It Say?* Are prophets and teachers the same men? "The two words are generic and specific terms applied to the same persons, one denoting their divine authority, and the other the precise way in which it was exercised." With this thought we agree. All prophets were teachers, but not all teachers were prophets. In the Antioch church, they were both prophets *and* teachers. The words of the Holy Spirit came during a period of "ministering to the Lord" and while they were fasting. The message of the Spirit came during some type of worship service. Perhaps it was on the Lord's day around the Lord's table. We do not know when or where or even to whom the Holy Spirit addressed these words, "Separate me Barnabas and Saul for the work where unto I have called them." Was this message given in an audible voice to the assembled group?; or by special revelations to one of the prophets? We do not know. It is enough to know He did speak. We would like to comment on the subject of fasting but this is not our purpose.

B. *What Does It Mean?* This passage teaches us the Holy Spirit spoke to certain persons, called them, and gave specific instructions. Is this an example for present-day Spirit-given calling and directing? Pause a moment and consider: (1) The Holy Spirit was calling an apostle and someone who had for a long time been closely associated with the apostles, (2) The question of apostolic authority was a very live issue. By speaking directly, the position of Paul as an apostle would be strengthened.

There was a task of evangelizing to be done; the Spirit's choice for this work was Barnabas and Saul. He had already called them for the task: 9:15; 22:14,15,21; 26:16. These considerations will help us to understand the previous commission of the Holy Spirit as related to Saul (whereas in these references the Lord Jesus is the spokesman we could assume this is the call to which the Holy Spirit made reference).

Another question poses itself to us: If Saul had been engaged in evangelistic work for the past 14 years (35 to 49 A.D.) why now call him to a work in which he was already working? The answer is either in the responsibility of the local church in Antioch or in the reconfirming of the apostleship of Paul. We do not know where or when the Holy Spirit had called Barnabas for the work. We are simply told He did.

C. *What Does It Mean To Me?* The Holy Spirit is a very real divine person with the power of thought and expression. He is vitally concerned about preaching the gospel. He will not preach it but has a great interest in those who do.

D. *How Can I Share It?* If we wanted to discuss the ordination of evangelists, or the subject of fasting in the early church, we could use these verses. But what shall we share in the work of the Spirit? Perhaps an assurance of His divinity and personality.

46. "Then, when they had fasted and prayed and laid their hands on them, they sent them away. So being sent out by the Holy Spirit, they went down to Seleucia and from there they sailed to Cyprus." (Acts 13:3,4)

A. *What Does It Say?* This text is the fulfillment of the one we have just studied. "Being sent out by the Holy Spirit" is the description of Luke as to action of the Antioch church. The Holy Spirit initiated the action and He is therefore logically described here as the source of the sending or the one who sent them. Whereas the hands of the elders of the church were doubtlessly laid on the heads of Paul and Barnabas and by this means the church approved and implemented the call of the Spirit, nonetheless, the Holy Spirit is indicated as the one who sent them.

B, C, D. We feel we can add nothing further to what we have already said on this text.

47. "But Elymas the magician (for thus his name is translated) was opposing them, seeking to turn the proconsul away from the faith. But Saul, who was also known as Paul, filled with the Holy Spirit, fixed his gaze upon him, . . ." (Acts 13:8,9)

A. *What Does It Say?* The action of the Holy Spirit in Paul must be associated with his credentials as an apostle. He said concerning this in II Corinthians 12:12: "The signs of a true apostle were performed among you with all perseverance, by signs and wonders and miracles." Paul takes the lead in the rest of the Acts account. This is the time and place for his move to leadership. Saul, who is from here on called Paul, was "filled with the Holy Spirit" from his conversion (9:17). We must conclude then that the expression used here refers to a fresh assertion or moving of the Holy Spirit within the apostle. We would assume this movement of the Holy Spirit was prompted by God, not Paul.

B. *What Does It Mean?* We think of a very similar incident with Peter and Ananias. In both cases the authority of an apostle was being tested. We can appreciate the need for such a move on the part of the Holy Spirit when we think of the alternative.

C. *What Does It Mean To Me?* There is little of personal application in this text. We see better the purposes of God.

D. *How Can I Share It?* See above comment.

48. "But the Jews aroused the devout women of prominence and the leading men of the city, and instigated a persecution against Paul and Barnabas, and drove them out of their district. But they shook off the dust of their feet in protest against them and went to Iconium. And the disciples were continually filled with joy and with the Holy Spirit." (Acts 13:50-52)

A. *What Does It Say?* "The expulsion is no way injured the disciples who were left destitute of these leaders. They had the best Paraclete, the Holy Spirit, who filled their hearts and also gave them joy. The imperfect describes this condition as one that continued indefinitely." (*Lenski*, p. 556) This text plainly states the Christians in Antioch of Pisidia were continually filled with joy and the Holy Spirit! Romans 15:13 seems to be a good companion verse: "Now may the God of hope fill you with all joy and peace in believing, that you may *abound in hope by the power of the Holy Spirit.*" Also Romans 14:17: "for the kingdom of God is not eating and drinking, but righteousness and peace and *joy in the Holy Spirit.*" Alexander well says: ". . . the primitive disciples are repeatedly described as rejoicing in the very circumstances which might seem peculiarly adapted to produce the opposite effect. That the cause of this effect was supernatural we learn from the concluding words." (p. 507)

B. *What Does It Mean?* It means these disciples had
a relationship to the Lord we have not yet found.
(I speak in the generic—where there are those who
are filled with joy and peace and hope, we gladly
exempt you.) Perhaps a letter I wrote to the Holy
Spirit would be appropriate just here. (I wrote
it as a soliloquy.)

Dear Unseen Guest:

There are several questions I have wanted to
ask for some time:

(1) What is your estimate or understanding
of the body (my body) in which you live?
Some answers He has given: (a.) This body is
wonderfully made, (b.) It is of dust to return
to it, (c.) It is full of desires; or *is* the body
the source of these desires?, or only the "mod-
us operandi"? These desires are (to name but
a few): (1) physical hunger, (2) sexual urge,
(3) need for warmth or cooling, (4) creativ-
ity. All these desires *must* be and *will* be expressed *through the body*. *How* such expression is carried out through the body deter-
mines if there will be joy and peace or grief
and wrath.

(2) How could one (myself) be indwelt with
or by the Spirit of another (You) and yet
not know it? The one indwelling (You) can
and does see, hear, speak, feel, and yet He
(You) never indicates in any way to me (to
my human spirit) that He is (You are) present. This seems strange if not almost impossible. Is it true? No demon ever so indwelt a
man. Or did he? Were the demon-possessed
aware of the indwelling or were only those
who knew them aware? I know I'll need to

read your word much more carefully to get answers here.

(3) Is not "self-consciousness" an intrinsic quality of being alive? (i.e. how can we know we are alive without a self-consciousness?) But then the Holy Spirit — (you) were alive long before you took up residence in me and you are aware of this whether I am or or not.

(4) Are you going to help me in any direct manner? (i.e. apart from the help I get by reading your word—?)

Answer: Read *Eph. 3:16; II Cor. 13:14; Phil. 2:1* and *Rom. 8:26,27* and answer for yourself. In each instance we are left responsible for the help or lack of it. How wonderful are the ways of the Spirit!

C. *What Does It Mean To Me?* We should have waited and placed the letter to the Holy Spirit under this heading. Suffice it to say here: there is a tragic need and at the same time a wonderful opportunity. We disciples of today can be and should be "continually filled with joy and with the Holy Spirit".

D. *How Can I Share It?* What a prize to share—Who among us has written, taught, or preached on "how to be filled with the Holy Spirit"? (i.e. apart from what is poorly substituted—the present day so-called miraculous manifestations.) We do not have a larger challenge.

49. "And after there had been much debate, Peter stood up and said to them, 'Brethren, you know that in the early days God made a choice among you, that by my mouth the Gentiles should hear the word of the gospel

and believe. And God, who knows the heart, bore witness to them, giving them the Holy Spirit, just as He also did to us." Acts 15:7, 8.

A. *What Does It Say?* This is yet another reference to the baptism in the Holy Spirit of the house of Cornelius. Please read 10:47 and in 11:17 and then this reference—the baptism in the Holy Spirit was a witness by God in favor or approval of these Gentiles. In the context in which it appears. (i.e. accepting the Gentiles without circumcision.) It is a very strong point.

B. *What Does It Mean?* In three references we are told the plain purpose of the happening at the house of Cornelius. (i.e. to convince the Jew of the acceptability of the Gentiles.) Are we not more than presumptuous to put some other meaning into this incident?

C. *What Does It Mean To Me?* We have discussed at length the meaning of Cornelius' experience to us; we refer the reader to that section.

D. *How Can I Share It?* See discussion above.

50. "For it seemed good to the Holy Spirit and to us to lay upon you no greater burden than these essentials! Acts. 15:28.

A. *What Does It Say?* It might come as somewhat of a surprise that these men felt they were under the direction and oversight of the Holy Spirit. We need to remember John 16:13—"But when He, the Spirit of truth, comes, He will guide you into all the truth . . ." This would seem to be a fulfillment of that promise. We would imagine the apostles: Peter, John, and Paul were the ones through whom the Holy Spirit especially worked. It is also worthy of note that upon writing the letter somehow James, Peter, John, Paul, Barnabus, and all others who might be the antecedents of the pronoun "us" felt the Holy Spirit had given them the decision or resolution as well as the contents of the letter. Just how they came to this conclusion, we are not told.

B. *What Does It Mean?* There were men who were under the direct supervision of the Holy Spirit. We do well to give heed to what they said and did.

C. *What Does It Mean To Me?* There are those who claim this relationship and direction today. Besides the fact that they do not have Biblical authority for the claim they do not produce a consistent pattern of life to support such a claim.

D. *How Can I Share It?* We should share the truth of apostolic authority. We can be always aware of God's providential direction which is vastly different than immediate guidance communicated to those being guided.

51. "And they passed through the Phrygian and Galatian region, having been forbidden by the Holy Spirit to speak the Word in Asia." Acts 16:6.

A. *What Does It Say?* It is worse than useless to speculate as to how the Holy Spirit communicated His will to these men. Was it directly through a voice that said—"no, not in Asia"? or was it though a set of circumstances from which this conclusion was drawn and attributed to the Holy Spirit? We do not know.

B. *What Does It Mean?* It is just as important to know we are led as it is to know where. Can we plan a move for our Lord and be perfectly confident we shall know whether we are forbidden or permitted? We are throughly persuaded God is at work in our lives but we know no way we can know His immediate will for a specific circumstance.

C. *What Does It Mean To Me?* There are always so many factors involved in our moves. We are never quite confident we have made the right one. (let alone be undeniably convinced the Holy Spirit directed the move.) It might be well to ask ourselves why Paul and Barnabas knew of the Spirit's leading and we do not. Perhaps they fasted and prayed more and were preconditioned to be led. Perhaps God had a special work for them to do that was a "one time" affair—never to be repeated. Was this direction of the Holy Spirit special apostolic equipment? Another large problem is our unwillingness to accept a set of circumstances as the will of the Spirit if we are displeased. We usually rationalize the Holy Spirit out and try until we are pleased.

D. *How Can I Share It?* It would be more than pleasant to tell someone else we are perfectly confident of the Spirit's leading in our lives and they can be in theirs. We wonder in the midst of this whole discussion how it could ever be the will of the Holy Spirit for the Word *Not* to be spoken anywhere at any time. But it was! Considering the responsibility of deciding *Not* to do something and making the Holy Spirit responsible we pause. What shall we say? I for one will blame myself for the mistakes and thank the Lord for the success. I do *Not* believe in any direct, infallible, immediate, personal instruction of the Holy Spirit today.

52. "And when they had come to Mysia, they were trying to go into Bithynia, and the Spirit of Jesus did not permit them." Acts 16:7.

A. B. C. D.—All we have said on the 49th reference can be applied to this one. We would add one thought: we do not believe Luke is writing this as historian making objective-historical observations. We believe he is saying that *at the time* of their arrival in Mysia the Holy Spirit in some direct-personal-intelligent manner let Paul and Barnabas know He did not want them to go to Bithynia.

53. "And it came about while Apollos was at Corinth, Paul having passed through the upper country came to Ephesus, and found certain disciples, and he said to them, "Did you receive the Holy Spirit when you believed?" and they said to him, "no, we have not even heard whether there is a Holy Spirit." (Acts 19:1, 2.)

A. *What Does It Say?* and *What Does It Mean?*

There is so very much to say on this text and the one to follow. We offer no infallible position. We try only to be close to the text and as consistent as possible. Several questions must be (will be) answered in the mind of the reader before he interprets this passage:

(1) Why did Paul ask the question? (i.e. "Did you receive the Holy Spirit when you believed?") (Note in passing that the text does *not* say "since" you believed. This use of "since" instead of "when" is entirely unwarranted by the Greek text. The term "believed" refers to saving faith.) We have read three answers to this question:

(a) Paul was asking about the supernatural gifts of the Spirit when he used the term "Holy Spirit" — He wanted to know from these twelve which supernatural power was manifested in their lives.

438

(b) Paul asked this as a greeting—with not more than "God bless you" in his intention—he of course expected an affirmative answer.

(c) Paul saw something in the attitude or actions of these men that caused him to ask this question—perhaps a total lack of the joy, peace, or love which was so prominent in the lives of others. Observing a lack of the fruit of the Spirit, he asked about the source. We would prefer this last reason but it is only a matter of conjecture at the same time it is very important.

(2) Why did Paul inquire into their baptism? Isn't there some essential connection between baptism and the Holy Spirit? Who were these twelve men? Were they disciples or converts of Apollos? Were they imperfectly taught by someone else?

Let's begin with the first question: What is meant by the term "Holy Spirit" as here used? We believe Paul was asking about the Holy Spirit Himself. Because of the lack of the Spirit produced virtues in the lives of these men he asked them if they had the Holy Spirit. Perhaps Paul sensed something wrong through the discernment given him by the Holy Spirit. In order to cause these men to see their own lack he asked a leading question. When they freely admitted their lack he inquired further.

Why did he ask about their baptism? Because it is in and through baptism we receive Him as a gift. It seemed inconceivable to Paul that anyone could be properly baptized without a knowledge of the Holy Spirit. Did not our Lord command us to be baptized into the name of (or by the authority of) the Father, Son, and *Holy Spirit*. (Matt.

28:19) Since the Holy Spirit is given at baptism, their lack of the Holy Spirit reflects on their baptism.

Their answer indicates they had not been baptized by the baptism Jesus commanded. Paul acknowledged the baptism of John had a purpose but it was not related to the reception of the Holy Spirit.

(3) Who were these men? Were they disciples of Apollos? If they were, why wasn't Apollos re-baptized? We do not know if they were disciples of Apollos and we do not know that Apollos was not re-baptized. We have no word on the subject of Apollos and his baptism; however simply because we have no account of his baptism does not at all preclude the possibility of his being baptized.

This passage—like Acts 8:12-24 gives us the entire scope of the Holy Spirit's work.

Notice: (1) The Holy Spirit is given to all Christians at baptism. These twelve men were improperly baptized therefore did not have Him. (2) The Spiritual gifts or supernatural powers such as speaking in other languages and prophesying were given by the hands of the apostles. This Paul gave to these men. (3) Paul was enabled to grant these powers because he was baptized in the Holy Spirit. We do not know when or where. Our opinion is at the time he was baptized in water. (Acts 9:17)

Why did Paul grant these two supernatural powers to the Holy Spirit within these men? They were chosen by God to help others through these gifts. Did some of the men later become elders of the Ephesian church? We do not know.

C. *What Does It Mean To Me?* What shall we say of persons today (and their name is legion) who do not know the Holy Spirit is given to Christians?

There are many, many members of the church who would answer much in the same thought (if not with the same words) to the question. "Did you receive the Holy Spirit when you became a Christian?" Perhaps we have overstated the case. It could be that such persons do know or have heard of the Holy Spirit but He is not at all real to them. He is only a name or some mysterious power. Many members of the church are hesitant to acknowledge the Holy Spirit because of the excess practiced by others. Such persons who do know there is a Holy Spirit but do not know of His relationship to them could hardly be present-day counterparts to those twelve of Ephesus. We do indeed need more information but not a re-baptism for such people.

D. *How Can I Share It?* We need to share first of all our concern for a lost world who is so very much in need of our wonderful unseen Guest. We need to so carefully understand the work of the Spirit as expressed in this passage that we can teach others also.

54. "And when Paul laid his hands upon them, the Holy Spirit came on them, and they began speaking with tongues and prophesying." Acts 19:6.

There is hardly any point of adding to what we have already written. This is a verse description of the giving of supernatural gifts or abilities from the Holy Spirit through the apostle's hands. The apostles were the agents God chose to grant these powers. In the absence of the only means of imparting these powers we do not today have these powers.

55, & 56. "And now, behold, bound in Spirit, I am on my way to Jerusalem, not knowing what will happen to me there, except that the Holy Spirit solemnly

441

testifies to me in every city, saying that bonds and afflictions await me." (Acts 20:23, 23)

A. *What Does It Say?* There is some question as to whether the word "Spirit" in verse 22 should be capitalized. This is because it is not clear if the human spirit of Paul or the Holy Spirit of God is involved. Perhaps it would be enough to say: if only the spirit of Paul is meant—yet he is constrained because of the Holy Spirit. It was because of the intimations of the Holy Spirit Paul felt as he did. Paul knew the *must* go to Jerusalem. He felt as a bound prisoner of the Holy Spirit, led along by the Spirit to the city. Just how Paul was informed by the Spirit concerning the bonds and afflictions, we are not told. Did God use inspired men like Agabus or did the Spirit grant internal revelations to Paul? By whatever manner, these warnings were repeated in city after city until Paul reached Ephesus.

B. *What Does It Mean?* Paul was consciously under the direction of the Holy Spirit—even in this there were areas of information kept from him—but he *did* know where and when God wanted him. He already knew his work—"to open their eyes in order to turn them from darkness to light and from the authority of Satan to God". But just where and when to do this work must be given to him as he goes.

C. *What Does It Mean To Me?* It is indeed marvelous to have this same message. Will we have the same Spirit-led journey? Was the direction by the Holy Spirit in the life of Paul a part of God's interest in the life of an apostle and therefore not to be expected in the work of lesser persons? If we were as committed as Paul—as "turned on" to

Christ's will in our life as he was would we then
expect His direction? Or are we hesitant because
we feel there is an unfair comparison involved. (i.e.
I am not an apostle and therefore will not expect
such directions.") We unavoidably struggle with
this question. What is your answer?

D. *How Can I Share It?* Shall we share the testimony
of God's grand direction in our preaching, teaching, living for Christ? Be careful! Do we read of
any misdirections in the N.T.? Do we learn that
Paul or Peter or James didn't understand the
directions of the Spirit and made several mistakes
until they found what they hoped was the will of
the Lord? If there is nothing more than a subjective judgment involved whose judgment is it?
Open your mind to two or three possible explanations. How can we be sure the Holy Spirit led here
or directed there? I am not adverse to such direction. I simply will not claim something I do not
have. How is it with you?

57. "Take heed unto yourselves, and to all the flock, in
which the Holy Spirit hath made you bishops, to feed
the church of the Lord which He purchased with His
own blood." Acts 20:28

A. *What Does It Say?* We would like very much to
give a careful exegesis of the entire verse; but our
purpose is to consider the Spirit's work. We do
consider the comments of J.A. Alexander of such
great value we reproduce them for your edification:

"Having thus affirmed his own fidelity, he urges them
to follow his example. *Take heed*, the same verb that is
used above, in 5, 35. 8, 6, 10. 11. 16, 14, and there explained. It denotes not mere attention but attendance,
serious and anxious care. *To yourselves*, to your own
safety and salvation, as a prerequisite of usefulness to others.

The flock, a term applied by Christ himself to his disciples (Luke 12, 32), and by Peter to the church already organized (I Pet. 5, 2, 3). It is a favorite figure with the prophets for the chosen people or the church of the Old Testament. (See Isai. 40, 11. 63, 11. Jer. 13, 17. 23, 2. 31, 10. 51, 23. Ezek. 34, 3. Mic. 7, 14. Zech. 10. 3. 11, 4. 7. 17.) Our Lord describes himself as the good shepherd, and believers as his sheep (John 10, 1-16.) Peter describes him as the shepherd and bishop (or overseer) of souls (I Pet. 2, 25), and as the chief shepherd (5, 4), to whom ministers are under-shepherds.

Over the which is not a correct version, as it makes the overseers entirely distinct from and superior to the flock, whereas the original makes them a part of it, although superior in office. *In which,* in the midst and as a part of which. *The Holy Ghost made,* literally, placed or set, not only by creating the office, but by choosing the incumbents, either by express designation (as in 13, 2), or by directing the choice of others 9 as in 6, 5).

> You will observe from the comment here the two possibilities in the Spirit's creating or placing elders in the flock. We must add: if the Holy Spirit also gave these men special directions in the gifts of "wisdom" and "knowledge" — not to mention "prophesy", we would understand the expression "made you bishops" to include the body of truth granted to them by the Holy Spirit. Without these special gifts, we cannot see how these men would be able to teach.

> B. *What Does It Mean?* Once again, we are tempted to discuss the larger subject of the work of the elders. We must limit ourselves to the Holy Spirit's work as related to bishops . . then and now. Is there any sense today in which the Holy Spirit makes elders? We believe there is. The Holy Spirit

has given the qualifications and the work to be done. We believe He has also provided the inward moral power to meet the qualifications and to carry out the work. Surely the Holy Spirit is waiting to add all who will answer His call through His Word to do the work of the elder.

D. *How Can I Share It?* There is no greater need than that of the Holy Spirit appointed elders. We refer you to our text THE CHURCH IN THE BIBLE, which contains much help and to our *Bible Study Textbook*, PAUL'S LETTERS TO TIMOTHY AND TITUS.

58, & 59. "And after looking up the disciples, we stayed there seven days, and they kept telling Paul through the Spirit not to set foot in Jerusalem." 21:4.

"And as we were staying there for some days, a certain prophet named Agabus came down from Judea— and coming to us, he took Paul's belt and bound his own feet and hands, and said, 'This is what the Holy Spirit says; 'In this way the Jews of Jerusalem will bind the man who owns this belt and deliver him into the hands of the Gentiles." 21:10, 11.

A. *What Does It Say?* It is important here to understand just what the Holy Spirit revealed to these disciples. Did He indeed say that Paul should not go to Jerusalem? How then could the same Spirit bind Paul to go to the city at all costs? We must conclude that what the Spirit revealed to the disciples was the danger into which Paul was going. The conclusion that he should not go because of these dangers was the judgment of the disciples, not the Holy Spirit. The dramatic action of Agabus was much more definite. He clearly revealed and defined the dangers and left the decision to Paul.

B. *What Does It Mean?* We would like to know *how* certain disciples at Tyre obtained this power from the Holy Spirit. If we just had one reference to their devotional life supplying this power we would be more than happy to suggest we have such gifted disciples in our present-day churches. In the absence of such an example, we must say again: the only way we know of obtaining the gift or power of prophesy was thru the hands of the apostles. We conclude then that both the Tyrian Christians and Agabus obtained their gifts from the hands of the apostles. Surely we would be presumptuous to say we know they didn't.

C. *What Does It Mean To Me?* The above comment will contribute to this answer. Please know that we are not negative in our attitude toward persons who cla'm the powers of these disciples and Agabus for today. We are stopped in our acceptance of those who claim these powers by the following: (1) No scripture promised of such powers through answer to prayer. (2) Contradictory directions on the part of the individuals. (3) Contradictory directions among several who claim such powers and are not Christian. (at least by our definition.)

D. *How Can I Share It?* Knowledge of God's immediate direction in the formation of the church is a large help.

60. "And when they did not agree with one another, they began leaving after Paul had spoken one parting word, 'The Holy Spirit rightly spoke through Isaiah the prophet to your father, . . .'" Acts 28:25.

What Does It Say? We have discussed earlier (point #5) the work of the Holy Spirit in the writing of the scriptures. We can add nothing else here.

Examination over Lesson Ten

1. How can we know that Holy Spirit is at work in our lives, particularly in our choices?

2. What was "the promise of the Father"? How does this relate to every Christian?

3. State and discuss three phrases to describe the experience of the apostles on Pentecost.

4. Please discuss the vast importance of the office of the twelve and show how Pentecost related.

5. Why are all to be filled with the Holy Spirit? How is this to happen? Why?

6. Where, when and how were certain "sons and daughters prophesying"?

7. Where, when and how did "all flesh" receive the Holy Spirit?

8. Discuss the alternate interpretation for what happened on Pentecost i.e. of those who feel it is an example for us today.

9. The presence of the Holy Spirit is a real reason for "seasons of refreshing". Explain.

10. Was Peter (and other apostles) permanently "filled with the Holy Spirit" or did this reoccur from time to time? How does this relate to us?

11. Give a clear definition of "inspiration" as it relates to the Scriptures.

12. There is a real lesson to learn in the sin of Ananias and Sapphira i.e. as related to the Holy Spirit. What is it?

13. There is a right and a wrong way to try the Spirit of God. Discuss.

14. Discuss carefully and personally the Holy Spirit as a witness.

15. If we were to select seven men from among one of our congregations, who we could describe as "full of the Holy Spirit", what would be the distinguishing characteristics?

16. A character study of Stephen would prove very helpful.
17. We have said of Acts 8:14-17, "they contain the whole system of the Holy Spirit's work". Discuss what is meant.
18. Discuss what Simon (the sorcerer) saw when the apostles laid their hands on the Samaritans.
19. Discuss the leading of the Holy Spirit in our present-day personal evangelism.
20. When and where and how was Paul baptized in the Holy Spirit?
21. Read Acts 9:31 and answer: "How did these persons obtain comfort from the Holy Spirit?"
22. Why did God use the Holy Spirit as a spokesman? (i.e. on certain occasions)
23. Are we anointed with the Holy Spirit? Discuss.
24. Please discuss in detail the reasons for the baptism in Holy Spirit of the household of Cornelius.
25. When did the house of Cornelius become Christians? Show how important is this question.
26. Barnabus is a grand example for us. Show how.
27. There were prophets in the church in the days of Paul and Peter. Are there prophets in today's church? Consider the high estimate Paul had of the gift of prophecy.
28. Does the Holy Spirit call, separate, and send men today? Discuss.
29. How can we be indwelt by the Holy Spirit and yet have no emotional, internal, immediate awareness of Him? Or is this the true circumstance? Discuss.
30. Why did Paul and Barnabus know of the Spirit's leading in their moves (choices) and we do not? Discuss.
31. Why did Paul ask certain men if they received the Holy Spirit when they believed?
32. Why did Paul inquire as to the baptism of the 12 at Ephesus?
33. Discuss how the Holy Spirit makes elders.